Armando Aliu
Editor

Artificial Intelligence and the Rule of Law

The Age of Legal Tech and Digital Governance in a Fractured Digital World

palgrave
macmillan

Editor
Armando Aliu
Institute of European Studies
Faculty of Social Sciences
University of Wrocław
Wrocław, Poland

ISBN 978-3-031-97388-8 ISBN 978-3-031-97389-5 (eBook)
https://doi.org/10.1007/978-3-031-97389-5

Cover credit: Anton Shaparenko/Alamy Stock Vector

This Palgrave Macmillan imprint is published by the registered company Springer Nature Switzerland AG
The registered company address is: Gewerbestrasse 11, 6330 Cham, Switzerland

Dedicated to
'(In memoriam of) Fiqiret' & 'Musa (Eja)'

Preface

Artificial intelligence (*AI*) is not a '*superorganismic deus ex machina*' to solve all global matters and social dilemmas. There is a constantly evolving technological evolution process in which generative *AI* (*GAI*) tools and practices extracting technological responses. This book argues the most pressing challenges in *AI* technologies and practices, the entanglements of '*AI and Law*' and '*AI and Rule of Law*' nexus and digitally transformed fracturing world that is shaped by digital governance and digital ethics. It contributes to an understanding of digital transformation in legal systems and the age of *LegalTech* inextricably intertwined in responsible, humancentric, explainable, and trustworthy *AI* technologies, *GAI*, and *AI interdisciplinarity*. It draws attention to unraveling the legal labyrinth of regulatory frameworks on *AI*, the rule of law, digital human rights, digital democracy, and how these *AI* regulations intervene to the digital transformation of *LegalTech* across the world. It emphasizes the necessity for a robust regulatory framework to mitigate the risks of *AI* and overcome legal hurdles. The book combines technology, law, ethics, and other technology-related research fields from an interdisciplinary point of view.

The book scrutinizes the issues, risks, and opportunities of *AI* to uphold the rule of law, promote human rights, enhance access to justice, protect people's rights and fundamental freedoms (including data privacy and data confidentiality principle), and strengthen the rule of law-based inclusive society. *AI* technologies and practices have a significant transformative impact on justice systems. These have transformed the administration of justice, law enforcement, civil and criminal investigations, and predictive justice (i.e., the use of algorithms to process cases supporting judges in their decision making).

The book sheds light on the impact of *AI* use on the development of the rule of law through considering the following issues: digitalization of justice systems, *AI*'s impact on safeguarding human rights, *AI* ethics, *AI* governance, *AI* use in justice systems, and so on. The book emphasizes that *AI*, rule of law, digital human rights, justice, and ethics are strongly interconnected from an interdisciplinary point of view. *AI* use in justice systems can increase the efficiency of judicial services for citizens, facilitate better access to justice, and reduce costs. Furthermore, the book delves into the challenges and risks of *AI* on its (in)consistency with ethical concerns, protection of privacy, personal data, and the General Data Protection Regulation (GDPR).

For this volume, we wanted to offer a wide scope across five dimensions. First, we began by presenting the relationship between *AI interdisciplinarity* and the rule of law. We distinguished '*AI and Rule of Law*' from '*AI and Law*' nexus and aligned *AI interdisciplinarity* with digital governance and digital ethics underpinned by *responsible AI*, and *AI4People* viewpoints. We highlighted the role of the arts and humanities in thinking about *AI* and history, present, and future of computational jurisprudence. Second, we argued the procedural fetishism and substantive due process in *AI* governance and digital constitutionalism, the right to be forgotten, and the legal feasibility of machine unlearning methods. Third, we particularly analyzed *GAI* governance and regulation for the future, and the shift from human vulnerability to digital vulnerability in the context of *AI* technologies and practices. Fourth, we argued interrelationships between the rule of algorithm and the rule of law by discussing *AI* systems and responsibility, the need for an international treaty on bio-technological ethics, international law between enhanced anthropocentrism and post-anthropocentrism, the EU *AI* Act, and the future of *AI* governance. Finally, we focused on the future of *AI* and the rule of law through discussing and prioritizing digital ethics, regulatory framework, and human rights-centered *AI* governance.[1]

Wrocław, Poland
June 2025

Armando Aliu

[1] *Ethics Statement: All chapter manuscripts were checked for plagiarism prior to publication through iThenticate as a part of Crossref Similarity Check. According to iThenticate Similarity Index analysis reports, all chapter manuscripts are highly original. All chapter manuscripts were evaluated for their intellectual content without discrimination or bias. The editor strictly maintained the confidentiality of submitted manuscripts, sharing information only with relevant parties (e.g., contributors and editorial staff) as part of the publication process, in accordance with the GDPR. No content generated by AI technologies has been used in the chapter manuscripts.*

Acknowledgements

I am filled with gratitude for the contributors to this edited volume for their perseverance and dedication in producing their chapters, their thoughtful and penetrating insights, and the quality of their scientific contribution. The strength of this book is a testament to their commitment and scientific efforts that comprise a blend of various theoretically innovative and methodologically diverse intellectual approaches.

The idea for this particular book started in the autumn of 2022 when I at started working at Jagiellonian University in Kraków (Poland). This book was developed within the framework of the NAWA/NCN Project (particularly in connection with the work package 2: digital geopolitics and digital governance in a fracturing world). 'The Project is co-financed by the Polish National Agency for Academic Exchange (*Narodowa Agencja Wymiany Akademickiej – NAWA*) under the *NAWA* Guest Professorship program' and the 'Polish National Agency for Academic Exchange within the *NAWA* Chair program'. I wish to acknowledge the financial assistance of the *NAWA* grant (*PPN/PRO/2020/1/00003/DEC/1*) from the Polish Academic Exchange Council and *NCN* grant (*ZARZADZENIE NCN 94/2020*) from the Polish National Science Council (*Narodowe Centrum Nauki– NCN*).

This edited book was also written in the framework of the *OPUS 26* project that is entitled '*Towards co-creative just transition at the urban level in Europe*' and conducted in the Institute of European Studies, Faculty of Social Sciences at the University of Wrocław (Poland).

The *OPUS 26* project is financed by the Polish National Science Council (*NCN*). I wish to acknowledge the financial assistance of the *OPUS 26* grant (*Reg. No: 2023/51/B/HS5/02581*) from the Polish National Science Council (*NCN*). I am grateful to *NAWA* and *NCN* for the funding that made the research collaboration possible. I am thankful to Aldona Wiktorska-Święcka (University of Wrocław, Poland), Shu-Chen Li (Dresden University of Technology, Germany), Ines Schmidt (Dresden University of Technology, Germany), Franziska Petri (KU Leuven, Belgium), Klaudia Proniewska (Jagiellonian University, Poland), and Tomasz Grodzicki (Jagiellonian University, Poland) for their help, guidance, and assistance during the *NAWA* and *NCN* projects lifetime. I am deeply indebted to the University of Wrocław, Faculty of Social Sciences, Institute of European Studies (Poland), Dresden University of Technology (Germany), the Europa-Kolleg Hamburg (Germany), Jagiellonian University, Faculty of Medicine, Department of Internal Medicine and Gerontology/Centre for Digital Medicine and Robotics (Poland), the Institute for Forecasting, Centre of Social and Psychological Sciences (CSPS), Slovak Academy of Sciences (Slovakia), and Inner-City Fund–ICF (USA) for ensuring research opportunities and having a productive and vibrant research ecosystem in which I could explore and develop the ideas that are central to the edited book.

I wish to express my sincere thanks to the European Cooperation in Science and Technology (*COST*) working group '*CA23114–Regaining linkage? Digital technologies improving civic engagement, political organizations and democracy (RELINK²)*', the *COST* working group '*CA23113–Climate change impacts on mental health in Europe* (*CliMent*)', the *COST* working group '*CA23118–Futures-oriented Governance of Outer Space: Towards Peace, Equity, and Environmental Integrity* (*FOGOS*)', and the *COST* working group '*CA18215–China in Europe research network (CHERN)*' for inviting me to group discussions and scientific events. I am thankful to Michał Jacuński (University of Wrocław, Poland), Elżbieta Szulc-Wałecka (University of Maria Curie-Skłodowska, Poland), Jasmin Fitzpatrick (Johannes Gutenberg University Mainz, Germany), Oscar Barbera (University of Valencia, Spain), Gabriela Borz (University of Strathclyde, UK), Marco Lisi (NOVA University Lisbon, Portugal), Isabelle Borucki (Philipps University of Marburg, Germany), Felix-Christopher von Nostitz (Lille Catholic Institute—ICL, France), Giulia Sandri (Free

University of Brussels–ULB, Belgium), Nana De Graaff (Vrije Universiteit Amsterdam, Netherlands), Jeffrey Henderson (University of Bristol, UK), Tim Ruhlig (Swedish Institute of International Affairs, Sweden), Nicholas Jepson (University of Manchester, UK), Nidhi Nagabhatla (Ghent University, Belgium), Sanae Okamoto (Maastricht University, Netherlands), Chiara Cadeddu (Erasmus University Rotterdam, Netherlands), Nidhi Nagabhatla (Ghent University, Belgium), Sanae Okamoto (Maastricht University, Netherlands), Xiao-Shan Yap (Utrecht University, Netherlands), Ioana Bratu (Vrije Universiteit Amsterdam, Netherlands), and Nikita SW Chiu (University of Durham, UK).

The autumn of 2022 was a stunning turning point for me. I was a participant of the *UNESCO MOOC* Seminar (TFS English) 'Artificial Intelligence and the Rule of Law'. The *UNESCO* seminar highlighted AI's application and impact on the rule of law and structured around six modules: (1) Why digital transformation and AI matter for justice systems? (2) AI adoption across justice systems, (3) the rise of online courts, (4) algorithmic bias and its implications for judicial decision making, (5) safeguarding human rights in the age of AI, and (6) AI ethics & governance concerning judicial operators. The seminar unpacked the opportunities and risks of the increasing adoption of AI technologies across justice systems and AI's impact on the administration of justice, particularly concerning human rights and AI ethics and governance issues. I am especially grateful to *UNESCO* and the *Future Society* for integrating the seminar participants with the activities of the '*Athens Roundtable on AI and the Rule of Law*' that is the premier international, multi-stakeholder gathering on artificial intelligence, legal systems and functions, regulatory compliance, and the rule of law. With the support and guidance of *UNESCO* and the *Future Society*, I was able to participate in the events and discussions of the *fourth* (2022), the *fifth* (2023), and the *sixth* (2024) '*Athens Roundtable on AI and the Rule of Law*'.

I am grateful to Palgrave Macmillan Commissioning Editor, Project Coordinators, and Production Editor Rachael Ballard, Naveen Dass, Claudia Petter, Cecile Schuetze Gaukel, and Karthika Sundar for their help, recommendations, and support. I would like to thank the Leuven Institute for Advanced Study (*LIAS*) and Metaforum at KU Leuven. As a member of the Association for the Advancement of Artificial Intelligence—*AAAI*, and the Academic Council on the United Nations System—*ACUNS*, I am likewise grateful to the *AAAI* and the *ACUNS* team members of who have nurtured and grown these organizations.

I also thank the Secretariat and panel participants of the '*39th Annual AAAI Conference on Artificial Intelligence* (February 25 and March 4, 2025, in Philadelphia, USA)', the '*ACUNS Annual Meeting* (23–25 June 2025 in Nairobi, Kenya)', the '*Social sciences 4 Climate change. From Knowledge to Action —Eurac Research—SOS4CC* (4–5 September 2025, Bolzano, Italy)', and the '29th Annual Conference of Central European Political Science Association (18–19 September 2025, Warsaw, Poland)'.

This edited book has a charity initiative. All earnings (e.g., one-time remuneration fee, royalties, net receipts of subsidiarity rights, etc.) that will be gained from this book will be donated to the United Nations International Children's Emergency Fund (*UNICEF*). I wish to extend my heartfelt gratitude and appreciation to *UNICEF*'s dedicated supporters worldwide for their unwavering commitment to improving the "*Lives of Children*". The statement "Children are our future" is somewhat incomplete. "*Children are the Present*".

Therefore, as one of the *UNICEF*'s supporters[1], I invite individuals to make a donation (https://help.unicef.org/gao/donate?country=31) to *UNICEF* to "*Save and Protect the World's Most Vulnerable Children*". *UNICEF* works to "*Save Children's Lives*". To "*Protect Children's Rights*". To "*Keep Children Safe*" from harm. To "*Give Children a Childhood*" in which they're protected, healthy, and educated. To "*Give Children a Fair Chance*" to fulfill their potential. Children are our future only if we "*Shape a Responsible, Sustainable, and Better/Brighter Future for Children*". Perhaps, *AI* and *automated/humanoid robots* will get smarter than our children in the future; however, machines will never be more important than human beings in this world.

[1] Further clarifications regarding how to be a volunteer with *UNICEF* are available at: https://www.unicef.org/careers/volunteers-unicef

Contents

Contributors

Ikran Abdirahman High Court of Kenya & the DIFA Legal, Nairobi, Kenya

Mohamed Ben Achour Centre de Recherche Léon Duguit (CRLD), Université Paris-Saclay, Paris, France

Armando Aliu Institute of European Studies, Faculty of Social Sciences, University of Wrocław, Wrocław, Poland

Dorian Aliu University of New York Tirana (UNYT), Tirana, Albania

Yunan Chen Beijing Foreign Studies University (BFSU), Beijing, People's Republic of China

Liane Rose Colonna Department of Law, Stockholm University, Stockholm, Sweden

Begoña Gonzalez Otero Max Planck Institute for Innovation and Competition, Munich, Germany;
The Governance Lab (GovLab), New York, USA

Sofia Klymchuk Ministry of Digital Transformation of Ukraine, Kyiv, Ukraine

David Krause Marquette University, Milwaukee, WI, USA

Hellen van der Kroef Law & Tech Lab, Faculty of Law, Maastricht University, Maastricht, Netherlands

Rūta Liepiņa ALMA-AI Bologna Interdisciplinary Research Center for AI and Law, University of Bologna, Bologna, Italy

Beatrice Panattoni Department of Law, University of Verona, Verona, Italy;
Faculty of Law, Economics and Finance, University of Luxembourg, Luxembourg, Luxembourg

Tobias Oechtering Division of Information Science and Engineering, KTH Royal Institute of Technology, Stockholm, Sweden

John Tasioulas Institute for Ethics in AI, Faculty of Philosophy, University of Oxford, Oxford, UK

Josh Lee Kok Thong Department School of Law, University of California, Berkeley, Berkeley, USA

Themistoklis Tzimas Aristotle University of Thessaloniki, Thessaloniki, Greece

Monika Zalnieriute Faculty of Law, Vilnius University, Vilnius, Lithuania;
Lithuanian Centre for Social Sciences, Vilnius, Lithuania

Surong Zhu Beijing Foreign Studies University (BFSU), Beijing, People's Republic of China

Abbreviations

AAAI	Association for the Advancement of Artificial Intelligence
ABA	American Bar Association
ACHR	African Charter of Human Rights
ACUNS	Academic Council on the United Nations System
ADM	Algorithmic Decision Making
AGI	Artificial General Intelligence
AI	Artificial Intelligence
AI4People	Artificial Intelligence for People
AI4S	Artificial Intelligence for Science
AIDP	International Association of Criminal Law (*Association Internationale de Droit Pénal*)
AI HLEG	High-Level Expert Group on Artificial Intelligence
ANI	Artificial Narrow Intelligence
ANN	Artificial Neural Network
AR	Augmented Reality
AU	African Union
AU AIS	African Union Continental AI Strategy
BDA	Big Data Analytics
CAD	Computer Aided Design
CAHAI	Council of Europe Ad Hoc Committee on Artificial Intelligence
CALR	Computer-Assisted Legal Research
CBR	Case-Based Reasoning
CFREU	Charter of Fundamental Rights of the EU
ChatGPT	Chat Generative Pre-trained Transformer
CJEU	Court of Justice of the EU

CMLRs	Computational Models of Legal Reasoning
CNN	Convolutional Neural Network
COBOT	Collaborative Robot
CoE	Council of Europe
CoE-CAHAI	Ad hoc Committee on Artificial Intelligence
COST	European Cooperation in Science and Technology
COVID-19	Coronavirus Disease 2019
DF	Deepfake
DL	Deep Learning
DNA	Deoxyribonucleic Acid
EAB	Ethics Advisory Board
EAG	Ethics Advisory Group
EbD	Ethics by Design
EC	European Commission
ECHR	European Convention on Human Rights
ECtHR	European Court of Human Rights
EGE	European Group on Ethics in Science and New Technologies
ESC	European Social Charter
EU	European Union
EU AI Act	The European Union's Artificial Intelligence Act, Regulation (EU) 2024/1689
FRIAs	Fundamental Rights Impact Assessments
FRT	Facial Recognition Technology
GAI	Generative AI
GANs	Generative Adversarial Networks
GDPR	General Data Protection Regulation
GPAI	General Purpose AI Systems
GPT	Generative Pre-trained Transformer
HGNT	Human Nuclear Genome Transfer
HITL	Human-in-the-Loop
HIV	Human Immunodeficiency Virus
HR	Humanoid Robot
HUDERAF	Human Rights, Democracy, and the Rule of Law Assurance Framework
IBA	International Bar Association
IBC	International Bioethics Committee
ICAIL	International Conference on AI and Law
IE	Information Extraction
Interpol	International Criminal Police Organization
IoT	Internet of Things
IRB	Institutional Review Board
IT	Information Technology
LegalTech	Legal Technology

LLM	Large Language Model
LLR	Log-Likelihood Ratio
(L)NLP	(Legal) Natural Language Processing
MITL	Machine-in-the-Loop
ML	Machine Learning
MNCs	Multinational Corporations
MOOC	Massive Open Online Course
NAWA	Polish National Agency for Academic Exchange (*Narodowa Agencja Wymiany Akademickiej*)
NCN	Polish National Science Council (*Narodowe Centrum Nauki*)
NCOB	Nuffield Council on Bioethics
PITL	Public-in-the-Loop
PSITL	Public-Servant-in-the-Loop
QA	Question Answering
QMS	Quality Management System
R&D	Research and Development
RAG	Retrieval-Augmented Generation
RBR	Rule-Based Reasoning
RL	Reinforcement Learning
RPA	Robotic Process Automation
RTBF	Right to be Forgotten
SMEs	Small and Medium-sized Enterprises
SSHA	Social Sciences, Humanities and Arts
STEM	Computer Science and Data Science
SWOT	Strengths, Weaknesses, Opportunities, and Threats
UDHR	Universal Declaration of Human Rights
UN	United Nations
UNESCO	UN Educational, Scientific and Cultural Organization
UNGPs	UN Guiding Principles on Business and Human Rights
UNICEF	UN International Children's Emergency Fund
UNICRI	UN Interregional Crime and Justice Research Institute
VR	Virtual Reality
WoS	Web of Science
XAI	Explainable Artificial Intelligence
WHO	World Health Organization
WTA	World Transhumanism Association
WWW	World Wide Web

List of Figures

CHAPTER 1

Introduction: *AI Interdisciplinarity* and the Rule of Law—The Age of Legal Tech and Digital Governance Shaped by Digital Ethics, *Responsible AI*, and *AI4People*

Armando Aliu and Dorian Aliu

'If you look around, there are very few examples of more intelligent things being controlled by less intelligent things, which makes you wonder whether when AI gets smarter than us, it's going to take over control.'
– Geoffrey E. Hinton

A. Aliu (✉)
Institute of European Studies, Faculty of Social Sciences, University of Wrocław, Wrocław, Poland
e-mail: armando.aliu@uwr.edu.pl

D. Aliu
University of New York Tirana (UNYT), Tirana, Albania
e-mail: dorianaliu@unyt.edu.al

A. Aliu (ed.), *Artificial Intelligence and the Rule of Law*,
https://doi.org/10.1007/978-3-031-97389-5_1

1.1 *AI* Interdisciplinarity and the Age of Legal Tech

Since John McCarthy coined the term '*Artificial Intelligence* (*AI*)' in 1956, *AI* has entered a broad spectrum of scientific disciplines and research fields.[1] *AI* in the legal research landscape first appeared in a research paper developed for the '*Mechanization of Thought Processes Conference*' that was held between November 24–27, 1958, in Teddington, England.[2] Through the digitalization of science, technology, and innovation, *AI*-based technologies, generative *AI* (*GAI*), computer-assisted legal research (*CALR*), machine learning (*ML*), deep learning (*DL*), artificial general intelligence (*AGI*), internet of thinks (*IoT*), collaborative robot (*COBOT*), humanoid robot (*HR*), robotic process automation (*RPA*), quantum computing technologies and super-computers, augmented reality (*AR*), virtual reality (*VR*), smart enhanced algorithms, big data analytics (*BDA*), facial recognition technology (*FRT*), and huge amounts of digital data enabled automated systems to perform tasks in digital universe and started undertaking the role of human intelligence.[3] The evolution of *AI* has four phases: (1) *rule-based AI* (i.e., using a set of prewritten rules to make decisions and solve problems),[4] (2) *ML* (i.e., a 'subfield of *AI* that studies the ability to improve performance based on experience, adapt to new circumstances and detect/extrapolate patterns'), (3) *DL* (i.e., *ML* using multiple layers of simple, adjustable computing elements), and (4) *GAI* (i.e., 'the ability

[1] McCarthy, J., Minsky, M. L., Rochester, N. & Shannon C. E. (1955). *A Proposal for the Dartmouth Summer Research Project on Artificial Intelligence*. Hanover, NH: Dartmouth College.

[2] Mehl, L. (1959). Automation in the legal world: From machine processing of legal information to the 'law machine' (pp. 755–787). November 24–27, 1958, the National Physical Laboratory, Teddington, England.

[3] OECD/Eurostat (2018). *Oslo Manual 2018: Guidelines for Collecting, Reporting and Using Data on Innovation: The Measurement of Scientific, Technological and Innovation Activities*. (4th Edition) Paris/Eurostat, Luxembourg: OECD Publishing, pp. 241–254; OECD (2020). *The Digitalisation of Science, Technology and Innovation: Key Developments and Policies*. Paris: OECD Publishing, pp. 84–86; Raj, P., Kumar, A., Dubey, A. K., Bhatia, S. & Manoj, O. (eds.) (2023). *Quantum Computing and Artificial Intelligence*. Berlin: Walter de Gruyter, pp. V–VI.

[4] Dawson, A. G. (2024). Algorithmic adjudication and constitutional AI—The promise of a better AI decision making future? *SMU Science and Technology Law Review*, *27*(1): 11–37, pp. 26–27.

of *AI* to generate content, speech, and action that is indistinguishable from human output').[5] There will always be *pros* and *cons* for the advancement of *AI* research and rapid expansion of digital universe in which human intelligence has entered the dominance of revolutionizing *AI*, anthropomorphizing the non-human, and rapid advancement stage of innovation in *AI*-based technologies.[6]

The '*AI interdisciplinarity*'[7] issue is crucial to knowledge production and the development of *AI* technologies and applications in specific research fields. According to Susskind, lawyers and legal theorists need to be more familiarized with the stunning advances in *AI* and certain crucial matters, such as knowledge-based systems in law, the potential, the limitations, and the dangers of *AI* and computer science to legal practice and research. *AI interdisciplinarity* created a synergy[8] and mutual understanding between lawyers, legal theorists, computer scientists, computer engineers, logicians, or mathematicians and triggered them to investigate further the applications of computer technology to

[5] Russell, S. J. & Norvig, P. (2022). *Artificial Intelligence: A Modern Approach. 4th Global Edition.* Harlow: Pearson, pp. 19–44; van der Sloot, B. (2024). *Regulating the Synthetic Society: Generative AI, Legal Questions and Societal Challenges.* Oxford: Bloomsbury, pp. 1–2.

[6] From an *AI SWOT* analysis perspective, *pros* will prioritize and praise the strengths and opportunities of *AI* in the short run, whereas *cons* will alert and harshly criticize threats (e.g., unacceptable and high risks of AI systems, etc.) and weaknesses of *AI* in the long run.

[7] Interdisciplinarity in *AI & Law* was unearthed in the 'Interdisciplinary Research Project' that was conducted by the Programing Research Group at the University of Oxford Computing Laboratory. The project was a part of a program of Research Council under grant GRA/A/43124. *See* Sufrin, B. (1981). Reading formal specifications. Oxford: University of Oxford Computing Laboratory.

[8] Susskind categorized two schools/approaches as '*ideal types*' (according to the terminology of Max Weber) in the field of *AI & Law*, such as '*pragmatism*' (i.e., the systems that can be operationalized/commercialized and excluded from theoretical problems) and '*purism*' (i.e., focusing on the nature of the law and intelligence with no regard for the delivery of commercially viable systems). Susskind's recommendation to encourage ideal collaboration between the '*pragmatists*' camp and the '*purists*' camp can be considered as an advancement strategy of *AI interdisciplinarity* to establish a holistic perspective in the field of *AI* and legal reasoning and accelerate knowledge production and development. *See* Susskind, R. (1989). Pragmatism and purism in artificial intelligence and legal reasoning. *AI & Society, 3*: 28–38, pp. 31–32.

the law.[9] *AI* has increased complexity[10] in interdisciplinary knowledge production in mathematics, technology, psychology, sociology, and law/ *LegalTech*[11]. Hence, complex issues require the collaboration of social scientists, natural scientists, engineers, legal experts, and business professionals[12]. In 2019, the *COVID-19* pandemic sparked a global research effort and encouraged diversified interdisciplinary research groups and interdisciplinary research clusters using *AI* technologies and applications and collaborate with each other to respond promptly to the early stages of the pandemic[13]. During the *COVID-19* pandemic, the use of large language models (*LLMs*)[14] in academia posed ethical dilemmas and

[9] Susskind, R. (1986). Expert systems in law: A jurisprudential approach to artificial intelligence and legal reasoning. *The Modern Law Review*, *49*: 168–194, pp. 168–170.

[10] Toulmin, S. E. (2003). *The Uses of Argument*. (updated edition) Cambridge: CUP, pp. 7–9; Verheij, B. (2020). Artificial intelligence as law. *Artificial Intelligence and Law*, *28*: 181–206, pp. 189–191.

[11] *LegalTech* is conceived as IT solutions which include both hardware and software utilized in the law. From interdisciplinary perspective, *LegalTech* has been misunderstood by non-legal professionals due to broad usage of its synonyms, such as 'Law Tech', 'Legal IT', or 'Legal Informatics' in the literature. There are three stages in *LegalTech*: *LegalTech 1.0* (technology [e.g., softwares, IT systems, online services, etc.] that supports the work of lawyers as professionals), *LegalTech 2.0* (advanced technology not only supporting lawyers, but also substituting itself for the work of humans and automating the acts to be taken—e.g., smart contracts, tokenization of processes, crypto-assets, etc.), and *LegalTech 3.0* (the higher tier where the decision is made by a system, on the basis of independently acquired data and self-learning—e.g., using *AI* or advanced algorithms utilizing *ML*). *See* Szostek, D. (2021). The concept of legal technology (LegalTech) and legal engineering. In: Szostek, D. & Załucki, M. (eds.) *Legal Tech: Information Technology Tools in the Administration of Justice* (pp. 19–28). Baden-Baden: Nomos, pp. 19–22.

[12] Lu, C. (2024). Rethinking artificial intelligence from the perspective of interdisciplinary knowledge production. *AI & Society*, *39*: 3059–3060, p. 3059.

[13] Abbonato, D., Bianchini, S., Gargiulo, F. & Venturini, T. (2024). Interdisciplinary research in artificial intelligence: Lessons from COVID-19. *Quantitative Science Studies*, *5*(4): 922–935, pp. 922–924.

[14] For instance, the utilization of some of *AI* tools (e.g., *ChatGPT* [by OpenAI], *Qwen* [by Alibaba], *Llama* [by Meta], *DeepSeek*, *Bing/Copilot*, *Research Rabbit*, *Mistral*, *Doubao*, etc.) as 'co-authors and/or reviewers' has been considered as a threat for the quality of scientific publications due to the specific reason that *AI* tools do not have legal/moral responsibility of an authorship. Enriched content of texts retrieved by GAI pose a risk of '*high sophistication*' that can be perceived as '*illusion*', a leak of meaning in a loophole of fuzzy data mixture and complex syntax, and a complexification handicap for *AI interdisciplinarity*.

raised serious concerns toward the responsibility, dignity, and credibility of science[15].

At the very beginning of the evolution process of *AI* in legal research domain, legal scholars and practitioners (except tort lawyers[16], information technology lawyers[17], and intellectual property lawyers) were resistant and reluctant to create a strong interrelationship between information technology and law[18]. They took little interest in embracing technology concepts due to the fuzzy tech terminologies and misconceptions[19] used in computer science and data science (*STEM*) and consider themselves strictly bound by 'national law'. Many jurists and legal theorists followed Hans Kelsen's argument (i.e., *the Pure Theory of Law [Reine Rechtslehre]* that syncretizes the *separability thesis* and the *normativity thesis*). Kelsen's '*Pure Theory of Law*' answers the question of '*what the law is*' (*de lege lata/lex lata*), not '*what the law ought to be*' (*de lege ferenda/lex ferenda*)—i.e., the separation of '*Law*' and '*Morals*'.[20] Kelsen

[15] Scimeca, M. & Bonfiglio, R. (2023). Dignity of science and the use of ChatGPT as a co-author. *ESMO Open*, *8*(4): 1–2, p. 1.

[16] Morgan, J. (2017). Torts and technology. In: Brownsword, R., Scotford, E. & Yeung, K. (Eds). *The Oxford Handbook of Law, Regulation and Technology* (pp. 523–546). Oxford: OUP, pp. 523–524.

[17] Valcke, P., Graef, I. & Clifford, D. (2018). iFairness –Constructing fairness in IT (and other areas of) law through intra- and interdisciplinarity. *Computer Law & Security Review*, *34*: 707–714, pp. 707–708.

[18] Dimatteo, L. A., Poncibò, C. & Cannarsa, M. (eds.) (2022). *The Cambridge Handbook of Artificial Intelligence: Global Perspectives on Law and Ethics*. Cambridge: CUP, pp. xxi–xxii.

[19] Buchanan, B. G. & Headrick, T. E. (1970). Some speculation about artificial intelligence and legal reasoning. *Stanford Law Review*, *23*(1): 40–62, pp. 40–41.

[20] Our intention is not to mull over the contradictory perspectives (of Hans Kelsen, H.L.A. Hart, Lon Fuller, Jeremy Bentham, John Austin, Jerome Hall, Hermann Heller, Gustav Radbruch, Joseph Raz, Ronald Dworkin, etc.) related to the separation of '*law*' and '*morals*' in legal positivism and philosophy of law. *See* Green, L. (2008). Positivism and inseparability of law and morals. *New York University Law Review*, *83*(4): 1035–1058; Spaak, T. (2005). Kelsen and Hart on the normativity of law. *Perspectives on Jurisprudence*, *48*: 397–414; Rooney, M. T. (1948). Law without justice?—The Kelsen and Hall theories compared. *Notre Dame Lawyer*, *23*(2): 140–172; Moore, J. G. (2020). Hart, Radbruch and the necessary connection between law and morals. *Law and Philosophy*, *39*(6): 691–704; Carlson, D. G. (2009). Hart avec Kant: On the inseparability of law and morality. *Washington University Jurisprudence Review*, *1*: 21–96; Pino, G. (2014). Positivism, legal validity, and the separation of law and morals. *Ratio Juris*, *27*(2): 190–217; Dyzenhaus, D. (1996). Hermann Heller—An introduction. *Cardozo Law Review*, *18*: 1129–1137.

sought to preclude from the cognition of positive law all elements foreign thereto[21]. This particular distinction requires considerable attention to identify the constraints of *AI* in law discipline, as well as normativity in the strictly legal sense and moral sense. For instance, *AI* technologies and applications can contribute to the technical aspects of law, such as case-based reasoning (*CBR*), rule-based reasoning (*RBR*), computational models of legal reasoning (*CMLRs*), etc.[22]; however, *AI* cannot quite tell us '*what the law ought to be*' or formulate an '*ideal legal order*'.[23] Kelsen suggested that the limits of the subject and its cognition must be clearly fixed as such: 'The specific science of law (i.e., jurisprudence) must be distinguished from the philosophy of justice, and from sociology, or cognition of social reality'[24]. Kelsen and his predecessors in the legal positivist camp resist the inclination to turn to '*ethics*[25]', psychology, and

21 Kelsen, H. (1941). The pure theory of law and analytical jurisprudence. *Harvard Law Review*, *55*(1): 44–70, pp. 44–45; Kelsen, H. (2002). *Introduction to the Problems of Legal Theory* (Translated by B. L. Paulson & S. L. Paulson) Oxford: Clarendon Press, pp. xxvi–xxix.

22 Ashley, K. D. & Bridge, D. G. (eds.) (2003). *Case-Based Reasoning Research and Development*. Berlin: Springer, p. v; Rissland, E. L., Ashley, K. D. & Branting, L. K. (2006). Case-based reasoning and law. *The Knowledge Engineering Review*, *20*(3): 293–298, pp. 293–295.

23 Essentially, *a monist approach à la Kelsen* and hierarchical relationship within the monist legal system structure (i.e., norms on a higher level authorize the creation of norms on a lower level) can form a more legitimate and effective ground for reconstruction of a global legal order. Kelsen asserted that international law and the various state legal systems taken together constitute a *unified normative system* (*monism*). *See* Spaak, T. (2013). Kelsen on monism and dualism. In: Novakovic M., (Ed.) *Basic Concepts of Public International Law: Monism & Dualism* (pp. 322–343). Belgrade: Alter DOO and Faculty of Law, University of Belgrade, Institute of Comparative Law.

24 Kelsen, H. (1941). The pure theory of law and analytical jurisprudence. *Harvard Law Review*, *55*(1): 44–70, p. 44; Kelsen, H. (2002). *Introduction to the Problems of Legal Theory* (Translated by B. L. Paulson & S. L. Paulson) Oxford: Clarendon Press, pp. xix–xxvi.

25 At this point, we refrain to enter into the historical debate of 'natural law' versus 'positive law/legal positivism'. *See* Kelsen, H. (2005). *General Theory of Law and State* (1st ed.). New York: Routledge; Raz, J. (1979). *The Authority of Law: Essays in Law and Morality*. Oxford: Clarendon Press; Hart, H. L. A. (1994). *The Concept of Law*. (2nd Edition) Oxford: Clarendon Press; Finnis, J. (1980). *Natural Law and Natural Rights*. Oxford: Clarendon Press; Alexy, R. (2008). On the concept and the nature of law. *Ratio Juris*, *21*(3): 281–99; Dworkin, R. A. (1982). "Natural" law revisited. *University of Florida Law Review*, 34(2): 165–188.

the like for help on legal questions. Therefore, there is a sharp distinction between the 'science of law', the 'philosophy of justice', and the 'sociology of law'.

In light of these considerations, *AI interdisciplinarity* and *AI & Rule of Law* entanglements can be considered apart from *AI & Law* that is more connected to the traditional legal positivism and legal practice using computational models. *AI & Law*, a subfield of '*AI/computer science* research', focuses on designing computer programs/computational models that perform legal reasoning. *AI & Law* interacted with each other and drew attention to *theoretical aspects* of computational frameworks/models for legal/automated reasoning, knowledge representation and reasoning, knowledge engineering, and legal philosophy[26] and *practical aspects* of intelligent legal information systems and (legal) natural-language processing—*(L)NLP*. In the mid-1980s, legal scholars and practitioners worked on *AI*-supported *CBR*, *RBR*, and legal argumentation. A synergy emerged not only between *AI & Law*, but also between *AI* and *AI & Law* that exceeds the boundaries of *AI* technologies and applications and covers learning, representation, and reasoning[27]. For instance, many *AI & Law* researchers adopted open-source text analysis tools and legal applications to identify argument-related information in legal texts and create a shift from legal information retrieval to legal argument retrieval through automated question answering (*QA*), information extraction (*IE*), and argument mining from legal texts. In other words, there is an interconnection between *CMLRs* and legal texts. Kevin Ashley highlighted that *AI & Law* clarifies how new technologies for

[26] Ashley, K. D. (2013). Teaching law and digital age legal practice with an AI and law seminar. *Chicago-Kent Law Review*, *88*(3): 783–844, pp. 783–786; Buchanan, B. G. & Headrick, T. E. (1970). Some speculation about artificial intelligence and legal reasoning. *Stanford Law Review*, *23*(1): 40–62, pp. 46–47; Gardner, A. (1987). *An Artificial Intelligence Approach to Legal Reasoning*. Cambridge, MA: The MIT Press, pp. 1–4; Rissland, E. L. (1988). Artificial intelligence and legal reasoning: A discussion of the field & Gardner's book. *AI Magazine*, *9*(3): 45–55, pp. 45–46; Verheij, B. (2020). Artificial intelligence as law. *Artificial Intelligence and Law*, *28*: 181–206, pp. 187–188.

[27] Ashley, K. D. (1990). *Modeling Legal Argument: Reasoning with Cases and Hypotheticals*. Cambridge, MA: The MIT Press; Ashley, K. D. & Rissland, E. L. (2003). Law, learning and representation. *Artificial Intelligence*, *150*: 17–58, pp. 17–18; McCarty, L. T. (1990). Artificial intelligence and law: How to get there from here. *Ratio Juris*, *3*(2): 189–200, pp. 193–194; Rissland, E. L., Ashley, K. D. & Loui, R. P. (2003). AI and law: A fruitful synergy. *Artificial Intelligence*, *150*(1–2): 1–15, pp. 1–2.

analyzing legal texts enable new tools for legal practice using computational models of legal reasoning and argumentation developed by *AI & Law* researchers. The main objective of much of the research in *AI & Law* has been to develop *CMLRs* that can make legal arguments and use them to predict the outcomes of legal disputes'[28]. A vast majority of the investigations on *AI & Law* are oriented toward the development of '*practical systems*' and only a small group of researchers are primarily interested in '*theoretical questions*'[29]. Overall, *AI and Law* is an intertwined research field and is uniquely positioned to integrate the *alpha*, *beta*, and *gamma* side of science, which corresponds roughly to humanities, experimental sciences, and social sciences. *AI & Law* benefits from the interdisciplinary aspects of different kinds of systems investigated: *theoretical systems* (e.g., mathematics and legal theory), *artificial systems* (e.g., software and statutes), and *natural systems* (e.g., human intelligence and the practices of law)[30].

The theory–practice gap in the *AI*-legal positivism landscape[31] can be filled with the applications of two theses[32] (i.e., the *normativity thesis*: separability of law and fact, and the *reductive thesis*: inseparability of law and fact) in *AI & Law* and *AI & Rule of Law*. However, *AI interdisciplinarity* in the framework of '*AI & Rule of Law*' is a complex issue to argue due to the reason that the '*Rule of Law*' stands in between 'law

[28] Ashley, K. D. (2017). *Artificial Intelligence and Legal Analytics: New Tools for Law Practice in the Digital Age*. (1st edition) Cambridge: CUP, pp. 3–4.

[29] McCarty, L. T. (1990). Artificial intelligence and law: How to get there from here. *Ratio Juris*, *3*(2): 189–200, pp. 190–193.

[30] Bench-Capon, T., Araszkiewicz, M., Ashley, K. et al. (2012). A history of AI and law in 50 papers: 25 years of the international conference on AI and law. *Artificial Intelligence and Law*, *20*: 215–319, pp. 308.

[31] Juškevičiūtė-Vilienė, A. (2024). Legal positivism, AI, and the modern legal landscape: Challenges in education, research, and practice. *Acta Universitatis Lodziensis. Folia Iuridica*, *109*: 25–41, pp. 28–29.

[32] From the *normativity thesis viewpoint*, *AI & Law* can be advanced through *Kelsen*'s arguments in which *AI* technologies and applications sterilize and enforce the technical aspects of law and contribute to the development of theoretical, artificial, and natural systems. Moreover, *à la Kelsen* precise distinction of '*AI & Law*' in *AI*-legal positivism landscape will enable legal context to become much more purified from complex transdisciplinary approaches and strictly bound on mechanistic aspect of *AI* tools for legal practice. From the *reductive thesis* point of view, '*AI & Rule of Law*' will encourage inter-/intra- disciplinary perspectives to develop knowledge production process.

as a science' (e.g., empirical law, computational law, etc.)' and 'justice' (*Aristotelian* virtue of justice and virtue of ethics, etc.).

LegalTech has a significant influence on *AI & Law* and *AI & Rule of Law* or vice versa. In the context of *AI* interdisciplinarity, this relationship interacts with legal practice, cognitive science, and legal theory and doctrine[33]. *LegalTech* fits well with *AI* interdisciplinarity because it improves the legal system for a broad diversified group—i.e., the general public, lawyers, the judiciary, etc.[34]

Consequently, there has been an increase in the exchange between *AI & Law* on the one hand, and *LegalTech* (and *AI & Rule of Law*) on the other hand, however, the increase has not been tremendous. The Legal Innovation & Technology Lab (LIT Lab) at Suffolk University Law School conducts *AI* projects that are relevant to *AI and Rule of Law*. Recently, Suffolk University Law School has launched an innovative online platform that allows users to practice their negotiation skills with *AI* bots that talk back. Unlike typical *AI* assistants that tend to be extremely accommodating, Suffolk's new tool presents users with *AI* negotiators that are programmed to employ a variety of tactics and strategies used by experienced lawyers[35].

1.2 *AI Interdisciplinarity* and the Rule of Law

There is rapidly growing literature on *AI & Rule of Law* prioritizing the adjudication. Lon L. Fuller asserted that adjudication default as an ordering principle if the established rules are insufficient to cover the area of possible controversy. He highlighted two approaches to adjudication: 'First rules, then courts (*civil law legal system*)', and 'first courts, then rules (*common law legal system*)'[36]. Courts deliver justice in accordance

[33] Araszkiewicz, M. (2021). Computational legal problem solving: What can legal tech learn from AI and law research, and beyond? In: Szostek, D. & Załucki, M. (eds.) *Legal Tech: Information Technology Tools in the Administration of Justice* (pp. 101–127). Baden-Baden: Nomos, pp. 126–127.

[34] Hartung, M., Bues, M. M. & Halbleib, G. (eds.) (2018). *Legal Tech: How Technology is Changing the Legal World—A Practitioner's Guide*. München: Beck, p. v.

[35] The Legal Innovation & Technology Lab (LIT Lab), Suffolk University Law School (2025). Digital dealmakers: Suffolk Law's new AI platform challenges student negotiators. Boston: Suffolk University.

[36] Fuller, L. L. (1960). Adjudication and the rule of law. *Proceedings of the American Society of International Law at Its Annual Meeting (1921–1969)*, *54*: 1–8, p. 6.

with the rule of law. Courts' prescriptions have shaped how technology can be used, and ethical rules impose a duty to the courts and the administration of justice. In this context, lawyers play a societal or structural role in upholding the rule of law. Thus, the use of *AI* and lawyers' ethical obligations interact symbiotically[37]. The use of *AI* to assist decisions made in the exercise of power by states increased discussion of *AI & Rule of Law*[38]. Frazier asserted that the 'rule of law[39]' is not self-sustaining, and society demands a more interdisciplinary legal system. Public authorities may undermine the rule-of-law principle when they implement and enforce the law through algorithmic regulation. The rule of law is a core interest of societies and individuals in constitutional democracies, and any adverse impact thereon can be conceptualized as harm on societies/ individuals[40].

Interdisciplinary approaches to *AI & Rule of Law* will reform the (algorithmic) adjudication of disputes related to *AI* and emerging new technologies and create a more reliable and accurate body of law in furtherance of the rule of law[41]. *AI & Rule of Law* scrutinizes *AI* tools (e.g., *ML* tools) applied in the pre-adjudicative phase of enforcing of the laws and during legal adjudication phase, and measures the impacts on fairness, transparency, compliance with the rule of law, and equity

[37] Legg, M. & Bell, F. (2020). *Artificial Intelligence and the Legal Profession.* Oxford: Bloomsbury, pp. 9–10.

[38] Burgess, P. (2022). The Rule of Law, Science Fiction and Fears of Artificial Intelligence. *Law, Technology and Humans*, *4*(2): 124–136, pp. 124–125.

[39] For historical evolution of the ambiguous concept of the 'rule of law', *See* Dicey, A. V. (1915). *Introduction to the Study of the Law of the Constitution.* London: Macmillan; Bingham, L. (2007). The rule of law. *Cambridge Law Journal*, *66*(1): 67–85; Venice Commission (2011). Report on the rule of law. Study No. 512/2009, Strasbourg: Venice Commission; Bingham, T. (2011). *The Rule of Law.* London: Penguin Books; Dworkin, R. (2013). The rule of law. *Law of Ukraine*, *2013*(4): 7–13; Venice Commission (2016). Rule of law checklist. Strasbourg: Venice Commission.

[40] Smuha, N. A. (2024). *Algorithmic Rule by Law: How Algorithmic Regulation in the Public Sector Erodes the Rule of Law.* Cambridge: CUP, p. 9.

[41] Frazier, K. (2023). A different alignment problem: AI, the rule of law, and outdated legal institutions and practices. *Journal of Business & Technology Law*, *19*(2): 331–372, pp. 331–332.

of adjudicative systems[42]. '*AI & Rule of Law*' is hinged on the principles of good democratic governance, such as ethics, accountability, transparency, fairness, etc. These governance principles have profoundly influenced *AI* in judicial reasoning, decision-making, and ethical implications of *AI* technologies and applications. *AI* has started to make its way into digital decision-making systems, replace human decision-makers, and assist judges in making judicial decisions. There is undoubtedly a lack of transparency in digital decision-making systems that contain extremely complex technology that is beyond the cognitive capacities of humans. Thus, the rule of law principles (i.e., transparency, fairness, and explainability, etc.) are endangered, and *AI* is challenging the ideals of the rule of law[43]. The use of *AI* has a significant influence on the development of the rule of law through considering the following issues: (1) algorithmic bias (e.g., data bias and design bias) and subjective bias (e.g., implicit and explicit biases based on gender, race, nationality, etc.), (2) digitalization of justice systems, (3) *AI*'s impact on safeguarding human rights, (4) *AI* ethics and governance, (5) *AI* use in justice systems, etc.

UNESCO's 'Global Judges Initiative (2014)' and the Initiative's '*AI and the Rule of Law Programme*' (2022)' engaged stakeholders in justice systems with the applications of *AI* and its impact on the '*Rule of Law*'. UNESCO and partners developed a Massive Open Online Course (MOOC) on *AI and the Rule of Law* in seven languages in 2022. UNESCO's MOOC on *AI and the Rule of Law* is indeed a milestone for the application of good practices on how courts are deciding *AI*-related cases, by considering human rights and ethical standards, and explicates the opportunities and risks of *AI* adoption by justice systems[44]. UNESCO's '*Recommendation on the Ethics of AI*' was adopted by UNESCO's 193 Member States in November 2021. The main action is for Member States to put in place effective measures, and to ensure

[42] Huq, A. Z. (2024). Artificial intelligence and the rule of law. In: Sevel, M. (Ed.) *Routledge Handbook of the Rule of Law* (pp. 260–272). Abingdon: Routledge, pp. 260–263; Tasioulas, J. (2023). The rule of algorithm and the rule of law. In: Bezemek, C., Potacs, M. & Somek, A. (eds.) *Vienna Lectures on Legal Philosophy, Volume 3 - Legal Reasoning* (pp. 17–40). London: Bloomsbury, pp. 17–20.

[43] Greenstein, S. (2022). Preserving the rule of law in the era of artificial intelligence (AI). *Artificial Intelligence and Law*, *30*: 291–323, pp. 291–292.

[44] UNESCO (2023). Global toolkit on AI and the rule of law for the judiciary. Paris: UNESCO, pp. 16–25.

adherence to them by encouraging all stakeholders to develop human rights, the rule of law, democracy, and ethical impact assessment and due diligence tools in line with guidance including the UN Guiding Principles on Business and Human Rights[45].

Since last decade, UNESCO's initiatives opened up *AI & Rule of Law* to 'broader normative considerations' as elaborated by international law and normative political theory and enabled the development of the consultation process of universally accepted values, principles, and standards. The term 'rule of law' is used to designate different ideals that the law should conform to, and the rule of law consists of principles that constrain the way government actions change and apply the law. Joseph Raz stated that the rule of law principles are not about the content of the law, but about its mode of generation and application[46]. Shared consensus rule-of-law components include principles such as the following: (1) The existence of rules, (2) consistency, (3) limitation of discretion, (4) prospectivity, (5) notice or publicity, (6) stability, (7) predictability, (8) democracy, (9) protections for human rights, and (10) free market economic system[47]. In an interview conducted by Armin von Bogdandy, Director of Max Planck Institute for Comparative Public Law and International Law in Heidelberg, Jürgen Habermas highlighted that the '*rule of law*' and '*sovereignty*' are the two most basic elements from which constitutional principles derive. Habermas supported a '*reconstructive approach*' to international law and put forward that the 'principles for building a community of free and equal citizens on national territories can and should also guide the transformation of international law'[48].

The '*AI & Rule of Law*' interactions and law enforcement by leveraging '*responsible AI technologies*', advanced *AI* tools, *AI* innovation, and high-tech applications enabled enhanced control mechanism of governmental bodies on technology and data for security and privacy reasons. In

[45] UNESCO (2022). Recommendation on the ethics of artificial intelligence. p. 26.

[46] Raz, J. (2019). The law's own virtue. *Oxford Journal of Legal Studies*, *39*(1): 1–15, pp. 1–2.

[47] Eyer, K. R. (2008). Administrative adjudication and the rule of law. *Administrative Law Review*, *60*(3): 647–706, p. 655–656.

[48] Von Bogdandy, A. & Habermas, J. (2013). Discourse theory and international law: An interview with Jürgen Habermas, *VerfBlog*, 2013/5/12.

this context, law enforcement agencies must take into account a responsible *AI* innovation approach by aligning with policing principles that are ethically sound and human rights compliant.[49]

1.3 Digital Ethics, '*Responsible AI*', and '*AI4People*' Through the Lens of *AI* Interdisciplinarity: '*Ethics by Design*' and Two Cultures of *STEM* and *SSHA*

AI interdisciplinarity navigates the practical terrain of science and the philosophy of technology. Technological ethics (*technoethics*) and biological ethics (*bioethics*) (e.g., in law, medicine, journalism, etc.) that employ *AI* systems require a philosophy of technology perspective of '*ethics by design (EbD)*' and an interdisciplinary approach to balance technical issues and forecast biases[50]. *EbD* is about the 'methods, algorithms, and tools needed to endow autonomous agents with the ability to reason about the ethical aspects of their decisions, and the methods, tools, and formalisms to ensure that an agent's behavior remains within the given moral bounds'[51].

Criticisms of modern technological design focus on the inherent consistency, and the rightness/wrongness of design maxims. However, it is quite difficult to address the issues inherent in the designed techno-lifeworld without the design process as a whole. The attempt to cultivate ethics within design starts with the attempt to articulate guidelines for that action called designing such that they already exist. The fundamental ethical issue of design is created by its essential separation from the 'inner'

[49] UNICRI & Interpol (2024). Toolkit for responsible AI innovation in law enforcement: Introduction to responsible AI innovation. Turin: UNICRI, pp. 13–14.

[50] Bisconti, P., and others (2023). Maximizing team synergy in AI-related interdisciplinary groups: An interdisciplinary-by-design iterative methodology. *AI & Society*, *38*: 1443–1452, pp. 1444–1445; Findeli, A. (1994). Ethics, aesthetics, and design. *Design Issues*, *10*(2): 49–68, pp. 50–51.

[51] Dignum, V. and others (2018). Ethics by design: Necessity or curse? *AIES '18: Proceedings of the 2018 AAAI/ACM Conference on AI, Ethics, and Society*, (pp. 60–66), p. 60.

and 'outer' worlds[52]. Thus, the dilemma of *EbD* with respect to *AI* interdisciplinarity encompasses two worlds of imagination: The one seeks for '*ethics and responsible design*' out there (*outer world*) and the other forms a biased view of '*ethics and design*' involving presumptions and presuppositions in the human mind or computer-aided design (*inner world*). In fact, a biased view of ethics and computer-aided design that is incorporated with a '*preference-based utilitarianism*' approach (i.e., focused on maximizing the fulfillment of human preferences) in the ethics of *AI*[53] can form hedonic loopholes in which ambiguities, anomalies, and controversies emerge as a consequence of designing *AI* systems that only purpose is the realization of human preferences[54].

Recently, the European Commission adopted the *EbD* and ethics of use approaches for *AI* as part of its ethics review procedure for *AI* projects. The objective of *EbD* is to incorporate ethical principles into the development process, ensuring that ethical issues are dealt with as soon as possible and are closely followed during research activities. In other words, *EbD* is aimed at preventing the occurrence of ethical problems first by treating them during the development stage rather than trying to resolve them later in the process.[55] The *EbD* framework contains the steps, such as assessment, instantiation, mapping, application, and implementation[56].

Fan designed an ethical hierarchy in turn from low order to high order[57]:

[52] Mitcham, C. (1995). Ethics into design. In: Buchanan, R. & Margolin, V. (eds.) *Discovering Design: Explorations in Design Studies* (pp. 173–189). Chicago: The University of Chicago Press, pp. 179–184.

[53] Tasioulas, J. (2022). Artificial intelligence, humanistic ethics. *Dædalus, the Journal of the American Academy of Arts & Sciences*, *151*(2): 232–243, pp. 232–234.

[54] Russell, S. J. (2019). *Human Compatible: AI and the Problem of Control*. London: Allen Lane, pp. 173–174.

[55] European Commission (2021). Ethics by design and ethics of use approaches for artificial intelligence (version 1.0). Brussels: European Commission–DG Research and Innovation, pp. 3–11.

[56] Brey, P. & Dainow, B. (2024). Ethics by design for artificial intelligence. AI and Ethics, 4:1265–1277, p. 1267.

[57] Fan, Y. (2024). The formation and implementation of ethical norms for artificial intelligence in the soil of the rule of law: Focusing on AI governance. *Applied Mathematics and Nonlinear Sciences*, *9*(1): 1–16, pp. 3–4.

- '*Ethical etiquette (1. Level: Maintain normal order)*' is the cornerstone of ethical development, a requirement of the workplace, and the guarantee of maintaining and operating order,
- '*Codes of ethics (2. Level: Basic principles that must be adhered to)*' are ethical norms that are the objective existence and the ethical normative requirements that must be followed,
- '*Ethical principle (3. Level: To guide the effective formulation and implementation of ethical protocols and codes of ethics)*' contain both objective ethical norms and individual subjective ethical attitudes,
- '*Ethical value (4. Level: The core of the whole ethical system, the essential characteristics of ethics)*' is the core of the ethical system and the high-level fruit of the development of ethical manners, ethical norms, and ethical principles.

Ethical inquiries can provide high-level principles as well as lower-level recommendations. Sartor clarified ethical considerations based on '*positive morality* (ethical practices with normative arguments aimed at supporting currently endorsed practices)' and '*critical morality* (criticizing ethical practices from the standpoint of a conception presented as superior, more rational, or supported by a stronger justification)'.[58]

Without imposing a hierarchy, the High-Level Expert Group on Artificial Intelligence (*AI HLEG*), set up by the European Commission, listed '*four ethical principles*' that are rooted in fundamental rights. These principles must be respected to ensure that *AI* systems are developed, deployed, and used in a trustworthy manner. They are specified as '*ethical imperatives*'[59]:

(a) *Respect for human autonomy*: Humans interacting with *AI* systems must be able to maintain full and effective self-determination over themselves. *AI* systems should not unjustifiably subordinate, coerce, deceive, manipulate, condition, or herd humans. Instead, they should be designed to augment, complement, and empower human cognitive, social, and cultural skills.

[58] Sartor, G. (2020). Artificial intelligence and human rights: Between law and ethics. *Maastricht Journal of European and Comparative Law*, *27*(6): 705–719, pp. 707–708.

[59] High-Level Expert Group on Artificial Intelligence—AI HLEG (2019). Ethics guidelines for trustworthy AI. Brussels: European Commission, pp. 11–13.

(b) *Prevention of harm*: Protection of human dignity as well as mental and physical integrity should be guaranteed. *AI* systems and the environments in which they operate must be safe and secure.
(c) *Fairness*: The development, deployment, and use of *AI* systems must be fair in both a substantive and a procedural dimension.
(d) Explicability: Algorithmic processes need to be transparent, the capabilities and purpose of *AI* systems openly communicated, and decisions explainable to those directly and indirectly affected.

Recently, there has been a substantial concentration on the responsible development and deployment of *AI* systems, and as a consequence, the *AI* community has become more concerned with assessing the influence of *AI* systems and mitigating risks for those affected[60]. In order to address the risks posed by *AI*, it is essential to identify the right basic ethical principles for the design, regulation, and use of *AI* and to use them for benefits and respect of individuals and societies. It is not easy, since ethical principles can vary depending on cultural contexts and analytical fields[61]. '*Responsible AI*' must align *AI* technologies and applications with the principles of governance, legal standards, and ethical principles to deal with biased or inaccurate *AI*-generated information and multilevel regulatory approaches to *AI*. '*Responsible AI*' ought to adopt a '*benefit-for-all principle*' and transform digital governance in favor of '*AI4People*' and a balance between '*AI4People*' and '*AI4S*'.

Public acceptance and adoption of digital technologies, including *AI*, only occur when benefits are considered meaningful and risks are considered potentially avoidable or minimized, or at least when something can be protected against them. These attitudes will depend on public participation in the development of digital technologies, the openness of their functioning, and the understandable and accessible regulatory and remedy mechanisms[62].

[60] Maslej, N., and others (2024). The AI index 2024 annual report. Stanford, CA: AI Index Steering Committee, Institute for Human-Centered AI, Stanford University, pp. 160–162.

[61] Taddeo, M., & Floridi, L. (2018). How AI can be a force for good. *Science*, *361*(6404), 751–752, p. 752.

[62] Floridi, L., and others (2018). AI4People—An ethical framework for a good AI society: Opportunities, risks, principles, and recommendations. *Minds and Machines*, *28*: 689–707, pp. 694–695.

Addressing societal and ethical concerns is vital for the responsible deployment of *AI* tools[63]. Thus, *AI interdisciplinarity* and the responsible deployment of *AI* tools must be in compliance with the principles and practices of *AI* ethics, such as data privacy and governance, accountability, transparency, fairness, explainability, inclusion, social and environmental impact, value alignment, human and moral agency, misinformation, power imbalance, etc.

The '*Responsible AI technologies*' fill the gap between computer science and data science (*STEM*) and the social sciences, humanities, and arts (*SSHA*). *AI interdisciplinarity* formed between '*Two Cultures*'[64]—cultures of science and literary intellectuals—has a vital role in knowledge production and, indeed, 'culture' as an 'input' could be expected to be at the heart of any divide between science, technology (industry), academia, and society. Thus, the role of '*responsible AI technologies*' in reconstructing, interrelating, and balancing this historical divide is quite significant.

The current situation is understandable and unacceptable. It is understandable, because the *R&D* of companies has driven *AI*-based innovation, and over the past decade, the industry has been leading discussions in collaboration with academia on how *AI* can be best applied for the benefit of society. Nevertheless, it is unacceptable to hand over these tasks to private or academic actors due to the lack of social and political responsibility and long-term planning with the aim of achieving a fair share of the benefits and opportunities for all. Meanwhile, the industry is developing its own *AI* principles or launching multistakeholder initiatives to develop best practices. They are also involved in regulating *AI*, whether through direct participation or lobbying. These industry efforts are admirable, but it is important to position them in light of three important issues. First, who sets the agenda for the governance of *AI*? Second, what is the cultural logic instantiated by this agenda, and third, what benefits are derived from it? The answer to these questions is important

[63] Hussain, T., Wang, D. & Li, B. (2024). The influence of the COVID-19 pandemic on the adoption and impact of AI ChatGPT: Challenges, applications, and ethical considerations. *Acta Psychologica*, *246*: 1–8, p. 7.

[64] Snow C. P. (1961). *The Two Cultures and the Scientific Revolution*. (7th ed.). Cambridge, UK: CUP, pp. 23–25.

because it highlights the risks of leaving the industry behind and reveals the shortcomings of current research efforts[65].

Institutionalization of *AI interdisciplinarity* can enrich the multi-faceted nature of *AI* and digital governance and ensure proximities between *STEM* and *SSHA*. *AI interdisciplinarity* inextricably is inter-twined with fuzzy tech terminologies and complexity thinking (CT), and it is embedded in social and cultural domains[66]. There is a lack of critical thinking and CT in the complex phenomena of *AI interdisciplinarity* and '*responsible AI technologies*' tend to explore generative knowledge and new paradigms for the future of *AI* from epistemological, ontological, and methodological perspectives. In the future, *GAI* will create highly sophisticated contents that guide us to unearth discrepancies, deficiencies, nature of complex phenomena, and accurateness of *AI* systems and the measures. Furthermore, diversified methodological approaches to *AI interdisciplinarity* by *STEM* and *SSHA* experts will have a profound influence on differentiate learning, instruction, and assessment that prioritize convergent and divergent interests of two cultures.

References

Abbonato, D., Bianchini, S., Gargiulo, F. & Venturini, T. (2024). Interdisciplinary research in artificial intelligence: Lessons from COVID-19. *Quantitative Science Studies*, *5*(4): 922–935. https://doi.org/10.1162/qss_a_00329

Aliu, A. (Ed.) (2024). *Complexity Thinking and China's Demography Within and Beyond Mainland China.* (1st edition) Singapore: Palgrave Macmillan. https://doi.org/10.1007/978-981-97-0172-8

Araszkiewicz, M. (2021). Computational legal problem solving: What can legal tech learn from AI and law research, and beyond? In: Szostek, D. & Załucki, M. (eds.) *Legal Tech: Information Technology Tools in the Administration of Justice* (pp. 101–127). Baden-Baden: Nomos.

[65] Cath, C., Wachter, S., Mittelstadt, B., Taddeo, M., & Floridi, L. (2018). Artificial intelligence and the 'good society': The US, EU, and UK approach. *Science and Engineering Ethics*, *24*: 505–528; Cath, C. (2018). Governing artificial intelligence: Ethical, legal and technical opportunities and challenges. *Philosophical Transactions of the Royal Society A: Mathematical, Physical and Engineering Sciences*, *376*: 3–4.

[66] Aliu, A. (Ed.) (2024). *Complexity Thinking and China's Demography Within and Beyond Mainland China.* (1st edition) Singapore: Palgrave Macmillan, pp. 16–17.

Ashley, K. D. (1990). *Modeling Legal Argument: Reasoning with Cases and Hypotheticals*. Cambridge, MA: The MIT Press.

Ashley, K. D. & Bridge, D. G. (eds.) (2003). *Case-Based Reasoning Research and Development*. Berlin: Springer.

Ashley, K. D. (2013). Teaching law and digital age legal practice with an AI and law seminar. *Chicago-Kent Law Review*, *88*(3): 783–844.

Ashley, K. D. (2017). *Artificial Intelligence and Legal Analytics: New Tools for Law Practice in the Digital Age*. (1st edition) Cambridge: CUP.

Ashley, K. D. & Rissland, E. L. (2003). Law, learning and representation. *Artificial Intelligence*, *150*: 17–58.

Bench-Capon, T., Araszkiewicz, M., Ashley, K. et al. (2012). A history of AI and law in 50 papers: 25 years of the international conference on AI and law. *Artificial Intelligence and Law*, *20*: 215–319. https://doi.org/10.1007/s10506-012-9131-x

Bisconti, P., Orsitto, D., Fedorczyk, F., Brau, F., Capasso, M., De Marinis, L., Eken, H., Merenda, F., Forti, M., Pacini, M. & Schettini, C. (2023). Maximizing team synergy in AI-related interdisciplinary groups: An interdisciplinary-by-design iterative methodology. *AI & Society*, *38*: 1443–1452. https://doi.org/10.1007/s00146-022-01518-8

Brey, P. & Dainow, B. (2024). Ethics by design for artificial intelligence. AI and Ethics, 4:1265–1277. https://doi.org/10.1007/s43681-023-00330-4

Buchanan, B. G. & Headrick, T. E. (1970). Some speculation about artificial intelligence and legal reasoning. *Stanford Law Review*, *23*(1): 40–62. https://doi.org/10.2307/1227753

Cath, C. (2018). Governing artificial intelligence: Ethical, legal and technical opportunities and challenges. *Philosophical Transactions of the Royal Society A: Mathematical, Physical and Engineering Sciences*, *376*: 3–4. https://doi.org/10.1098/rsta.2018.0080

Cath, C., Wachter, S., Mittelstadt, B., Taddeo, M., & Floridi, L. (2018). Artificial intelligence and the 'good society': The US, EU, and UK approach. *Science and Engineering Ethics*, *24*: 505–528. https://doi.org/10.1007/s11948-017-9901-7

Dignum, V. and others (2018). Ethics by design: Necessity or curse? *AIES '18: Proceedings of the 2018 AAAI/ACM Conference on AI, Ethics, and Society*, (pp. 60–66). ACM. https://doi.org/10.1145/3278721.3278745

Dimatteo, L. A., Poncibò, C. & Cannarsa, M. (eds.) (2022). *The Cambridge Handbook of Artificial Intelligence: Global Perspectives on Law and Ethics*. Cambridge: CUP.

European Commission (2021). Ethics by design and ethics of use approaches for artificial intelligence (version 1.0). Brussels: European Commission–DG Research and Innovation. https://ec.europa.eu/info/funding-tenders/opportunities/docs/2021-2027/horizon/guidance/ethics-by-design-and-ethics-of-use-approaches-for-artificial-intelligence_he_en.pdf March 21, 2025.

Eyer, K. R. (2008). Administrative adjudication and the rule of law. *Administrative Law Review*, *60*(3): 647–706.

Findeli, A. (1994). Ethics, aesthetics, and design. *Design Issues*, *10*(2): 49–68. https://doi.org/10.2307/1511628

Floridi, L., Cowls, J., Beltrametti, M., Chatila, R., Chazerand, P., Dignum, V., Luetge, C., Madelin, R., Pagallo, U., Rossi, F., Schafer, B., Valcke, P. & Vayena, E. (2018). AI4People—An ethical framework for a good AI society: Opportunities, risks, principles, and recommendations. *Minds and Machines*, 28: 689–707.

Frazier, K. (2023). A different alignment problem: AI, the rule of law, and outdated legal institutions and practices. *Journal of Business & Technology Law*, *19*(2): 331–372.

Fuller, L. L. (1960). Adjudication and the rule of law. *Proceedings of the American Society of International Law at Its Annual Meeting (1921–1969)*, *54*: 1–8.

Gardner, A. (1987). An Artificial Intelligence Approach to Legal Reasoning. Cambridge, MA: The MIT Press.

Greenstein, S. (2022). Preserving the rule of law in the era of artificial intelligence (AI). *Artificial Intelligence and Law*, *30*: 291–323. https://doi.org/10.1007/s10506-021-09294-4 Accessed December 6, 2024.

Hartung, M., Bues, M. M. & Halbleib, G. (eds.) (2018). *Legal Tech: How Technology is Changing the Legal World—A Practitioner's Guide*. München: Beck.

High-Level Expert Group on Artificial Intelligence—AI HLEG (2019). Ethics guidelines for trustworthy AI. Brussels: European Commission. https://ec.europa.eu/newsroom/dae/document.cfm?doc_id=60419 March 16, 2025.

Hinton, G. E. (2024). University of Toronto press conference: Professor Geoffrey Hinton, Nobel prize in physics 2024. https://www.utoronto.ca/news/geoffrey-hinton-wins-nobel-prize Accessed January 16, 2025.

Hussain, T., Wang, D. & Li, B. (2024). The influence of the COVID-19 pandemic on the adoption and impact of AI ChatGPT: Challenges, applications, and ethical considerations. *Acta Psychologica*, 246: 1–8.

Huq, A. Z. (2024). Artificial intelligence and the rule of law. In: Sevel, M. (Ed.) Routledge Handbook of the Rule of Law (pp. 260–272). Abingdon: Routledge. https://doi.org/10.4324/9781351237185

Juškevičiūtė-Vilienė, A. (2024). Legal positivism, AI, and the modern legal landscape: Challenges in education, research, and practice. *Acta Universitatis Lodziensis. Folia Iuridica*, 109: 25–41. https://doi.org/10.18778/0208-6069.109.02 Accessed January 16, 2025.

Kelsen, H. (1941). The pure theory of law and analytical jurisprudence. *Harvard Law Review*, *55*(1): 44–70. https://doi.org/10.2307/1334739 Accessed December 6, 2024.

Kelsen, H. (2002). *Introduction to the Problems of Legal Theory* (Translated by B. L. Paulson & S. L. Paulson) Oxford: Clarendon Press.

Legg, M. & Bell, F. (2020). *Artificial Intelligence and the Legal Profession*. Oxford: Bloomsbury.

Lu, C. (2024). Rethinking artificial intelligence from the perspective of interdisciplinary knowledge production. *AI & Society*, *39*: 3059–3060. https://doi.org/10.1007/s00146-023-01839-2

Maslej, N., Fattorini, L., Perrault, R., Parli, V., Reuel, A., Brynjolfsson, E., Etchemendy, J., Ligett, K., Lyons, T., Manyika, J., Niebles, J. C., Shoham, Y., Wald, R. & Clark, J. (2024). The AI index 2024 annual report. Stanford, CA: AI Index Steering Committee, Institute for Human-Centered AI, Stanford University. https://aiindex.stanford.edu/wp-content/uploads/2024/05/HAI_AI-Index-Report-2024.pdf Accessed January 27, 2025.

McCarthy, J., Minsky, M. L., Rochester, N. & Shannon C. E. (1955). A Proposal for the Dartmouth Summer Research Project on Artificial Intelligence. http://jmc.stanford.edu/articles/dartmouth/dartmouth.pdf Accessed November 10, 2024.

McCarty, L. T. (1990). Artificial intelligence and law: How to get there from here. *Ratio Juris*, *3*(2): 189–200. https://doi.org/10.1111/j.1467-9337.1990.tb00057.x

Mehl, L. (1959). Automation in the legal world: From machine processing of legal information to the 'law machine' (pp. 755–787). November 24 to 27, 1958, the National Physical Laboratory, Teddington, England. https://aitopics.org/download/classics:97D0F0CA Accessed December 6, 2024.

Mitcham, C. (1995). Ethics into design. In: Buchanan, R. & Margolin, V. (eds.) *Discovering Design: Explorations in Design Studies* (pp. 173–189). Chicago: The University of Chicago Press.

Morgan, J. (2017). Torts and technology. In: Brownsword, R., Scotford, E. & Yeung, K. (Eds). *The Oxford Handbook of Law, Regulation and Technology* (pp. 523–546). Oxford: OUP.

OECD/Eurostat (2018). Oslo Manual 2018: Guidelines for Collecting, Reporting and Using Data on Innovation: The Measurement of Scientific, Technological and Innovation Activities. (4th Edition) Paris/Eurostat, Luxembourg: OECD Publishing. https://doi.org/10.1787/9789264304604-en

OECD (2020). The Digitalisation of Science, Technology and Innovation: Key Developments and Policies. Paris: OECD Publishing. https://doi.org/10.1787/b9e4a2c0-en Accessed December 15, 2024.

Raj, P., Kumar, A., Dubey, A. K., Bhatia, S. & Manoj, O. (eds.) (2023). *Quantum Computing and Artificial Intelligence*. Berlin: Walter de Gruyter.

Raz, J. (2019). The law's own virtue. *Oxford Journal of Legal Studies*, *39*(1): 1–15. https://doi.org/10.1093/ojls/gqy041 Accessed December 15, 2024.

Rissland, E. L. (1988). Artificial intelligence and legal reasoning: A discussion of the field & Gardner's book. *AI Magazine*, *9*(3): 45–55. https://doi.org/10.1609/aimag.v9i3.942 Accessed December 6, 2024.

Rissland, E. L., Ashley, K. D. & Loui, R. P. (2003). AI and law: A fruitful synergy. *Artificial Intelligence*, 150(1–2): 1–15. https://doi.org/10.1016/S0004-3702(03)00122-X Accessed December 6, 2024.

Rissland, E. L., Ashley, K. D. & Branting, L. K. (2006). Case-based reasoning and law. *The Knowledge Engineering Review*, *20*(3): 293–298. https://doi.org/10.1017/S0269888906000701 Accessed December 6, 2024.

Russell, S. J. (2019). *Human Compatible: AI and the Problem of Control*. London: Allen Lane.

Russell, S. J. & Norvig, P. (2022). *Artificial Intelligence: A Modern Approach*. 4th Global Edition. Harlow: Pearson.

Sartor, G. (2020). Artificial intelligence and human rights: Between law and ethics. *Maastricht Journal of European and Comparative Law*, *27*(6): 705–719.

Scimeca, M. & Bonfiglio, R. (2023). Dignity of science and the use of ChatGPT as a co-author. *ESMO Open*, *8*(4): 1–2.

Smuha, N. A. (2024). *Algorithmic Rule By Law: How Algorithmic Regulation in the Public Sector Erodes the Rule of Law*. Cambridge: CUP.

Snow C. P. (1961). *The Two Cultures and the Scientific Revolution*. (7th ed.). Cambridge, UK: CUP.

Sufrin, B. (1981). Reading formal specifications. Oxford: University of Oxford Computing Laboratory. https://www.cs.ox.ac.uk/files/6410/prg24.pdf Accessed December 6, 2024.

Susskind, R. (1986). Expert systems in in law: A jurisprudential approach to artificial intelligence and legal reasoning. *The Modern Law Review*, *49*: 168–194.

Susskind, R. (1989). Pragmatism and purism in artificial intelligence and legal reasoning. *AI & Society*, *3*: 28–38.

Szostek, D. (2021). The concept of legal technology (LegalTech) and legal engineering. In: Szostek, D. & Załucki, M. (eds.) *Legal Tech: Information Technology Tools in the Administration of Justice* (pp. 19–28). Baden-Baden: Nomos.

Taddeo, M., & Floridi, L. (2018). How AI can be a force for good. *Science*, *361*(6404), 751–752.

Tasioulas, J. (2022). Artificial intelligence, humanistic ethics. *Dædalus, the Journal of the American Academy of Arts & Sciences*, *151*(2): 232–243.

Tasioulas, J. (2023). The rule of algorithm and the rule of law. In: Bezemek, C., Potacs, M. & Somek, A. (eds.) *Vienna Lectures on Legal Philosophy, Volume 3—Legal Reasoning* (pp. 17–40). London: Bloomsbury.

The Legal Innovation & Technology Lab (LIT Lab), Suffolk University Law School (2025). Digital Dealmakers: Suffolk Law's New AI Platform Challenges Student Negotiators. Boston: Suffolk University. https://www.suffolk.edu/news-features/news/2025/03/18/20/19/ai-negotiation-tool Accessed April 5, 2025.

Toulmin, S. E. (2003). The Uses of Argument. (updated edition) Cambridge: CUP.

UNESCO (2022). Recommendation on the ethics of artificial intelligence. https://unesdoc.unesco.org/ark:/48223/pf0000381137 Accessed February 6, 2025.

UNESCO (2023). Global toolkit on AI and the rule of law for the judiciary. Paris: UNESCO. https://unesdoc.unesco.org/ark:/48223/pf0000387331 Accessed February 6, 2025.

UNICRI & Interpol (2024). Toolkit for responsible AI innovation in law enforcement: Introduction to responsible AI innovation. Turin: UNICRI, https://unicri.org/sites/default/files/2025-03/Intro_Resp_AI_Innovation_Mar25.pdf Accessed March 6, 2025.

Valcke, P., Graef, I. & Clifford, D. (2018). iFairness –Constructing fairness in IT (and other areas of) law through intra- and interdisciplinarity. *Computer Law & Security Review*, *34*: 707–714.

van der Sloot, B. (2024). *Regulating the Synthetic Society: Generative AI, Legal Questions and Societal Challenges*. Oxford: Bloomsbury.

Verheij, B. (2020). Artificial intelligence as law. *Artificial Intelligence and Law*, *28*: 181–206. https://doi.org/10.1007/s10506-020-09266-0

von Bogdandy, A. & Habermas, J. (2013). Discourse Theory and International Law: An Interview with Jürgen Habermas, VerfBlog, 2013/5/12, https://verfassungsblog.de/discourse-theory-and-international-law-an-interview-with-jurgen-habermas/, https://doi.org/10.17176/20170216-185041. Accessed December 12, 2024.

CHAPTER 2

The Role of the Arts and Humanities in Thinking About AI

John Tasioulas

2.1 Choice

Perhaps the most fundamental contribution of the arts and humanities is to make vivid the fact that the development of AI is not a matter of destiny, but instead involves successive waves of highly consequential human choices. It's important to identify the choices, to frame them in the right way, and to raise the question: who gets to make them and how?

This is important because AI, and digital technology generally, has become the latest focus of the historicist myth that social evolution is preordained, that our social world is determined by independent variables over which we, as individuals or societies, are able to exert little control. So we either go with the flow or go under. As Aristotle put it: 'No one deliberates about things that are invariable, nor about things that it is impossible for him to do'.[1]

[1] Aristotle, Nicomachean Ethics Book VI, 5.

J. Tasioulas (✉)
Institute for Ethics in AI, Faculty of Philosophy, University of Oxford, Oxford, UK
e-mail: john.tasioulas@philosophy.ox.ac.uk

A. Aliu (ed.), *Artificial Intelligence and the Rule of Law*,
https://doi.org/10.1007/978-3-031-97389-5_2

Not long ago, processes of economic globalisation were being presented as invariable in this way until a populist backlash and then the COVID-19 pandemic kicked in. Today, it is technological developments that are portrayed in this deterministic fashion. An illustration of this trend is a recent speech by Tony Blair identifying the '21st-century technological revolution' as defining the progressive task. As the political scientist Helen Thompson pointed out, technology has replaced globalisation in Blair's rhetoric of historicist progressivism.[2]

The humanities are vital to combatting this historicist tendency, which is profoundly disempowering for individuals and democratic publics alike. They can do so by reminding us, for example, of other technological developments that arose the day before yesterday—such as the harnessing of nuclear power—and how their development and deployment were always contingent on human choices, and therefore hostage to systems of value and to power structures that could have been otherwise.

2.2 Ethics

Having highlighted the necessity for choice, the second contribution the arts and humanities can make is to emphasise the inescapability of ethics in framing and thinking through these choices.

Ethics is inescapable because it concerns the ultimate values in which our choices are anchored, whether we realise it or not. These are values that define what it is to have a good life, and what we owe to others, including non-human animals and to nature. Therefore, all forms of 'regulation' that might be proposed for AI, whether one's self-regulation in deciding whether to use a social robot to keep one's aged mother company, or the content of the social and legal norms that should govern the use of such robots, ultimately implicate choices that reflect ethical judgments about salient values and their prioritisation.

The arts and humanities in general, and not just philosophy, engage directly with the question of ethics—the ultimate ends of human life. And, in the context of AI, it is vital for them to fight against a worrying contraction that the notion of ethics is apt to undergo. Thanks in part

[2] Helen Thompson, 'In Blair-World, Tech is the Bright New Progressive Cause. But He Ignores the Real Reason for Change', New Statesman, May 19, 2021. Retrieved from: https://www.newstatesman.com/politics/uk/2021/05/blair-world-tech-bright-new-progressive-cause-he-ignores-real-reasons-change.

to the incursion of big tech into the AI ethics space, 'ethics' is often interpreted in an unduly diminished way. For example, as a form of soft, self-regulation lacking legal enforceability. Or, even more strangely, it is identified with a narrow sub-set of ethical values.

So, for example, in her recent book, *Atlas of AI*, Kate Crawford writes, 'we must focus less on ethics and more on power' because 'AI is invariably designed to amplify and reproduce the forms of power it has been deployed to optimize'.[3] But what would the recommended focus on power entail? Crawford tells us it would interrogate the power structures in which AI is embedded, in terms of ideas of equality, justice, and democracy. The irony here is that these ideas are either themselves core ethical values, or—in the case of democracy—to be explicated and defended in terms of such values. We must appeal to them to frame what it is to live a flourishing human life and what we owe to others engaged in the same enterprise; only this can provide an adequate critical standpoint from which to engage with power structures.

It would be a hugely damaging capitulation to the distortions wrought by big tech to adopt their anaemic understanding of ethics as essentially self-regulation, at best, or corporate PR, at worst. Reclaiming a broad and foundational understanding of ethics in the AI domain, with radical implications for the re-ordering of social power, will be an important task of the arts and humanities.

This, of course, is easier said than done, because there are traditions within the humanities themselves that purport to be sceptical of ethics as such, but on closer inspection, it seems to me that even these sceptical traditions cannot escape ethical commitments of their own—even if it is just the commitment to confronting grim realities unflinchingly.

2.3 The Dominant Approach

The next question we might ask is: what is the shape of the ethical self-understanding that the arts and humanities can help to generate? The starting-point, I think, is to recognise that there is already a dominant approach in this area, that it has grave deficiencies, and that a key task for the humanities is to help us elaborate a more robust and capacious

[3] Kate Crawford, Atlas of AI: Power, Politics, and the Planetary Costs of Artificial Intelligence (Yale University Press, 2021), p. 224.

approach to ethics that overcomes these deficiencies. I take the dominant approach to be that which is found most congenial by the powerful scientific, economic, and governmental actors in this field.

Like anyone else, AI scientists are prone to the illusion that the intellectual tools at their disposal have a far greater problem-solving purchase than is actually warranted. This is a phenomenon that Plato diagnosed long ago with respect to the technical experts of his day, such as cobblers and ship-builders. The mind-set of scientists working in AI tends to be data-driven, it places great emphasis on optimisation as the core operation of rationality, and it prioritises formal and quantitative techniques.

Given that intellectual framework, it is little wonder that a leading AI scientist like Stuart Russell, in his book *Human Compatible*, finds himself drawn to a preference-based utilitarianism as his overarching ethics. Russell's book is concerned with the worry that AI will eventually spiral out of control—no longer constrained by human morality—with cataclysmic consequences. But what is human morality? According to Russell, the morally right thing to do is that which will maximise the fulfilment of human preferences.[4] So, ethics is reduced to an exercise in prediction and optimisation—predicting which act or policy is likely to lead to the optimal fulfilment of human preferences.

But this view of ethics is, of course, notoriously open to serious challenge. Its concern with aggregating preferences threatens to override important rights that erect strong barriers to what can be done to individuals. And that's even before we start observing that some human preferences may themselves be infected with racist, sexist, or other prejudices. Ethics operates in the crucial space of reflection on what our preferences should be, a vital consideration that makes a belated appearance in the last few pages of Russell's book.[5] It does not take those preferences as ultimate determinants of value.

Small wonder, too, that Russell accepts a conception of intelligence—effectively, as means-ends reasoning which makes choice of ends extraneous to the operations of intelligence—according to which superintelligence is compatible with the worst forms of sociopathy. On this degraded view of intelligence, which Russell treats as 'just a given', a

[4] Stuart Russell, Human Compatible: AI and the Problem of Control (Allen Lane, 2019), p. 178.

[5] Id, p. 255.

machine that annihilated humanity in order to maximise the number of paper clips in existence could nonetheless qualify as super-intelligent.[6]

This crude, preference-based utilitarianism also exerts considerable power as an ideology among leading economic and governmental actors. This is less easy to see, because the doctrine has been modified by positing wealth-maximisation as the more readily measureable proxy for preference-satisfaction. Hence the tendency of GDP to hijack governmental decision-making around economically consequential technologies such as AI, with the consequent side-lining of values that are not readily expressed by market demand. Hence, also, the legitimation of profit-maximisation by corporations as the most effective institutional means to societal wealth-maximisation.

2.4 The Three Ps: Pluralism, Procedures, and Participation

So the kind of ethics we should hope the arts and humanities steer us towards is one that ameliorates and transcends the limitations and distortions of this dominant paradigm derived from science and economics. I think such a humanistic ethic, informed by the arts and humanities, would have at least the following three features (the three Ps):

1. *Pluralism*: it would emphasise the plurality of values, both in terms of the elements of human wellbeing and the core components of morality. This pluralism calls into question the availability of some optimising function in determining what is all-things-considered the right thing to do. It also undermines the facile assumption that the key to the ethics of AI will be found in one single master-concept, whether that be trustworthiness or human rights or something else. How could human rights be the overarching framework for AI ethics when, for example, AI has a serious environmental impact that cannot be exclusively cashed out in terms of its bearing on anthropocentric concerns? And what about those human values to which we do not think of ourselves as having a right but which are nonetheless important, such as mercy or solidarity? Nor can trustworthiness be the master value, despite the emphasis that it

[6] Id, p. 167.

is repeatedly given in documents on AI ethics. Trustworthiness is at best parasitic on compliance with more basic values, it cannot displace the need to investigate those values. Admitting the existence of a plurality of values, with their nuanced relations and messy conflicts, heightens the need for choice adverted to previously, and accentuates the question of whose decision will prevail. This sensitive exploration of a plurality of values and their interactions is what the arts and humanities, at their best, do. I say at their best because, of course, they often fail in this task. My own discipline, philosophy, has itself in recent years often propagated the highly systematising and formal approach to ethics that I have condemned. I feel philosophers have a lot to learn from closer engagement with other humanities disciplines, like classics and history, and with the arts, especially fiction, which often gets to the heart of issues like the significance of distinctively human interactions, or the nature of human emotion, in ways that the more discursive methods of philosophy cannot.

2. *Procedures not just outcomes*: I come now to the second feature of a humanistic approach to ethics, which is the importance of procedures not just outcomes. Of course, we want AI to achieve valuable social goals, such as improving access to education, justice, and health care, in an effective and efficient way. The COVID-19 pandemic has cast into sharp relief the question of what outcomes AI is being used to pursue—is it helping us, for example, to reduce the need for our fellow citizens to undertake dangerous and mind-numbing labour in the delivery of vital services, or is it engaged in profit-making activities, like vacuuming up people's attention online, that have little or no redeeming social value? The second feature of a humanistic approach to ethics is to drive home the important point that what we rightly care about is not just the value of the outcomes that AI can deliver, but the processes through which it does so. Take the example of the use of AI in cancer diagnosis and its use in the sentencing of criminals. Intuitively, the two cases seem to exhibit a difference in the comparative valuing of the soundness of the eventual decision or diagnosis and the process through which it is reached. When it comes to cancer, what may be all-important is getting the most accurate diagnosis, and it is largely a matter of indifference whether this comes through the use of an AI diagnostic tool or the exercise of human judgement. In criminal sentencing, however, there is a powerful intuition that being

sentenced by the robot judge—even if the sentence is likely to be less biassed or more consistent than one rendered by a human counterpart—means sacrificing important values relating to the process of decision. This point is familiar, of course, in relation to such process values as transparency, procedural fairness, and explainability. But it goes even deeper, because of the dread many understandably feel in contemplating a dehumanised world in which judgements that bear on our deepest interests and moral standing have, at least as their proximate decision-makers, autonomous machines that do not have a share in human solidarity and cannot be held accountable for their decisions in the way that a human judge can.

3. *Participation*: The third feature relates to the importance of participation in the process of decision-making with respect to AI, whether participation as an individual or as part of a group of self-governing democratic citizens. At the level of individual wellbeing, this takes the focus away from theories that equate human wellbeing with some end-state, such as pleasure or preference-satisfaction. Such end states could in principle be brought about through a process in which the person who enjoys them is entirely passive, for example, by putting some anti-depressant drug in the water supply. Contrary to this passive view of wellbeing, it would stress, as Alasdair MacIntyre did in *After Virtue*, that the 'good life for man is the life spent in seeking for the good life for man'.[7] Or, put slightly differently, that successful engagement with valuable pursuits is at the core of human wellbeing. If the conception of human wellbeing that emerges is deeply participatory, then this has immense relevance for assessing the significance of increased delegations of decision-making power to AI. One of the most important sites of participation in constructing a good life, in modern societies, is the workplace. According to a McKinsey study, around 30% of all work activities in 60% of occupations are capable of being automated.[8] Can we accept the idea that the large-scale elimination of job opportunities, due to automation, can be compensated for by the extra 'goodies' that automation makes available? The answer depends on

[7] Alasdair MacIntyre, After Virtue (Bloomsbury Revelations, 2013), p. 254.

[8] James Manyika and Kevin Sneader, 'AI, automation, and the future of work: Ten things to solve for', June 1, 2018. Retrieved from: https://www.mckinsey.com/featured-insights/future-of-work/ai-automation-and-the-future-of-work-ten-things-to-solve-for.

whether the participatory self-fulfilment of work can, any time soon, be feasibly replaced by other activities, such as art, friendship, play, or religion. If it cannot, addressing the problem with a mechanism like universal basic income (UBI), which involves the passive receipt of a benefit, will not be enough. Similarly, we value citizen participation as part of collective democratic self-government. And, arguably, we do so not just because of the instrumental benefits of democratic decision-making in reaching better decisions ('the wisdom of crowds' factor), but because of the way in which participatory decision-making processes affirm the status of citizens as free and equal members of the community. This is an essential plank in the defence against the tendency of AI to be co-opted by technocratic modes of decision-making that erode democratic values by seeking to convert matters of political judgement into questions of technical expertise. At present, much of the culture in which AI is embedded is distinctly technocratic, with decisions regarding the 'values' encoded in AI applications being taken by elites within the corporate or bureaucratic sectors, often largely shielded from democratic control.[9] Indeed, a small group of tech giants accounts for the lion's share of investment in AI research, dictating its overall direction. Meanwhile, we know that AI-enabled social media poses risks to the quality of public deliberation that a genuine democracy involves by promoting the spread of disinformation, aggravating political polarisation, and so on. Similarly, the use of AI as part of corporate and governmental attempts to monitor and manipulate individuals undermines privacy and threatens the exercise of basic liberties, effectively discouraging citizen participation in democratic politics. We need to think seriously about how AI and digital technology more generally can enable, rather than hinder and distort, democratic participation.[10] This is all the more urgent given the declining faith in democracy across the globe in recent years, including in long-established democracies such as the United Kingdom and the United States. Indeed, the disillusionment is such

[9] Glen Weyl, 'Why I Am Not a Technocrat', August 19, 2019. Retrieved from: https://www.radicalxchange.org/media/blog/2019-08-19-bv61r6/

[10] For some positive thinking along these lines, see Hélène Landemore, 'Open Democracy and Digital Technologies', in L. Bernholz, H. Landemore, R. Reich (eds), Digital Technology and Democratic Theory (University of Chicago Press, 2021).

> that a recent report found that 51% of Europeans favoured replacing at least some of their parliamentarians with AI.[11] Most enthusiastic were the Spaniards at 66%. Outside Europe, 75% of people surveyed in China supported the proposal. Fortunately, in the UK 69% of respondents opposed the idea, the number falling to 60% in the United States. There is still time to salvage the democratic ideal that an essential part of citizen dignity is active participation in self-government.

Which brings me to my final point. If the arts and humanities are to advance the agenda of the kind of humanistic AI ethics I have sketched, then they themselves need to be democratised. In a democracy, it's not enough to give people a vote while effectively excluding them from deliberation; and if they are to deliberate as equals, they have to have access to the key sites in which basic ideas about justice and the good are worked out.

The arts and humanities are prominent among those sites. Hence the wisdom of Article 27 of the Universal Declaration of Human Rights, which includes a right to participation in science and culture over and above purely political participation. We can see manifestations of this right, enabled by digital technology, in the resurgent citizen science movement.

But we also have to address the exclusion of our fellow citizens, itself often highly discriminatory in nature, from the domains of artistic creativity and humanistic enquiry. This means that the kind of research we should aim to do on AI within the arts and humanities should not merely be accessible to a wider public, nor should it merely model civil and rational debate for that public—however vital both of those things are. It should also afford ordinary citizens the opportunity to articulate their views in dialogue with others. I think one of the most important goals for the arts and humanities is to develop formats that facilitate such wide-ranging democratic dialogue.

[11] 'More Than Half of Europeans Want to Replace Lawmakers with AI, Study Finds', May 27, 2021. Retrieved from: https://www.cnbc.com/2021/05/27/europeans-want-to-replace-lawmakers-with-ai.html.

References

Aristotle, *Nicomachean Ethics* Book VI.

Helen Thompson, 'In Blair-World, Tech is the Bright New Progressive Cause. But He Ignores the Real Reason for Change', *New Statesman*, May 19, 2021. https://www.newstatesman.com/politics/uk/2021/05/blair-world-tech-bright-new-progressive-cause-he-ignores-real-reasons-change.

Kate Crawford, *Atlas of AI: Power, Politics, and the Planetary Costs of Artificial Intelligence* (Yale University Press, 2021).

Stuart Russell, *Human Compatible: AI and the Problem of Control* (Allen Lane, 2019).

Alasdair MacIntyre, *After Virtue* (Bloomsbury Revelations, 2013).

James Manyika and Kevin Sneader, 'AI, automation, and the future of work: Ten things to solve for', June 1, 2018 https://www.mckinsey.com/featured-insights/future-of-work/ai-automation-and-the-future-of-work-ten-things-to-solve-for.

Glen Weyl, 'Why I Am Not a Technocrat', August 19, 2019 https://www.radicalxchange.org/media/blog/2019-08-19-bv61r6/

For some positive thinking along these lines, see Hélène Landemore, 'Open Democracy and Digital Technologies', in L. Bernholz, H. Landemore, R. Reich (eds), Digital Technology and Democratic Theory (University of Chicago Press, 2021).

'More Than Half of Europeans Want to Replace Lawmakers with AI, Study Finds', May 27, 2021 https://www.cnbc.com/2021/05/27/europeans-want-to-replace-lawmakers-with-ai.html

CHAPTER 3

The Trio of Computational Jurisprudence: History, Present, and Future

Surong Zhu and *Yunan Chen*

3.1 Introduction

Since the modern era, the scientific status of the humanities and social sciences has been a topic of continuous debate. In response, legal scholars have persistently sought to establish law as a science—from the emergence of "legal metrology" in 1949 to the contemporary concept of "computational law". Computational law represents both an emerging interdisciplinary field and a novel approach to legal research through disciplinary integration. Broadly defined, computational law encompasses all intersections between information technology and law. More narrowly, it comprises three main aspects: (1) employing computational technology to

S. Zhu (✉) · Y. Chen
Beijing Foreign Studies University (BFSU), Beijing, People's Republic of China
e-mail: zhu_su_rong@163.com

Y. Chen
e-mail: chenyunan0713@163.com

A. Aliu (ed.), *Artificial Intelligence and the Rule of Law*,
https://doi.org/10.1007/978-3-031-97389-5_3

identify patterns in legal practice and analyze data for valuable insights[1]; (2) applying computational technology to legal reasoning, encompassing both legal analysis and the automation of adjudication[2]; and (3) investigating new forms of social relations emerging from advances in computational technology.[3] In this chapter, we adopt the broad definition of computational law, whose scope includes, but is not limited to, the digital storage and retrieval of legal information, the automated analysis of legal texts, the formalization and intelligent processing of legal reasoning, the development of legal decision-support systems, and the examination of legal issues arising from new technological applications.

The evolution of computational law dates back to the mid-twentieth century. From the early concept of legal metrology to the contemporary exploration of generative artificial intelligence's impact and potential applications in judicial activities, the field has progressed through multiple stages—including theoretical conception, initial practice, and rapid development. Each technological advancement has profoundly shaped its evolution. Today, with the widespread implementation of big data, cloud computing, and artificial intelligence, computational law is poised to confront new challenges and seize emerging opportunities for further advancement.

This chapter systematically reviews the development of computational law by analyzing its key research areas and evolutionary trajectory. Additionally, it employs the "prompt reasoning" method to examine the capabilities and limitations of generative artificial intelligence in supporting judicial processes and to offer insights into future development trends. By assessing both the historical progression and current state of computational law, this study aims to delineate a clearer direction for its future evolution.

[1] See Zuo Weimin, Towards Big Data Legal Research, Legal Studies, Issue 4, 2018, pp. 139–140.

[2] For a detailed introduction, refer to the CodeX official website: https://law.stanford.edu/codex-the-stanford-center-for-legal-informatics/, accessed on March 13, 2024.

[3] See Shen Weixing & Liu Yun, A New Paradigm in Legal Studies: The Connotation, Scope, and Methods of Computational Law, Legal Studies, Issue 5, 2020, p. 13.

3.2 The Evolution of Computational Law: From Theoretical Conception to Practical Application

The evolution of computational law has traversed multiple stages—from its theoretical inception to practical application. This section provides a systematic review of its development, focusing on shifting research priorities and technological applications across different periods, and examines how advancements in information technology have shaped its trajectory.

3.2.1 *The Pioneer of Legal Scientification: Legal Metrology (1940s)*

The origins of integrating quantitative reasoning with legal studies can be traced back to 1666, when Gottfried Wilhelm Leibniz first proposed establishing a connection between quantitative analysis and legal inquiry. Leibniz argued that legal studies could benefit from incorporating the modular structures inherent in legal rules with various quantitative methods, including statistics, mathematics, computer science, data science, machine learning, and artificial intelligence.[4] In 1709, Nicolas I. Bernoulli published a paper exploring the application of quantitative methods in law, addressing topics such as lottery and insurance pricing, inheritance, witness reliability, the probability of innocence, and human survival.[5] Later, in 1785, Marquis de Condorcet introduced the "Condorcet Jury Theorem",[6] which has since found widespread application in fields ranging from sociology to machine learning. Between 1827 and 1835, French scholar Adolphe Quetelet and his colleagues began analyzing the statistical patterns underlying social phenomena such as drunkenness, insanity, suicide, and crime, and they examined conviction rates using data collected by the French criminal justice administration.[7]

[4] Leibniz, Gottfried Wilhelm, and Friedrich Heer. Gottfried Wilhelm Leibniz. Gütersloh, Germany: Fischer Bücherei, 1958.

[5] Bernoulli, Nicolaus. De usu artis conjectandi in jure:... typis Johannis Conradi à Mechel, 1709.

[6] De Condorcet, Nicolas. Essai sur l'application de l'analyse à la probabilité des décisions rendues à la pluralité des voix. Cambridge University Press, 2014.

[7] Stigler, Stephen M. The History of Statistics: The Measurement of Uncertainty Before 1900. Harvard University Press, 1990.

In 1949, Lee Loevinger introduced the term "jurimetrics",[8] arguing that humanity's progress must shift from jurisprudence—merely speculative legal reasoning—to jurimetrics, defined as the scientific study of legal issues.[9] Between the 1950s and 1960s, Loevinger published numerous articles on the intersection of science and law. In 1961, he underscored the significance of advancements in electronic technology for data retrieval in legal research.[10] Moreover, he emphasized that statistics is the most practically valuable branch of mathematics for both law and the behavioral sciences, noting that many statistical concepts have direct applications in everyday legal problems. He argued that statistics should be an integral component of every law school curriculum. In 1963, Loevinger introduced the concept of electronic data retrieval, describing it as an innovative and promising field. He further elaborated on key principles of text processing and clarified the association factor proposed by H. Edmund Stiles.[11] Additionally, Loevinger discussed the probabilistic indexing approach introduced by Maron and Kuhns and examined the "LEX" legal indexing system developed by the U.S. Department of Justice's Antitrust Division. Concurrently, he provided a detailed description of modern data processing methods.[12]

3.2.2 *The Emergence of Legal Automation: Conceptual Introduction (1950s)*

The year 1956 marked the official birth of both the field and term "artificial intelligence" (AI). Following the emergence of this new research domain, in 1958, its pioneers, John McCarthy and Marvin Minsky, organized the "Mechanization of Thought Processes" symposium. The purpose of this event was to consolidate, plan, and present the work of

[8] Garner, Bryan A. (2001). "jurimetrics." A Dictionary of Modern Legal Usage. Oxford University Press, p. 488.

[9] Loevinger, Lee. "Jurimetrics—The Next Step Forward." Minn. L. Rev. 33 (1948): 455.

[10] Loevinger, Lee. "Jurimetrics: Science and Prediction in the Field of Law." Minn. L. Rev. 46 (1961): 255.

[11] Stiles, H. Edmund. "The Association Factor in Information Retrieval." Journal of the ACM (JACM) 8.2 (1961): 271–279.

[12] Loevinger, Lee. "Jurimetrics: The Methodology of Legal Inquiry." Law and Contemporary Problems 28.1 (1963): 5–35.

numerous scientists from various disciplines who were exploring ways to mechanize thought processes. During this symposium, Lucien Mehl from the French Council of State delivered a presentation titled "Automation in the Legal World".[13] In his presentation, Mehl proposed that legal automation could be achieved through two fundamentally distinct yet interrelated types of machines: (1) a "document or information machine", designed to enable legal researchers to rapidly access relevant case law and legal scholarship; and (2) a "consultation machine", capable of addressing a wide range of legal questions. According to Mehl, the consultation machine could essentially perform much of a lawyer's work by providing "precise answers to legal questions".

Although the concept of legal automation had emerged, academic research on the subject remained limited. One of the few pioneering studies was "Storage and Retrieval of Legal Information: Possibilities of Automation", published in 1960 by Layman E. Allen and colleagues at Yale University.[14] This study estimated the scope of legal information processing challenges and provided a framework for distinguishing tasks amenable to automation from those requiring human judgment. Additionally, it outlined the legal research process, offering detailed descriptions to guide future investigations.

Following 1958, legal practitioners began to explore information retrieval and database development. John Horty, a lawyer in Western Pennsylvania, pioneered the use of Computer-Assisted Legal Research (CALR) technology at the University of Pittsburgh Health Law Research Center for comparative hospital law research. In 1959, Horty, Nathan Hershey, and Eric Springer developed the "Pittsburgh System", a legal information retrieval method that, unlike other contemporary approaches, did not rely on existing indexes. Instead, it searched the full text of legal materials—such as statutes, regulations, and case law. A defining feature

[13] Mehl, L., "Automation in the Legal World: From the Machine Processing of Legal Information to the 'Law Machine,'" Mechanisation of Thought Processes: Proceedings of a Symposium Held at the National Physical Laboratory on 24th–27th November 1958 (1959, Vol. II, Her Majesty's Stationery Office, London), pp. 755–787.

[14] Allen, Layman E., Robin Brooks, and Patricia A. James. "Storage and Retrieval of Legal Information: Possibilities of Automation." MULL Mod. Uses Log. L. 2 (1960): 68.

of the Pittsburgh System was its focus on resolving specific statutory law research questions from the outset.[15]

3.2.3 *The Large-Scale Exploration of Legal Informatization: Theoretical Inquiry and Initial Practice (1960s)*

In the early 1960s, legal informatization flourished, with academic research and judicial practice advancing in parallel. In 1961, Roy N. Freed, in *Prepare Now for Machine-Assisted Legal Research*,[16] advocated for machine-assisted legal research to alleviate lawyers' workloads. In 1962, Frederick Bernays Wiener, in *Decision Prediction by Computers: Nonsense Cubed—And Worse*,[17] explored computer-based prediction of Supreme Court decisions while also highlighting its limitations. In 1963, Joan M. Covey, in *Information Retrieval in Law: Problems and Progress with Legal Computers*,[18] observed that although traditional legal indexing systems were reliable, the rapidly growing volume of legal materials rendered them increasingly impractical. While computers offered promising solutions, skepticism persisted—particularly regarding their impact on legal reasoning—with the authors arguing that the key challenge lay in improving indexing methods rather than storage technology. In 1964, Carroll D. French, in *An Electronic Forms File: New Assistance for Legal Drafting*,[19] proposed electronic systems for law firms managing large volumes of legal forms and documents, thereby enabling more efficient retrieval and drafting. In 1967, W. Ronald Robins, in *Automated Legal Information Retrieval*,[20] highlighted the overwhelming growth of

[15] William B. Eldridge & Sally F. Dennis, "The Computer as a Tool for Legal Research," 28 Law & Contemp. Probs. 1, 88 (1963).

[16] Freed, Roy N. "Prepare now for machine-assisted legal research." ABAJ 47 (1961): 764.

[17] Wiener, Frederick Bernays. "Decision prediction by computers: Nonsense cubed—and worse." American Bar Association Journal (1962): 1023–1028.

[18] Covey, Joan M. "Information retrieval in law: Problems and progress with legal computers." Dick. L. Rev. 67 (1962): 353.

[19] French, Carroll D. "An Electronic Forms File: New Assistance for Legal Drafting." ABAJ 50 (1964): 41.

[20] Robins, W. Ronald. "Automated legal information retrieval." Hous. L. Rev. 5 (1967): 691.

legal materials, which rendered research increasingly inefficient as traditional indexing methods struggled to keep pace, thus impeding lawyers' ability to retrieve precise legal information. The authors suggested that computer-assisted legal research could soon offer a transformative solution, revolutionizing the legal research process. In the same year, the article *Computerized Law Retrieval: Present and Future*[21] discussed the advantages and convenience of computerized case citation retrieval services, while emphasizing that these systems were merely a starting point rather than the ultimate goal of legal information retrieval. With advancements in computer hardware and indexing technology, further improvements in these systems were anticipated.

During the 1960s, courts increasingly embraced automated legal technology. In 1962, the St. Louis County Probate Court in Missouri became the first to employ punched cards for managing court minutes and statutory records. The following year, in 1963, a lawyer in Cleveland, Ohio, utilized a computer system to prepare cross-examination questions in a medical malpractice case.[22] In 1964, the Court of Common Pleas of Allegheny County, Pennsylvania, implemented data processing to manage personal injury case schedules.[23] In 1965, the Superior Court of Suffolk County, Massachusetts, initiated a project to explore modern data processing for court statistics.[24] In 1966, the New York Judicial Conference considered using computers to assess statewide sentencing practices, aiming to improve sentencing consistency.[25]

Overall, during this phase, legal informatization was in its exploratory and early implementation stage. Research and applications primarily focused on information retrieval, document management, data analysis, and basic decision-support systems. Both academic and legal practitioners expressed strong interest in the potential of artificial intelligence in law, which fostered the emergence of interdisciplinary collaboration and research.

[21] Franz, J. Noland. "Computerized Law Retrieval: Present and Future." U. Mo. Kan. City L. Rev. 35 (1967): 219.

[22] Morris, Crawford. "Hospital Computers in Court." MULL: Modern Uses of Logic in Law (1963): 61–66.

[23] Ellenbogen, Henry. "Automation in the Courts." ABAJ 50 (1964): 655.

[24] N.Y. Jud. Law § 234-a (Supp. 1965).

[25] Interview with Lawrence N. Marcus, Counsel to the Judicial Conference of New York State, March 3, 1966.

3.2.4 Breakthroughs in Legal Informatization: Information Service Systems and Automated Analysis (1970s)

Following the 1970s, legal informatization experienced significant advancements. Initially, direct legal information services began to emerge. In 1973, MDC launched LEXIS at a press conference in New York City, enabling online searches of New York and Ohio case law as well as federal tax materials. By the end of that year, LEXIS had expanded to encompass 2 billion characters, incorporating the United States Code and U.S. Reports from 1938 to 1973.[26] In 1975, West Publishing introduced Westlaw to provide comprehensive legal research and database services. Concurrently, case management systems began to emerge. In the same year, the Federal Judicial Center initiated the COURTRAN project to electronically record court proceedings—initially for criminal cases and subsequently for civil cases.[27] In 1976, Michael Shrayer developed Electric Pencil, the first PC-based word processor, which subsequently became widely used by law firms for document drafting. In 1977, McCarty developed TAXMAN, one of the first AI-assisted legal analysis systems, which applied artificial intelligence techniques to corporate tax law.[28] In 1978, Chicago-Kent College of Law, in collaboration with Northwestern University, developed Sprowl—a questionnaire system designed to generate legal inquiries based on standardized statutes.[29] Meanwhile, academic research increasingly explored the role of AI in legal reasoning. A notable example is a 1970 Stanford Law Review article that introduced AI into legal reasoning by arguing that existing legal retrieval systems lacked advanced reasoning capabilities.[30] The study proposed two models: one for interpreting facts and laws to protect a party's interests,

[26] Bourne, Charles P.; Hahn, Trudi Bellardo (2003). A History of Online Information Services, 1963–1976. MIT Press, pp. 300–301. ISBN 978-0-262-02538-6. Available through IEEE Xplore.

[27] Forrester, J. Owen. "The History of the Federal Judiciary's Automation Program." Am. UL Rev. 44 (1994): 1483.

[28] McCarty, L. Thome. "Reflections on TAXMAN: An Experiment in Artificial Intelligence and Legal Reasoning." Scientific Models of Legal Reasoning. Routledge, 2013. 145–202.

[29] See Allen, Layman E., and C. Rudy Engholm. "Normalized legal drafting and the query method." J. Legal Educ. 29 (1977): 380.

[30] Buchanan, Bruce G., and Thomas E. Headrick. "Some speculation about artificial intelligence and legal reasoning." Stan. L. Rev. 23 (1970): 40.

and another for recommending legal actions that achieve client objectives while mitigating risks. It further identified four key aspects of legal reasoning—conceptual relationships, fact recognition, rule conflict resolution, and analogical reasoning—and examined both the potential and the challenges of applying AI in these areas.

3.2.5 The Early Development of Legal Artificial Intelligence: Expert Systems and Reasoning Mechanisms (1980s)

Since the 1980s, academia has endeavored to formalize legal reasoning by rendering legal information computable for complex tasks. In 1987, the inaugural International Conference on Artificial Intelligence and Law (ICAIL) marked a turning point, as discussions increasingly centered on legal expert systems. In *Expert Systems in Law: Out of the Research Laboratory and into the Marketplace*,[31] the author introduced a 1983 project at Oxford University that developed a Scottish divorce law expert system, examined the role of digital technology in law, and scrutinized the jurisprudential aspects of constructing expert systems. This study emphasized the expansion of access to legal expertise and the transition from research to market applications. In *The Datalex Project*,[32] the authors underscored key differences between legal expert systems and those in other fields, advocating for specialized development approaches to simulate lawyer-client interactions, legal argumentation, and judicial decision-making. In *EPS: An Estate Planning Expert System*,[33] the authors presented EPS—a prototype designed to assist estate planning through direct interaction with clients and lawyers. Unlike typical expert systems, EPS also functioned as an educational tool, elucidating legal concepts for users without specialized knowledge. At the same conference, further exploration of legal reasoning and information systems ensued. In *Conceptual Organization of Case Law Knowledge Bases*, the author outlined a three-component model for case law knowledge bases, integrating legal concepts, case descriptors, and decision trees to

[31] R. E. Susskind. 1987. Proceedings of ICAIL '87. ACM, New York, NY, USA, 1–8. https://doi.org/10.1145/41735.41736.

[32] G. Greenleaf, A. Mowbray, and A. L. Tyree. 1987. Proceedings of ICAIL '87. ACM, New York, NY, USA, 9–17. https://doi.org/10.1145/41735.41737.

[33] D. A. Schlobohm and D. A. Waterman. 1987. Proceedings of ICAIL '87. ACM, New York, NY, USA, 18–27. https://doi.org/10.1145/41735.41738.

enhance conceptual retrieval. In *A Process Specification of Expert Lawyer Reasoning*,[34] the author examined expert legal reasoning, highlighting the construction of mental models and the role of narrative reasoning as crucial for legal problem-solving and case retrieval, thereby influencing the development of AI-driven legal tools.

By the 1980s, legal AI research had entered its nascent development phase, concentrating on the formalization of legal reasoning and the development of expert systems. During this period, researchers examined practical applications, fostered interdisciplinary collaboration, and enhanced system functionalities, thereby laying the foundation for future advancements in legal AI.

3.2.6 The Diversified Development of Computational Law: Network Connectivity and Artificial Intelligence (1990s–Present)

British computer scientist Tim Berners-Lee proposed the World Wide Web (WWW) in 1989, implemented its first version at CERN in 1990, and opened it to the public in 1991.[35] The advent of the World Wide Web enabled documents and media to be uploaded to servers and accessed through web browsers, which in turn spurred explosive growth in legal databases and data sources. To analyze the progress of computational law after 1990, this study utilizes the Web of Science (WoS) as its data source. Data retrieval was conducted for the period from 1990 to August 1, 2024, using the search query: TS = (Automation OR Information Storage OR Retrieval Assistance OR Artificial Intelligence OR Technology OR Computers OR Expert Systems) AND TS = (Legal). Filtering for articles, review articles, and open-access papers initially yielded 13,896 documents. After data cleaning to remove duplicates and irrelevant studies (e.g., those related to biological research or genetic testing), 7806 relevant documents remained. For data analysis and visualization, CiteSpace was employed to explore the evolution of computational law research through co-citation analysis, keyword co-occurrence, and clustering techniques to identify key trends.

[34] D. P. O'Neil. 1987. Proceedings of ICAIL '87. ACM, New York, NY, USA, 52–59. https://doi.org/10.1145/41735.41742.

[35] Berners-Lee, Timothy J. Information Management: A Proposal. No. CERN-DD-89-001-OC. 1989.

Keyword Co-occurrence Analysis. Keywords effectively summarize an article's theme and core content. Keyword co-occurrence analysis facilitates the identification of research hotspots over a specified period. As illustrated by the co-occurrence network of computational law research hotspots (Fig. 3.1), high-frequency keywords include information technology, intellectual property, privacy, human rights, machine learning, data protection, big data, and artificial intelligence—each appearing over 100 times, with centrality values ranging from 0.03 to 0.26. Notably, the keywords "information", "machine learning", "model", and "artificial intelligence" are represented by larger nodes with centrality values exceeding 0.1, indicating strong interconnections with other keywords. This suggests that these areas have been key focal points in computational law research during this period.

Keyword Clustering Analysis. To gain a deeper understanding of research hotspots and developments in computational law during this period, the log-likelihood ratio (LLR) algorithm was employed to cluster high-frequency keywords, resulting in the keyword clustering network shown in Fig. 3.2. The clustering structure exhibits a modularity index (Q) of 0.4852 and a mean silhouette index (S) of 0.7646. Because $Q > 0.3$ and $S > 0.7$, the clustering structure is statistically significant and

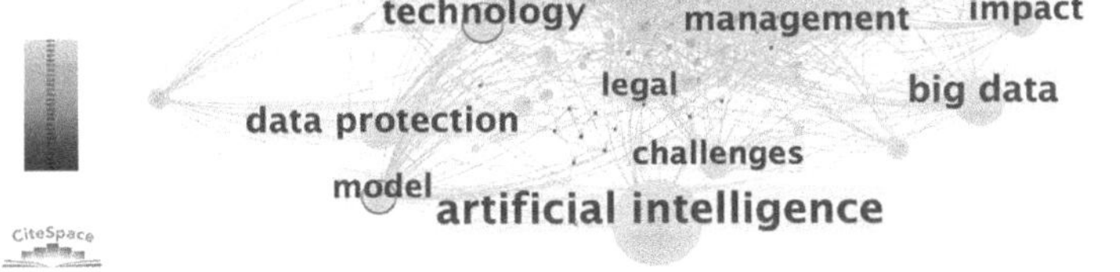

Fig. 3.1 Keyword co-occurrence network of research hotspots in computational law

demonstrates high homogeneity among cluster members, indicating reliable and meaningful results.[36] Table 3.1 provides a detailed breakdown of cluster size, silhouette scores, log-likelihood ratio (LLR) values, and the top five cluster label terms with the highest LLR values.

Based on the results of the keyword clustering analysis and a review of the relevant literature, research during this phase primarily concentrates on three interconnected areas.

First, risk governance in the digital era has emerged as a major research hotspot, with a particular emphasis on data protection and privacy issues. As big data, cloud computing, and artificial intelligence become increasingly pervasive, the challenge of balancing technological advancements with robust data and privacy safeguards has garnered significant academic attention.[37] Additionally, intellectual property (IP) law in the digital age is undergoing substantial challenges and transformations—especially with the advent of AI and large language models. Scholars have been actively

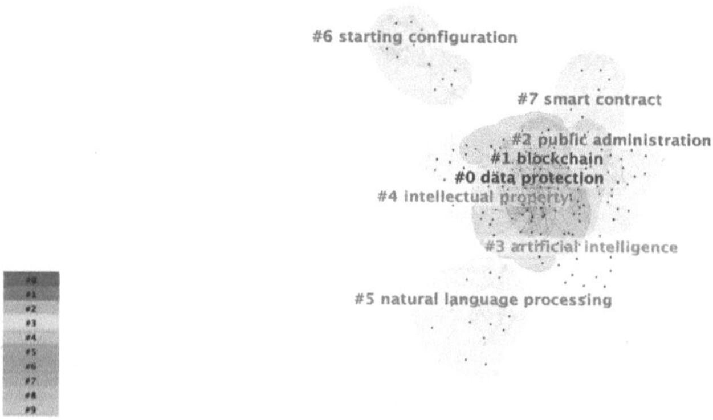

Fig. 3.2 Keyword clustering network of research hotspots in computational law

[36] Chen Yue, Chen Chaomei, Liu Zeyuan, et al. "Methodological Functions of CiteSpace Knowledge Mapping." Studies in Science of Science, No. 2, 2015.

[37] Bygrave, Lee A. "Privacy and data protection in an international perspective." Scandinavian Studies in Law 56.8 (2010): 165–200.; Hoofnagle, Chris Jay, Bart Van Der Sloot, and Frederik Zuiderveen Borgesius. "The European Union General Data Protection Regulation: What it is and what it means." Information & Communications Technology Law 28.1 (2019): 65–98.; Taylor, Linnet. "What is data justice? The case for connecting digital rights and freedoms globally." Big Data & Society 4.2 (2017): 2053951717736335.

Table 3.1 Keyword clustering table of research hotspots in computational law

Cluster ID and name	*Size*	*Silhouette score*	*Top five cluster labels (highest LLR values)*
#0 Data protection	48	0.596	Data protection; big data; privacy; artificial intelligence; law
#1 Blockchain	43	0.521	Blockchain; knowledge; data protection; innovation; smart contract
#2 Public administration	28	0.804	Public administration; information; European integration; international economic relations; humanitarian space
#3 Artificial intelligence	19	0.879	Artificial intelligence; legal regulation; digital technologies; digital economy; legal personhood
#4 Intellectual property	18	0.874	Intellectual property; artificial intelligence; patents; science; large language models
#5 Natural language processing	16	0.986	Natural language processing; deep learning; machine learning; privacy; neural networks
#6 Starting configuration	13	0.995	Starting configuration; Markov Chain Monte Carlo; Gibbs sampling; complex Bayesian networks; artificial intelligence
#7 Smart contract	9	0.823	Smart contract; electronic commerce; business; artificial intelligence; acceptance

discussing how patent and copyright laws should evolve in response to these advancements.[38]

Second, the application, progress, and regulation of digital technology in legal practice constitute a critical research direction. The emergence

[38] Davies, Colin R. "An evolutionary step in intellectual property rights–Artificial intelligence and intellectual property." Computer Law & Security Review 27.6 (2011): 601–619; Franceschelli, Giorgio, and Mirco Musolesi. "Copyright in generative deep learning." Data & Policy 4 (2022): e17.

of blockchain technology has introduced novel possibilities in legal practice, particularly in the realms of data protection[39] and smart contracts.[40] Concurrently, the legal regulation of AI is gaining importance, with growing attention to issues such as legal liability in AI systems,[41] algorithmic fairness,[42] transparency in AI decision-making,[43] and explainability.[44] Moreover, the rapid expansion of the digital economy has prompted scholars to explore and propose legal frameworks for its effective governance.[45]

Third, there is a significant focus on technological advancements in legal applications. Technologies such as natural language processing (NLP),[46] deep learning,[47] and machine learning[48] have been widely

[39] Zyskind, Guy, and Oz Nathan. "Decentralizing privacy: Using blockchain to protect personal data." 2015 IEEE Security and Privacy Workshops. IEEE, 2015.

[40] Christidis, Konstantinos, and Michael Devetsikiotis. "Blockchains and smart contracts for the Internet of Things." IEEE Access 4 (2016): 2292–2303.

[41] O'Sullivan, Shane, et al. "Legal, regulatory, and ethical frameworks for the development of standards in artificial intelligence (AI) and autonomous robotic surgery." The International Journal of Medical Robotics and Computer-Assisted Surgery 15.1 (2019): e1968.

[42] Bird, Sarah, et al. "Fairness-aware machine learning: Practical challenges and lessons learned." Proceedings of the Twelfth ACM International Conference on Web Search and Data Mining. 2019.

[43] Winfield, Alan FT, and Marina Jirotka. "Ethical governance is essential to building trust in robotics and artificial intelligence systems." Philosophical Transactions of the Royal Society A: Mathematical, Physical and Engineering Sciences 376.2133 (2018): 20180085.

[44] Brkan, Maja. "Do algorithms rule the world? Algorithmic decision-making and data protection in the framework of the GDPR and beyond." International Journal of Law and Information Technology 27.2 (2019): 91–121.

[45] Cath, Corinne. "Governing artificial intelligence: Ethical, legal and technical opportunities and challenges." Philosophical Transactions of the Royal Society A: Mathematical, Physical and Engineering Sciences 376.2133 (2018): 20180080.

[46] Jallan, Yashovardhan, et al. "Application of natural language processing and text mining to identify patterns in construction-defect litigation cases." Journal of Legal Affairs and Dispute Resolution in Engineering and Construction 11.4 (2019): 04519024.

[47] Chalkidis, Ilias, and Dimitrios Kampas. "Deep learning in law: Early adaptation and legal word embeddings trained on large corpora." Artificial Intelligence and Law 27.2 (2019): 171–198.

[48] Medvedeva, Masha, Michel Vols, and Martijn Wieling. "Using machine learning to predict decisions of the European Court of Human Rights." Artificial Intelligence and Law 28.2 (2020): 237–266.

applied in legal text analysis, case retrieval, and legal reasoning. Furthermore, advanced statistical methods—such as Bayesian network[49]and Markov Chain Monte Carlo (MCMC)[50]—are increasingly being integrated into legal analysis, providing novel quantitative tools for legal research.

Lastly, the digital transformation of public administration has become an important research hotspot.[51] The adoption of digital technologies in public management has enhanced administrative efficiency and spurred innovative governance models. At the international level, scholars have closely examined digital challenges related to European integration, digitalization in international economic relations, and the transformation of humanitarian spaces.[52] It is important to note that these research directions are not isolated but rather deeply interconnected. For example, AI applications in law often intersect with issues of data protection, intellectual property rights, and legal regulation. Future research is expected to become even more diversified, with an increased emphasis on interdisciplinary approaches to tackle the complex legal challenges of the digital era. Reflecting on the evolution of computational law—from the early days of jurimetrics to today's AI-assisted judicial activities—it is evident that the field has continuously adapted in response to technological advancements. This evolution not only mirrors innovations in legal research methodologies but also demonstrates the legal system's ongoing efforts to adapt to emerging technologies.

[49] Fenton, Norman, Martin Neil, and David A. Lagnado. "A general structure for legal arguments about evidence using Bayesian networks." Cognitive Science 37.1 (2013): 61–102.

[50] Yildirim, Engin, Aziz Kutlar, and Serdar Gulener. "Estimating Judicial Ideal Points of the Justices of the Turkish Constitutional Court between 1962 and 1982." Amme Idaresi Dergisi 50.4 (2017): 1–31.

[51] Suksi, Markku. "Administrative due process when using automated decision-making in public administration: Some notes from a Finnish perspective." Artificial Intelligence and Law 29.1 (2021): 87–110.

[52] Bellanova, Rocco, Helena Carrapico, and Denis Duez. "Digital/sovereignty and European security integration: An introduction." European Security 31.3 (2022): 337–355.

3.3 Current Status and Assessment of Computational Law: Generative Artificial Intelligence Empowering Judicial Activities

On November 30, 2022, OpenAI publicly launched ChatGPT, heralding a new era in artificial intelligence.[53] As a representative of next-generation generative AI, ChatGPT engages users in natural language conversations and is capable of tasks such as drafting emails, translating texts, and compiling code. This technological breakthrough has garnered significant attention across various fields, including legal research. Scholars have begun exploring the application of generative AI in judicial activities[54] and risk prevention.[55] However, existing research exhibits notable limitations. For instance, investigations into generative AI's role in judicial assistance have yet to thoroughly assess its performance in judicial decision-making. Current studies predominantly emphasize risks—such as the algorithmic black box phenomenon and inherent biases—while lacking detailed analyses of how these issues manifest in judicial practice and how generative AI performs across different judicial stages. Moreover, research on specific application scenarios of generative AI in judicial practice remains insufficient.[56] Although the literature notes its potential in legal document drafting, case retrieval, and judicial assistance, there is a paucity of concrete case studies and empirical analyses to fully illustrate its advantages and limitations.[57]

[53] Roumeliotis, Konstantinos I., and Nikolaos D. Tselikas. "ChatGPT and Open-AI Models: A Preliminary Review." Future Internet 15.6 (2023): 192.

[54] Wang Lusheng. "From Evolution to Revolution: The Impact of ChatGPT-like Technology on the Legal Industry." Dongfang Law Journal, No. 4, 2023.Gong Shanyao. "Practical Reflections and Improvements in AI Judicial Applications." Journal of the National Prosecutors College, No. 5, 2023.

[55] Wang Xiuping. "Legal Risks of AI Judicial Applications and the Rule-of-Law Response." Political and Legal Forum, No. 2, 2024.Chen Yongwei. "Beyond ChatGPT: Opportunities, Risks, and Challenges of Generative AI." Journal of Shandong University (Philosophy and Social Sciences), No. 3, 2023.

[56] Atkinson, Katie, Trevor Bench-Capon, and Danushka Bollegala. "Explanation in AI and Law: Past, Present, and Future." Artificial Intelligence 289 (2020): 103387.

[57] Armour, John, and Mari Sako. "AI-Enabled Business Models in Legal Services: From Traditional Law Firms to Next-Generation Law Companies?" Journal of Professions and Organization 7.1 (2020): 27–46.

This study, based on data extracted from China's judicial case database, investigates the practical capabilities of generative AI in judicial activities. It focuses on how generative AI integrates detailed case information, retrieves relevant legal documents and regulations, extracts key individuals and legal relationships, and assists in judicial decision-making and legal document generation. To achieve this, the study employs a prompt-based reasoning approach, utilizing specific prompts to activate the legal document processing capabilities of large language models, thereby guiding them to efficiently complete judicial tasks.

Specifically, an evaluation framework was initially established based on the Opinions of the Supreme People's Court on Regulating and Strengthening AI Judicial Applications. This framework integrates judicial practice requirements with large language model evaluation systems to propose assessment metrics for generative AI-assisted judicial decision-making. The proposed metrics include keyword extraction ability, legal provision citation ability, event structuring ability, judgment generation ability, and legal opinion generation ability—each serving as a fundamental component to ensure the accuracy and fairness of judicial decisions.

For evaluation, entity annotation and legal provision extraction were measured using precision, recall, and $F1$ score. Precision reflects the proportion of correct predictions made by the model; recall measures how comprehensively the model identifies correct results; and the $F1$ score provides a balanced evaluation of both precision and recall. Event structuring was assessed using sentence segmentation models and edit distance metrics, the latter evaluating the similarity between predicted and reference texts. Judgment generation ability was measured through relation extraction and numerical distance metrics, while legal opinion generation was evaluated based on the accuracy of cited legal provisions in conjunction with the judgment generation assessment.

Regarding data sources, the study selected 215 cases from PKULaw, consisting of 110 criminal cases, 82 civil cases, and 21 administrative cases. To ensure high-quality annotations, 10 legal experts manually labeled the dataset, covering entity annotation (e.g., names, legal terms, dates, and numbers), legal provision extraction, event structuring, judgment annotation, and legal opinion formulation.

During the evaluation phase, multiple large language models were tested, including ChatGPT (3.5-turbo), ChatLaw, Claude (3-sonnet), Doubao, Kimi, Wenxin Yiyan (ERNIE), GLM, Qianfan, Qianwen, Xuanyuan, and Lingyi Wanwu. The results revealed notable variations in model performance and accuracy in legal document processing, underscoring differences in their capabilities to assist judicial activities.

This study evaluates the performance of generative artificial intelligence in judicial assistance tasks, encompassing keyword extraction, legal provision citation, event structuring, judgment generation, and legal opinion generation. The evaluation of keyword extraction indicates that Wenxin Yiyan (ERNIE) achieves superior performance in extracting person names and time-related information, with $F1$ scores of 0.916 and 0.815, respectively—demonstrating robust Chinese language comprehension and effective keyword extraction capabilities. However, all models exhibit suboptimal performance in recognizing legal terminology, with $F1$ scores below 0.3, which highlights significant room for improvement in legal term identification.

Regarding legal provision citation, most models perform poorly. The Doubao model attains relatively better accuracy (0.335) and recall (0.365), yet its $F1$ score remains below 0.3, indicating that both the accuracy and comprehensiveness of citing legal provisions require substantial enhancement, especially in complex legal reasoning scenarios. In event structuring, although the Lingyi Wanwu model shows some advantage with an accuracy of 0.562 and a recall of 0.515, its overall performance remains moderate, suggesting that large language models struggle to capture entity relationships and contextual backgrounds in complex cases.

For judgment generation, the Kimi model achieves notable accuracy (0.520) and recall (0.515); however, its $F1$ score of 0.490 remains below the desired level, reflecting challenges in legal logical reasoning and fact verification. In legal opinion generation, the Kimi and Qianfan models exhibit the highest accuracy and recall, with $F1$ scores of 0.549 and 0.541, respectively, yet improvements are still needed when handling complex legal issues.

Finally, correlation analysis among the five tasks reveals a strong positive correlation between event structuring, legal opinion writing, and judgment generation, whereas the correlation between legal provision citation and judgment generation is weaker. This finding underscores the limitations of current generative AI models in legal reasoning and application. Overall, while generative AI demonstrates potential in processing legal documents, extracting key information, and generating preliminary legal opinions, it continues to face significant challenges in complex legal reasoning, fact verification, and the precise application of legal provisions.

Enhancing performance in these areas will require higher-quality data and further model optimization.

Because this study is based on a Chinese judicial database, the evaluation may be biased against large language models predominantly trained on English-language datasets. This limitation could impair their ability to accurately process Chinese legal texts—especially in understanding legal terminology, sentence structures, and cultural nuances. Future research should incorporate cross-linguistic model evaluations to further enhance AI performance across diverse languages and legal systems.

3.4 Future Prospects of Computational Law: Development Directions and Optimization Strategies for Legal Artificial Intelligence

The evolution of computational law has been inextricably linked to technological advancements. From the advent of jurimetrics in the 1940s, through the emergence of legal automation concepts in the 1950s and the breakthroughs in legal informatization during the 1960s and 1970s, to the early development of legal expert systems in the 1980s and the current experimentation with general-purpose large models assisting judicial activities, computational law has evolved along a continuum from quantitative analysis to intelligent applications. As the field continues to progress, the application of AI in judicial assistance remains a central research focus. Nevertheless, the stark contrast between early expert systems—which excelled in narrowly defined tasks—and the inconsistent performance of current large models in complex legal scenarios raises a critical question: What qualities and capabilities should an ideal legal AI system possess? In other words, what form of judicial AI can truly meet the multifaceted needs of legal practice? Addressing this question requires a comprehensive evaluation that encompasses technological factors, legal practice, ethical norms, and societal impact. Building upon the empirical findings presented earlier and informed by ongoing technological advancements, this section explores the construction of an ideal legal AI system and outlines strategies for enhancing existing models.

From a judicial practice perspective, an effective legal AI system should encompass five core capabilities: keyword extraction, legal provision citation, relationship analysis, judgment generation, and legal opinion drafting. These components constitute the fundamental framework of a legal AI system, and an ideal large-scale legal model should excel in all these tasks.

From a practical application standpoint, an ideal legal AI model must demonstrate robust adaptability and resilience. Evaluation results indicate that model performance varies significantly across different case types. For example, administrative case processing exhibits substantially higher judgment error rates compared to civil and criminal cases, suggesting that legal AI models struggle to handle diverse legal contexts—including varying case types, legal systems, and linguistic environments. Given the rigorous nature of legal practice and its minimal tolerance for errors, a legal AI model should incorporate mechanisms for self-assessment and uncertainty quantification, enabling it to recognize when a case exceeds its capabilities and to prompt human expert intervention when necessary. Finally, an ideal legal AI model must ensure high explainability and transparency. Although this study does not directly evaluate these aspects, the unique nature of the legal field demands that the decision-making process of a legal AI model be traceable and auditable—a requirement that is crucial not only for ensuring judicial fairness but also for maintaining public trust in AI-assisted judicial processes.

In conclusion, an ideal legal AI system must integrate high-precision analysis, superior content generation, and robust explainability to effectively support legal professionals, enhance judicial efficiency, and serve as a valuable auxiliary tool. Future research and development should focus on the following key areas:

First, fundamental legal capabilities. A judicial AI system must excel in basic text processing tasks—such as keyword extraction, legal provision citation, and event structuring—which form the foundation of all legal AI applications. However, current large models exhibit inconsistent performance in these core areas, underscoring the need for further optimization.

Second, legal reasoning ability. Beyond basic text processing, judgment generation and legal opinion drafting reveal that existing models lack advanced legal reasoning. Current AI models struggle with abstracting legal concepts, flexibly applying legal principles, and performing case-based analogical reasoning. These limitations arise because large models primarily rely on statistical learning and pattern matching rather than true understanding. Enhancing legal-specific reasoning capabilities should, therefore, be a top priority for future AI research and design.

Third, legal language generation. AI-generated legal documents often suffer from logical inconsistencies, unprofessional phrasing, and improper formatting—reflecting deficiencies in deep semantic comprehension and specialized writing skills. To address these issues, legal rhetoric principles should be integrated into AI models to encode legal argumentation and rhetorical structures, thereby enhancing persuasiveness and professionalism. Implementing a multi-stage generation model—encompassing outline generation, content expansion, and logic verification—and training on high-quality legal document templates could further improve structural coherence and stylistic accuracy.

Fourth, ethical and fairness considerations. AI models may inadvertently inherit or amplify existing societal biases, leading to unjust judicial decisions. Moreover, the opacity of AI decision-making processes complicates ethical review and oversight. Future AI systems should record and explain each decision-making step to enable ethical audits and incorporate fairness constraints to balance competing interests across demographic groups. The involvement of ethics experts in AI development and deployment is essential to ensure responsible usage in the legal domain.

Fifth, specialized and scientific evaluation methods. While this study identifies five core capabilities for legal AI and evaluates existing models accordingly, technological advances and deeper integration of AI into judicial workflows necessitate a more comprehensive and standardized evaluation system. Such evaluations should also incorporate feedback from legal practitioners to ensure that AI tools effectively address real-world professional needs.

Sixth, enhancing human-AI collaboration. Effective human-AI collaboration requires synergistic interaction between legal professionals and AI systems.[58] Achieving this necessitates not only high-performance, reliable AI models but also optimized legal workflows and well-trained practitioners. Developing interactive judicial AI systems—capable of natural language communication, real-time instruction processing, and prompt feedback—along with redesigning workflows to clearly delineate the division of labor between AI and human professionals, is essential. Additionally, integrating AI training into legal education will equip future legal professionals with the necessary skills to effectively leverage AI tools.

[58] Liu Qian, Gui Jianjun, Yang Xiaowei, et al. "Research Status and Development Trends of Industrial Robot Sensing and Control Technology—A Patent Literature Analysis Perspective." Journal of Robotics, No. 5, 2016.

Seventh, improving security and privacy protection. Judicial activities involve handling highly sensitive data, and breaches or misuse can have serious consequences. AI systems may also become targets of cyber-attacks. To mitigate these risks, techniques such as federated learning—which enables models to learn from distributed datasets without direct access to raw data—and differential privacy should be employed. Enhancing AI robustness against adversarial inputs is also crucial to prevent manipulation or deception.

Eighth, establishing an interdisciplinary research framework. Computational law is inherently interdisciplinary, requiring collaboration among experts in law, computer science, ethics, and cognitive science. However, current interdisciplinary cooperation remains limited. Establishing dedicated computational law research centers in universities and research institutions, as well as developing specialized degree programs, would help cultivate legal professionals with expertise in both AI and technology. Closer collaboration between academia, legal practitioners, and technology companies is essential for translating research findings into practical applications.

Addressing these key areas will be instrumental in developing a legal AI system that not only meets the rigorous demands of legal practice but also fosters trust, fairness, and innovation in the legal domain.

3.5 Conclusion

Over the past 70 years, computational law has emerged as an indispensable branch of legal research. By tracing its developmental trajectory and examining its close ties with technological advancements, this study underscores the transformative impact of next-generation generative AI on judicial activities. Although current AI models offer notable benefits in legal text processing and case retrieval, they continue to exhibit significant shortcomings in addressing complex legal problems and executing precise legal reasoning.

Today, computational law is evolving rapidly, as technological progress brings both opportunities and challenges. With ongoing advances in AI technology and the expansion of legal knowledge bases, the field is poised for further breakthroughs. Interdisciplinary and cross-domain collaboration will be essential to drive this progress, ensuring that computational law better serves legal practice and societal needs.

At the same time, it is crucial to remain vigilant regarding the potential risks and challenges introduced by technological progress. Only by harnessing these technological strengths while steadfastly upholding the rule of law and maintaining a commitment to human-centered values can computational law contribute positively to legal modernization and foster the development of a fairer, more efficient legal system.

References

Zuo Weimin, Towards Big Data Legal Research, Legal Studies, Issue 4, 2018, pp. 139–140.

Shen Weixing & Liu Yun, A New Paradigm in Legal Studies: The Connotation, Scope, and Methods of Computational Law, Legal Studies, Issue 5, 2020.

Leibniz, Gottfried Wilhelm, and Friedrich Heer. Gottfried Wilhelm Leibniz. Gütersloh, Germany: Fischer Bücherei, 1958.

Bernoulli, Nicolaus. De usu artis conjectandi in jure:... typis Johannis Conradi à Mechel, 1709.

De Condorcet, Nicolas. Essai sur l'application de l'analyse à la probabilité des décisions rendues à la pluralité des voix. Cambridge University Press, 2014.

Stigler, Stephen M. The History of Statistics: The Measurement of Uncertainty Before 1900. Harvard University Press, 1990.

Garner, Bryan A. (2001). "jurimetrics." A Dictionary of Modern Legal Usage. Oxford University Press.

Loevinger, Lee. "Jurimetrics—The Next Step Forward." Minn. L. Rev. 33 (1948): 455.

Loevinger, Lee. "Jurimetrics: Science and Prediction in the Field of Law." Minn. L. Rev. 46 (1961): 255.

Stiles, H. Edmund. "The Association Factor in Information Retrieval." Journal of the ACM (JACM) 8.2 (1961): 271–279.

Loevinger, Lee. "Jurimetrics: The Methodology of Legal Inquiry." Law and Contemporary Problems 28.1 (1963): 5–35.

Mehl, L., "Automation in the Legal World: From the Machine Processing of Legal Information to the 'Law Machine,'" Mechanisation of Thought Processes: Proceedings of a Symposium Held at the National Physical Laboratory on 24th–27th November 1958 (1959, Vol. II, Her Majesty's Stationery Office, London), pp. 755–787.

Allen, Layman E., Robin Brooks, and Patricia A. James. "Storage and Retrieval of Legal Information: Possibilities of Automation." MULL Mod. Uses Log. L. 2 (1960): 68.

William B. Eldridge & Sally F. Dennis, "The Computer as a Tool for Legal Research," 28 Law & Contemp. Probs. 1, 88 (1963).

Freed, Roy N. "Prepare now for machine-assisted legal research." ABAJ 47 (1961): 764.

Wiener, Frederick Bernays. "Decision prediction by computers: Nonsense cubed—and worse." American Bar Association Journal (1962): 1023–1028.

Covey, Joan M. "Information retrieval in law: Problems and progress with legal computers." Dick. L. Rev. 67 (1962): 353.

French, Carroll D. "An Electronic Forms File: New Assistance for Legal Drafting." ABAJ 50 (1964): 41.

Robins, W. Ronald. "Automated legal information retrieval." Hous. L. Rev. 5 (1967): 691.

Franz, J. Noland. "Computerized Law Retrieval: Present and Future." U. Mo. Kan. City L. Rev. 35 (1967): 219.

Morris, Crawford. "Hospital Computers in Court." MULL: Modern Uses of Logic in Law (1963): 61–66.

Ellenbogen, Henry. "Automation in the Courts." ABAJ 50 (1964): 655.

N.Y. Jud. Law § 234-a (Supp. 1965).

Interview with Lawrence N. Marcus, Counsel to the Judicial Conference of New York State, March 3, 1966.

Bourne, Charles P.; Hahn, Trudi Bellardo (2003). A History of Online Information Services, 1963–1976. MIT Press, pp. 300–301. ISBN 978-0-262-02538-6. Available through IEEE Xplore.

Forrester, J. Owen. "The History of the Federal Judiciary's Automation Program." Am. UL Rev. 44 (1994): 1483.

McCarty, L. Thome. "Reflections on TAXMAN: An Experiment in Artificial Intelligence and Legal Reasoning." Scientific Models of Legal Reasoning. Routledge, 2013. 145–202.

Allen, Layman E., and C. Rudy Engholm. "Normalized legal drafting and the query method." J. Legal Educ. 29 (1977): 380.

Buchanan, Bruce G., and Thomas E. Headrick. "Some speculation about artificial intelligence and legal reasoning." Stan. L. Rev. 23 (1970): 40.

R. E. Susskind. 1987. Proceedings of ICAIL '87. ACM, New York, NY, USA, 1–8. https://doi.org/10.1145/41735.41736

G. Greenleaf, A. Mowbray, and A. L. Tyree. 1987. Proceedings of ICAIL '87. ACM, New York, NY, USA, 9–17. https://doi.org/10.1145/41735.41737

D. A. Schlobohm and D. A. Waterman. 1987. Proceedings of ICAIL '87. ACM, New York, NY, USA, 18–27. https://doi.org/10.1145/41735.41738

D. P. O'Neil. 1987. Proceedings of ICAIL '87. ACM, New York, NY, USA, 52–59. https://doi.org/10.1145/41735.41742

Berners-Lee, Timothy J. Information Management: A Proposal. No. CERN-DD-89-001-OC. 1989.

Chen Yue, Chen Chaomei, Liu Zeyuan, et al. "Methodological Functions of CiteSpace Knowledge Mapping." Studies in Science of Science, No. 2, 2015.

Bygrave, Lee A. "Privacy and data protection in an international perspective." Scandinavian Studies in Law 56.8 (2010): 165–200.

Hoofnagle, Chris Jay, Bart Van Der Sloot, and Frederik Zuiderveen Borgesius. "The European Union General Data Protection Regulation: What it is and what it means." Information & Communications Technology Law 28.1 (2019): 65–98.

Taylor, Linnet. "What is data justice? The case for connecting digital rights and freedoms globally." Big Data & Society 4.2 (2017): 2053951717736335.

Davies, Colin R. "An evolutionary step in intellectual property rights–Artificial intelligence and intellectual property." Computer Law & Security Review 27.6 (2011): 601–619.

Franceschelli, Giorgio, and Mirco Musolesi. "Copyright in generative deep learning." Data & Policy 4 (2022): e17.

Zyskind, Guy, and Oz Nathan. "Decentralizing privacy: Using blockchain to protect personal data." 2015 IEEE Security and Privacy Workshops. IEEE, 2015.

Christidis, Konstantinos, and Michael Devetsikiotis. "Blockchains and smart contracts for the Internet of Things." IEEE Access 4 (2016): 2292–2303.

O'Sullivan, Shane, et al. "Legal, regulatory, and ethical frameworks for the development of standards in artificial intelligence (AI) and autonomous robotic surgery." The International Journal of Medical Robotics and Computer-Assisted Surgery 15.1 (2019): e1968.

Bird, Sarah, et al. "Fairness-aware machine learning: Practical challenges and lessons learned." Proceedings of the Twelfth ACM International Conference on Web Search and Data Mining. 2019.

Winfield, Alan FT, and Marina Jirotka. "Ethical governance is essential to building trust in robotics and artificial intelligence systems." Philosophical Transactions of the Royal Society A: Mathematical, Physical and Engineering Sciences 376.2133 (2018): 20180085.

Brkan, Maja. "Do algorithms rule the world? Algorithmic decision-making and data protection in the framework of the GDPR and beyond." International Journal of Law and Information Technology 27.2 (2019): 91–121.

Cath, Corinne. "Governing artificial intelligence: Ethical, legal and technical opportunities and challenges." Philosophical Transactions of the Royal Society A: Mathematical, Physical and Engineering Sciences 376.2133 (2018): 20180080.

Jallan, Yashovardhan, et al. "Application of natural language processing and text mining to identify patterns in construction-defect litigation cases." Journal of Legal Affairs and Dispute Resolution in Engineering and Construction 11.4 (2019): 04519024.

Chalkidis, Ilias, and Dimitrios Kampas. "Deep learning in law: Early adaptation and legal word embeddings trained on large corpora." Artificial Intelligence and Law 27.2 (2019): 171–198.

Medvedeva, Masha, Michel Vols, and Martijn Wieling. "Using machine learning to predict decisions of the European Court of Human Rights." Artificial Intelligence and Law 28.2 (2020): 237–266.

Fenton, Norman, Martin Neil, and David A. Lagnado. "A general structure for legal arguments about evidence using Bayesian networks." Cognitive Science 37.1 (2013): 61–102.

Yildirim, Engin, Aziz Kutlar, and Serdar Gulener. "Estimating Judicial Ideal Points of the Justices of the Turkish Constitutional Court between 1962 and 1982." Amme Idaresi Dergisi 50.4 (2017): 1–31.

Suksi, Markku. "Administrative due process when using automated decision-making in public administration: Some notes from a Finnish perspective." Artificial Intelligence and Law 29.1 (2021): 87–110.

Bellanova, Rocco, Helena Carrapico, and Denis Duez. "Digital/sovereignty and European security integration: An introduction." European Security 31.3 (2022): 337-355.

Roumeliotis, Konstantinos I., and Nikolaos D. Tselikas. "ChatGPT and Open-AI Models: A Preliminary Review." Future Internet 15.6 (2023): 192.

Wang Lusheng. "From Evolution to Revolution: The Impact of ChatGPT-like Technology on the Legal Industry." Dongfang Law Journal, No. 4, 2023.Gong Shanyao. "Practical Reflections and Improvements in AI Judicial Applications." Journal of the National Prosecutors College, No. 5, 2023.

Wang Xiuping. "Legal Risks of AI Judicial Applications and the Rule-of-Law Response." Political and Legal Forum, No. 2, 2024.

Chen Yongwei. "Beyond ChatGPT: Opportunities, Risks, and Challenges of Generative AI." Journal of Shandong University (Philosophy and Social Sciences), No. 3, 2023.

Atkinson, Katie, Trevor Bench-Capon, and Danushka Bollegala. "Explanation in AI and Law: Past, Present, and Future." Artificial Intelligence 289 (2020): 103387.

Armour, John, and Mari Sako. "AI-Enabled Business Models in Legal Services: From Traditional Law Firms to Next-Generation Law Companies?" Journal of Professions and Organization 7.1 (2020): 27–46.

Liu Qian, Gui Jianjun, Yang Xiaowei, et al. "Research Status and Development Trends of Industrial Robot Sensing and Control Technology—A Patent Literature Analysis Perspective." Journal of Robotics, No. 5, 2016.

CHAPTER 4

Contribution to an Algorithm for the Rule of Law

Mohamed Ben Achour

Through algorithmic modeling, the author simulates basic interactions between legal and political institutions in a recursive computational process. The contribution serves both as a proof-of-concept and a philosophical foundation, offering a scalable framework for institutional modeling and user interface design. Beyond its possible software applications, the chapter aims to build a method for translating abstract legal theory into computable logic through Niklas Luhmann's systems theory. This computational perspective aims to revitalize the *Rechtsstaat's* projective, programmatic dimension, eclipsed by modern legal positivism, and provides a dynamic tool for advancing governance and institutional design in the digital age.

M. B. Achour (✉)
Centre de Recherche Léon Duguit (CRLD), Université Paris-Saclay, Paris, France
e-mail: mohamed.ben-achour@universite-paris-saclay.fr

A. Aliu (ed.), *Artificial Intelligence and the Rule of Law*,
https://doi.org/10.1007/978-3-031-97389-5_4

4.1 Introduction

4.1.1 Historical and Conceptual Background of the Rechtsstaat

The concept of the *Rechtsstaat*[1] as we understand it today, traces its intellectual roots back to the *Vormärz* period of nineteenth-century Germany.[2] During this era, law professors such as Welker, Rotteck, and Robert von Mohl, used Kant's a priori doctrine of law and freedom as a framework to build a system of foundational concepts for a liberal and anti-authoritarian State. Kant's doctrine, outlined in the *Metaphysics of Morals*, starts with a distinction between empirically enacted statutory laws, and a priori principles of right, grounded in autonomy and practical reason[3] with which a fair State must be constituted. A series of principles, such as universality and freedom, deriving their validity internally from their conformity to the universal principle of right[4] as a foundation. According to Kant, a fair State can only be realized when its legal framework is modeled through these principles. The aim of his work was to create a rational framework for the State that articulates the harmony between individual liberty and social order.

Kantian jusnaturalism was significantly critiqued by the rise of legal positivism in the late nineteenth and early twentieth centuries. Positivist scholars dismissed the naturalist notion of a "higher" rational principle, arguing instead that positive law, empirically proven, also derives its validity internally through the scientific coherence of legal theory. Therefore, it does not need any metaphysical grounding other than positive law. State content and legal order became inherently one and the same for

[1] Or État de droit or Rule of Law, or any theory that posits the independence of political and judicial powers as a condition for a fair State. We will explain more later on (Sect. 4.1.3.1).

[2] Olivier Jouanjan provides a good introduction to the conceptual history of the Rechtsstaat. See Olivier Jouanjan, *Figures de l'État de droit: Le Rechtsstaat dans l'histoire intellectuelle et constitutionnelle de l'Allemagne* (Strasbourg: Presses Universitaires de Strasbourg, 2001), 25.

[3] Immanuel Kant, *Metaphysics of Morals: The Philosophy of Law*, translated by William Hastie, in *Collected Works of Immanuel Kant* (Hastings: Delphi Classics, 2016), §§41–44. In these paragraphs, Kant distinguishes between empirical statutory laws, and universal principles of rational law.

[4] *Any action is right if it can coexist with everyone's freedom in accordance with a universal law.*

positivist legal science.[5] Hans Kelsen, in his *Pure Theory of Law*, posited that any distinction between the State and the law was a false dualism.[6] For Kelsen, the State is a legal order itself, with law serving as the product of political decisions, inseparably linked to the State's structure. Because of this radical separation between law as a positive object and law as a metaphysical construction, ontological questions on law as a "rational idea" were disregarded to the benefit to the study of actual positive law as an empirical object. As all State actions are, by definition, legal, the concept of a Rechtsstaat became perceived as a sad pleonasm, a vague concept used to legitimize the political power instead of a rigorously grounded scientific observation.

While positivism successfully identified the insufficient moral groundings of jusnaturalism and operated a scientific revolution by making the empirical norm as its sole object of study, this shift led also to the marginalization of the *projective* dimension of it. The *Rechtsstaat* was more than a theory; it was a constitutional project. The influence of axiological neutrality and anti-metaphysics trends reduced legal science to a pure observation of positive laws, devoid of broader constitutive, projective, even perfectionist intent. The focus shifted from rationally *modeling* a fair society (*Rechtsstaat*) to strictly deduce a general theory of the State based on the positive law it produced (*Staatsrecht*). This loss of intentionality reduced legal science to a synthesis of existing laws rather than a modeling science using concepts to construct and shape legal cognition.

In his works on the construction of legal theory, Olivier Jouanjan insists on the fact that modeling and constructing have long been instruments of legal thought. Jouanjan's research shows that nineteenth-century German Kantian jurists constructed the modern naturalist legal science in a manner like how one might assemble a machine. Their rationalist approach validates a theoretical construct by its internal logical

[5] Michael Stolleis provides a detailed exploration of positivists contributed to the consolidation of legal positivism by detaching the judicial system from external, normative constraints. He writes: "The more that the methodological ideals of legal positivism were recognized as a goal to strive for (that is the distancing of historical, economic, and political reflection from legal work 'in and of itself') the more that the 'real disciplines' lost their place as helping sciences." See Michael Stolleis, *Public Law in Germany, 1800–1914* (New York: Berghahn Books, 2001), 213.

[6] Kelsen exposes his view on the traditional dualism of state and law in a specific chapter. See Hans Kelsen, *Pure Theory of Law*, 2nd ed., translated by Max Knight (Berkeley: University of California Press, 1967), 279–318.

consistency and ability to generate coherent legal doctrines. Legal science has been built by axioms and principles from which derive a functional producing concrete output such as projects, doctrine, constitutional models, foundational theories, etc. This process of construction shares serious similarities with computer programming. Both disciplines rest on conceptualization rather than verification: just as jurists built legal science from principles, programmers construct software from code, assuming that, coding is only but a construction work based on logical connections, the same cognitive tool that has been used by nineteenth-century legal scholars. The question of the serendipity or the determination of the intent itself is irrelevant. The shift is on the construction itself and its internal validity. A computer code's validity is determined by its ability to execute without errors and produce the intended output. The same goes for rationalist legal theory: a theory is valid if its internal consistency produces a coherent discourse on law that holds.

We hypothesize that, in the context of contemporary legal and political thought, modern tools such as programming and systemic modeling might offer a new opportunity to revisit and revitalize the projective dimension of the *Rechtsstaat*. Just as nineteenth-century jurists constructed rational machines to construct theories of the State, today's programming languages and algorithms allow for the construction of dynamic, adaptable cognitive tools capable of simulating societal logic in real-time. Formalizing legal and political processes through algorithms allows for their translation into a computable logic. The act of writing the concepts in code rather than natural language activates the concepts in a recursive computer process capable of generating the concept's output in its runtime. This act will display the philosophical concept in real-time as computer output instead of words printed on paper. Instead of static textual description, concepts become active, generative processes that can be immediately experienced and manipulated through computational output.

4.1.2 Goal of the Chapter

The central aim of this chapter is to revive the project of the Rule of Law, obscured by positivism, using systemic modeling and computational tools. To accomplish this, we need to conceptualize the Rechtsstaat not as a rigid framework of principles, but as a dynamic computational system capable of simulating the autonomous functioning of legal and political logic in real-time. Systems theory provides the conceptual lens through which the differentiation, autonomy, and interdependence of legal and political subsystems of society can be understood. An algorithmic modeling of this differentiation will be used to simulate the interaction of autonomous systems within an environment. We argue that computational simulation is highly adaptable to systems theory. We argue also that this constructed simulation of the political and judicial systems interactions in a dynamic, recursive program demonstrates a continuity between legal philosophy and computational logic. Computational methods allow us to simulate the institutional behavior of law, politics, and society in a cognitively exploitable way, like a theory tool.[7] The approach first begins with philosophical reasoning and results in a computational model. We open with a critique of the latest major refutation of the Rule of Law concept, Kelsen's theory of the "identity" of the State and Law. Then, we will present Niklas Luhmann's systems theory as an alternative, which grounds a theory of "difference" of State and Law (2). This theory of difference of State and Law allows us to model the Rule of Law in code (3). Finally, the practical contributions of this modeling, along with its potential for future research will be discussed (4). The full code and its output will be exposed in the annex.

4.1.3 Scope

4.1.3.1 Rechtsstaat or Rule of Law?

For the sake of clarity in this article, we will not pick up on the infinite differences between *Rechtsstaat* and *Rule of Law*. We acknowledge that these terms arise from distinct historical and cultural traditions. The *Rechtsstaat*, stemming from German legal theory, emphasizes the rational organizational principles as an inherent structure for limiting State authority and protecting individual rights and freedoms. In contrast, the Anglo-Saxon *Rule of Law* tradition places greater focus on procedural fairness and legal certainty, framing the law itself as a check against arbitrary authority rather than a systemic construct of governance. But in the

[7] Sebastian Benthall and Katherine J. Strandburg, "Agent-Based Modeling as a Legal Theory Tool," *Frontiers in Physics* 9 (2021): 666386, https://doi.org/10.3389/fphy.2021.666386.

end, despite these distinctions, both traditions aim for same general principle: opposing arbitrary decisions through assuring the independence of powers from each other.

Although our approach first originates from the *Rechtsstaat* tradition because of its focus on the institutional interaction between political and judicial systems, the research ultimately yields a result that internally synthesizes key features of both traditions. We will however use the term "Rule of Law" throughout this chapter for simplicity and accessibility. By Rule of Law, we mean a state model that: guarantees the independence of judicial institutions; ensures that laws produced by legitimate political powers are considered as norms by the judicial institution; establishes a balance between judicial independence and political power, and, in general, a stable and fair governance system that guarantees both political and judicial autonomy.

4.1.3.2 Python Model as a Proof of Concept

The algorithmic model of the Rule of Law presented in this chapter is a proof of concept aimed at translating the theoretical foundations of the Rule of Law into computational logic.[8] A proof of concept is a basic version of an idea that includes only its core, fundamental features, a demonstration that shows a technology can work in practice. It is not intended as a fully developed, exhaustive system but rather as a foundational step in demonstrating the feasibility of the project, that is modeling interacting legal and political systems through a systemic approach. The focus of this chapter is on capturing the essential computable dynamics between legal and political subsystems rather than giving the fully developed potential of the model. It is designed to illustrate the key interactions: the production of laws and regulations by the political system, their interpretation by the judicial system, and their recursive adjustment through checks and balances. This proof of concept serves as a testing ground for refining the model, integrating real-world data, and eventually scaling toward more sophisticated and comprehensive simulations connected to the real institutions.

[8] The project kept evolving past the proof-of-concept. For a closer look into the more complex computational models and advanced implementations of the concept, refer to my repository available on GitHub: GitHub, "OPTIMUS Projects Repository," accessed September 16th, 2025, https://github.com/mbenachour24/OPTIMUS_projects.

4.1.4 Literature Review

4.1.4.1 Systems Theory in Law and Organizational Studies

Systems theory offers a framework for understanding the complexity of dynamic systems. Originally founded on contributions from Norbert Wiener in cybernetics and Heinz von Foerster in second-order cybernetics, systems theory posits autonomy and self-regulation as fundamental mechanism in dynamic systems.[9] Humberto Maturana and Francisco Varela extended these principles through the concept of autopoiesis, describing systems as self-reproducing entities. The notion is later adapted to sociology and philosophy by Niklas Luhmann.[10] Gunther Teubner further extended legal autopoiesis to address global legal pluralism in complex societies[11]. The concept of autopoiesis is law has been both fertile and subject to critiques.

We must acknowledge the limitations of purely autopoietic conceptions of systems. As Capps and Palmer Olsen argue[12], overly closed (autopoietic) views of legal systems are insensitive to causal processes operating in society and history, thus affecting practical reasoning and reducing human agency. Similarly, criticisms of cybernetics in general often insist on the need for empirical data and the recognition of the impact of history and society on such modeling, as well as the potential for organizational variation through substantial methods that are simply "out of the system".

For the conceptual critique, we can answer that our framework incorporates further reflexivity by shifting from autopoiesis to structural coupling as a focal point. This work is based on *minimum of two autopoietic systems interacting through structural coupling*, e.g., a least two systems that remain internally coherent while engaging in mutual perturbation through coupling. The emphasis is therefore not on the

[9] Michael Pateau provides a thorough research on the link between Luhmann's social systems theory and its link with foundational cybernetics. See Michael Paetau, "Niklas Luhmann and Cybernetics," *Journal of Sociocybernetics* 11 (2013): 75–103.

[10] Luhmann very frequently references the work of Maturana and Varela. For instance, in *Essays on Self-Reference*, he directly cites their definition of autopoiesis in the first pages as a canonical definition. See Niklas Luhmann, *Essays on Self-Reference* (New York: Columbia University Press, 1990), 3.

[11] See Gunther Teubner, *Constitutional Fragments: Societal Constitutionalism and Globalization* (Oxford: Oxford University Press, 2012).

[12] Patrick Capps and Henrik Palmer Olsen, "Legal Autonomy and Reflexive Rationality in Complex Societies," *Social & Legal Studies* 11, no. 4 (2002): 547–567.

closure of the system, but the modalities of its cooperation within its environment. We propose that elevating structural coupling to the status of primary analytical operator enables a conceptual breakthrough for systemic approaches. It allows us to move beyond the limitations of closed autopoietic models by acknowledging the presence and relevance of other social systems, and thus, other causalities.

For the empirical critique, we argue that the logical modeling exposed in this work permits the connection to empirical data in a new way for empirical legal studies: real-time data. Beyond the simulations, the structuring of real-time data opens new methods of empirical research. The "recursive" logical formalism at the heart of our model enables a direct connection with real-time data flows. Modeled institutions can ingest, filter, and respond to empirical signals extracted from databases and APIs, updated instantaneously, and structured through legal theoretic algorithmic rules. This enables not only simulation but the actual operationalization of legal theory on living data.

4.1.4.2 On the Computational Modeling of Legal Principles

L. Thorne McCarty's Taxman Project laid the foundation for modeling legal principles in ways that computers could both analyze and apply. Since the Taxman project, "Computational Law" became this multidisciplinary field that exploits algorithms, simulations, and data-driven analysis to study, automate, and predict legal processes. It somehow became evident that *legal reasoning is computable*[13], and that lead to the densification of research in that direction. Since then, the question of employing these algorithms as law per se has been raised.

Nathalie Smuha[14] has offered one of the most compelling critiques of algorithmic governance in concrete governing contexts and warned about how these methods can erode principles of the Rule of Law as legality, transparency, and democratic accountability.

However, her critique targets the operational deployment of algorithms in *governing* society, not the *conceptual modeling* of legal principles

[13] Giovanni Contissa and Giovanni Sartor, "How the Law Has Become Computable," in *Effective Protection of the Rights of the Accused in the EU Directives*, ed. Giovanni Contissa, Giulia Lasagni, Michele Caianiello, and Giovanni Sartor (Leiden: Brill | Nijhoff, 2022), 27–41.

[14] Nathalie A. Smuha, *Algorithmic Rule by Law: How Algorithmic Regulation in the Public Sector Erodes the Rule of Law* (Cambridge: Cambridge University Press, 2024).

via algorithmic logic. For our work, this distinction matters: critique of algorithmic "governance" does not automatically apply to the algorithmic "modeling" of the Rule of Law. Smuha's work addresses the real-world institutional use of algorithms to apply the law, especially in liberal democracies where opacity, bias, and loss of accountability have become tangible risks. She warns against the erosion of due process, and the rise of a techno-legal Leviathan that outsources legal authority to black-box systems. But she does not directly address whether the theory of the Rule of Law itself (its structural logic, axioms, and dynamics) can be translated into a computable model. In that sense, her reliance on legal-philosophical frameworks such as those of Dicey or Raz affirms an axiomatic approach, but stops short of exploring how such axioms could be implemented computationally.

We argue that, instead of algorithmic governance, algorithmic modeling can be very interesting, not only because it models the logic of the concepts themselves instead of their execution, but also reverses the dynamic on surveillance: an algorithmic model of the State does not surveil the citizen, but the Institutions. In doing so, it transforms computation from an instrument of control into a mechanism of institutional reflexivity and transparency. Yet, in the current literature, the question of assessing if the concept of Rule of Law *itself* could become a computational model remains unexplored, and this type of work remains simply outside of the current epistemic horizon, related more to software engineering than to legal philosophy.

In this approach, we aim to address this epistemological void by introducing computational simulations of societal dynamics as a method for examining the computable dynamic interactions within judicial and political systems.

Computational simulations represent "algorithmic systems" as networks of autonomous agents interacting within defined environments. These algorithmic simulations can be used to represent social actors. Stemming from interdisciplinary research across sociology, economics, and physics, pioneers like Joshua Epstein and Robert Axtell[15] demonstrated the power of such models in revealing how individual behaviors governed by simple rules can aggregate into complex macro-level social

[15] See Joshua M. Epstein, "Growing Adaptive Organizations: An Agent-Based Computational Approach," in *Generative Social Science: Studies in Agent-Based Computational Modeling*, by Joshua M. Epstein (Princeton: Princeton University Press, 2006), 309–342.

patterns. Agent-Based Modeling, for example, "grows societies from the bottom up", through recursive local interactions governed by simple behavioral rules to study the emergent behaviors of recursive operations. Computational simulations potentially contain tools for analyzing institutional dynamics and systemic responses to normative changes that have not yet been explored.

Computational simulations are especially suited for examining emergent behaviors by modeling interactions between autonomous "agents", which are defined as autonomous individuals interacting within their environment. The "Luhmannian" expansion of this simulation consists in proposing that these agents do not need to only model individuals to simulate societies; instead, they can model a social system as one autopoietic unit. As long as these systems possess their own self-referential logic and own operations, they can be differentiated as units and interact with each other through couplings. Luhmann's systems theory translates here: it simulates social systems, much like individuals, as subjective units capable of self-referential behavior and interactions[16].

Sebastian Benthall and Katherine J. Strandburg have highlighted the potential for simulation within financial regulation and institutional behavior, yet its broader applications, particularly in exploring the dynamic of political and judicial systems and the production of norms, remain underexplored[17]. We will simulate the interaction between political and judicial institutions and observe their evolution. In doing so, we intend to use computational simulation like a *theory tool* to model the Rule of Law as a set of behaviors emerging from two interacting agents: the political system and the judicial system.

[16] In *Social Systems*, Luhmann expands the notion of subjectivity by stating: "If one wishes to retain a 'subject' terminology, one can still say: a consciousness is the subject of the world, alongside which there are other kinds of subjects, above all social systems". Luhmann affirms that social systems are as much "subjects" as individuals, i.e., agents capable of self-referential behavior and interactions with their environment. The essence of Luhmann's contribution to continental philosophy is extending the traditional framework of subjectivity beyond individuals. See Niklas Luhmann, *Social Systems*, translated by John Bednarz Jr., with Dirk Baecker (Stanford: Stanford University Press, 1995), 438.

[17] Sebastian Benthall and Katherine Strandburg note that: "the legal literature seems surprisingly oblivious to ABM's [Agent-Based Modeling] potential to inform the evaluation of proposals for legal and regulatory change. Because ABM is an increasingly important social scientific tool, its lackluster uptake by legal scholars who aim to predict the effects of regulatory proposals is disappointing". Sebastian Benthall, Katherine Strandburg, "Agent-Based Modeling as a Legal Theory Tool", 2.

Introducing this method to simulate the interaction of political and judicial systems requires treating law and politics as two distinct (yet interacting) autonomous units. However, in legal theory, this perspective is incompatible with Hans Kelsen's theory of the identity of law and state. Kelsen's monist hypothesis presents an important obstacle in legal theory to considering the political system and the judicial system as two distinct agents, and therefore should be addressed. We will need to present the problematic arguments of Kelsen (Sect. 4.2.1), to which we will present Luhmann's systems theory as an alternative (Sect. 4.2.2).

4.2 The Theory of the Identity of Law and State and the Theory of the Difference of Law and State

4.2.1 *Theory of the Identity of State and Law: The Insufficiency of the Monolithic Perspective*

In the *Pure Theory of Law*, Hans Kelsen[18] affirms that the identity between the State and law is the necessary condition for the development of legal science. According to the author, the State is essentially a legal order, and the distinction between the State and law is viewed as an ideological fiction. He asserts that the State is not an entity separate from the law but rather a personification of the legal system. The political power does not have a form: its form is the legal order. Therefore, the State, or the "legal order", is the perfect form of the subjective, unbounded political power. Kelsen qualifies the very notion of "Rule of Law" as useless[19], because since every State is a legal order, it is inherently a rule-of-law State. As compelling as Kelsenian theory might be on this point, it does although simplify the complex relationship between a "political form" such as a parliament or a council, and the judicial form, which is the tribunals, into an ontological unity. By affirming that the

[18] Kelsen bases his thesis precisely on the fact that the State is the object of legal science. In this sense, the State is not a natural object but the Law itself. "The identification of law and state (the recognition that the state is a legal order) [is] the presupposition of a true science of law". Hans Kelsen, *Pure Theory of Law,* 318.

[19] "And then the attempt to legitimize the state as governed by law, as a Rechtsstaat, is revealed as entirely useless because, as we have said, every state is 'governed by law' in the sense that every state is a legal order". Hans Kelsen, *Pure Theory of Law*, 319.

State is nothing but the personification of the legal order or, conversely, that the form that the law is inherently the State itself, Kelsen's epistemology, normativism, forecloses possibility of internal differentiation and fails to capture the operational dynamics and autonomy of institutional systems inside the State itself. A monistic view reduces the legal science to an instrument of observing the normative hierarchical structure, but the organizational functions of the institutional actors are simply disregarded. In computer science, this is akin to trying to understand a program based only on its logging output. The fact that we started studying the log output (positivism) is a good step forward, but radically insufficient to understand the full dynamic at play (that systems theory begins to unveil).

In legal theory, saying that the judiciary system does only mechanically apply norms dictated by political power is an incomplete and highly critiqued vision. This critique of normativism is shared by Carl Schmitt for example, who argued that judicial work also has a voluntarist aspect, where positive norms are nothing but a part of the judge's decision. Courts produce other things than political decisions: they render judgments[20]. This fundamental differentiation in the dynamic between an institutional logic that creates the norms, and another one that applies them, is entirely overlooked in a model that identifies law and State as one single monolith. The identity theory ignores the structural tensions that arise when distinct systems interact, due to their distinct functioning. The judicial system operates according to its own logic to produce judgments, while the political system operates on a separate logic to produce political acts (laws, regulations, etc.). This operational divergence cannot be adequately captured within a normativist framework. What happens when political power does not respect the judgment of a court? What happens

20 "Neither the individual judge nor the judiciary as a whole are thereby elevated into a legislator, not even when a case is decided that is not covered by any positive statute. If a judge is told, in the event that there are doubts about the content of or gaps in a statute, that he ought to imagine himself to be a legislator and to decide in the way he would decide if he were the legislator, that usage of the word 'legislator' has significance only as a heuristic principle. The question of the correctness of the decision has nothing to do with an appraisal, in state law, of a judge's constitutional position. The judge is neither a legislator nor the mouth of the statute [...] The judge was not supposed to engage in 'legal-political' deliberations, or to be influenced by them; he is to be onguard against them as an *occasio proxima* ['proximate occasion']." Carl Schmitt, "Statute and Judgment," in *Carl Schmitt's Early Legal-Theoretical Writings*, ed. and trans. Lars Vinx and Samuel Garrett Zeitlin, Cambridge Studies in Constitutional Law (Cambridge: Cambridge University Press, 2021), 126–127.

when a court does not ground its judgment on a positive norm? Are we still in a rule-of-law State then? Moreover, society often encounters situations where the normative output of the political system cannot be easily integrated into the judicial system, like legislative inflation and legal complexity, yet normativist legal science cannot answer on these specific organizational, "systemic" behaviors.

4.2.2 *Functional Differentiation of Social Systems: A Theory of Difference of State and Law*

Niklas Luhmann's systems theory is based on the idea that modern society is composed of functionally differentiated, autopoietic social systems, each with its own specific structures, logics, operations, and functions[21]. This functional differentiation also applies to political and judicial systems[22]. Each system is considered an independent operational system within a society. For the political system, this means that political content is reproduced through political operations: the will of political power is communicated in the binding political acts it produces such as laws and regulations. For the judicial system, this means that the processing of cases through judicial norms, interpretations, doctrines, and values is communicated through judicial operations, the judgments. Luhmann presents social systems as "autopoietic" systems, that is, self-referential entities that reproduce themselves through their own operations. Etymologically, "autopoiesis" comes from the ancient Greek "auto" meaning "self" and "poiesis" meaning "creation" or "production". Thus, "autopoiesis" literally translates to "self-creation". Major concept of the second-order cybernetics, it was first introduced by biologists Humberto Maturana

[21] Luhmann's notion of functional differentiation of society can be summarized as follows: "Functional differentiation creates societal part systems for the resolution of specific societal problems". Niklas Luhmann, *A Sociological Theory of Law*, 2nd ed., translated by Elizabeth King-Utz and Martin Albrow (London: A Glasshouse Book, 2014), 22.

[22] "Our proposition will be that there is not one system under the heading of the concept of the state but there are two different systems, both operationally closed, having different functions, different codes, and different code-dependent programmes" Niklas Luhmann, *Law as a Social System*, translated by Klaus A. Ziegert (Oxford: Oxford University Press, 2004), 364.

and Francisco Varela[23], who defined an autopoietic system as a system that self-reproduces itself, through the internal communication of its own components. These exclusive interactions simultaneously establish the system's boundaries within its environment, the environment being *everything that is not internal communication*. Building on this biological foundation, Luhmann applies the concept of autopoiesis to social systems. He argues that social systems are operationally closed: they operate according to their own internal logic and cannot directly perform the functions of other systems since they can observe the world only through their own communication[24]. They produce and reproduce their own reality through their own operations and with reference to their own objects[25].

However, social systems are not isolated. Through what systems theory calls a "structural coupling", it is possible to understand how social systems can cooperate despite their "autopoietic" autonomy. A structural coupling is a specific operation that guarantees a possibility of cooperation between two distinct systems, allowing them to influence and adapt to each other's conditions while maintaining their autonomy. For example, the cooperation between the distinct powers of the State according to the separation of powers: judicial power has the authority to review and control legislative and executive acts, while remaining subject to the

[23] Autopoietic systems "are systems that are defined as unities as networks of productions of components that recursively, through their interactions, generate and realize the network that produces them and constitute, in the space in which they exist, the boundaries of the network as components that participate in the realization of the network" Humberto Maturana, *Autopoiesis: A Theory of Living Organization* (New York: North Holland, 1981), 21.

[24] What this primarily means is that the reality of social systems refers to itself: modern economics views everything from an economic perspective, modern politics from a political perspective, modern science from a scientific perspective, and so on. Economics sees politics as an economic problem, and politics sees economics as a political problem, etc. Therefore, Politics will act with political acts on the economic field by regulating markets, and economy will act with economical acts on the political field by not including banned items on the market, etc. Hugues Rabault provides a thorough analysis of how social systems theory deconstructs the ontological constructions of legal concepts, see Hugues Rabault, "Théorie des systèmes :vers une théorie fonctionnaliste du droit," *Droit et société,* no. 86 (2014): 221.

[25] Self-referential systems are systems "qui produisent eux-mêmes en tant qu'unité par toutes choses qu'ils utilisent comme unité" [that produce themselves as a unity with everything they use as a unit.]. Niklas Luhmann, "L'unité du système juridique", in *Archives de la Philosophie du Droit,* Paris: Sirey, 1986, 165.

enforcement of those acts upon itself. This structural link between these separated powers does not affect their autonomous functioning. Systems theory builds on this very idea. Political content (e.g., the creation of laws) provides the framework within which legal judgments are formed, while legal decisions (e.g., constitutional reviews) can recalibrate political actions by verifying their legality or suppressing abuses of power. The "Rule of Law" structural coupling is that the judgments are necessarily produced in reference to the positive law produced by the political system[26], and that the positive law is reviewed, interpreted, and applied by the judicial system. One system creates the norms, and the other system controls and enforces them[27].

In summary, it is possible to "differentiate" the political system and the judicial system as two distinguished social systems through their distinct operations: On one hand, a judicial system, that is a social system operating through legal communications called judgments. It processes society's judicial requests by distinguishing in its judgments between the legal and the illegal matters in the case (legal/illegal code). This system is operationally closed, meaning it operates according to its own binary logic (legal/illegal) and cannot directly interfere with the operations of other systems, such as the political or economic systems. On the other hand, the political system operates through political communications (norms), through a logic that determines the creation of a norm (government/opposition). Power reproduces the will and constraints of the political system and feeds the positive law of the judicial system. The judicial system responds to the social expectation of handling cases and controlling political will.

[26] In the case of the modern French Republican Constitution, the positive law is fed by structural coupling with the political system (Parliament) through the principle of legality, which binds judges to apply laws enacted by Parliament (e.g., Articles 4 and 5 of the Civil Code). However, without this 'constitutional pact,' the judicial system can still produce its own doctrine of judgment (precedents) and form its own valid rules, as is the case with the Common Law tradition.

[27] Laurence Diver briefly touches on this interplay between legal and political systems. His analysis deconstructs the Rule of Law into two essential components: a generative pattern (that we consider as the political system) and a procedural pattern (for us, the judicial system). See Laurence Diver, "Using Design Patterns to Build and Maintain the Rule of Law," *Digital Society* 3, no. 2 (2024). https://doi.org/10.1007/s44206-024-00132-z.

4.3 An Algorithm for the Rule of Law

4.3.1 Systemic Modeling of the Rule of Law

Having explored the theoretical foundations of systems theory, specifically Luhmann's concepts of functional differentiation and structural coupling, we now turn to the practical challenge of modeling these dynamics. This section outlines a systemic approach to modeling the Rule of Law. The systemic modeling that will be exposed will serve as a pivot, moving from abstract legal theory to the concrete algorithmic representation of legal thought.

To model the Rule of Law using a systemic method, we should consider two levels of observation:

- First, **the first-order observation**: From an objective point of view, the distinction between the judge and the norm (Sect. 4.3.1.1).
- Then, **the second-order observation**: From a systemic point of view, the distinction between the judicial system and the political system (Sect. 4.3.1.2) (Fig. 4.1).

4.3.1.1 First-Order Observation: The Distinction Between Judge and Norm

Rudimentarily and fundamentally, the judicial system can be reduced to two essential elements:

- On one hand, **the "subject" judge**, the human element, the "human resource" of the judicial system. The judge is responsible for basing their judgment on a **norm**.
- On the other hand, **the "object" norm** (constitutional norm, positive law, regulation, and, generally, any valid rule). The norm serves as a reference object for the **judge**, providing a foundation for the judgment to be made.

Within a systemic analysis, the goal is to study the interaction link between the subject and the object. This interaction link is the judge's reference to the norm. The judge refers to the norm to ground their judgment, and it is only after this necessary reference to the norm that the judgment is considered legal. Thus, **from the perspective of positivism, a judgment is considered valid if and only if it is produced through the judge's**

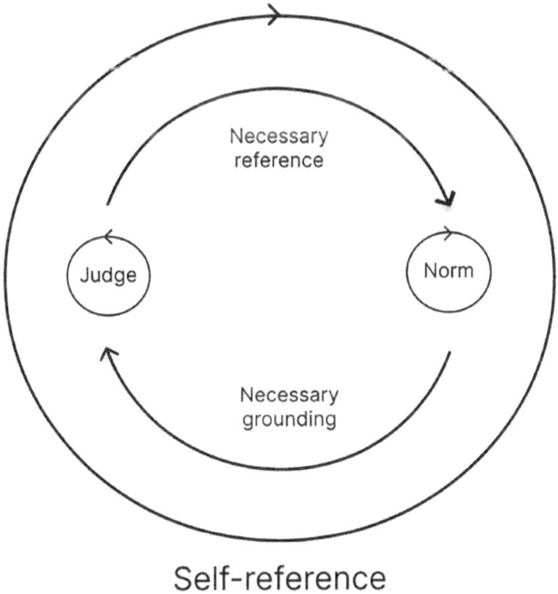

Fig. 4.1 Interaction between the norm and the judge first-order observation (reference) and second-order observation (self-reference)

reference to the norm[28], meaning a judicial decision is valid only if it's based on positive law.

The production of the judicial system, **the "judgment",** is the product of the judge's reference to the positive law. This is considered a legal self-reference if we accept that the positive law produced by the political system is used as a grounding by the judicial system, and the judge, the independent operator of the judicial system ("Rule", from Rule of Law), takes it into account to render the judgment.

Based on this systemic logic, we can infer that **the judge is structurally linked to the norm through the reference operation.** The proposition is equally valid in both directions: **the norm is structurally linked to the**

[28] This proposition remains, of course, rudimentary and does not aim to critique the validity of case law, nor the empiricist legal studies that emphasize the interpretive activity of judges in the production of norms. However, it does explain the constitutional phenomenon in which the judge is bound by the positive law produced by political power.

judge through the reference operation. In other words, the role of the judge in the application of norms (the judge "enlivens" the norm through interpretation and application) and the role of the norm in the existence of the judge (the norm grounds the judge's interpretation and application) are intrinsically connected. In this sense, **there is no norm without a judge (voluntarism), and no judge without a norm (normativism).** The dialectic between *rationalism* and *voluntarism* on which twentieth-century legal theory was founded does not concern systems theory. There is a fundamental **interaction** between judges (voluntarist element) and norms (rational element). The interpretative activity of judges plays a central role in the application of norms, and the positive existence of norms grounds the function of the judge. The interaction between these two elements, rather their annulment of one another, is too serious to be not considered.

4.3.1.2 Second-Order Observation: The Distinction Between the Legal System and the Political System

The four rules of second-order observations, as synthesized from Luhmann's work, and broadly from systems theory, are: functional differentiation, autopoiesis, structural coupling, and society.

1. **Functional Differentiation**: Institutions are divided into distinct, autonomous units, each serving a specific function. Legal and political branches, for example, operate as independent parts essential to the coherence of the entire system.
2. **Autopoiesis**: Each unit self-regulates according to its own binary logic. The legal system, for instance, operates on valid/invalid distinctions, while the political system is driven by government/opposition decisions. This internal regulation keeps each unit stable and consistent.
3. **Structural Coupling**: Although each unit remains autonomous, they interact through stable, flexible mechanisms. These interactions enable the institution to evolve cohesively, allowing separate units to maintain independence while staying interdependent.
4. **Society (Temporal Recursion)**: Society acts as a temporal orchestrator that ensures that all units function recursively, iterating over time to adapt the system to new information. This is the condition for social evolution, where recursive interactions between units and dynamic adjustment is a condition for the existence of society.

Applying these four rules, these are the results we get (Fig. 4.2):

- **The Political System**: Positioned on the left, the political system is depicted as the generator of norms through its legislative and policy-making processes. The system operates autonomously, following its own logic (government/opposition) to produce the norms.
- **The Judicial System**: On the right, the judicial system is represented as responsible for case processing: creating judgments in which it will be applying and interpreting the norms produced by the political system. This system operates autonomously, following its own logic (legal/illegal) while processing cases by producing judgments.
- **Their Structural Coupling**: The reform arrow represents the binding influence of political reforms on judicial courts. In the structural coupling between the political and judicial systems, political reforms, such as the enactment of new laws or amendments to existing ones, create a framework that judicial courts should adhere to when interpreting and applying the law in judgments.

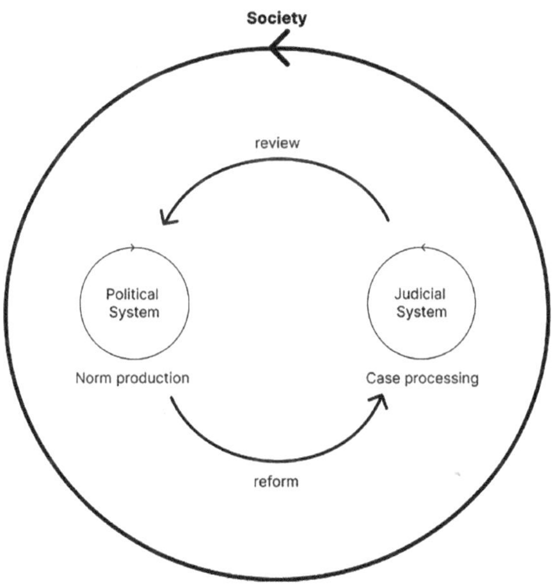

Fig. 4.2 Autonomy and structural coupling of legal and political systems

This demonstrates how political decisions, once formalized as norms, shape the parameters within which judicial decisions are made. The review arrow, going from the political system to the judicial system, reflects the role of judicial review in assessing and validating political outputs, such as laws and regulations. This ensures that political decisions align with constitutional and legal frameworks. For example, court rulings can identify gaps, ambiguities, or constitutional issues in legislation, prompting the political system to revise or reform existing norms.

- **Society**: Encircling the entire diagram, society serves as the temporal recursion within which these systems interact. It acts as the source of social demands to produce norms and judgments: every iteration, cases are brought before the courts, while the norms are the translation of political will demanded by the citizen political needs of society and articulated through legislative or regulatory processes. The circular representation emphasizes the iterative and reciprocal nature of these processes. The functioning of society lies in its temporal iterative element, that serves as the condition for the interaction between the distinct processes of judicial and political systems: every day, the court should open their doors and process new cases while parliaments should legislate on the pressing matters of daily governance.

It is important to note that the structural coupling between the judicial system and the political system is not automatic; it results from the fundamental principle of the Rule of Law, and its establishment can only be achieved through constitutional means. The political system should be constitutionally authorized to produce norms, while the judicial system, also constitutionally mandated, has the mission of rendering judgments by referring to the existing political norms.

4.3.1.3 Fundamental Rules of the Rule of Law

Four fundamental rules for algorithmic modeling of the Rule of Law are directly deduced from the four elements of the second-order distinction: functional differentiation, autopoiesis, structural coupling, and the functioning of society.

1. **Rule of Legality (Differentiation & Autopoiesis of the Political System)**: Every political decision should be considered a norm and be applicable within society. This is consistent with the requirements of the Rule of Law tradition, which emphasizes the primacy of the law, legal certainty, non-arbitrariness, etc.
2. **Rule of Due Process (Differentiation & Autopoiesis of the Judicial System)**: Courts are required to produce judgments. Norms should be interpreted by the courts based on specific cases. This is equivalent to the requirements of the *Rechtsstaat* tradition, which focuses on the formal organization of powers guaranteeing the independence of the judiciary.
3. **Rule of Checks and Balances (Structural Coupling)**: Judicial decisions can influence future political decisions, and political decisions can influence future judicial decisions.
4. **Rule of Temporality (Functioning of Society)**: For the system to remain "alive", the operation of the judge referencing the norm should be iterated in time. Social temporality paces the operations of the judicial system. Without the judge's active and repeated reference to the norm, the norm cannot be applied in society. The recursive functioning of society (typically, the flow of days, the work calendar) should happen, for the Rule of Law to exist. This is commonly met with legal notions such as prescription, reasonable time, various procedural timelines, contractual durations, penalties, or the "*principe de continuité du service public*" (principle of continuity of public service) a French constitutional principle based on the need to respond to the needs of general interest without interruption. In politics, it is operationalized through electoral calendars, terms of office, constitutionally prescribed deadlines, etc. Simply put: everyday, the court must open its doors in the morning and accept cases. Politicians must achieve their calendars one day at a time.

4.3.2 *Algorithmic Translation of the Specific Systemic Rules Applicable to the Rule of Law*

The four concepts to define and convert into code are: functional differentiation, autopoiesis, structural coupling, and society.

4.3.2.1 Functional Differentiation

Functional differentiation is the process by which social systems specialize and distinguish themselves according to their specific roles in society. In the context of the Rule of Law, this means that the judicial system and the political system have distinct, yet interdependent functions: the political system fulfills a decision-making function (represented by the `PoliticalSystem` class and the `make_decision` method), while the judicial system is dedicated to producing judgments (represented by the `JudicialSystem` class and the `produce_cases` method) (Fig. 4.3).

Python formalization:

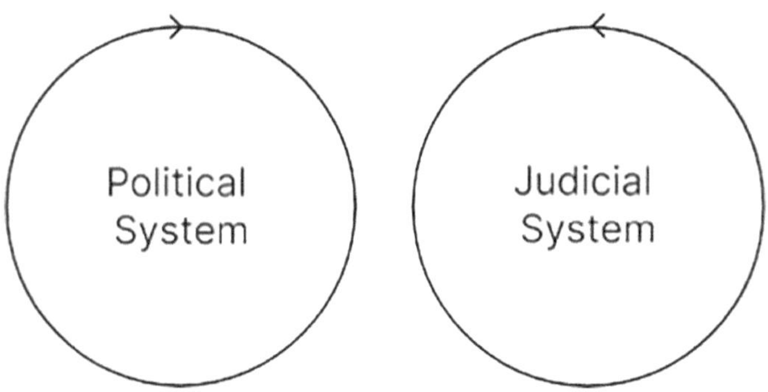

Fig. 4.3 The judicial system and the political system as two differentiated systems

```
class PoliticalSystem:
    def __init__(self):
        self.norm_counter = 0
        self.norms = []

    def make_decision(self):
        """Simulates the creation of a norm by the political system."""
        self.norm_counter += 1
        norm = f"Norm {self.norm_counter}"
        self.norms.append(norm)
        print(f"Political System: Created {norm}")

class JudicialSystem:
    def __init__(self):
        self.case_counter = 0
        self.cases = []

    def produce_cases(self, norms):
        """Simulates the creation of cases based on norms provided by the political system."""
        for norm in norms:
            self.case_counter += 1
            case = f"Case {self.case_counter} based on {norm}"
            self.cases.append(case)
            print(f"Judicial System: Processed {case}")
```

Explanations:

- The political system makes decisions (represented by the `PoliticalSystem` class with the `make_decision` method).
- The judicial system produces judgments (represented by the `JudicialSystem` class with the `produce_cases` method).
- The `PoliticalSystem` class has a `make_decision` method that creates norms.
- The `JudicialSystem` class has a `produce_cases` method that creates judgments based on norms.

4.3.2.2 Autopoiesis

Autopoiesis, in the context of legal and political systems, describes how these systems generate and maintain themselves. The political system produces norms, while the judicial system generates judgments, including a reference to the norms.

In the Python formalization, this dynamic is captured through several classes. The `Norm` class represents the norms created by the political system. Each norm is defined by attributes such as `id`, `text`, and `valid`, which determine the formal validity and content of the norm:

```
class Norm:
    def __init__(self, norm_id, text, valid=True, complexity=1):
        self.id = norm_id
        self.text = text
        self.valid = valid
        self.complexity = complexity

    def invalidate(self):
        self.valid = False
        self.history.append("Invalidated by court")
```

The `Case` class represents the judgments produced by the judicial system. Each judgment is linked to a specific norm via the `norm_id` attribute (Fig. 4.4).

```
class Case:
    def __init__(self, case_id, text, norm_id)
        self.id = case_id
        self.text = text
        self.norm_id = norm_id
```

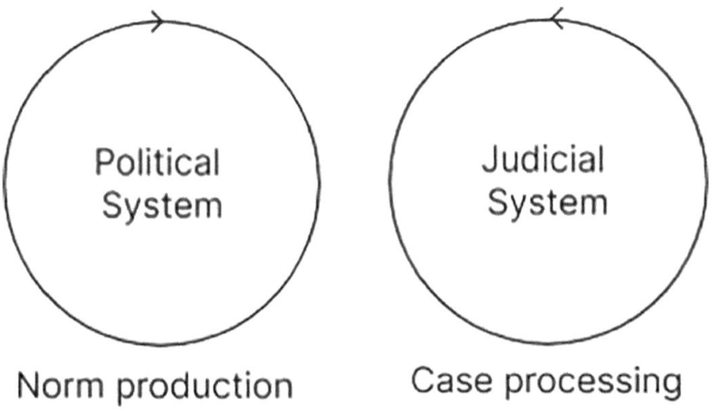

Fig. 4.4 The two functionally differentiated systems produce operational units by which they reproduce their systemic unity

The political system is modeled by the `PoliticalSystem` class, which contains a `make_decision` method to simulate the production of norms:

```
class PoliticalSystem:
    def make_decision(self):
        norm = Norm()
        # Norm production logic
```

Similarly, the `JudicialSystem` class uses the `produce_cases` method to generate judgments in reference to existing norms:

```
class JudicialSystem:
    def produce_cases(self):
        case = Case()
        # Case processing logic
```

Norms are created by the political system, while judgments are produced by the judicial system. This model reflects the self-reproduction of systems by their reference to their own objects (self-reference).

- Norms are created by the political system and have attributes such as `id` (norm number), `text` (content), `validity`, and `complexity`.
- Judgments are created by the judicial system and have attributes such as `id` (judgment number), `text` (content of the judgment), `norm_id` (reference norm), constitutionality, and complexity.

4.3.2.3 Structural Coupling

Structural coupling refers to how two distinct systems, although operationally closed, can interact and influence each other's internal structures. For example, political decisions that produce norms should be interpreted and applied by the judicial system. Conversely, judicial decisions can impact future political decisions.

In the Python formalization, this interaction is represented by the fact that, on the one hand, the `JudicialSystem` class plays a key role in controlling the constitutionality of norms. The `check_constitutionality` method allows the judicial system to verify the validity of norms created by the political system and invalidate them if they do not meet constitutional criteria (Fig. 4.5):

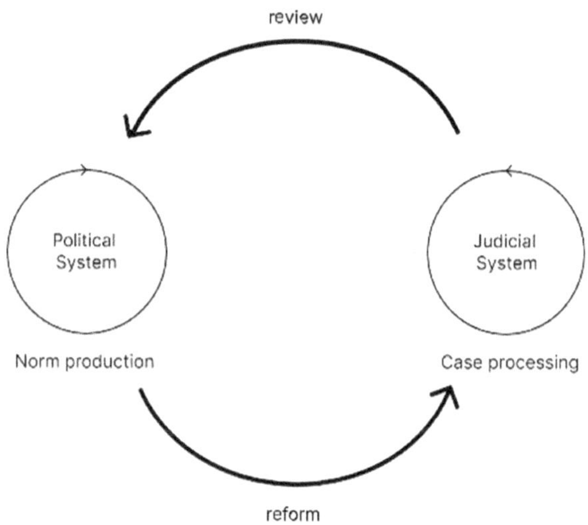

Fig. 4.5 The two functionally differentiated systems are structurally coupled

```
class JudicialSystem:
        def check_constitutionality(self, norm):
                if not norm.valid:
                  norm.invalidate()
  # The judicial system checks the constitutionality of Law and has the power to invalidate
unconstitutional norms
```

Additionally, the `produce_cases` method in the same class illustrates how judgments are produced within the judicial system in direct reference to norms established by the political system:

```
def produce_cases(self):
        case = Case(case_id, text, norm_id)
```

On the other hand, from the political side, political decisions, once made, are transformed into norms that are then applied and interpreted by the judicial system. This is reflected in the production of laws and regulations as part of a reform.

Python formalization:

```
class PoliticalSystem:
    def __init__(self):
        self.norm_pool = []
        self.norm_counter = 0

    def make_decision(self):
        new_norms = self.produce_norms_decision()
        for norm in new_norms:
            self.norm_pool.append(norm)
            norm.log_event("Created by political decision")
        return new_norms

    def produce_norms_decision(self):
        norm_id = self.norm_counter
        new_law = Law(
            norm_id=norm_id,
            text=f"Law {norm_id}",
            valid=True,
        self.norm_counter += 1
        return [new_law]
```

Explanations:

Production of Norms: The `produce_norms_decision` method in the `PoliticalSystem` class simulates the creation of new norms (Laws) following a political decision. These norms are then added to a list of norms (`norm_pool`) and may be subject to constitutional review by the judicial system.

Reform of Norms: The `reform_norm` method illustrates how an existing norm can be revised (e.g., in this version of the code, by changing its complexity) through a political decision. This demonstrates the ongoing influence of the political system on the existing legal corpus.

4.3.2.4 Society

Society is the environment in which the political and judicial systems operate and interact. Its iterative process creates the necessary conditions for the existence and functioning of its subsystems by formulating expectations and exerting pressures that influence political and legal decisions. In this simulation, the `Society` class orchestrates the interaction between the political system and the judicial system by modeling social dynamics through computable iteration (Fig. 4.6).

Python formalization:

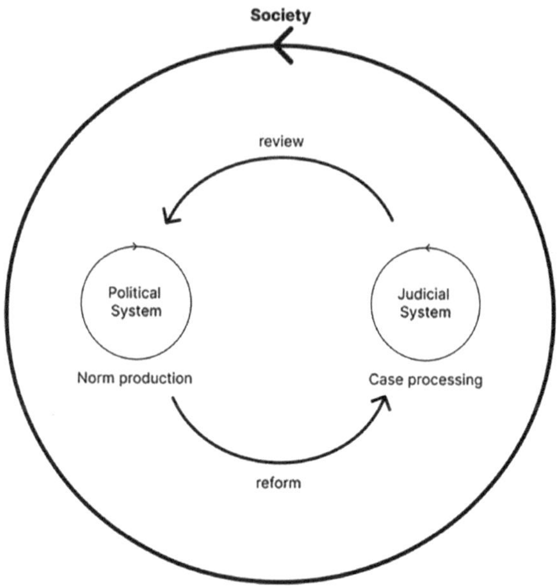

Fig. 4.6 The iterative functioning of society is a necessary condition for the functioning of both systems and their coupling

```
class Society:
    def __init__(self):
        self.political_system = PoliticalSystem()
        self.judicial_system = JudicialSystem()
        self.iteration = 0

    async def simulate(self):
        while self.iteration < SIMULATION_DAYS:
            self.iteration += 1
            log("DAY " + str(self.iteration))

            # Random event
            event   =   random.choice(["Economic   Crisis",   "Elections",   "Natural
Disaster"])
            log("Event: " + event)

            # Interaction: Political system produces norms
            new_norms = self.political_system.make_decision()

            # Judicial system processes those norms
            self.judicial_system.produce_cases(new_norms)

            wait(0.1)  # Simulated time delay

        log("Simulation completed.")

async def main():
    society = Society()
    await society.simulate()

run(main())
```

Explanations:

Initialization: The `Society` class initializes society by creating instances of the `PoliticalSystem` and `JudicialSystem`. These systems are responsible for producing norms and processing legal cases, respectively.

Simulation of Days: Each iteration of the `simulate` method represents a day in the simulation, where political and judicial systems interact to generate norms and judgments.

Random Events: Random events, such as an economic crisis or social movement, are introduced into the simulation to add uncertainty and model the inherent variability of any society. These events can disrupt systems and lead to adjustments in political and judicial decisions.

Delay: A delay is added to each iteration to realistically simulate the passage of time and prevent the simulation from running too quickly.

`society = Society(); society.simulate().`: **This part initiates the simulation by calling the Society method. It is the condition for the functioning of all the operations inside it.** I like to see this as the computational translation of Luhmann's last book's title and seminal phrase: "*die Gesellschaft der Gesellschaft*" (the society of society) (Fig. 4.7).

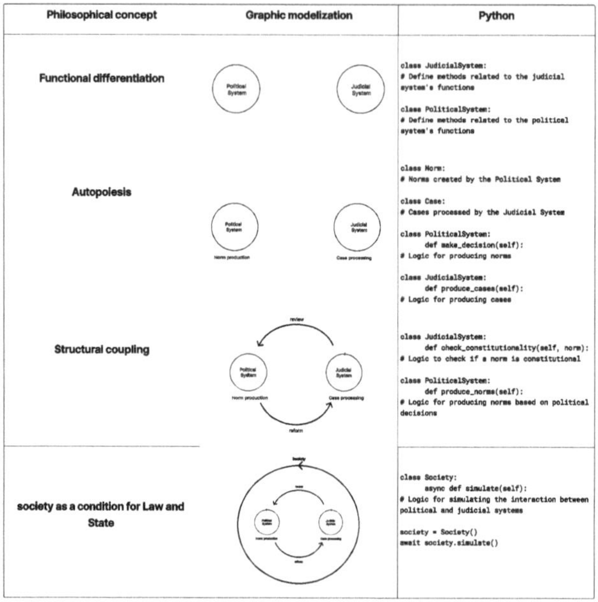

Fig. 4.7 The comparative illustrations

4.4 Conclusion

4.4.1 This Code as a Software Model

The algorithm version presented in this chapter is in its initial phase of development. Its main function is to offer proof-of-concept for translating the Rule of Law into computational logic. By simulating the interactions between political and judicial systems, the model operationalizes systemic theory and offers a computational perspective on the computable dynamics of governance systems. While this "mini" model demonstrates the feasibility of modeling these interactions, future developments could transform it into a fully integrated software platform potentially capable of real-time analysis and simulation. A tool based on this method would cross theoretical insights with practical applications by bringing two kinds of utilities: scientific analysis and engineering deployments. From a scientific perspective, such a platform would allow us to model a system, feed it data (such as livestreams and real-time updates) and observe its evolution over time. From an engineering perspective, if the model is implemented in a real-world governance system, it would enable virtues such as traceability, transparency, identification of systemic bottlenecks, "what-if" scenario simulations, and could lead to better optimizations of institutional processes.

The modular architecture and computational capacity, as demonstrated in earlier developments, holds the potential to evolve into a platform for operationalizing the Rule of Law. As an open-ended software system, it invites iterative contributions from researchers and practitioners, enabling continuous refinement and adaptation to the complexities of modern governance.

4.4.2 Scalability

This proof of concept represents what a "concept" is in both theory and practice. For instance, Lon Fuller proposed eight rules for the Rule of Law that serve as a foundational framework, despite subsuming thousands of specific rules under their scope[29]. Similarly, this model presents a core set of processes that permits complex extensions while maintaining its fundamental logic. Its scalability resides in the inheritance capabilities offered by the programming language. For example, the `Norm` class can be expanded into subclasses such as `Law` and `Regulation`, while the `PoliticalSystem` can be further developed into `Government` and `Parliament` subclasses. This would allow for a more granular modeling of structural coupling, where the government (a subclass of the political system) produces regulations (a subclass of norms).

Also, the power of the model resides in its readiness to be connected to real-time data streams. The simulation that the algorithm runs is based on stochastic methods, but algorithmic structure of the code can structure real data. With APIs, databases, and other data integration methods, the algorithm could evolve into an instant decision-support tool, connected to real-time data sources directly from legal and political governance. If the data sources are found, this could have the potential, for example, to make possible an instant, direct version of an official law register, instead of it being printed once every 24 h.

[29] Lon L. Fuller, *The Morality of Law*, Revised edition (New Haven: Yale University Press, 1969).

4.4.3 Code as Legal Ontology

The algorithm can be understood as a cognitive tool that navigates the complexity of legal and political systems by modeling their interactions with potential for real-time precision. Unlike traditional theoretical approaches, which tend to freeze phenomena in static words printed in pages, this algorithm, written in actionable words, uses the power of dynamic calculations to reflect the ongoing processes of normative production and judicial decision-making. We believe this could potentially offer a more accurate mirror of social reality than static philosophical representations in words. This translation opens up a new method for computational law: the concept of Rule of Law ceases to be fixed in time and becomes dynamic, potentially reflecting data about society in *real-time*.

Instead of confining itself to static concepts, new "philosophical tools", such as this algorithm, focus on operational dynamics rather than accurate static descriptions of law. There is here a philosophical transition, where human does not longer *think* in terms of immutable entities, where concepts are treated as objects, but *simulate* operational loops constructed in perpetual iterative, recursive accomplishments. This passage from thinking legal theory to simulating legal systems has the potential to transform ontology of law as a science: it moves from contemplating what *is* law to simulating what recursively *becomes* law, *communicates* as law, *operates* as law, *functions* as law, or, in more ontological terms, what is *in-the-process-of-being* law (*en-train-d'être, im-werden-sein*).

In this algorithm, law is not represented, but executed, in the computational sense of the term. When systems like this one are eventually connected to real data and deployed in real environments, they could cease to be philosophical tools and become cognitive infrastructures, i.e., tools for governance, reflection, and institutional design, evolving exactly at the same time as the institutions they mirror. The legal engineer therefore does not longer think about law; he builds computational systems that perform its logic. In this framework, code becomes the grammar of a legal ontology, not because it describes norms, but because it is the site where normativity is enacted.

When we recognize that legal thinking becomes a recursive pattern of cognition, *actualization* becomes the most fundamental task. Real-time cognition supposes that the information is maintained "correct" as long as the process of observation (interaction) between the observer (subject) and the actual existence of the information (object) is maintained. In the same way, it is admitted that judicial monitoring should focus on actualizing the knower on the last "legal news" by getting freshest information about it. Our understanding of legal and political realities constantly adapts to the evolving data and structures that these systems operate. Therefore, just as "legal news" does not simply describe law but gives information about its latest state, systems that could be deployed on this algorithm would not just stately describe the Rule of Law as all the previous theories of the Rule of Law, they "embody" the Rule of Law as a dynamic real-time entity, evolving and reacting to new inputs. Just as social media platforms update feeds to reflect the latest content, the algorithm updates the status of legal and political systems, reflecting the changes as soon as they happen. Actualizing, updating, loading, refreshing, this is not new for Internet's "interactive" culture. Refreshing a web page, actualizing it, brings the newest, more accurate information about the logged state of its components. This isn't a simple metaphor; this is part of the same broader epistemic shift, from ink to digital, that impacted humanity's cognition process from everyday life to the most rigorous sciences.

If ontology's task is fundamentally the study of what *is*, then the real-time cognition is part of ontology, whether it is in natural language or in computer code. Classes, functions, attributes, variables, each module can represent a real information about society and embed it within a project containing numerous other information. Luhmann suggested that each system creates its own reality through its operations. We propose that even our conceptual tools could potentially become as fluid and dynamic as the systems they describe. The reality of cognition is fully modulable, and even natural language is not a constant. In fact, coding the Rule of Law simply meant that *legal philosophy has simply changed its brush*, moving from natural language to computer language. We believe that this transition could potentially open the door to a new way of doing philosophy that no longer seeks to describe the state of things, but actively understands and intervenes in the processes of the world's becoming, in phase with every twenty-first-century social technologies.

Acknowledgements This chapter contains a dataset that was published by the Institute for Quantitative Social Sciences (IQSS) at Harvard University, Harvard Dataverse: Achour, Mohamed Ben (2025). '*Contribution to an Algorithm for the Rule of Law (Annex)*', Harvard Dataverse, V1, https://dataverse.harvard.edu/.

References

Benthall, Sebastian, and Katherine J. Strandburg. "Agent-Based Modeling as a Legal Theory Tool." Frontiers in Physics 9 (2021): Article 666386. https://doi.org/10.3389/fphy.2021.666386.

Capps, Patrick, and Henrik Palmer Olsen. "Legal Autonomy and Reflexive Rationality in Complex Societies." Social & Legal Studies 11, no. 4 (2002): 547–67.

COHUBICOL. "Vocabulary of the Rule of Law." Accessed January 15, 2025. https://publications.cohubicol.com/vocabularies/law/rule-of-law/.

Contissa, Giovanni, and Giovanni Sartor. "How the Law Has Become Computable." In Effective Protection of the Rights of the Accused in the EU Directives, edited by Giovanni Contissa, Giulia Lasagni, Michele Caianiello, and Giovanni Sartor, 27–41. Leiden: Brill | Nijhoff, 2022.

Diver, Laurence. "Using Design Patterns to Build and Maintain the Rule of Law." Digital Society 3, no. 2 (2024): Article 132. https://doi.org/10.1007/s44206-024-00132-z.

Epstein, Joshua M. "Growing Adaptive Organizations: An Agent-Based Computational Approach." In Generative Social Science: Studies in Agent-Based Computational Modeling, 309–42. Princeton: Princeton University Press, 2006.

Fuller, Lon L. The Morality of Law. Revised ed. New Haven: Yale University Press, 1969.

Hildebrandt, Mireille. "Algorithmic Regulation and the Rule of Law." Philosophical Transactions of the Royal Society A: Mathematical, Physical and Engineering Sciences 276, no. 2128 (2018): Article 20170355. https://doi.org/10.1098/rsta.2017.0355.

Jouanjan, Olivier. Figures de l'État de droit: Le Rechtsstaat dans l'histoire intellectuelle et constitutionnelle de l'Allemagne. Strasbourg: Presses Universitaires de Strasbourg, 2001.

Kant, Immanuel. Metaphysics of Morals: The Philosophy of Law, translated by William Hastie. In Collected Works of Immanuel Kant, §§41–44. Hastings: Delphi Classics, 2016.

Kelsen, Hans. Pure Theory of Law. 2nd ed., translated by Max Knight. Berkeley: University of California Press, 1967.

Luhmann, Niklas. A Sociological Theory of Law. 2nd ed., translated by Elizabeth King-Utz and Martin Albrow. London: A Glasshouse Book, 2014.

Luhmann, Niklas. Essays on Self-Reference. New York: Columbia University Press, 1990.

Luhmann, Niklas. Law as a Social System. Translated by Klaus A. Ziegert. Oxford: Oxford University Press, 2004.

Luhmann, Niklas. "L'unité du système juridique." In Archives de la Philosophie du Droit, 165. Paris: Sirey, 1986.

Luhmann, Niklas. Social Systems, translated by John Bednarz Jr., with Dirk Baecker. Stanford: Stanford University Press, 1995.
Maturana, Humberto. Autopoiesis: A Theory of Living Organization. New York: North Holland, 1981.
Paetau, Michael. "Niklas Luhmann and Cybernetics." Journal of Sociocybernetics 11 (2013): 75–103.
Rabault, Hugues. "Théorie des systèmes: Vers une théorie fonctionnaliste du droit." Droit et société, no. 86 (2014): 221.
Schmitt, Carl. "Statute and Judgment." In Carl Schmitt's Early Legal-Theoretical Writings, edited and translated by Lars Vinx and Samuel Garrett Zeitlin. Cambridge: Cambridge University Press, 2021.
Smuha, Nathalie A. Algorithmic Rule by Law: How Algorithmic Regulation in the Public Sector Erodes the Rule of Law. Cambridge: Cambridge University Press, 2024.
Stolleis, Michael. Public Law in Germany, 1800–1914. New York: Berghahn Books, 2001.
Teubner, Gunther. Constitutional Fragments: Societal Constitutionalism and Globalization. Oxford: Oxford University Press, 2012.
Wittgenstein, Ludwig. Philosophical Investigations. Translated by G. E. M. Anscombe, P. M. S. Hacker, and Joachim Schulte. Revised 4th ed. Chichester, UK: Wiley-Blackwell, 2009.

CHAPTER 5

From Procedural Fetishism to Substantive Due Process in AI Governance and Digital Constitutionalism

Monika Zalnieriute

"We should have equivalent due-process protections for algorithmic decisions as for human decisions."
– Kate Crawford[1]
University of Southern California (USC) Annenberg School for Communication and Journalism, California, USA

[1] Kate Crawford, quoted in Tom Simonite, "AI Experts Want to End 'Black Box' Algorithms in Government," Wired (18 October 2017), https://www.wired.com/story/ai-experts-want-to-end-black-box-algorithms-in-government/ accessed: 10 April 2025.

M. Zalnieriute (✉)
Faculty of Law, Vilnius University, Vilnius, Lithuania
e-mail: monika.zalnieriute@tf.vu.lt

Lithuanian Centre for Social Sciences, Vilnius, Lithuania

A. Aliu (ed.), *Artificial Intelligence and the Rule of Law*,
https://doi.org/10.1007/978-3-031-97389-5_5

5.1 Introduction

In 2016, Nathen Kearney received two false notices from Centrelink (Australian welfare agency) regarding a combined $6000 debt that he had allegedly accrued due to welfare overpayments. A series of phone calls from debt collectors and the withholding of his tax rebate followed, and it took over 5 years for him to recover both financially and mentally from this incident.[2] Rhys Cauzzo and Jarrad Madgwick also received several notices of welfare debts ($28,000 and $1795.85, respectively).[3] However, unable to talk to anyone in government about the mistake, both men took their lives.[4] These people were just three of the 443,000 people embroiled in what was coined the "Robo-debt" controversy—where, between July 2015 and November 2019, welfare recipients received letters from the Australian government falsely declaring that they had accrued significant amounts of personal debt to the public welfare agency, Centrelink.[5]

These administrative errors occurred due to the implementation of an automated welfare compliance and debt system in the Department of Human Services (DHS). The "Robo-debt" scheme replaced manual review of individual bank records, instead simply ensuring compliance by comparing the annual income figure provided by the Australian Taxation Office (ATO) to the fortnightly income reported to Centrelink.[6] If

[2] Seb Starcevic, 'Australian Robodebt Scandal Shows the Risk of Rule by Algorithm', Context, 2022 https://www.context.news/surveillance/australian-robodebt-scandal-shows-the-risk-of-rule-by-algorithm accessed: 20 September 2023.

[3] Olivia Ireland Keoghan Sarah, 'Jennifer Miller Lost Her Son to Suicide after He Was Chased by Debt Collectors. She Is Ready for Justice', The Sydney Morning Herald, 2023 <https://www.smh.com.au/politics/federal/felicity-had-11-500-wrongly-taken-from-her-bank-account-she-s-ready-for-vindication-20230706-p5dm3i.html> [accessed 20 September 2023]; article:author, 'Qld Mum of Robodebt Victim Jarrad Madgwick "Vindicated" after Four-Year Battle', News.Com.Au, 7 July 2023, section News Life <https://www.news.com.au/lifestyle/real-life/news-life/qld-mum-of-robodebt-victim-jarrad-madgwick-vindicated-after-fouryear-battle/news-story/05e10c9f42f7a5a65bab09d0a782de9b> [accessed 20 September 2023].

[4] 'Robodebt: Illegal Australian Welfare Hunt Drove People to Despair', BBC News, 7 July 2023, section Australia <https://www.bbc.com/news/world-australia-66130105> [accessed 20 September 2023].

[5] Starcevic, 'Australian Robodebt Scandal Shows the Risk of Rule by Algorithm'.

[6] Monika Zalnieriute, Lyria Bennett Moses and George Williams, 'The Rule of Law and Automation of Government Decision-Making', The Modern Law Review, 82/3 (2019), 436; Luke Henriques-Gomes, 'Robodebt: Five Years of Lies, Mistakes and Failures That Caused a $1.8bn Scandal', The Guardian, 10 March 2023, section Australia

these figures did not line up—or if individuals had not correctly updated any variations in earnings over the year (a fact which Centrelink did not make known)[7]—the individual would automatically be issued with a debt notice. Given the inaccuracy of the algorithm and its significant negative effects, a Royal Commission into the scheme was instigated—the findings have been handed down in July 2023.[8]

The "Robo-debt" story above is not an exception, but rather a typical illustration of the issues faced by individuals when dealing with AI and automation in public administration and government services. For example, in late 2024, the French government faced legal action over its use of an AI-driven algorithm designed to detect welfare fraud.[9] This system, operational since the 2010s, assigned risk scores to welfare recipients based on personal data, flagging individuals for potential fraud investigations. However, a coalition of 15 human rights organisations, including Amnesty International and La Quadrature du Net, filed a lawsuit alleging that the algorithm disproportionately targeted marginalised groups, such as disabled individuals and single mothers, thereby violating European privacy and anti-discrimination laws.[10]

Many scholars have been unequivocal about how we need to temper such abusive power in the digital age: we need due process safeguards.[11]

news <https://www.theguardian.com/australia-news/2023/mar/11/robodebt-five-years-of-lies-mistakes-and-failures-that-caused-a-18bn-scandal> [accessed 20 September 2023].

[7] Zalnieriute, Bennett Moses and Williams, 'The Rule of Law and Automation of Government Decision-Making', 436.

[8] 'The Robodebt Findings Have Been Handed down—What Happens Next?', ABC News, 7 July 2023 <https://www.abc.net.au/news/2023-07-08/robodebt-royal-commission-report-handed-down-what-next-explainer/102571876> [accessed 20 September 2023].

[9] Morgan Meaker, 'Algorithms Policed Welfare Systems for Years. Now They're Under Fire for Bias' WIRED (16 October 2024) https://www.wired.com/story/algorithms-policed-welfare-systems-for-years-now-theyre-under-fire-for-bias, accessed 10 April 2025.

[10] Ibid.

[11] Citron, 'Technological Due Process', 1249–1314; Danielle Keats Citron and Frank A. Pasquale, 'The Scored Society: Due Process for Automated Predictions', Washington Law Review, 89 (2014), 1–35; Frank Pasquale, 'Inalienable Due Process in an Age of AI: Limiting the Contractual Creep toward Automated Adjudication', in Constitutional Challenges in the Algorithmic Society, ed. by Amnon Reichman and others (Cambridge, 2021), 42–56; Nicolas P Suzor, Lawless: The Secret Rules That Govern Our Digital Lives (2019).

And we need them against both the state and private actors.[12] Digital due process is not however just a scholarly idea; many organisations emerged in recent years aim to ensure due process in the automated state. For example, a Cornell University's Digital Due Process Clinic, established in 2020, is comprised of multidisciplinary students who both provide pro bono services for those impacted by automated decisions, as well as conduct research on current issues within the realm of technology and due process.[13]

The concept of due process is particularly popular amongst digital constitutionalist scholars. Digital constitutionalism is a strand of scholarship that seeks to understand the impact of digital technologies on the rights of individuals vis a vis the state, but also *vis-à-vis* private actors. Digital constitutionalists adopt many different approaches,[14] yet many emphasise the importance of due process. In this chapter, I argue that while due process and procedural safeguards are useful in managing power abuse in the automated state, nonetheless, due process is not a panacea that can alone temper power in the digital age. I argue that even if states and companies follow due process safeguards, such safeguards are not alone sufficient to address the power imbalance between individuals and citizens on the one hand, and the state and companies on the other. In fact, an obsession with due process in digital constitutionalist discourse is part of the phenomenon which I have called *procedural fetishism*—an overemphasis on the ability of procedural safeguards to limit state and

[12] Oreste Pollicino, Judicial Protection of Fundamental Rights on the Internet: A Road Towards Digital Constitutionalism? (2021); Oreste Pollicino, 'The Quadrangular Shape of the Geometry of Digital Power(s) and the Move towards a Procedural Digital Constitutionalism', European Law Journal, n/a/n/a <https://onlinelibrary.wiley.com/doi/abs/10.1111/eulj.12472> [accessed 27 September 2023]; Giovanni De Gregorio, Digital Constitutionalism in Europe: Reframing Rights and Powers in the Algorithmic Society, Cambridge Studies in European Law and Policy (Cambridge, 2022a); Kate Crawford and Jason Schultz, 'Big Data and Due Process: Toward a Framework to Redress Predictive Privacy Harms', Boston College Law Review, 55/1 (2014), 93–128.

[13] 'About Us', Digital Due Process Clinic <https://dueprocess.sts.cornell.edu/about/> [accessed 26 September 2023].

[14] De Abreu Duarte, Francisco; De Gregorio, Giovanni and Golia, Angelo Jr, Perspectives on Digital Constitutionalism (2023) in O. Kanevskaia, P. Palka, B. Brozek, Handbook on Law and Technology (Edward Elgar) Forthcoming, available at SSRN: https://ssrn.com/abstract=4508600 or http://dx.doi.org/10.2139/ssrn.4508600.

corporate power.[15] Procedural fetishism distracts the public from substantive questions as to the appropriateness and concentration of state and corporate power, and redirects them to the micro-level issues. I argue that an overemphasis on due process reinforces procedural fetishism and distracts from the significant dangers that AI tools, digital technologies, and tech companies pose to constitutional values, fundamental rights, and the rule of law, as well as our environment and social equality. To counter procedural fetishism, digital constitutionalism must revive the substantive conceptions of due process, which focus on limits of—and not just the procedures for—power in the digital age.

Section 5.2 of this chapter first introduces the concept of due process and overviews its legal roots and meaning in a historical and contemporary context. Section 5.3 then moves on to discuss due process in digital constitutionalism: how AI tools and automated decision-making challenge the concept of due process and how scholars have sought to address those challenges. Section 5.4 focuses on the dangers of the tendency to overemphasise due process—what I have termed *procedural fetishism*—in digital constitutionalism. It discusses why procedural conceptions of due process alone are insufficient to guard against the expansion of power in the digital age, before Sect. 5.5 concludes by arguing for revival of substantive due process to counter procedural fetishism in the digital age.

5.2 Due Process

The modern conceptions of due process stem from the principle of equality before the law, which is a fundamental tenet of legal systems, seeking to ensure that all humans are subject to the same legal rules regardless of their background or status.[16] The notion of due process—a fundamental constitutional value which stipulates not only that the same legal rules apply to all individuals, but that institutions must also treat individuals fairly during the judicial process by conducting "legal proceedings according to rules and principles that have been established in a system of jurisprudence for the enforcement and protection of private

[15] Monika Zalnieriute, 'Against Procedural Fetishism: A Call for a New Digital Constitution', Indiana Journal of Global Legal Studies, 30(2) (2023), 230.

[16] Zalnieriute, Bennett Moses and Williams, 'The Rule of Law and Automation of Government Decision-Making', 431.

rights".[17] While the concept of due process is somewhat ill-defined, particularly in England where the concept is less contested than in the United States (where a wealth of jurisprudence exists surrounding the Fifth Amendment), it essentially "provides a necessary check on the exercise of state power over its citizens".[18] Due process constrains the processes of adjudication,[19] which is of utmost importance in common law systems which rely heavily on the discretion of judges, lawyers and police.[20] In the eyes of Zedner and Stuckenberg, due process "underpins the very authority of the state to enact and enforce the criminal law"—only where process is strictly adhered to can the state maintain the authority to enforce criminal law.[21]

Such modern notions of due process have their origins in two main sources—the Magna Carta in England, and the Constitution in the United States.[22] When the Magna Carta was written in 1215, Article XXIX stated that "[n]o freemen shall be taken or imprisoned or disseised or exile or in any way destroyed, nor will we go upon him nor send upon him, except by the lawful judgement of his peers or by the law of the land".[23] This provision recognised that citizens had a right to fairness through uniform procedures and establishes "the requirement of procedural regularity as an essential facet of good governance"[24]—thus enshrining elements of due process that still exist in society today. Moreover, this idea also resonated in the United States, where the Fifth

[17] Adam Augustyn, 'Due Process', Britannica, 2023.

[18] Lucia Zedner and Carl-Friedrich Stuckenberg, 'Due Process', in Core Concepts in Criminal Law and Criminal Justice: Volume I, ed. by Alexander Heinze and others (Cambridge, 2020), I, 305 <https://www.cambridge.org/core/books/core-concepts-in-criminal-law-and-criminal-justice/due-process/DB991C16B8CC45DB4CB5D60105CC34ED> [accessed 20 September 2023].

[19] Crawford and Schultz, 'Big Data and Due Process', 110.

[20] Zedner and Stuckenberg, 'Due Process', I, 307.

[21] Zedner and Stuckenberg, 'Due Process', I, 306.

[22] Crawford and Schultz, 'Big Data and Due Process', 110; Zedner and Stuckenberg, 'Due Process', I, 308.

[23] Magna Carta, England and Wales, 1297 <http://www.legislation.gov.uk/aep/Edw1cc1929/25/9/section/XXIX?view=extent> .

[24] Zedner and Stuckenberg, 'Due Process', I, 308.

Amendment of the US Constitution articulated that "no person shall...be deprived of life, liberty, or property, without due process of law".[25] Both of these sources emphasise not only the fundamental principles that constitute citizenship (i.e. life, liberty and property), but it also imposes a significant burden on the government to respect these values through extensive processes.

In contemporary context, due process is generally regarded as the idea that in order for governments to deprive someone of liberty or take away their property, there must be both "notice and the opportunity for a hearing on the matter before an impartial adjudicator".[26] This often means providing individuals with notice of their decisions before they are made and allowing them to be heard by presenting further information or affording them a hearing.[27] International treaties and law has significantly bolstered the recognition of due process rights: for example, the *United Nations' International Covenant on Civil and Political Rights* has an extensive outline of due process rights (Articles 6–15),[28] and the *European Convention on Human Rights* outlines prohibitions on human rights including the right to liberty and a fair trial (Articles 5 and 6).[29]

Moreover, due to the post-colonial context within the United States, the US Constitution approached the protections against state power more vigorously than in England, meaning that more jurisprudence has developed in this location than in any other around the world.[30] Both courts and judges alike from the United States have greatly influenced our modern understanding of due process. For example, cases such as *Goldberg v. Kelly*[31] and *Mathews v. Eldridge*[32] in the 1970s have outlined what

[25] United States Constitution, 1787 <https://www.archives.gov/founding-docs/constitution-transcript> [accessed 31 July 2020] amend. V.

[26] Crawford and Schultz, 'Big Data and Due Process', 111.

[27] Citron, 'Technological Due Process', 1249.

[28] International Covenant on Civil and Political Rights, General Assembly Resolution 2200A (XXI), 1966 <https://www.ohchr.org/en/professionalinterest/pages/ccpr.aspx> [accessed 11 August 2020].

[29] Council of Europe, Convention for the Protection of Human Rights and Fundamental Freedoms (European Convention on Human Rights), ETS 5, 1953 <https://www.echr.coe.int/Documents/Convention_ENG.pdf> .

[30] Zedner and Stuckenberg, 'Due Process', I, 309.

[31] Goldberg v. Kelly, 397 U.S. 254 (1970).

[32] Mathews v. Eldridge, 424 U.S. 319 (1976).

due process requirements look like for governments. *Goldberg* established that adequate notice alongside the opportunity to have a meaningful hearing with arguments and evidence was required to satisfy due process. *Mathews* further clarified that the requirements for due process depend on balancing the private interest government interest and risk of erroneous deprivation.

Scholars and judges have also been active in further elaborating the due process conceptions. For example, in the 1970s US Judge Henry Friendly detailed eleven elements that could assist in establishing due process in a hearing, including an unbiased tribunal, notice of the proposed action, opportunity to present reasons why proposed action should be taken, right to call witnesses, right to know evidence against oneself, right to have decision based on the evidence presented, right to counsel, making of a record, a statement of reasons, public attendance and judicial review.[33] More recently, in 2021, Frank Pasquale has suggested that due process rights are comprised of four equally important "core features" that should be present in all cases—"the ability to explain one's case, a judgement by a human decision maker, and explanation for that judgement, and the ability to appeal".[34] While there may indeed be other elements of due process, it is these notions that are fundamental to our modern understanding of this concept.

5.3 Due Process in Digital Constitutionalism

5.3.1 How AI and Automated Decision-Making Undermine Due Process

"Automated systems jeopardize due process norms."
– Danielle K. Citron[35]
University of Virginia, School of Law (UVA Law), LawTech Center, Charlottesville, Virginia, USA

[33] Judge Henry J. Friendly, United States Court of Appeal for the Second Circuit, 'Some Kind of Hearing', University of Pennsylvania Law Review, 123 (1975), 1267; Crawford and Schultz, 'Big Data and Due Process', 116.

[34] Pasquale, 'Inalienable Due Process in an Age of AI', 45.

[35] Danielle Keats Citron, 'Technological Due Process', Washington University Law Review, 85/6 (2007), 1249.

However, as the "Robodebt" examples at the start of this chapter demonstrate, AI tools and automated decision-making pose significant challenges to due process. Vast array of literature has discussed how automation of public and private processes threatens due process rights.[36] Allowing AI tools and other automated decision-making systems to make administrative decisions creates issues within all of the four key aspects of due process identified by Frank Pasquale. For example, as I have argued in my earlier work, AI tools and systems often reduce or eliminate notice of government decisions, reverse the onus of proof in a way that undermines the ability of individuals to be heard, are either so opaque or technical that the ability to challenge decisions is eroded and can also contain inaccuracies or discriminatory elements that threaten the validity of the decisions themselves.[37] I discuss these challenges in turn.

First, AI tools and automated decision-making systems challenge fundamental aspects of due process because they often fail to give sufficient notice of both the outcome of an administrative decision as well as the intended charges or actions to be taken by an agency.[38] Not only does this deprive individuals from receiving notice from a human being,[39] but also their adoption has led to an abandonment of any form of anticipatory notice regarding government actions in various instances.[40] For example, Danielle Citron identifies that automated public benefits schemes such as TIERS in Texas and CalWIN in California have tended to halt public benefits to individuals without informing them.[41] Where notice is provided under such schemes, it is often lacklustre; providing insufficient information to allow individuals to both understand the reasoning of the decision or challenge the claims made.[42] Moreover,

[36] See, for example, Pasquale, 'Inalienable Due Process in an Age of AI', 42–56; Citron, 'Technological Due Process', 1249–1314; Zalnieriute, Bennett Moses and Williams, 'The Rule of Law and Automation of Government Decision-Making', 425–55.

[37] Zalnieriute, Bennett Moses and Williams, 'The Rule of Law and Automation of Government Decision-Making', 425–55, M. Zalnieriute, L. Bennett Moses and G. Williams, 'The Rule of Law "By Design"?' Tulane Law Review, Vol 95 (5) 2021, pp. 1063–1101.

[38] Citron, 'Technological Due Process', 1281.

[39] Pasquale, 'Inalienable Due Process in an Age of AI', 46.

[40] Citron, 'Technological Due Process', 1282.

[41] Citron, 'Technological Due Process', 1282.

[42] Citron, 'Technological Due Process', 1282.

other US schemes have gone as far as to take positive action against individuals without providing any notice—a key example being the Transportation Security Administration's "No Fly" list which uses automated data-matching software to identify terrorists, but misidentifies approximately 1500 individuals a week without notifying them of this adverse finding.[43]

Second, even where adequate notice is provided, AI tools and automated decision-making systems often reverse the onus of proof from governmental agencies to individual citizens. The lack of information surrounding a decision forces individuals to engage in fact-finding—a burden which would traditionally rest on the government department making the decision.[44] For instance, in the Robo-debt example, the Australian government issued the debt notices before either the calculations had been checked or the debts had been verified. This essentially reversed the fact-finding burden which previously rested on the Department, in that individuals had to take steps to investigate their debts and if they were accurate (which—in most cases—they were not).[45]

Another fundamental tenet of due process—the ability to adequately challenge decisions through hearings—is further undermined by AI tools and automated decision-making systems. This largely occurs where the systems used by governments to automate their decisions are not transparent, meaning individuals either cannot access the information used to make a decision or determine its accuracy.[46] This can be seen in the Robodebt example discussed above, as the debt collection notice failed to explain how the overpayment of welfare benefits was calculated and the importance of updating income variation across the year,[47] meaning individuals were not adequately equipped to challenge the adverse finding against them. The fact that any published code or outcomes of automated decision-making software may be extremely technical also exacerbates this

[43] Citron, 'Technological Due Process', 1256.

[44] Zalnieriute, Bennett Moses and Williams, 'The Rule of Law and Automation of Government Decision-Making', 451.

[45] Peter Hanks, 'Administrative Law and Welfare Rights: A 40-Year Story from "Green v Daniels" to "Robot Debt Recovery"', AIAL Forum 1, 89 (2017), 1–15.

[46] Zalnieriute, Bennett Moses and Williams, 'The Rule of Law and Automation of Government Decision-Making', 449.

[47] Zalnieriute, Bennett Moses and Williams, 'The Rule of Law and Automation of Government Decision-Making', 449.

tension with due process rights. While affording access to the source code of the system may assist individuals in successfully challenging decisions made about them,[48] this still assumes that all affected individuals are technologically literate and capable of understanding what is often complex software programming. For example, even if the Robo-debt code had been provided, it would need to be presented in a relatively simple fashion in order for due process rights to be upheld. As such, automated systems often fail to afford individuals "with a genuine opportunity to correct the erroneous data held on them effectively den[ying] them due process rights and hence equal treatment under the law".[49] Finally, automation can also introduce significant inaccuracies, biases, and discriminatory elements into decision-making systems that erode the core notion that individuals should be subject to the same procedures and have equal access to their rights within the legal system. Such automated systems often fail to meet these standards, by not ensuring "like cases be treated alike".[50] Instead—as automated decision-making systems are often informed by demographic data—this information is simply applied without questioning the potential for discrimination amongst certain groups. This may happen in a variety of ways, including by: explicitly using statistical factors or immutable factors (i.e. age, gender, socioeconomic status, employment) into the analyses; or implicitly making correlations between the them through the machine learning.[51] The latter process is particularly dangerous, in that it not only becomes impossible to determine the actual basis of decision-making in the machine, but it also creates a set of "rules" by the automated system that produce discriminatory outcomes based on historical data.[52]

One relevant example is the Correctional Offender Management Profiling for Alternative Sanctions (COMPAS) used in the United States—as this uses historical data to determine the risk of a particular

[48] Citron, 'Technological Due Process', 1284.

[49] Zalnieriute, Bennett Moses and Williams, 'The Rule of Law and Automation of Government Decision-Making', 449.

[50] Zalnieriute, Bennett Moses and Williams, 'The Rule of Law and Automation of Government Decision-Making', 451.

[51] Zalnieriute, Bennett Moses and Williams, 'The Rule of Law and Automation of Government Decision-Making', 452.

[52] Zalnieriute, Bennett Moses and Williams, 'The Rule of Law and Automation of Government Decision-Making', 452.

defendant re-offending in the future.[53] This undermines equal treatment before the law in the sense that it explicitly incorporates factors such as socioeconomic status, employment, gender into the decision-making process in inappropriate ways, as well as increasing the potential that the software is biased towards minorities due to its "learning" processes.[54] Moreover, at a higher level, other people involved in the judicial process (i.e. hearing officers, witnesses or judges) may also become biased when confronted with the data from automated systems. This effect is called "automation bias", when individuals may attribute more validity to automated data in the hearing process than individual testimony or arguments. This ultimately undermines not only an individual's opportunity to be heard, but also their right to an impartial adjudicator.[55]

5.3.2 *The Procedural "Fix": Digital Constitutionalism as a Means of Restoring Due Process*

To understand and conceptualise these various challenges to due process in the digital age, scholars and institutions have often turned to the notion of digital constitutionalism. First defined by Nic Suzor in 2010 as the "the work of articulating limits on the exercise of power in a networked society",[56] digital constitutionalism aims to find ways to restrain private and public power in digital spaces. This largely involves integrating the core principles of constitutionalism (i.e. democracy, rule of law, due process) into the context of technology and private actors.[57] Digital constitutionalism has also been defined as a "constellation of initiatives that have sought to articulate a set of political rights, governance norms,

[53] Zalnieriute, Bennett Moses and Williams, 'The Rule of Law and Automation of Government Decision-Making', 425–55.

[54] Zalnieriute, Bennett Moses and Williams, 'The Rule of Law and Automation of Government Decision-Making', 452.

[55] Citron, 'Technological Due Process', 1283.

[56] Nicolas Suzor, 'Digital Constitutionalism: Using the Rule of Law to Evaluate the Legitimacy of Governance by Platforms', Social Media and Society, 4/3 (2018), 4; Nicolas Suzor, 'Digital Constitutionalism and the Role of the Rule of Law in Virtual Communities' (unpublished PhD Thesis, Queensland University of Technology, 2010).

[57] Edoardo Celeste, 'What Is Digital Constitutionalism?', The Digital Constitutionalist, 2022 <https://digi-con.org/what-is-digital-constitutionalism/> [accessed 14 September 2023].

and limitations on the exercise of power on the Internet".[58] Recent examples of digital constitutionalist efforts at policy level covers various national and regional laws and proposals, such as the "A Stronger Online Economy: Opportunity, Innovation and Choice" Bills in the United States,[59] the Artificial Intelligence Act,[60] Digital Services Act,[61] Digital Markets Act,[62] as well as self-regulation through pseudo-courts like the Facebook Oversight Board.[63]

Many scholars have suggested that digital constitutionalist initiatives may be a useful means to prevent new decision-making technologies from undermining due process rights. In particular, the concept of *digital/technological due process* has been proposed as a way to stave off any negative due process ramifications that may arise from the integration of automated systems into private and public sectors. For example, Danielle Citron's seminal 2008 piece suggests that the appearance of automation in the public sectors of judicial and administrative decision-making requires a new model of "technological due process" to be developed.[64] This framework aims to systematise when agencies should turn to automated decision-making, and when they do, propose new mechanisms and

[58] Dennis Redeker, Lex Gill and Urs Gasser, 'Towards Digital Constitutionalism? Mapping Attempts to Craft an Internet Bill of Rights', International Communication Gazette, 80/4 (2018), 303.

[59] The bills include the American Innovation and Choice Online Act, the Platform Competition and Opportunity Act, the Ending Platform Monopolies Act, the Augmenting Compatibility and Competition by Enabling Service Switching (ACCESS) Act, and the Merger Filing Fee Modernization Act, see 'House Lawmakers Release Anti-Monopoly Agenda for "A Stronger Online Economy: Opportunity, Innovation, Choice"', U.S. House Judiciary Committee, 2021 <https://judiciary.house.gov/news/documentsingle.aspx?DocumentID=4591> [accessed 13 October 2021].

[60] Proposal for a Regulation of the European Parliament and of the Council laying down harmonised rules on artificial intelligence (Artificial Intelligence Act) and amending certain Union legislative acts COM (2021) 206 final (Apr. 21, 2021).

[61] Council Regulation (EC) 2022/2065 of 19 October 2022 on a Single Market for Digital Services and Amending Directive 2000/31/EC (Digital Services Act) [2022] L227/1.

[62] Council Regulation (EC) 2022/1925 of 14 September 2022 on Contestable and Fair Markets in the Digital Sector and Amending Directives (EU) 2019/1937 and (EU) 2020/1828 (Digital Markets Act) [2022] L265/1.

[63] Monika Zalnieriute, 'Against Procedural Fetishism: A Call for a New Digital Constitution', Indiana Journal of Global Legal Studies, 30(2) (2023), 230.

[64] Citron, 'Technological Due Process', 1249–1314.

procedures which will act as a proxy for the elements of due process (such as transparency, accountability, and fairness) that are endangered by such automation.[65] Citron suggests that this could take the form of a "rules-versus-standard" approach to determining when automation can be used without undermining due process, such that only decisions involving rules (i.e. a prescribed ex-ante outcome) should be subject to automation.[66] Additionally, she also proposes procedures that aim to combat the undermining of due process by automated decisions—including mandating audit trails for automated systems, educating hearings officers about automation bias, and requiring the release of source code and testing of software before use.[67] Citron and Pasquale then expand on this framework in their subsequent work,[68] which argues that a "right to inspect, correct, and dispute inaccurate data and to know the sources (furnishers) of the data[69]", would remedy the due process concerns raised by such automation.

More recently, Frank Pasquale also examined the ability of AI systems to further undermine due process in the administrative sector, particularly the possibility of automated systems becoming engrained into the contractual bargains between the state and individuals (e.g. by adding addendums onto contracts for disability payment schemes that warns the individual that AI will be used to determine eligibility for the scheme and no recourse will be provided).[70] He suggests that to do so would significantly undermine due process, and instead proposes a similar technological due process framework which would require governments to either refrain from integrating such contractual bargains for automated systems while also ensuring transparency and accountability for such systems where integrated.[71] In his work, De Gregorio also examines the principle of "human-in-the-loop" for algorithmic decision-making—i.e. where humans are required to make review the decision of automation before implementing the final outcome, such as in the General

[65] Citron, 'Technological Due Process', 1258.

[66] Citron, 'Technological Due Process', 1301–4.

[67] Citron, 'Technological Due Process', 1305–12.

[68] Citron and Pasquale, 'The Scored Society', 1–35.

[69] Citron and Pasquale, 'The Scored Society', 20.

[70] Pasquale, 'Inalienable Due Process in an Age of AI', 44.

[71] Pasquale, 'Inalienable Due Process in an Age of AI', 42–56.

Data Protection Regulations.[72] He sees this principle as a "paradigmatic attempt to introduce procedural safeguards" and indicates that it functions as a means to "remedy the lack of transparency oversight on algorithmic technologies".[73]

These notions of digital/technological due process have also been conceptualised for the private sector. For example, Crawford and Schultz proposed a similar framework to Citron and Pasquale, aimed at the private sector, arguing that similar procedural mechanisms could be applied to ensure that due process is also not undermined by big tech companies.[74] The framework comprises three major procedural suggestions, including: introducing a requirement for data companies to provide notice of the predictions they make as well as the personal data relied upon, providing opportunities to "challenge the fairness of the predictive process employed" and allowing for a "neutral data arbiter" who fields the complaints and thus performs a quasi-judicial review role.[75] These recommendations function to ensure that individuals maintain the same rights of due process that they are (supposed to be) regularly afforded by the legal system.

Other scholars have also focused on the ability of legislation and the judiciary to enforce the laws of digital constitutionalism against private companies.[76] For example, Giulia Gentile considers the European Union standards for due process to determine how the offline and online realms of due process interact with one another.[77] She proposes that due process procedures in both the offline and online realms should remain distinct, in order to avoid issues with compliance and the blurring of remedies provided by courts and private actors.[78]

Oreste Pollicino, on the other hand, has explored private power within the digital landscape, suggesting that private tech companies have

[72] De Gregorio, Digital Constitutionalism in Europe.

[73] De Gregorio, Digital Constitutionalism in Europe, 269.

[74] Crawford and Schultz, 'Big Data and Due Process', 93–128.

[75] Crawford and Schultz, 'Big Data and Due Process', 125–28.

[76] Giulia Gentile, 'Between Online and Offline Due Process: The Digital Services Act' (Rochester, NY, 2023) <https://papers.ssrn.com/abstract=4550655> [accessed 27 September 2023]; Pollicino, 'The Quadrangular Shape of the Geometry of Digital Power(s) and the Move towards a Procedural Digital Constitutionalism'.

[77] Gentile, 'Between Online and Offline Due Process'.

[78] Gentile, 'Between Online and Offline Due Process'.

expanded their power through four "quadrangular" dimensions: space (the "territory" of digital spaces), values (judicial and political approaches to technology), actors (the transmutation of major platforms), and remedies (political limitations on private digital power).[79] Pollicino, discusses what countries are doing to prevent abuse of power in the digital age and how effective these mechanisms are, and he proposes to pay more attention to procedural, rather than just substantive normative aspects of what he calls digital remedies.[80] Altogether, many different scholars have aimed to constrain public and private actors from abusing AI systems and digital technologies.

5.4 One Dimensional Due Process: The Procedural Fetishism of Digital Constitutionalism

However, many strands within digital constitutionalism have elaborated frameworks that can be described as one dimensional—they advocate for more procedures, more safeguards, more checklists, but do not engage with substantial questions whether certain AI systems or tools should be used at all. I argue that proceduralist interpretations of due process are dangerous for their tendency to ignore the substantive legality of AI systems and tech regimes, and drawing attention to the micro-level issues of implementing procedural safeguards, such as audits and impact assessments.[81] I suggest that this tendency to overemphasise procedural dimensions of due process results in procedural fetishism which has dominated the digital constitutionalist discourse.

Many of the aforementioned frameworks propose procedural safeguards as the sole mechanism for restoring the principles of due process that have been undermined by recent automation efforts. For example,

[79] Pollicino, 'The Quadrangular Shape of the Geometry of Digital Power(s) and the Move towards a Procedural Digital Constitutionalism', 2.

[80] Pollicino, 'The Quadrangular Shape of the Geometry of Digital Power(s) and the Move towards a Procedural Digital Constitutionalism', 17.

[81] Zalnieriute, 'Against Procedural Fetishism: A Call for a New Digital Constitution', 227–64; Monika Zalnieriute, 'Procedural Fetishism and Mass Surveillance under the ECHR: Big Brother Watch v. UK', Verfassungsblog: On Matters Constitutional, 2021 <https://verfassungsblog.de/big-b-v-uk/> [accessed 9 August 2021]; Monika Zalnieriute, '"Transparency Washing" in the Digital Age: A Corporate Agenda of Procedural Fetishism', Critical Analysis of Law, 8/1 (2021), 139–53.

Citron argues that an "inquisitorial model of quality control can partially replace aspects of adversarial justice that automation renders ineffectual"[82] Crawford and Schultz suggest that "procedural data due process" will "ensure protections that are both fair and feasible for those at risk from this new form of privacy harm"[83]; Pollicino concludes that "it is desirable to provide users of these instruments both with information and also with procedures that can rebalance the unilateral asymmetries of the power of platforms".[84] He also states that evolving digital constitutionalism from a sectoral approach to a "horizontal and procedure-based one" is beneficial in that "it is potentially able to help consolidate a (necessary) trans-Atlantic bridge".[85] Similarly, other scholars, such as Giovanni De Gregorio also highlight the importance of procedural safeguards in digital constitutionalism: "The possibility to rely on procedural safeguards would mitigate disproportionate effects resulting from the exercise of public powers or private determinations. Due process would play a crucial role even beyond the boundaries of public powers".[86]

In this sense, such frameworks rely significantly on regulating the procedural micro-issues rather than engaging with the substantive questions of whether AI tools and digital technologies should find the place in administrative and private decision-making processes in the first place. This is the core of procedural fetishism—assuming the need, the usefulness of the technologies, and then maintaining the status quo by diverting attention from substantive accountability to micro-issues which are inefficient or wholly inadequate to deal with changing legal and political power dynamics.[87]

Such a proceduralist approach to due process is problematic since it rests on the fundamental assumption that procedural safeguards, in both the private and public spheres, will be sufficient to constrain power in the digital space. However, this is not necessarily the case. Primarily, the bulk

[82] Citron, 'Technological Due Process', 1250.

[83] Crawford and Schultz, 'Big Data and Due Process', 128.

[84] Pollicino, Judicial Protection of Fundamental Rights on the Internet, 20.

[85] Ibid, 1.

[86] De Gregorio, Digital Constitutionalism in Europe, 267 citing Giacinto Della Cananea, Due Process of Law Beyond the State: Requirements of Administrative Procedure (Oxford University Press 2016).

[87] Zalnieriute, 'Against Procedural Fetishism: A Call for a New Digital Constitution', 229.

of procedures suggested as a means of limiting corporate power (such as audits, impact assessments, and transparency measures) aim to achieve due process by fostering transparency around the automated decision-making process. Such dependence on the ideal of transparency rests on the idea that if something can be seen, it can be trusted.[88] However, attempts to restrain power in the digital age are often fruitless—they are either exploited strategically "to distract from, and even legitimise, the substantial policies and actions[89]" of the companies which infringe due process norms, or to promote a model of "controllability, measurability and agency" while "in practice maintaining a degree of secrecy[90]". For example, Maroni identifies the Digital Services Act (DSA),[91] General Data Protection Regulations (GDPR),[92] and E-Commerce Directive[93] as fitting examples of legislation which aims to prevent corporate power but end up legitimising it. For example, she points to the use of transparency reports by platforms generally (and as mandated in Articles 14 & 15 of the DSA), suggesting that these procedural measures "embod[y] early cyber-libertarian narratives"[94] which merely enables companies to act as if they are promoting human rights while actively undermining them in practice. This is particularly concerning for due process rights, as these legislative instruments (especially the DSA) often take a "data-centric approach and

[88] Subhanya Sivajothy, 'With and Against Transparency: Taking a Critical Look at How "Transparency" Is Taken Up in Data Justice Discourses', The iJournal: Graduate Student Journal of the Faculty of Information, 5/1 (2020), 57–66; Zalnieriute, '"Transparency Washing" in the Digital Age', 139–53; Marta Maroni, '"Mediated Transparency": The Digital Services Act and the Legitimisation of Platform Power' (Rochester, NY, 2023) <https://papers.ssrn.com/abstract=4413531> [accessed 13 October 2023].

[89] Zalnieriute, '"Transparency Washing" in the Digital Age', 150.

[90] Maroni, '"Mediated Transparency": The Digital Services Act and the Legitimisation of Platform Power', 20.

[91] Council Regulation (EC) 2022/2065 of 19 October 2022 on a Single Market for Digital Services and Amending Directive 2000/31/EC (Digital Services Act) [2022] L227/1.

[92] European Parliament and European Council, General Data Protection Regulation (GDPR), OJ L 119, 2016 <https://gdpr-info.eu/> [accessed 14 August 2020].

[93] Directive 2000/31/EC of the European Parliament and of the Council of 8 June 2000 on Certain Legal Aspects of Information Society Services, in Particular Electronic Commerce, in the Internal Market ('Directive on Electronic Commerce').

[94] Maroni, '"Mediated Transparency": The Digital Services Act and the Legitimisation of Platform Power'.

leave[s] aside issues of algorithmic transparency"[95] as the latter is deemed to be too closely connected to the company's business model and thus are protected under Article 40 of the DSA.[96]

In this sense, proceduralist interventions often fail because they not only maintain respect for the business model of tech companies and highly depend on corporate self-regulation—what Maroni suggests "has been the preferred model of regulation"[97] within the digital space. Companies can thus apply the "transparency" ideal selectively by disclosing only what is commercially desirable for them to disclose and concealing anything that is not, regardless of how transparent they promise the public and regulators they will be.[98] As such, any procedures mandated in an effort to enable digital constitutionalism end up as mere box-ticking exercises to exploit "transparency" for marketing and branding purposes.[99]

By implementing these procedures, companies using automated decision-making can also proactively prevent any regulation of their activities. Frank Pasquale argues that this weak or almost non-existent regulation has enables companies to position themselves as decision-making authorities that exercise juridical power, which results in a shift of the identity of digital companies from participants *in* the market to makers *of* the market, creating a new political economy and concentrating power in the hands of corporations rather than governments.[100] Companies can then depict themselves as their own regulators. For example, private companies have created coalitions aimed to uphold due process—such as the Digital Due Process Organisation, which aims to "simplify,

[95] Maroni, '"Mediated Transparency": The Digital Services Act and the Legitimisation of Platform Power', 3.

[96] Maroni, '"Mediated Transparency": The Digital Services Act and the Legitimisation of Platform Power', 19–20.

[97] Maroni, '"Mediated Transparency": The Digital Services Act and the Legitimisation of Platform Power', 2.

[98] Mikkel Flyverbom, The Digital Prism: Transparency and Managed Visibilities in a Datafied World, 1st edn (2019), 15.

[99] Christina Garsten and Monica Lindh De Montoya, 'The Naked Corporation: Visualization, Veiling and the Ethico-Politics of Organizational Transparency', in Transparency in a New Global Order: Unveiling Organizational Visions, ed. by Christina Garsten and Monica Lindh De Montoya (Cheltenham, 2008), 87.

[100] Frank Pasquale, 'From Territorial to Functional Sovereignty: The Case of Amazon', Law and Political Economy, 2017 <https://lpeblog.org/2017/12/06/from-territorial-to-functional-sovereignty-the-case-of-amazon/> [accessed 17 June 2020].

clarify and unify the ECPA (Electronic Communications Privacy Act)[101] standards, providing stronger privacy protections for communications and associated data in response to changes in technology and new services and usage patterns".[102] This coalition is formed predominantly by "privacy advocates, major companies and think tanks" such as Facebook, Apple, Snapchat, and Google.[103] While this initiative indeed appears to be tackling the problems of due process arising out of the development of new technologies, the fact that its members include companies like Facebook (who has a significant history of privacy issues as well as due process concerns, such as the integration of "Community Standards" which exhibit bias and disproportionately target minority individual's content with little opportunity to appeal the decisions)[104] challenges its legitimacy. Rather than being a genuine attempt to prevent the undermining of due process in digital spaces, such initiatives become hijacked by companies with a history of contributing to the problem—a form of *corporate due process washing*, where consumers are fed the narrative that companies are attempting to fortify due process concerns even though their intentions and behaviours demonstrate otherwise.[105] Due process thus devolves into an exercise in company branding, rather than a genuine means by which corporate power can be limited in digital age.

In sum, digital constitutionalism is being plagued by procedural fetishism and corporate due process washing. While there are no easy

[101] Electronic Communications Privacy Act of 1986 (ECPA), 18 U.S.C. §§ 2510–2523 <https://bja.ojp.gov/program/it/privacy-civil-liberties/authorities/statutes/1285> [accessed 26 September 2023].

[102] 'Our Principles', Digital Due Process <https://digitaldueprocess.org/our-principles/> [accessed 26 September 2023].

[103] 'Who We Are', Digital Due Process <https://digitaldueprocess.org/who-we-are/> [accessed 26 September 2023].

[104] Adi Robertson, 'Human Rights Groups Want Facebook to Offer "Due Process" for Takedowns', The Verge, 2018 <https://www.theverge.com/2018/11/14/18095447/facebook-mark-zuckerberg-santa-clara-principles-moderation-open-letter-due-process-eff-aclu> [accessed 27 September 2023]; David Lat, 'Facebook Banishment and Due Process—Above the Law', 2008 <https://abovethelaw.com/2008/03/facebook-banishment-and-due-process/> [accessed 27 September 2023].

[105] See, for example, another perspective on corporate 'washing' attempts in Zalnieriute, '"Transparency Washing" in the Digital Age', 139–53.

fixes to this plague, one thing is clear: we need to start reviving substantive conceptions of due process if we want digital constitutionalism to be more than just a power legitimization tool.

5.5 The Future of Digital Constitutionalism: Re-Instating Substantive Dimensions of Due Process

What are these substantive conceptions of due process? For example, Issacharoff highlighted that due process has moved through three central phases in the modern era: 1) substantive, 2) procedural and 3) functional due process.[106] Substantive due process is defined as the "question of whether the government's deprivation of a person's life, liberty or property is justified by a sufficient purpose[107]", which in turn gives rise to a set of presumed individual claims or rights which cannot be infringed upon by public or private actors.[108] This phase of due process was ultimately "positive" in nature, as it focused on recognising new substantive rights. Conversely, procedural due process is "negative" in that it merely asks whether the incursion on a right by the government conformed with existing procedures before a benefit was denied.[109]

Digital constitutionalist approach to regulating AI and automated decision-making in both sectors has been largely proceduralist—it has focused on ensuring institutions must jump through procedural hurdles before exercising power, rather than questioning the legitimacy of the power itself. These solely proceduralist approaches, alongside the due process washing attempts of companies, should be rejected for they fundamentally misunderstand the theoretical foundations of due process. Not only do these frameworks conflate the implementation of due process

[106] S. Issacharoff, 'Due Process in Law', in International Encyclopedia of the Social & Behavioral Sciences, ed. by Neil J. Smelser and Paul B. Baltes (Oxford, 2001), 3894–97 <https://www.sciencedirect.com/science/article/pii/B0080430767028527> [accessed 20 September 2023].

[107] Erwin Chemerinsky, 'Substantive Due Process Practising Law Institute Section 1983 Civil Rights Litigation Symposium', Touro Law Review, 15/4 (1998), 1501.

[108] Issacharoff, 'Due Process in Law', 697.

[109] Chemerinsky, 'Substantive Due Process Practising Law Institute Section 1983 Civil Rights Litigation Symposium', 1501; Issacharoff, 'Due Process in Law', 697.

(i.e. the procedures which ensure it) with its content (i.e. the substantive reasons underlying the restraint of power[110]), but also they ignore the normative foundations of due process.

Indeed, due process is a normative assessment—while it limits state (or corporate) power by detailing the processes by which lawful decisions can be made, in doing so it also incorporates the norms of "regularity, fairness, rationality"[111] and asks where governments have a "good reason" to surveill or impact the lives of individuals through automated decision-making. The US Constitution provides a good example, as its due process clause functions to restrain government power where its exercise would be arbitrary, without sufficient reasoning or corrupt—all of which are normative considerations.[112] Substantive due process thus recognises that there are both substantive and formal criteria by which due process attempts to judge government decisions,[113] while proceduralist due process only recognises the validity of formal processes in creating lawful actions. As noted by Timothy Sandefur, the latter approach is doomed because it fails to attach procedures to a "broader normative commitment" to law and justice.[114]

In this sense, approaches to due process in digital constitutionalism that only focus on procedural dimensions ignore the significant informational asymmetries between individuals and companies in the digital age mean that norms of fairness (which ground the principle of due process) cannot be upheld in these situations. Introducing formalistic restrictions on private and public decision-making may ensure regularity, but it does not attach to normative foundations. As noted by Oreste Pollicino, due process in digital constitutionalism "is destined to degenerate into a sterile exercise of "procedural fetishism'" if it detaches significantly

110 Issacharoff, 'Due Process in Law', 3894-97.

111 Timothy Sandefur, 'In Defense of Substantive Due Process, or the Promise of Lawful Rule', Harvard Journal of Law & Public Policy, 35/1 (2012), 285.

112 Sandefur, 'In Defense of Substantive Due Process, or the Promise of Lawful Rule', 285.

113 Sandefur, 'In Defense of Substantive Due Process, or the Promise of Lawful Rule', 314.

114 Sandefur, 'In Defense of Substantive Due Process, or the Promise of Lawful Rule', 314.

from the reference values that are intimately connected to achieving due process.[115]

Therefore, digital constitutionalist approach to due process should focus on substantive attempts at limiting power in the digital space. While this of course includes procedural safeguards, these should all be grounded in normative considerations of ensuring fairness between the individuals on the one hand and the state and companies on the other. For example, Zalnieriute has suggested that tangible legal obligations and novel ambitious laws may be one means by which the project of digital constitutionalism can be redirected towards a more substantive outlook.[116] This can be achieved by various means, I briefly outline several of them here.

First, a binding international treaty on data privacy represents one of the most promising avenues for advancing substantive due process in the age of AI beyond the patchwork of national regulatory regimes. While the General Data Protection Regulation (GDPR)[117] has set a global benchmark, its regional scope and extraterritorial claims raise concerns about uneven enforcement and jurisdictional legitimacy. A global treaty, grounded in international human rights law and negotiated under multilateral institutions such as the United Nations or the Council of Europe, could establish a minimum threshold for data protection obligations, applicable to both states and AI and tech companies. Such an international treaty should not merely replicate existing regulatory models but embed enforceable duties on companies as direct duty-bearers—particularly in relation to automated decision-making, algorithmic profiling.[118] By doing so, international law could move from a state-centric framework

[115] Pollicino, *Judicial Protection of Fundamental Rights on the Internet*, 20.

[116] Zalnieriute, 'Against Procedural Fetishism: A Call for a New Digital Constitution', 227-64.

[117] Regulation (EU) 2016/679 of the European Parliament and of the Council of 27 April 2016 on the protection of natural persons with regard to the processing of personal data and on the free movement of such data, and repealing Directive 95/46/EC (General Data Protection Regulation) (2016) OJ L 119/1.

[118] See especially Monika Zalnieriute, From Human Rights Aspirations to Enforceable Obligations by Non-State Actors in the Digital Age: The Case of Internet Governance and ICANN, 21 YALE J.L. & TECH. 278 (2019).

towards a pluralistic governance model that acknowledges the private power and responsibility of corporate actors.[119]

Second, the growing political influence of AI companies necessitates more robust democratic oversight of their practices. Expanding political and legal scrutiny through novel ambiotious legislation—would help recalibrate power asymmetries between individuals and platforms. This includes legislative bans on particularly invasive or manipulative uses of AI technologies, such as real-time facial recognition, biometric surveillance, or algorithmic content suppression, which have disproportionate effects on racialised, gendered, and otherwise marginalised communities.[120] Crucially, as I explain in my other work, such laws must transcend the formalist paradigms of procedural fairness and engage with the socio-material impacts of AI systems.[121]

Third, the unprecedented concentration of data, infrastructure, and capital in the hands of a few AI companies has revived calls for structural interventions akin to the antitrust movements of the early twentieth century.[122] Applying anti-monopoly tools to AI comapnies requires legal innovation, particularly in reconceptualising market dominance in the context of platform economics and data extraction.[123] Traditional competition law frameworks—such as the Sherman Act in the United States[124]

[119] Ibid.

[120] See Rita Matulionyte and Monika Zalnieriute (eds), The Cambridge Handbook of Facial Recognition in the Modern State (Cambridge University Press 2024).

[121] M. Zalnieriute, 'Compliance without Constraint: Procedural Fetishism of Big Tech in the Age of AI' in A. Andhov (ed) Rethinking Big Tech, Hart Publishing, 2026 (forthcoming).

[122] See, e.g., Manuel Wörsdörfer, Big Tech and Antitrust: An Ordoliberal Analysis, 35 PHILOS. TECHNOL. 65 (2022); ZEPHYR TEACHOUT, BREAK'EM UP: RECOVERING OUR FREEDOM FROM BIG AG, BIG TECH, AND BIG MONEY (2020); NICOLAS PETIT, BIG TECH AND THE DIGITAL ECONOMY: THE MOLIGOPOLY SCENARIO (2020), https://cadmus.eui.eu/handle/1814/68567 (last visited Sep 25, 2022); Dina Srinivasan, The Antitrust Case against Facebook: A Monopolist's Journey towards Pervasive Surveillance in Spite of Consumers' Preference for Privacy, 16 BERKELEY BUS. L.J. 39 (2019).

[123] Lina M Khan, 'Amazon's Antitrust Paradox' (2017) 126 Yale Law Journal 710; Zephyr Teachout, Break'Em Up: Recovering Our Freedom from Big Ag, Big Tech, and Big Money (All Points Books 2020).

[124] The Sherman Antitrust Act of 1890 (26 Stat. 209, 15 U.S.C. §§ 1–7).

or Article 102 TFEU in the EU[125]—must be updated to account for non price harms and algorithmic gatekeeping. In addition to structural separations (e.g. breaking up giants like Amazon or Meta), taxation regimes must be redesigned to capture digital value production and redistribute profits derived from public infrastructures and social data. This includes the adoption of digital services taxes, global minimum corporate tax rates, and public benefit levies. For example, the OECD/G20 has announced an Inclusive Framework on Base Erosion and Profit Shifting, which has now been adopted by over 140 jurisdictions, setting a global minimum corporate tax rate of 15%, which took effect in 2024.[126] These fiscal tools are essential not only for economic justice but also for curbing the political influence of AI companies over law and public discourse.

When traditional regulatory mechanisms prove insufficient, more radical democratic approaches must be considered, such as mandating corporate governance reforms that embed worker, user, and public participation in platform governance. Such proposals are grounded in long-standing traditions of cooperative governance, drawing from labour law, corporate social responsibility frameworks, and public interest law. This could take the form of algorithmic accountability boards, user co-determination rights, or democratic data trusts that shift decision-making power away from executives and shareholders. Embedding democratic norms into the internal governance structures of AI companies would align them with constitutional values of participation and pluralism.

The reclassification of AI companies as public utilities represents the most radical yet potentially transformative legal intervention. Critical scholars have argued that essential digital infrastructures—search engines, cloud services, social media platforms—should be treated as public utilities.[127] This approach is rooted in the idea that certain digital

[125] Consolidated Version of the Treaty on the Functioning of the European Union [2012] OJ C326/47, art 102.

[126] Organisation for Economic Co-operation and Development (OECD), Base Erosion and Profit Shifting (beps)https://www.oecd.org/tax/beps/, accessed 10 April 2025. See also OECD, International community strikes a ground-breaking tax deal for the digital age, (2021), https://www.oecd.org/tax/international-community-strikes-a-ground-breaking-tax-deal-for-the-digital-age.htm (last visited 10 April, 2025).

[127] See Dan Schiller, Reconstructing Public Utility Networks: A Program for Action, 14 INTERNATIONAL JOURNAL OF COMMUNICATION 12 (2020); VINCENT MOSCO, BECOMING DIGITAL: TOWARD A POST-INTERNET SOCIETY (2017);

infrastructures—such as search engines, social networks, or app stores—have become essential to the exercise of rights and participation in public life. As such, they ought to be governed by the same legal principles that apply to utilities like electricity, water, or telecommunications.

Public utility regulation would impose strict non-discrimination obligations, mandate interoperability and access, and prohibit arbitrary content moderation or data collection practices. In extreme cases, it may require public ownership or stewardship of core infrastructures to insulate them from market logics. Such an approach shifts the paradigm from market repair to democratic control, aiming not just to foster competition but to confront the deeper political economy of surveillance, manipulation, and data extraction.[128] While such proposals face significant legal and political hurdles, they reflect a growing consensus that digital power must be subjected to democratic control, particularly when it intersects with public services, civil liberties, and the rule of law.

5.6 Conclusion

As this chapter has argued, digital constitutionalism and AI governance must move beyond its current proceduralist orientation and confront the structural injustices embedded in the deployment of AI and automated systems. While due process remains a cornerstone of constitutional governance, its over-reliance in digital contexts often legitimises rather than limits power. The proliferation of procedural safeguards—audits, impact assessments, transparency reports—risks becoming an empty shell if not rooted in substantive limits on power. Procedural fetishism, as critiqued here, distracts from the deeper normative questions that AI raises about the concentration of economic, and political power in the hands of a few AI companies.

To reclaim due process as a meaningful constraint on power, I have argued, we must revive its substantive dimensions. This requires legal and regulatory transformations that not only mandate fairness in procedure

JAMES MULDOON, PLATFORM SOCIALISM: HOW TO RECLAIM OUR DIGITAL FUTURE FROM BIG TECH (2022).

[128] Thomas M Hanna & Michael Brennan, There's No Solution to Big Tech Without Public Ownership of Tech Companies, JACOBIN (2020), https://jacobin.com/2020/12/big-tech-public-ownership-surveillance-capitalism-platform-corporations (last visited Sep 25, 2022).

but also challenge the legitimacy of certain automated practices altogether. Binding international treaties, structural competition law reforms, democratic co-governance of platforms, and reimagining digital infrastructures as public utilities are not merely technical options—they are constitutional imperatives. These measures are essential to reverse the erosion of rights in the automated state and to restore the balance between private innovation, public accountability, and individual dignity.

Ultimately, the future of digital constitutionalism will depend on its ability to disrupt the procedural status quo and to articulate a new social contract for the age of AI—one that affirms right to shape the conditions under which justice in the age of AI is imagined, claimed, and delivered. Only then can due process reclaim its emancipatory potential in the age of AI.

References

Kate Crawford, quoted in Tom Simonite, "AI Experts Want to End 'Black Box' Algorithms in Government," Wired (18 October 2017), https://www.wired.com/story/ai-experts-want-to-end-black-box-algorithms-in-government/ accessed: 10 April 2025.

Olivia Ireland Keoghan Sarah, 'Jennifer Miller Lost Her Son to Suicide after He Was Chased by Debt Collectors. She Is Ready for Justice', The Sydney Morning Herald, 2023 <https://www.smh.com.au/politics/federal/felicity-had-11-500-wrongly-taken-from-her-bank-account-she-s-ready-for-vindication-20230706-p5dm3i.html> [accessed 20 September 2023]

Seb Starcevic, 'Australian Robodebt Scandal Shows the Risk of Rule by Algorithm', Context, 2022 https://www.context.news/surveillance/australian-robodebt-scandal-shows-the-risk-of-rule-by-algorithm accessed: 20 September 2023.

'Qld Mum of Robodebt Victim Jarrad Madgwick "Vindicated" after Four-Year Battle', News.Com.Au, 7 July 2023, section News Life <https://www.news.com.au/lifestyle/real-life/news-life/qld-mum-of-robodebt-victim-jarrad-madgwick-vindicated-after-fouryear-battle/news-story/05e10c9f42f7a5a65bab09d0a782de9b> [accessed 20 September 2023]

'Robodebt: Illegal Australian Welfare Hunt Drove People to Despair', BBC News, 7 July 2023, section Australia <https://www.bbc.com/news/world-australia-66130105> [accessed 20 September 2023]

Monika Zalnieriute, Lyria Bennett Moses and George Williams, 'The Rule of Law and Automation of Government Decision-Making', The Modern Law Review, 82/3 (2019), 436.

Luke Henriques-Gomes, 'Robodebt: Five Years of Lies, Mistakes and Failures That Caused a $1.8bn Scandal', The Guardian, 10 March 2023, section Australia news <https://www.theguardian.com/australia-news/2023/mar/11/robodebt-five-years-of-lies-mistakes-and-failures-that-caused-a-18bn-scandal> [accessed 20 September 2023]

'The Robodebt Findings Have Been Handed down—What Happens Next?', ABC News, 7 July 2023 <https://www.abc.net.au/news/2023-07-08/robodebt-royal-commission-report-handed-down-what-next-explainer/102571876> [accessed 20 September 2023]

Morgan Meaker, 'Algorithms Policed Welfare Systems for Years. Now They're Under Fire for Bias' WIRED (16 October 2024) https://www.wired.com/story/algorithms-policed-welfare-systems-for-years-now-theyre-under-fire-for-bias, accessed 10 April 2025.

Citron, 'Technological Due Process', 1249–1314; Danielle Keats Citron and Frank A. Pasquale, 'The Scored Society: Due Process for Automated Predictions', Washington Law Review, 89 (2014), 1–35.

Frank Pasquale, 'Inalienable Due Process in an Age of AI: Limiting the Contractual Creep toward Automated Adjudication', in Constitutional Challenges in the Algorithmic Society, ed. by Amnon Reichman and others (Cambridge, 2021), 42–56.

Nicolas P Suzor, Lawless: The Secret Rules That Govern Our Digital Lives (2019).

Oreste Pollicino, Judicial Protection of Fundamental Rights on the Internet: A Road Towards Digital Constitutionalism? (2021); Oreste Pollicino, 'The Quadrangular Shape of the Geometry of Digital Power(s) and the Move towards a Procedural Digital Constitutionalism', European Law Journal, n/a/n/a <https://onlinelibrary.wiley.com/doi/abs/https://doi.org/10.1111/eulj.12472> [accessed 27 September 2023]

Giovanni De Gregorio, Digital Constitutionalism in Europe: Reframing Rights and Powers in the Algorithmic Society, Cambridge Studies in European Law and Policy (Cambridge, 2022a)

Kate Crawford and Jason Schultz, 'Big Data and Due Process: Toward a Framework to Redress Predictive Privacy Harms', Boston College Law Review, 55/1 (2014), 93–128.

'About Us', Digital Due Process Clinic <https://dueprocess.sts.cornell.edu/about/> [accessed 26 September 2023].

de Abreu Duarte, Francisco; De Gregorio, Giovanni and Golia, Angelo Jr, Perspectives on Digital Constitutionalism (2023) in O. Kanevskaia, P. Palka, B. Brozek, Handbook on Law and Technology (Edward Elgar) Forthcoming, available at SSRN: https://ssrn.com/abstract=4508600 or https://doi.org/10.2139/ssrn.4508600.

Monika Zalnieriute, 'Against Procedural Fetishism: A Call for a New Digital Constitution', Indiana Journal of Global Legal Studies, 30(2) (2023), 227–64.

Adam Augustyn, 'Due Process', Britannica, 2023.

Lucia Zedner and Carl-Friedrich Stuckenberg, 'Due Process', in Core Concepts in Criminal Law and Criminal Justice: Volume I, ed. by Alexander Heinze and others (Cambridge, 2020), I, 305 <https://www.cambridge.org/core/books/core-concepts-in-criminal-law-and-criminal-justice/due-process/DB991C16B8CC45DB4CB5D60105CC34ED> [accessed 20 September 2023].

Crawford and Schultz, 'Big Data and Due Process', 110.

Magna Carta, England and Wales, 1297 <http://www.legislation.gov.uk/aep/Edw1cc1929/25/9/section/XXIX?view=extent>.

United States Constitution, 1787 <https://www.archives.gov/founding-docs/constitution-transcript> [accessed 31 July 2020] amend. V.

International Covenant on Civil and Political Rights, General Assembly Resolution 2200A (XXI), 1966 <https://www.ohchr.org/en/professionalinterest/pages/ccpr.aspx> [accessed 11 August 2020].

Council of Europe, Convention for the Protection of Human Rights and Fundamental Freedoms (European Convention on Human Rights), ETS 5, 1953 <https://www.echr.coe.int/Documents/Convention_ENG.pdf>.

Goldberg v. Kelly, 397 U.S. 254 (1970).

Mathews v. Eldridge, 424 U.S. 319 (1976).

Judge Henry J. Friendly, United States Court of Appeal for the Second Circuit, 'Some Kind of Hearing', University of Pennsylvania Law Review, 123 (1975), 1267.

Pasquale, 'Inalienable Due Process in an Age of AI', 42–56.

Danielle Keats Citron, 'Technological Due Process', Washington University Law Review, 85/6 (2007), 1249.

Zalnieriute, Bennett Moses and Williams, 'The Rule of Law and Automation of Government Decision-Making', 425–55.

M. Zalnieriute, L. Bennett Moses and G. Williams, 'The Rule of Law "By Design"?' Tulane Law Review, Vol 95 (5) 2021, pp. 1063–1101.

Peter Hanks, 'Administrative Law and Welfare Rights: A 40-Year Story from "Green v Daniels" to "Robot Debt Recovery"', AIAL Forum 1, 89 (2017), 1–15.

Nicolas Suzor, 'Digital Constitutionalism: Using the Rule of Law to Evaluate the Legitimacy of Governance by Platforms', Social Media and Society, 4/3 (2018), 4.

Nicolas Suzor, 'Digital Constitutionalism and the Role of the Rule of Law in Virtual Communities' (unpublished PhD Thesis, Queensland University of Technology, 2010).

Edoardo Celeste, 'What Is Digital Constitutionalism?', The Digital Constitutionalist, 2022 <https://digi-con.org/what-is-digital-constitutionalism/> [accessed 14 September 2023].

Dennis Redeker, Lex Gill and Urs Gasser, 'Towards Digital Constitutionalism? Mapping Attempts to Craft an Internet Bill of Rights', International Communication Gazette, 80/4 (2018), 303.

The bills include the American Innovation and Choice Online Act, the Platform Competition and Opportunity Act, the Ending Platform Monopolies Act, the Augmenting Compatibility and Competition by Enabling Service Switching (ACCESS) Act, and the Merger Filing Fee Modernization Act, see 'House Lawmakers Release Anti-Monopoly Agenda for "A Stronger Online Economy: Opportunity, Innovation, Choice"', U.S. House Judiciary Committee, 2021 <https://judiciary.house.gov/news/documentsingle.aspx?DocumentID=4591> [accessed 13 October 2021].

Proposal for a Regulation of the European Parliament and of the Council laying down harmonised rules on artificial intelligence (Artificial Intelligence Act) and amending certain Union legislative acts COM (2021) 206 final (Apr. 21, 2021).

Council Regulation (EC) 2022/2065 of 19 October 2022 on a Single Market for Digital Services and Amending Directive 2000/31/EC (Digital Services Act) [2022] L227/1.

Council Regulation (EC) 2022/1925 of 14 September 2022 on Contestable and Fair Markets in the Digital Sector and Amending Directives (EU) 2019/1937 and (EU) 2020/1828 (Digital Markets Act) [2022] L265/1.

Giulia Gentile, 'Between Online and Offline Due Process: The Digital Services Act' (Rochester, NY, 2023) <https://papers.ssrn.com/abstract=4550655> [accessed 27 September 2023]

Monika Zalnieriute, 'Procedural Fetishism and Mass Surveillance under the ECHR: Big Brother Watch v. UK', Verfassungsblog: On Matters Constitutional, 2021 <https://verfassungsblog.de/big-b-v-uk/> [accessed 9 August 2021]

Monika Zalnieriute, '"Transparency Washing" in the Digital Age: A Corporate Agenda of Procedural Fetishism', Critical Analysis of Law, 8/1 (2021), 139–53.

Giacinto Della Cananea, Due Process of Law Beyond the State: Requirements of Administrative Procedure (Oxford University Press 2016).

Subhanya Sivajothy, 'With and Against Transparency: Taking a Critical Look at How "Transparency" Is Taken Up in Data Justice Discourses', The iJournal: Graduate Student Journal of the Faculty of Information, 5/1 (2020), 57–66.

Marta Maroni, '"Mediated Transparency": The Digital Services Act and the Legitimisation of Platform Power' (Rochester, NY, 2023) <https://papers.ssrn.com/abstract=4413531> [accessed 13 October 2023].

European Parliament and European Council, General Data Protection Regulation (GDPR), OJ L 119, 2016 <https://gdpr-info.eu/> [accessed 14 August 2020].

Directive 2000/31/EC of the European Parliament and of the Council of 8 June 2000 on Certain Legal Aspects of Information Society Services, in Particular Electronic Commerce, in the Internal Market ('Directive on Electronic Commerce').

Mikkel Flyverbom, The Digital Prism: Transparency and Managed Visibilities in a Datafied World, 1st edn (2019), 15.

Christina Garsten and Monica Lindh De Montoya, 'The Naked Corporation: Visualization, Veiling and the Ethico-Politics of Organizational Transparency', in Transparency in a New Global Order: Unveiling Organizational Visions, ed. by Christina Garsten and Monica Lindh De Montoya (Cheltenham, 2008), 87.

Frank Pasquale, 'From Territorial to Functional Sovereignty: The Case of Amazon', Law and Political Economy, 2017 <https://lpeblog.org/2017/12/06/from-territorial-to-functional-sovereignty-the-case-of-amazon/> [accessed 17 June 2020].

Electronic Communications Privacy Act of 1986 (ECPA), 18 U.S.C. §§ 2510–2523 <https://bja.ojp.gov/program/it/privacy-civil-liberties/authorities/statutes/1285> [accessed 26 September 2023].

'Our Principles', Digital Due Process <https://digitaldueprocess.org/our-principles/> [accessed 26 September 2023].

'Who We Are', Digital Due Process <https://digitaldueprocess.org/who-we-are/> [accessed 26 September 2023].

Adi Robertson, 'Human Rights Groups Want Facebook to Offer "Due Process" for Takedowns', The Verge, 2018 <https://www.theverge.com/2018/11/14/18095447/facebook-mark-zuckerberg-santa-clara-principles-moderation-open-letter-due-process-eff-aclu> [accessed 27 September 2023]

David Lat, 'Facebook Banishment and Due Process—Above the Law', 2008 <https://abovethelaw.com/2008/03/facebook-banishment-and-due-process/> [accessed 27 September 2023].

S. Issacharoff, 'Due Process in Law', in International Encyclopedia of the Social & Behavioral Sciences, ed. by Neil J. Smelser and Paul B. Baltes (Oxford, 2001), 3894–97 <https://www.sciencedirect.com/science/article/pii/B0080430767028527> [accessed 20 September 2023].

Erwin Chemerinsky, 'Substantive Due Process Practising Law Institute Section 1983 Civil Rights Litigation Symposium', Touro Law Review, 15/4 (1998), 1501.

Timothy Sandefur, 'In Defense of Substantive Due Process, or the Promise of Lawful Rule', Harvard Journal of Law & Public Policy, 35/1 (2012), 285.

Regulation (EU) 2016/679 of the European Parliament and of the Council of 27 April 2016 on the protection of natural persons with regard to the processing of personal data and on the free movement of such data, and repealing Directive 95/46/EC (General Data Protection Regulation) (2016) OJ L 119/1.

Monika Zalnieriute, From Human Rights Aspirations to Enforceable Obligations by Non-State Actors in the Digital Age: The Case of Internet Governance and ICANN, 21 YALE J.L. & TECH. 278 (2019).

Rita Matulionyte and Monika Zalnieriute (eds), The Cambridge Handbook of Facial Recognition in the Modern State (Cambridge University Press 2024).

M. Zalnieriute, 'Compliance without Constraint: Procedural Fetishism of Big Tech in the Age of AI' in A. Andhov (ed) Rethinking Big Tech, Hart Publishing, 2026 (forthcoming).

Manuel Wörsdörfer, Big Tech and Antitrust: An Ordoliberal Analysis, 35 PHILOS. TECHNOL. 65 (2022).

Nicolas Petit, Big Tech and the Digital Economy: The Moligopoly Scenario (2020), https://cadmus.eui.eu/handle/1814/68567 (last visited Sep 25, 2022)

Dina Srinivasan, The Antitrust Case against Facebook: A Monopolist's Journey towards Pervasive Surveillance in Spite of Consumers' Preference for Privacy, 16 BERKELEY BUS. L.J. 39 (2019).

Lina M Khan, 'Amazon's Antitrust Paradox' (2017) 126 Yale Law Journal 710.

Zephyr Teachout, Break 'Em Up: Recovering Our Freedom from Big Ag, Big Tech, and Big Money (All Points Books 2020).

The Sherman Antitrust Act of 1890 (26 Stat. 209, 15 U.S.C. §§ 1–7).

Consolidated Version of the Treaty on the Functioning of the European Union [2012] OJ C326/47.

Organisation for Economic Co-operation and Development (OECD), Base Erosion and Profit Shifting (beps) https://www.oecd.org/tax/beps/, accessed 10 April 2025.

OECD, International community strikes a ground-breaking tax deal for the digital age, (2021), https://www.oecd.org/tax/international-community-strikes-a-ground-breaking-tax-deal-for-the-digital-age.htm (last visited 10 April, 2025).

Dan Schiller, Reconstructing Public Utility Networks: A Program for Action, 14 International Journal of Communication 12 (2020).

Vincent Mosco, Becoming Digital: Toward a Post-internet Society (2017).

James Muldoon, Platform Socialism: How to Reclaim Our Digital Future From Big Tech (2022).

Thomas M Hanna & Michael Brennan, There's No Solution to Big Tech Without Public Ownership of Tech Companies, JACOBIN (2020), https://jacobin.com/2020/12/big-tech-public-ownership-surveillance-capitalism-platform-corporations (last visited Sep 25, 2022).

CHAPTER 6

The Right to Be Forgotten Meets Machine Learning: Evaluating the Legal Feasibility of Unlearning Methods

Liane Rose Colonna and *Tobias Oechtering*

Liane Colonna's contribution to this chapter is partially supported by the Wallenberg AI, Autonomous Systems and Software Program—Humanity and Society (WASP-HS) funded by the Marianne and Marcus Wallenberg Foundation and the Marcus and Amalia Wallenberg Foundation. Both authors also owe gratitude to Professor Mikael Johansson who we had wonderful conversations with about the nature of machine unlearning and provided extremely helpful comments on the manuscript, or parts thereof, at various stages in its development. As far as shortcomings are concerned, they are all attributable to the authors.

L. R. Colonna (✉)
Department of Law, Stockholm University, Stockholm, Sweden
e-mail: liane.colonna@juridicum.su.se

T. Oechtering
Division of Information Science and Engineering, KTH Royal Institute of Technology, Stockholm, Sweden
e-mail: oech@kth.se

A. Aliu (ed.), *Artificial Intelligence and the Rule of Law*,
https://doi.org/10.1007/978-3-031-97389-5_6

6.1 Introduction

The rapid advancement of machine learning (ML) technology is exposing a critical mismatch between the pace of technological advancement and the capacity of existing legal frameworks to effectively regulate it.[1] As ML technologies advance, driving major changes across all sectors of society, traditional regulatory mechanisms—such as notice-and-comment rule-making, legislation, and judicial review—are increasingly inadequate to address its unique and complex challenges.[2] These established legal tools were designed for a slower, more predictable regulatory landscape, and they now struggle to respond to the ethical, privacy, and accountability questions that ML raises.[3] This disconnect not only limits the ability of regulators to manage the societal impacts of ML effectively but also fuels a growing concern that outdated legal approaches may inhibit innovation by imposing rigid and often impractical constraints.

An urgent example of this regulatory gap lies within the General Data Protection Regulation's (GDPR) "right to be forgotten"(RTBF), which grants individuals the right to request the deletion of their personal data once it is no longer necessary for processing purposes.[4] As ML systems become increasingly integrated into vital sectors like healthcare, finance, and education, fulfilling these requests has become a critical concern for data controllers. Naive retraining, the process of rebuilding a ML model from scratch to remove a single data point, is typically impractical due to the extensive computational resources, significant labor, and time it

[1] See Roger Brownsword (2008) Rights, Regulation, and the technological revolution (Oxford University Press).

[2] Gary E. Marchant, The growing gap between emerging technologies and the law (2011). In: Gary E. Marchant, Braden R. Allenby, Joseph R. Herkert (eds) The growing gap between emerging technologies and legal-ethical oversight. Springer Dordrecht, 19–33, 19.

[3] See more generally Tobias J. Oechtering, Sara Saeidian and Cecilia Magnusson Sjöberg (2023) Calculated privacy: tech meets law and law meets tech. Florida International University Law Review 17: 383–398, 386.

[4] Regulation (EU) 2016/679 of the European Parliament and of the Council of 27 April 2016 on the protection of natural persons with regard to the processing of personal data and on the free movement of such data, and repealing directive 95/46/EC (General Data Protection Regulation, "GDPR") (2016) OJ L 119., Article 17.

requires.[5] This highlights the immediate need for more efficient solutions that can address such requests without compromising the accuracy and effectiveness of algorithmic outputs or risking the leakage of personal data. In personalized medicine, for example, unlearning strategies are in critical need due to the complexity of ML models and the impracticality of retraining them from scratch, given the immense costs and computational resources involved.

The current state of the art in machine unlearning can be categorized into two broad approaches, which differ not only in how unlearning is implemented but also in how the concept of "unlearning" itself is defined and understood.[6] The first approach employs exact unlearning methods, which utilize techniques enabling the system to remove specific data points without necessitating a complete retraining of the model.[7] This may be done, for example, by partitioning the deployed model into smaller sub-models, allowing for the retraining of only the sub-model containing the personal data subject to an erasure request, rather than retraining the entire model.[8] An alternative approach is active machine unlearning or approximate unlearning, where the aim is to selectively remove the impact of specific data points from the model without

[5] Katie Hawkins, Nora Alhuwaish, Sana Belguith, Asma Vranaki and Andrew Charlesworth (2024) A decision-making process to implement the 'Right to Be Forgotten' in machine learning. In: K. Rannenberg, P. Drogkaris, C. Lauradoux (eds) Privacy Technologies and Policy. APF 2023. Lecture Notes in Computer Science, vol 13888. Springer, Cham, 20–38, 30.

[6] Anvith Thudi, Hengrui Jia, Ilia Shumailov, Nicolas Papernot (2022) On the necessity of auditable algorithmic definitions for machine unlearning. 31st USENIX Security Symposium (USENIX Security 22), 4007-4022.

[7] Haibo Zhang, Toru Nakamura, Takamasa Isohara and Kouichi Sakurai (2023) A review on machine unlearning. SN Computer Science 4: 337, 1-13,6 (explaining, "Exact unlearning means that the model outputs after removing the sample x is the same as the one that was never trained on the removed sample x.").

[8] Lucas Bourtoule, Varun Chandrasekaran, Cristopher A. Choquette-Choo, Hengrui Jia, Adelin Travers, Baiwu Zhang, David Lie and Nicolas Papernot (2021) Machine unlearning. In 2021 IEEE Symposium on Security and Privacy, 141–159.

the need to retrain it at the algorithmic level.[9] Using advanced post-processing algorithms, this method seeks to efficiently update the model to eliminate the influence of the deleted data while, at least theoretically, preserving the integrity of the model's performance. Active unlearning seeks to be a much faster and less resource-intensive approach than passive unlearning, making it a potentially more practical solution for real-world applications where frequent data deletions may be required.

Despite the potential of machine unlearning, there are critical research gaps surrounding both its legal and technical implications. From a legal perspective, the adequacy of unlearning solutions in meeting legal standards is unclear, especially given the lack of established precedents and guidelines on how machine unlearning should be implemented and evaluated. From a technical perspective, the field remains in its infancy, with significant uncertainties surrounding its feasibility. Current approaches to unlearning almost always face a tradeoff: either the model continues to memorize personal information, or the removal process compromises its performance. This means that if machine unlearning is conducted in a way that compromises model accuracy and reliability after data removal, it may paradoxically address the legal requirement of complying with the RTBF but create other legal problems, namely violating the obligations to ensure accuracy under the GDPR,[10] as well as the robustness and safety requirements set forth in the AI Act.[11]

This chapter examines how evolving legal and technical frameworks can more effectively navigate the complexities of implementing the RTBF in the ML context, aiming to suggest an approach that can protect individual

[9] Min Chen, Zhikun Zhang, Tianhao Wang, Michael Backes, Mathias Humbert, Yang Zhang (2021) When machine unlearning jeopardizes privacy. In Proceedings of the 2021 ACM SIGSAC Conference on Computer and Communications Security (CCS'21), November 15–19, 2021, Virtual Event, Republic of Korea. ACM, New York, NY, USA, 16 pages.

[10] GDPR, Article 5(1)(d)(stating, "Personal data shall be … accurate and, where necessary, kept up to date…").

[11] Regulation (EU) 2024/1689 of the European Parliament and of the Council of 13 June 2024 laying down harmonised rules on artificial intelligence and amending Regulations (EC) No 300/2008, (EU) No 167/2013, (EU) No 168/2013, (EU) 2018/858, (EU) 2018/1139 and (EU) 2019/2144 and Directives 2014/90/EU, (EU) 2016/797 and (EU) 2020/1828 ("AI Act")(2024) OJ L 1689, Article 15 (stating, "High-risk AI systems shall be designed and developed in such a way that they achieve an appropriate level of accuracy, robustness, and cybersecurity, and that they perform consistently in those respects throughout their lifecycle.").

rights while enabling continued technological innovation. It begins by offering a doctrinal analysis of the RTBF, exploring its legal origins, evolution, and general application. The chapter then explores four challenges that exist within the context of machine unlearning: data fragmentation, the persistence of learned patterns in ML systems, accuracy trade-offs in unlearning, and technical barriers to auditing, all which impact compliance and accountability. Finally, the chapter critically evaluates both active and passive machine unlearning under available legal guidelines, precedents, and scholarship. Ultimately, it seeks to help bridge the gap between legal requirements and technological reality, offering insights into how the RTBF might be adapted to ensure meaningful data privacy in the age of ML.

6.2 Right to Be Forgotten

The RTBF has its origins in the EU's 1995 Data Protection Directive (95/46/EC) and the 2000 Directive on Electronic Commerce (2000/31/EC).[12] These directives established the legal basis for search engine providers' obligation to remove links within the EU, which was solidified in 2014 by the Court of Justice of the European Union (CJEU) in *Google Spain v. Gonzales*.[13] In this case, a man requested the removal of search results related to a past real estate auction, arguing that the information published was outdated and no longer relevant to the public or to him personally.[14] Citing Article 12(b) of Directive 95/46/EC, the CJEU ruled that when information processed by search engines is deemed inadequate, irrelevant, or excessive in relation to the purpose of the data processing, the associated links must be removed.[15]

[12] Council Directive No. 95/46/EC of 24 October 1995 on the Protection of Individuals with Regard to the Processing of Personal Data and on the Free Movement of Such Data, art. 2(c), OJ. L 281/31 (1995); Directive 2000/31/EC, of the European Parliament and of the Council of 8 June 2000 on Certain Legal Aspects of Information Society Services, in Particular Electronic Commerce, in the Internal Market, 2000 O.J. L 178 1, 1.

[13] Case C-131/12 Google Spain SL, Google Inc. v Agencia Española de Protección de Datos (AEPD), Mario Costeja González [2014] ECLI:EU:C:2014:317.

[14] Id. para. 14–15.

[15] Id. para. 94.

Importantly, the CJEU did not clarify whether the removal obligation extended to erasing the information entirely from the internet, as the Court focused solely on Google's responsibilities as a search engine and did not address the role of the original publisher.[16] The Court distinguished between making the information less accessible through search engines and fully deleting the data from its source, suggesting that the obligation can be satisfied by limiting public visibility, even if the original data remains intact. In other words, *Google Spain* established the right to be delisted—not a complete RTBF because the ruling focused only on the removal of search results linked to the data subject's name, rather than erasing all traces of the original content itself.[17] It is further important to observe that in its decision, the Court explicitly weighed the data protection rights of individuals against the commercial interests of search engines and the public's right to information which highlights the importance of the principle of proportionality in defining the scope of the RTBF.[18] The Court found that Google's economic interests and the public's interest in access to the personal data did not outweigh the fundamental rights of the data subject.[19]

In 2018, however, the GDPR explicitly recognized the RTBF, going far beyond the "right to be delisted" established in *Google Spain*.[20] Article 17 distinguishes between the "right to erasure," which focuses on the controller's obligation to delete data, and the "right to be forgotten," which implies deletion must extend to all possible sources where parts of

[16] Herke Kranenborg (2020) Article 17 Right to erasure ('right to be forgotten'). In: Christopher Kuner, Lee A Bygrave, Christopher Docksey, Laura Drechsler (eds) The EU General Data Protection Regulation (GDPR): A commentary, Oxford, 475–484, 479–480.

[17] Eugenia Politou, Alexandra Michota, Efthimios Alepis, Matthias Pocs, Constantinos Patsakis (2018) Backups and the Right to Be Forgotten in the GDPR: An uneasy relationship. Computer Law & Security Review Volume 34: 1247–1257, 1248.

[18] Case C-131/12 Google Spain SL, Google Inc. v Agencia Española de Protección de Datos (AEPD), Mario Costeja González [2014] ECLI:EU:C:2014:317, para. 81.

[19] Id.

[20] Eugenia Politou, Alexandra Michota, Efthimios Alepis, Matthias Pocs, Constantinos Patsakis (2018) Backups and the Right to Be Forgotten in the GDPR: An uneasy relationship. Computer Law & Security Review 34: 1247–1257, 1248; Aleksandra Kuczerawy and Jef Ausloos (2016) From notice-and-takedown to notice-and delist: Implementing Google Spain Colorado Technology Law Journal 14: 219–258, 224 (explaining that "(the Court) did not rule that search engines can be compelled to interfere with the source itself, nor that search engines can be compelled to delist a search result entirely (i.e. on the basis of any search term").

the data may exist.[21] That is, the right to forget ensures that individuals are not perpetually tied to their past, allowing them to be "forgotten" to protect their dignity while the right to delete grants individuals control over their personal information, enabling them to manage how their data are processed.[22]

The RTBF aligns with privacy as control first defined by Westin.[23] This is because it grants individuals the authority to dictate the dissemination and use of their personal information, particularly in relation to data protection, while also embodying the concept of informational self-determination by empowering individuals to decide whether their data should be processed or shared.[24] Furthermore, it connects to human dignity by restricting the dissemination of personal data, protecting individuals from being treated as objects in commercial exploitation, and enhancing consumer protection.[25]

Article 17(1) sets forward six situations where a person has the right to ask for personal data to be erased by the data controller. Three of the grounds overlap, such as when personal data are no longer necessary for the purpose for which they were collected or otherwise processed,[26] consent is withdrawn,[27] or the data were processed unlawfully.[28] This is because "they all assume the lack of a basis for processing."[29] Article 17(1)(d) acts as a general clause, confirmed by recital 65, which states

[21] Eugenia Politou, Efthimios Alepis and Constantinos Patsakis (2018) Forgetting personal data and revoking consent under the GDPR: Challenges and proposed solutions, Journal of Cybersecurity 4:1–20, 11.

[22] Jay Kaganoff (2021) Send the word over there: An offshore solution to the Right to Be Forgotten, Northwestern Journal of International Law and Business 41: 245–271, 249–50.

[23] Alan Westin, *Privacy and Freedom* (New York, Atheneum: 1967).

[24] Helena U. Vrabec (2021) The Right to Be Forgotten, data subject rights under the GDPR. In: Helena U. Vrabec (ed) Data subject rights under the GDPR, Oxford, 2021; online edn, Oxford Academic, 129–158, 130–131.

[25] Id.

[26] GDPR Article 17(1)(a).

[27] GDPR Article 17(1)(b).

[28] GDPR, Article 17(1)(d).

[29] Herke Kranenborg (2020) Article 17 Right to erasure ('right to be forgotten'). In: Christopher Kuner, Lee A Bygrave, Christopher Docksey, Laura Drechsler (eds) The EU General Data Protection Regulation (GDPR): A commentary, Oxford, 475–484, 481.

that the right to erasure can be used when the processing does not comply with the GDPR.[30]

Article 17(1)(c) is linked to the right to object under Article 21, applicable when processing is based on Article 6(1)(e) or (f) of the GDPR. Under Article 21(1), the burden of proof shifts to the data controller, who must demonstrate compelling legitimate grounds to continue processing the data.[31] If the controller cannot provide such justification, the data must be erased.[32] The fourth and fifth grounds include the requirement to erase personal data to comply with legal obligations under Union or Member State law,[33] and when the data were collected in connection with the provision of information society services, particularly when the personal data pertains to a child and was processed based on the child's consent.[34]

Article 17(3) provides for exceptions to the RTBF such as where processing is necessary for exercising the right of freedom of expression and information as well as for reasons of public interest in the area of public health. Additionally, the RTBF may be restricted for scientific, archiving, statistical, and historical research purposes if erasure would make it impossible or significantly hinder the objectives of such processing.[35] The GDPR requires data erasure "without undue delay" using effective measures, but determining how quickly data can be erased from deployed ML models remains an important, unresolved question.[36]

Koops highlights a common phenomenon on the internet where content that is deemed funny or embarrassing is frequently copied and shared, often exacerbating the spread of the material.[37] He notes that

[30] Id.

[31] Id.

[32] Id.

[33] GDPR, Article 17(1)(e).

[34] GDPR, Article 17(1)(f).

[35] GDPR, Article 17(3)(d).

[36] Sebastian Schelter, Stefan Grafberger, and Ted Dunning (2021) HedgeCut: Maintaining randomised Trees for Low-Latency Machine Unlearning. In Proceedings of the 2021 International Conference on management of data (SIGMOD'21). Association for Computing Machinery, New York, NY, USA, 1545–1557. https://doi.org/10.1145/3448016.3457239.

[37] Bert-Japp Koops (2011) Forgetting footprints, shunning shadows: A critical analysis of the "right to be forgotten" in Big Data Practice. SCRIPTed 8: 229-256, 244; Helena

when official requests are made to remove such content at its source, some individuals or groups, motivated by a strong belief in the freedom of expression, intentionally replicate the material to ensure it remains available to the online community.[38] This practice can undermine efforts to protect privacy or enforce the RTBF, as the act of copying disperses the content across various platforms, making it more difficult to completely remove.

In 2018, Fosch Villaronga et. al further explain that the core challenge with the RTBF lies in the disconnect between the well-intentioned goals of regulators, who draft laws in abstract terms, and the practical complexities of modern technical systems.[39] The vague language of the RTBF suggests that personal data can simply be deleted, as if digital data were as straightforward to erase as "a physical file that can simply be destroyed."[40] Years later, this observation rings even truer as the challenges of implementing the RTBF have only grown more pronounced with the increasing complexity of data ecosystems.

6.3 Machine Unlearning and the RTBF: The Challenges

Even before the rise of highly advanced ML models and systems, there have been numerous legal and technical difficulties associated with data deletion. These challenges include the persistence of data in backup systems and archives, where copies of personal data may continue to exist even after deletion requests have been processed.[41] Another obstacle lies in ensuring that third-party processors and data-sharing partners comply

U. Vrabec (2021) The Right to Be Forgotten, data subject rights under the GDPR. In: Helena U. Vrabec (ed) Data subject rights under the GDPR, Oxford, 2021; online edn, Oxford Academic, 129-158, 141–142.

[38] Id.

[39] Eduard Fosch Villaronga, Peter Kieseberg, Tiffany Li (2018), Machines remember: Artificial intelligence and the Right to Be Forgotten. Computer Law & Security Review 34: 304–313, 304.

[40] Id. at 307.

[41] Eugenia Politou, Alexandra Michota, Efthimios Alepis, Matthias Pocs, Constantinos Patsakis (2018) Backups and the Right to Be Forgotten in the GDPR: An uneasy relationship. Computer Law & Security Review Volume 34: 1247-1257.

with data deletion requests.[42] Even if a data controller removes data from its systems, ensuring that all third-party recipients do the same introduces complexity, especially when data has been shared across a chain of processors or across borders.[43] Regulatory compliance across different legal jurisdictions adds another layer of difficulty, as data protection laws and obligations may differ, potentially slowing or complicating the deletion process.

The emergence of ML models has further compounded these long-standing issues, adding more layers of complexity to the task of ensuring that data, once incorporated into model training, can be effectively removed. Unlike relational databases, which support relatively straightforward transactional deletes and updates, ML models lack built-in deletion mechanisms.[44] As a result, the erasure of personal data has shifted from a fairly simple task to a difficult procedure, complicated by the "opaque and nondeterministic nature of ML" models and their inherent ability to learn and evolve based on previously processed personal data.[45]

Machine unlearning has emerged as a potential solution for implementing the RTBF in the digital age, offering a range of techniques to selectively remove data from ML models, although it is crucial to acknowledge that the field remains in its early stages, and no single technique offers a definitive solution to ensuring data privacy. Beyond meeting data protection compliance, unlearning provides a pathway to eliminate copyrighted, toxic, dangerous, or otherwise harmful content, supporting ethical and responsible AI use.[46] Furthermore, as large language models

[42] Id. at 1250; Jef Ausloos (2011) The 'Right to Be Forgotten'—Worth remembering? Computer Law & Security Review 28: 143–152, 146–147.

[43] Jef Ausloos (2011) The 'Right to Be Forgotten'—Worth remembering? Computer Law & Security Review 28: 143–152, 146–147.

[44] Sebastian Schelter, Stefan Grafberger, and Ted Dunning (2021) HedgeCut: Maintaining randomised Trees for Low-Latency Machine Unlearning. In Proceedings of the 2021 International Conference on management of data (SIGMOD'21). Association for Computing Machinery, New York, NY, USA, 1545–1557, 1545; Meem Arafat Manab (2024) Eternal sunshine of the mechanical mind: The irreconcilability of machine learning and the Right to be Forgotten. arXiv:2403.05592.

[45] Bjørn Aslak Juliussen, Jon Petter Rui, Dag Johansen (2023) Algorithms that forget: Machine unlearning and the right to erasure. Computer Law & Security Review 51:105885, 1–12, 2.

[46] Luciano Floridi (2023) Machine unlearning: Its nature, scope, and importance for a "delete culture". Philosophy & Technology 36: 42.

(LLMs) are particularly prone to issues like hallucinations, unlearning allows for the removal of factually incorrect information.[47] Models trained on static historical data also risk becoming outdated as data distributions shift—such as evolving customer preferences in recommendation systems—resulting in performance degradation over time.[48] Unlearning, therefore, is essential not only for privacy but also for maintaining model relevance in dynamic environments.

As noted at the outset, passive or exact unlearning seeks to fully eliminate the influence of specific data points from a model by retraining it at the algorithmic level.[49] Xu et. al explain, "Exact unlearning guarantees that the distribution of an unlearned model and a retrained model are indistinguishable."[50] The benefit of this approach is that the model behaves as though the removed data had never been part of the training process.[51] Although this method offers strong guarantees of data removal, it typically requires significant computational and storage resources, generally making it only suitable for simpler models.[52] In other words, retraining a model with exact unlearning techniques may "suffer inefficiency similar to naive retraining, and may also yield poorer

[47] Id.

[48] Jie Xu, Zihan Wu, Cong Wang, and Xiaohua Jia (2024) Machine unlearning: Solutions and challenges. IEEE Transactions on Emerging Topics in Computational Intelligence 8: 2150–2168, 2150.

[49] Luciano Floridi (2023) Machine unlearning: Its nature, scope, and importance for a "delete culture". Philosophy & Technology 36: 42 (observing that that exact unlearning is a actually a misnomer because it is really re-learning); Jie Xu, Zihan Wu, Cong Wang, and Xiaohua Jia (2024) Machine unlearning: Solutions and challenges. IEEE Transactions on Emerging Topics in Computational Intelligence 8: 2150–2168, 2150 (stating, "Exact unlearning aims to completely remove the influence of targeted data points from the model through algorithmic-level retraining.").

[50] Heng Xu, Tianqing Zhu, Lefeng Zhang, Wanlei Zhou, and Philip S. Yu. 2023. Machine unlearning: A survey. ACM Computing Surveys 56, 1, Article 9 (January 2024), 1–36, 6.

[51] Jie Xu, Zihan Wu, Cong Wang, and Xiaohua Jia (2024) Machine unlearning: Solutions and challenges. IEEE Transactions on Emerging Topics in Computational Intelligence 8: 2150–2168, 2150.

[52] Id.

performance."[53] That said, research in this field is advancing with techniques like Sharded, Isolated, Sliced, and Aggregated training making exact unlearning more viable, at least for simpler models.[54]

In contrast, active machine unlearning or approximate unlearning aims to reduce the influence of targeted data points by efficiently updating the model's parameters.[55] That is, unlike passive unlearning which defines unlearning at the algorithmic level and can guarantee "all the data subjects' personal data has been removed," it defines unlearning at the level of model parameters and provides "a statistical bound as to its ability to remove the requested data from the existing deployed model."[56] It is a practical approach that seeks to reduce the influence of specified data points in a model rather than fully removing them, involving steps such as calculating data influence, optionally adjusting model parameters to negate that influence, optionally adding noise to protect data confidentiality, and validating the updated model's performance, making it a resource-efficient alternative to exact unlearning.[57]

[53] Kairan Zhao, What makes unlearning hard and what to do about it, https://arxiv.org/html/2406.01257v1.

[54] Lucas Bourtoule, Varun Chandrasekaran, Cristopher A. Choquette-Choo, Hengrui Jia, Adelin Travers, Baiwu Zhang, David Lie and Nicolas Papernot. (2021). Machine unlearning. In 2021 IEEE Symposium on Security and Privacy, 141–159; but see further Korbinian Koch; Marcus Soll, No matter how you slice it: Machine unlearning with SISA comes at the expense of minority classes," 2023 IEEE Conference on Secure and Trustworthy Machine Learning (SaTML), Raleigh, NC, USA, 2023, pp. 622–637.

[55] Jie Xu, Zihan Wu, Cong Wang, and Xiaohua Jia (2024) Machine unlearning: Solutions and challenges. IEEE Transactions on Emerging Topics in Computational Intelligence 8: 2150–2168, 2150.

[56] Katie Hawkins, Nora Alhuwaish, Sana Belguith, Asma Vranaki and Andrew Charlesworth (2024) A decision-making process to implement the 'Right to Be Forgotten' in machine learning. In: K. Rannenberg, P. Drogkaris, C. Lauradoux (eds) Privacy Technologies and Policy. APF 2023. Lecture Notes in Computer Science, vol 13888. Springer, Cham, 20–38, 31.

[57] Jie Xu, Zihan Wu, Cong Wang, and Xiaohua Jia (2024) Machine unlearning: Solutions and challenges. IEEE Transactions on Emerging Topics in Computational Intelligence 8: 2150–2168.

While it does not completely remove the influence,[58] this approach significantly lowers computational, storage, and time requirements.[59] It is particularly promising for large-scale and complex models where exact unlearning may be impractical.[60] Xu et al. succinctly explain approximate unlearning as a method that reduces the influence of unlearned data to an acceptable level, offering advantages over exact unlearning, such as greater computational efficiency, reduced storage costs, and increased flexibility.[61]

While machine unlearning possibly offers a solution to the implementation of the RTBF in the digital age, its successful integration into existing regulatory and technical frameworks requires overcoming several complex challenges. Set forth below is a discussion of four key challenges of machine unlearning which have legal implications. These include data fragmentation, the retention of learned patterns in machine learning systems, trade-offs in accuracy during unlearning, and technical limitations in auditing.

6.3.1 Challenge 1: Data and Information Fragmentation

The interconnected, layered, correlated, and fragmented nature of the data that exists within the ML context adds complexity to defining the scope of personal data under the GDPR, raising an initial question about whether the RTBF can be invoked at all. Personal data can exist in various stages within the development of an ML model, from its presence in the training set to its influence on the learned parameters and on the outputs generated by the model. Moreover, even the model itself may potentially

[58] Anvith Thudi, Hengrui Jia, Ilia Shumailov, Nicolas Papernot (2022) On the necessity of auditable algorithmic definitions for machine unlearning, 31st USENIX Security Symposium (USENIX Security 22), 4007-4022, 4009 (explaining that a disadvantage of approximate unlearning "comes from the fact that the unlearning property provided is harder to understand (especially to the end user): the data points to be unlearned are still involved in some of the decisions made to obtain the final model.").

[59] Jie Xu, Zihan Wu, Cong Wang, and Xiaohua Jia (2024) Machine unlearning: Solutions and challenges. IEEE Transactions on Emerging Topics in Computational Intelligence 8: 2150–2168, 2150.

[60] Id.

[61] Id. at 2156.

be considered personal data, further challenging the boundaries of data protection regulation.[62]

It is well understood that European data protection law revolves around the concept of personal data, as the GDPR's rights and protections apply only to such data. The GDPR defines personal data broadly as any information related to an identified or identifiable person, and this scope has been interpreted expansively, with commentators like Purtova arguing that almost any piece of information could qualify as personal data.[63] Both the Article 29 Working Party and the CJEU have extended the definitions of "identifiability" and "relating to," encompassing data that could potentially identify a person or influence their rights, behavior, or status, even if the data controller has no interest or ability to re-identify the individual.[64]

This expansive interpretation of personal data is illustrated in several landmark cases, which clarify how even indirect or inferred information can fall within the GDPR's scope. In Lindqvist (C-101/01), the CJEU held that references to a minor foot injury and part-time medical leave constituted "data concerning health," indicating that even seemingly trivial health details warrant special protection.[65] In Breyer (C-582/14), the Court determined that IP addresses, while not directly identifying users, could still be classified as personal data if re-identification were technically possible through third-party cooperation.[66] This decision

[62] Bjørn Aslak Juliussen, Jon Petter Rui, Dag Johansen (2023) Algorithms that forget: Machine unlearning and the right to erasure. Computer Law & Security Review 51:105885, 1–12, 3–6; Lilian Edwards and Michael Veale (2017) Slave to the algorithm? Why a "Right to an Explanation" is probably not the remedy you are looking for. Duke Law and Technology Review 16: 18–84, 70–71; Maria Rigaki and Sebastian Garcia (2023) A survey of privacy attacks in machine learning. ACM Computing Surveys 56, 4, Article 101, 1–34, 2.

[63] Nadezhda Purtova (2018) The law of everything. Broad concept of personal data and the future of EU data protection law. Law, Innovation and Technology 10: 40–81, 41.

[64] See Article 29 Data Protection Working Party Opinion 04/2007 on the Concept of Personal Data, at 10 (June 10, 2007), https://ec.europa.eu/justice/article-29/documentation/opinion-recommendation/files/2007/wp136_en.pdf [https://perma.cc/W6Y4-DM39.

[65] Criminal proceedings against Bodil Lindqvist Case C-101/01, 2003 ECR I-12971 (Nov. 6, 2003).

[66] Patrick Breyer v Bundesrepublik Deutschland. Case C-582/14. ECLI:EU:C:2016:779.

implies that if key-coded or de-identified information can be indirectly linked back to an identifiable person, a data controller may be obligated to treat it as personal data. The Nowak case (Case C-434/16) further emphasized an expansive understanding of personal data, with the Court ruling that even an exam script and examiner comments related sufficiently to the candidate to be considered personal data.[67] Finally, in Vyriausioji (C-184/20), the CJEU recognized that information on a declarant's relationships, such as a spouse or partner, could reveal sensitive personal data, such as sexual orientation, thus requiring data controllers to account for potential inferences that could expose sensitive information.[68] Collectively, these cases highlight that machine unlearning mechanisms must address not only direct identifiers but also certain data fragments and residual traces, ensuring compliance with the GDPR's broad interpretation of personal data.

The abstraction and fragmentation of information in the ML context make the implementation of the RTBF a highly complex task because models are built on data aggregated from many individuals, not easily traceable to any single user. When ML systems use data inferred from large datasets to generate insights or perform tasks, the impact of removing one person's data often hinges on how unique that data point is within the training dataset. In many cases, especially with large and diverse datasets and models with complex architectures, an individual's data is diffused within the broader dataset, resulting in minimal observable changes to the model's outputs.[69] However, what matters most is not the size of the dataset but the uniqueness of a data point within it: highly detailed data, like a human gene or fingerprint, remains unique even in large datasets.

[67] Peter Nowak v Data Protection Commissioner. Case C-434/16. ECLI:EU:C:2017:994.

[68] OT v. Vyriausioji tarnybinės etikos komisija. Case C-184/20. ECLI:EU:C:2022:601.

[69] Helena U. Vrabec, The Right to Be Forgotten, data subject rights under the GDPR. In: Helena U. Vrabec (ed) Data subject rights under the GDPR, Oxford, 2021; online edn, Oxford Academic, 129–158, 130–131; Lilian Edwards and Michael Veale (2017) Slave to the algorithm? Why a "Right to an Explanation" is probably not the remedy you are looking for. Duke Law and Technology Review 16: 18–84.

Edwards and Veale explain that ML systems often need numerous examples to recognize patterns effectively.[70] These systems are calibrated, or "regularized," to avoid focusing on random "noise" in the data, instead capturing the primary "signal" to enhance the model's usefulness in analyzing future cases.[71] Consequently, retraining a model to exclude a single user's data is both resource-intensive and technically challenging, largely due to the absence of efficient methods for implementing such changes. Yet, in many cases, depending on the task, such retraining would likely result in negligible changes to predictions or commercial outcomes. Meaningful changes in a model's behavior would likely require a substantial number of users—or even entire cohorts—requesting data removal simultaneously, a scenario that remains practically unlikely.[72]

In the data-driven environment, it is critical to highlight that algorithms do not generate information from "meaningful elements" as humans do; instead, they process data to identify correlations, patterns, and statistical associations.[73] Data without context lacks inherent meaning; it is simply numeric differences that gain relevance only in specific contexts and for particular users, as Bateson describes information as a "difference that makes a difference."[74] Algorithms process these raw "differences" into patterns, which can later become informative when contextualized and communicated to users, often without the users needing to know the specific data points involved.[75] In this way, algorithms "produce" information by identifying previously unnoticed correlations and patterns within large datasets.[76] This process highlights how data-driven technologies extract valuable insights from data, underpinning the foundation of the information society.

[70] Lilian Edwards and Michael Veale (2017) Slave to the algorithm? Why a "Right to an Explanation" is probably not the remedy you are looking for. Duke Law and Technology Review 16: 18–84, 69.

[71] Id.

[72] Id.

[73] Elena Esposito (2017) Algorithmic memory and the Right to Be Forgotten on the web. Big Data and Society 4: 1–11, 5.

[74] Id. citing Bateson G (1972) Steps to an Ecology of Mind. New York: Ballantine Books, 582.

[75] Elena Esposito (2017) Algorithmic memory and the Right to Be Forgotten on the web. Big Data and Society 4: 1–11, 5.

[76] Id.

6.3.2 *Challenge 2: The Retention of Learned Patterns in Machine Learning Systems*

A broad interpretation of "forgetting"under the RTBF poses challenges in ML, where data deeply ingrained within the structure of ML models influences outputs, making complete removal difficult, if not impossible, to achieve.[77] In other words, ML models have a "memory," retaining traces of data that continue to shape their behavior even after attempts to delete or "forget" that information.[78] Two Microsoft researchers aptly compare the challenge of removing specific data from a ML model to extracting individual ingredients from a baked cake.[79] Similarly, Dang likens it to asking a person to forget a single lesson from their entire educational history.[80]

Removed data can persist in a model's parameters because the goal of ML training is to create a model capable of performing specific tasks or making accurate predictions, which often requires the intentional memorization of certain data points to improve performance.[81] For example, models like K-nearest neighbor classifiers use data points as

[77] Eduard Fosch Villaronga, Peter Kieseberg, Tiffany Li (2018) Humans forget, machines remember: Artificial intelligence and the Right to Be Forgotten. Computer Law & Security Review 34: 304–313; Stephen Pastis, A.I. trained on private user data never really "forgets," Fortune Eur. (2023), https://fortune.com/europe/2023/08/30/researchers-impossible-remove-private-user-data-delete-trained-ai-models/

[78] Stephen Pastis (2023) A.I. trained on private user data never really "forgets," Fortune Eur., https://fortune.com/europe/2023/08/30/researchers-impossible-remove-private-user-data-delete-trained-ai-models/; Claudio Novelli, Federico Casolari, Philipp Hacker, Giorgio Spedicato, Luciano Floridi (2024) Generative AI in EU law: Liability, privacy, intellectual property, and cybersecurity. Computer Law & Security Review 55: 106066.

[79] Ronen Eldan and Mark Russinovich (2023) Who's Harry Potter? Making LLMs forget, Physics of AGI, https://www.microsoft.com/en-us/research/articles/whos-harry-potter-making-llms-forget-2/.

[80] Quang-Vinh Dang (2021) Right to Be Forgotten in the age of machine learning. In: T. Antipova (ed.) Advances in Digital Science. Springer International Publishing, Cham, pp. 403–411.

[81] Claudio Novelli, Federico Casolari, Philipp Hacker, Giorgio Spedicato, Luciano Floridi (2024) Generative AI in EU law: Liability, privacy, intellectual property, and cybersecurity. Computer Law & Security Review 55: 106066; Bjørn Aslak Juliussen, Jon Petter Rui, Dag Johansen (2023) Algorithms that forget: Machine unlearning and the right to erasure. Computer Law & Security Review 51:105885, 1–12, 5.

direct encoders, making individual data an integral part of the model.[82] In other ML approaches, however, the retention of personal information is unintentional and occurs as an accidental byproduct of the training process, specifically connected to the overfitting problem.[83] Juliussen et. al explains, “Unintended memorization takes place during model training when a specific data point, for instance, a credit card number, in the training data are assigned a significantly higher likelihood in the model than what would be expected by random chance.”[84] To put it differently, unintended memorization occurs when a model, during training, disproportionately retains certain data points, embedding them within its structure in ways that were not deliberately designed.

Ultimately, in ML models, even when data are "forgotten," remnants of that data can still influence future outputs because of how the learning process integrates data. During training, ML models absorb patterns, relationships, and features from the data, which become embedded in the algorithm’s parameters. This results in a form of "memory" where the effects of the data persist, even if the original data point is removed. These traces can affect how the model continues to make decisions or generate predictions, meaning that the influence of forgotten data can linger, making it difficult to eliminate its impact on the system’s behavior. This inherent characteristic of ML poses challenges to implementing a full RTBF, as the data becomes entangled with the very structure of the model. This memorization behavior is further supported by studies on adversarial attacks, which have shown that private information can be extracted from trained models targeting specific data points.[85]

[82] Bjørn Aslak Juliussen, Jon Petter Rui, Dag Johansen (2023) Algorithms that forget: Machine unlearning and the right to erasure. Computer Law & Security Review 51:105885, 1–12, 5.

[83] Id.

[84] Id. citing Nicholas Carlini, Evaluating and testing unintended memorization in neural networks, https://bair.berkeley.edu/blog/2019/08/13/memorization/ accessed: 15.07.2023.

[85] Chang, Yi, Zhao Ren, Thanh Tam Nguyen, Wolfgang Nejdl, and Björn W Schuller (2022) Example-based explanations with adversarial attacks for respiratory sound analysis. In Interspeech 2022 September 2022, Incheon, Korea, 18–22.

6.3.3 *Challenge 3: Trade-Offs in Accuracy During Unlearning*

Machine unlearning, aimed at removing specific data from ML models, poses challenges that can degrade model accuracy. One major issue is catastrophic unlearning, where the removal of data leads to catastrophic drops in performance.[86] According to the current state of the art, models subjected to unlearning often perform far worse than models retrained without the removed data, and the more data points removed, the greater the decline.[87] Each unlearned piece disrupts the model's structural coherence, making it harder to maintain the accuracy of predictions. While some methods can reduce this decline, preventing catastrophic unlearning remains an unresolved challenge, particularly as the volume of removed data increases.[88] As the inner mechanisms of ML techniques like neural networks remain largely opaque, their black-box nature may inherently contribute to the persistence of catastrophic unlearning.

A different perspective is that approximate unlearning is vulnerable to the issue of over-unlearning, where more data than necessary may be removed, leading to a significant decline in the model's performance and overall efficacy.[89] Here, it is important to recognize that there will almost always be a tradeoff between data removal and model accuracy. This tradeoff arises as a direct consequence of the data processing inequality, which essentially states that any post-processing of data cannot increase

[86] Quoc Phong Nguyen, Bryan Kian, Hsiang Low, Patrick Jaillet (2020) Variational Bayesian unlearning. In Proceedings of the 34th International Conference on Neural Information Processing Systems (NIPS'20). Curran Associates Inc., Red Hook, NY, USA, Article 1344, 16025–16036 (explaining, "A trained ML model is said to experience catastrophic unlearning from the erased data when its resulting performance is considerably worse than that from retraining with the remaining data.").

[87] Id.

[88] Chunxiao Li, Haipeng Jiang, Jiankang Chen, Yu Zhao, Shuxuan Fu, Fangming Jing, Yu Guo (2024) An overview of machine unlearning. High-Confidence Computing 100254, 1–11, 2; Weiqi Wang, Zhiyi Tian, Chenhan Zhang, Shui Yu (2024) Machine unlearning: A comprehensive survey arXiv:2405.07406.

[89] Hongsheng Hu, Shuo Wang, Jiamin Chang, Haonan Zhong, Ruoxi Sun, Shuang Hao, Haojin Zhu, Minhui Xue (2023) A Duty to Forget, a Right to be Assured? Exposing Vulnerabilities in Machine Unlearning Services, https://arxiv.org/abs/2309.08230.

the information content of the original dataset.[90] In other words, any modification—such as removing data points—will typically degrade the model's performance, as the process reduces the information available for the model to draw from. This tradeoff between accuracy and the extent of data removal is not just a possibility but a fundamental rule in the context of ML. As the level of data removal increases, the impact on the model's accuracy typically becomes more pronounced. If this loss of accuracy is deemed unacceptable for a given application, then deleting the entire model and retraining it from scratch may become the only viable alternative. To address this challenge, it is essential to develop approaches that minimize the degradation effect, ensuring that data removal processes maintain a sufficient balance between compliance and model performance.

Finally, it is important to observe that machine unlearning may affect different groups in varying ways, raising concerns about fairness.[91] The European Data Protection Supervisor raises concerns that machine unlearning may disproportionately affect the accuracy of predictions for certain demographic sub-populations, potentially introducing new biases or amplifying existing ones, ultimately compromising the model's overall fairness.[92] In fact, this risk of introducing or exacerbating biases may highlight a need to retain certain data points, even when there is a request to delete them.

6.3.4 *Challenge 4: Technical Limitations in Auditing*

Hine et. al. contend that certifiability is essential within the context of machine unlearning.[93] More specifically, they assert that unlearning

[90] Chuteng Zhou, Quntao Zhuang, Matthew Mattina and Paul N. Whatmoug, "Strong data processing inequality in neural networks with noisy neurons and its implications," 2021 IEEE International Symposium on Information Theory (ISIT), Melbourne, Australia, 2021, pp. 1170–1175, 1170.

[91] Saskia Keskpaik, Machine unlearning, European Data Protection Supervisor, https://www.edps.europa.eu/data-protection/technology-monitoring/techsonar/machine-unlearning_en.

[92] Id.

[93] Emmie Hine, Claudio Novelli, Mariarosaria Taddeo and Luciano Floridi (2024) Supporting trustworthy AI through machine unlearning. Science and Engineering Ethics 30: 43, 1–13; see also Anvith Thudi, Hengrui Jia, Ilia Shumailov, Nicolas Papernot (2022) On the necessity of auditable algorithmic definitions for machine

processes must be "certifiable" to ensure that affected entities are aware that unlearning has been successfully completed and that the resulting model closely resembles one that was never trained on the removed data.[94] A certifiable machine unlearning framework should equip users, regulators, and auditors with the necessary tools and tests to verify the effectiveness of the unlearning process.[95]

While requiring machine unlearning to be certifiable is in line with the accountability principle set forward in the GDPR, current approaches generally lack formal guarantees on data removal, although this is a rapid area of technological research.[96] Without the technical possibility to ensure that a model has been updated with the personal data approximately removed, a platform may falsely assert full compliance with the RTBF, claiming all possible steps have been taken, while, in truth, residual data remains intact.[97] This gap highlights a critical challenge: without verifiable mechanisms for ensuring true data removal, there is a risk that residual data traces persist, undermining the law.

In support of certifiable machine unlearning, at least three key aspects are key: unlearning effectiveness, efficiency, and model utility.[98] Unlearning effectiveness assesses how thoroughly data has been removed, potentially using measures such as data removal completeness (to confirm

unlearning, 31st USENIX Security Symposium (USENIX Security 22), 4007–4022, 4020; see also Saskia Keskpaik, Machine unlearning, European Data Protection Supervisor, https://www.edps.europa.eu/data-protection/technology-monitoring/techsonar/machine-unlearning_en (stating, "Machine unlearning necessitates auditability and verification to ensure that personal data has been successfully deleted from the models. This requirement for transparency can increase trust in these systems. When users and regulatory bodies can verify that data has been properly unlearned, it fosters confidence in the privacy practices of the organisations utilising these models.").

[94] Emmie Hine, Claudio Novelli, Mariarosaria Taddeo and Luciano Floridi (2024). Supporting trustworthy AI through machine unlearning. Science and Engineering Ethics 30: 43.

[95] Id.

[96] Alex Oesterling, Jiaqi Ma, Flavio Calmon, Himabindu Lakkaraju (2024) Fair machine unlearning: Data removal while mitigating disparities. Proceedings of The 27th International Conference on Artificial Intelligence and Statistics, PMLR 238:3736–3744.

[97] Ivan Visconti (2024) The right to be zero-knowledge forgotten. In Proceedings of the 19th International Conference on Availability, Reliability and Security (ARES'24). Association for Computing Machinery, New York, NY, USA, Article 110, 1–9.

[98] Cassandra Lindstrom (2024) Evaluation metrics for machine unlearning. Preprints 2024, 2024091925, https://www.preprints.org/manuscript/202409.1925/v1.

that the influence of removed data is eliminated), privacy leakage (to detect any residual data), and influence reduction and perturbation analysis (to ensure no lingering effects).[99] Efficiency addresses computational feasibility, especially for large-scale applications where cost and processing time matter.[100] Model utility ensures that the model remains functional post-unlearning, with checks on accuracy, robustness, fairness, and more.[101] Together, these metrics might provide a structured approach for verifying that unlearning is effective and certifiable, aligning with the GDPR's accountability principle by ensuring verifiable data removal without compromising model performance.[102]

6.4 Legal Interpretations of the RTBF in ML Contexts

Article 17 mandates that a data controller erases personal data under specified circumstances, but what exactly this entails within the context of ML is ambiguous. In some cases, compliance might be interpreted as merely removing the data from the database which contains the training data, and any backups. This may be acceptable based on a plain reading of the black-letter law, which appears to require only the erasure of the data itself, without extending to outputs or the model itself. However, such a narrow interpretation of the RTBF of course may not "effectively and completely" safeguard the data subject's fundamental rights in line with established CJEU case law, as it overlooks the persistent influence of the erased personal data on the model.[103]

Juliussen et. al propose a general rule: if a trained ML model is shown to leak personal data and the data subject requests erasure, merely removing the data from the training set is insufficient. In such cases,

[99] Id.

[100] Id.

[101] Id.

[102] Id.

[103] Case C-131/12 Google Spain SL, Google Inc. v Agencia Española de Protección de Datos (AEPD), Mario Costeja González [2014] ECLI:EU:C:2014:317, para 34.

exact machine unlearning methods must be applied to the model itself.[104] They further explain, "In a situation where the ML model is trained on personal data, but there is not any evidence that identifiability is possible only from the ML model, a request for erasure could be complied with through an approximation unlearning method."[105] While this proposal certainly provides a practical and possible solution, it is somewhat problematic because it presupposes an incident where data is leaked or that data subjects have the ability to prove that their personal data can be inferred from the ML model through, for example, relying on research on inference attacks.[106] This approach does not take a proactive approach to law which seeks to avoid harm through preventive measures rather than reacting to incidents after they occur.[107] Furthermore, most data subjects will lack the technical skills to prove their data is being leaked by a ML model, although this is debated in the literature.[108]

Ultimately, many questions remain about the adequacy of these unlearning techniques—specifically, whether exact machine unlearning, which fully removes data traces, is necessary, or if approximate unlearning, which reduces the model's dependency on the data without completely eliminating residual effects, might suffice.[109] This distinction is crucial,

[104] Bjørn Aslak Juliussen, Jon Petter Rui, Dag Johansen (2023) Algorithms that forget: Machine unlearning and the right to erasure. Computer Law & Security Review 51:105885, 1–12, 11.

[105] Id.

[106] Katie Hawkins, Nora Alhuwaish, Sana Belguith, Asma Vranaki and Andrew Charlesworth (2024) A decision-making process to implement the 'Right to Be Forgotten' in machine learning. In: K. Rannenberg, P. Drogkaris, C. Lauradoux (eds) Privacy Technologies and Policy. APF 2023. Lecture Notes in Computer Science, vol 13888. Springer, Cham, 20–38, 30.

[107] See e.g. Peter Seipel (2006) "Nordic School of Proactive Law Conference, June 2005 Closing Comments," In: Peter Wahlgren (ed.), *A Proactive Approach, Scandinavian Studies in Law Volume 49* (Stockholm Institute for Scandinavian Law): 359–363.

[108] *But see* Katie Hawkins, Nora Alhuwaish, Sana Belguith, Asma Vranaki and Andrew Charlesworth (2024) A decision-making process to implement the 'Right to Be Forgotten' in machine learning. In: K. Rannenberg, P. Drogkaris, C. Lauradoux (eds) Privacy Technologies and Policy. APF 2023. Lecture Notes in Computer Science, vol 13888. Springer, Cham, 20–38, 30 (arguing that data subjects and DPAs may be able to rely on "recent publications" to provide them with the technical capabilities to provide evidence that their data exists in a ML model).

[109] Katie Hawkins, Nora Alhuwaish, Sana Belguith, Asma Vranaki and Andrew Charlesworth (2024) A decision-making process to implement the 'Right to Be Forgotten'

as exact unlearning can be technically demanding and resource-intensive, while approximate unlearning may strike a balance between compliance and practical feasibility, though its sufficiency under legal standards remains uncertain. Set forth below is a legal discussion of these two possible approaches: Exact unlearning and approximate unlearning.

6.5 Exact Unlearning

The European Network and Information Security Agency ("ENISA") proposes several interpretations of what it might mean to erase data for purposes of GDPR compliance, albeit in 2011 and long before the recent advances in ML. First, it explains, "A strict interpretation would require that all copies of the data be erased and removed from any derived or aggregated representations to the point where recovering the data is impossible by any known technical means."[110] In other words, under a strict interpretation, data erasure would involve eliminating all instances of the data, including any derived or aggregated forms, to such an extent that recovery would be technically impossible using any current methods.

A similar understanding of erasure is proposed by Garg et. al who describe the "leave no trace" approach as ensuring that "a deletion request should leave the data collector and the rest of the system in a state equivalent (or at least very similar) to what it would have been had the deleted data never been provided to the data collector in the first place."[111] They further explain that this approach places "several constraints" on the data controller. First, the requested data must be

in machine learning. In: K. Rannenberg, P. Drogkaris, C. Lauradoux (eds) Privacy Technologies and Policy. APF 2023. Lecture Notes in Computer Science, vol 13888. Springer, Cham, 20–38, 26 (explaining, "Even if the RTBF applies to all phases and throughout the life cycles of the ML system, it is still questionable whether the law requires an exact or approximate degree of erasure from the deployed model, as it can be technically difficult to guarantee 100% erasure. The GDPR neither requires complete erasure nor prevents it.").

[110] Peter Druschel, Michael Backes, Rodica Tirtea (2011) The Right to be Forgotten–Between expectations and practice, ENISA-European Union Agency for Cybersecurity, 1–22, 9, https://www.enisa.europa.eu/publications/the-right-to-be-forgotten

[111] Sanjam Garg, Shafi Goldwasser and Prashant Nalini Vasudeva (2016) Formalizing data deletion in the context of the Right to Be Forgotten. In: Anne Canteaut, Yuval Ishai (eds) Advances in Cryptology—EUROCRYPT 2020. EUROCRYPT 2020. Lecture Notes in Computer Science, vol 12106. Springer, Cham.

entirely removed from the data collector's memory once processed.[112] Second, any dependencies that other data may have on the deleted information should also be removed.[113] Finally, the data collector must refrain from sharing collected data with external entities, as this compromises the ability to honor future deletion requests.[114] Once data are shared externally, the data collector can no longer ensure its complete removal, as it loses control over data locations beyond its direct oversight.[115]

A recent Federal Trade Commission case in the United States involving Everalbum, Inc. illustrates the "leave no trace" approach by mandating that the company retrain its model from scratch, thereby completely removing any residual influence of the deleted data on the system.[116] In this case, the FTC found that the company had misled consumers about how it used facial recognition in its photo storage app, particularly in how it retained and used personal data after deletion requests. By mandating a full model retrain, the FTC ensured that any residual data or derived outputs based on previously deleted information were entirely removed from the system. This strict measure aligns with the "leave no trace" principle, which demands that a data deletion request should return the system to a state as if the deleted data had never been collected in the first place. Furthermore, one could argue that this approach was reasonable, given the current limitations of approximate unlearning methods, which are not yet capable of reliably ensuring the complete removal of residual data influences from ML models.

112 Id.

113 Id.

114 Id.

115 Id.

116 In the Matter of Everalbum, Inc., United States of America Before the Federal Trade Commision (May 7, 2021), available at https://www.ftc.gov/system/files/documents/cases/1923172_-_everalbum_complaint_final.pdf; US Federal Trade Commission Press Release (2021) California Company Settles FTC Allegations It Deceived Consumers about use of Facial Recognition in Photo Storage App (January 11, 2021) available at https://www.ftc.gov/news-events/news/press-releases/2021/01/california-company-settles-ftc-allegations-it-deceived-consumers-about-use-facial-recognition-photo; see further Tiffany C. Li (2022) Algorithmic destruction, SMU Law Review 75: 479, 499–501; Joshua A. Goland (2023) Algorithmic disgorgement: destruction of artificial intelligence models as the Ftc's newest enforcement tool for bad data, Richmond Journal of Law and Technology 29: 1, 17–27.

There is also some evidence of the "leave no trace" approach in Europe. The most notable case concerns Clearview AI. In May 2020, the French data protection authority, Commission nationale de l'informatique et des libertés (CNIL), began investigating Clearview AI's facial recognition software following complaints from individuals about its unauthorized collection and use of the personal data of several tens of millions of citizens' data. By November 2021, the CNIL formally notified Clearview AI to cease processing personal data of individuals in France without a legal basis and to comply with requests for data erasure, but the company failed to respond.[117] Subsequently, the CNIL's restricted committee imposed a €20 million fine, citing breaches of GDPR Articles 6, 12, 15, 17, and 31, and ordered Clearview AI to stop unlawful data processing and delete collected data within 2 months, with a penalty of €100,000 per day for non-compliance.

In its order, the CNIL ordered Clearview "to delete all the personal data of these individuals, in particular, the data of the complainant in question who requested erasure."[118] However, the supervisory authority (SA) did not explicitly address the critical question of how controllers should approach the erasure of personal data that has already been integrated into ML models.[119] That said, "erasing the entire model" is likely what the CNIL intended, as simply deleting the training database of facial images, without addressing the deployed model, would be insufficient.[120] The deployed model would still retain the ability to recognize the erased images since the biometric templates derived during training would remain unchanged.[121]

[117] European Data Protection Board, The French SA fines Clearview AI EUR 20 million (20 October 2022), https://www.edpb.europa.eu/news/national-news/2022/french-sa-fines-clearview-ai-eur-20-million_en.

[118] Restricted Committee Deliberation No. SAN-2022-019 of 17 October 2022 concerning CLEARVIEW AI, https://www.cnil.fr/sites/cnil/files/atoms/files/deliberation_of_the_restricted_committee_no_san-2022-019_of_17_october_2022_concerning_clearview_ai.pdf.

[119] Katie Hawkins, Nora Alhuwaish, Sana Belguith, Asma Vranaki and Andrew Charlesworth (2024) A decision-making process to implement the 'Right to Be Forgotten' in machine learning. In: K. Rannenberg, P. Drogkaris, C. Lauradoux (eds) Privacy Technologies and Policy. APF 2023. Lecture Notes in Computer Science, vol 13888. Springer, Cham, 20–38, 21.

[120] Id. at 34.

[121] Id.

It is further important to mention that in December 2024, the European Data Protection Board (EDPB) issued an opinion on the use of personal data in the development and deployment of AI models.[122] This opinion addresses several key issues, including the implications of developing AI models with personal data that has been unlawfully processed. According to the EDPB, SAs can impose corrective measures to remediate such unlawful processing. These measures may include erasing the unlawfully processed portion of a dataset, erasing the entire dataset, or *even deleting the AI model itself*, depending on the circumstances and proportionality of the case.[123] In its opinion, the EDPB further emphasizes that unlawfully processed personal data can be deleted upon a data subject's request under Article 17 GDPR or by an ex officio order from a SA (i.e., an order issued independently by the authority without a prior request).[124]

6.6 Approximate Unlearning

The "beyond use"test provides an alternative to full data deletion when it is not technically feasible or practical. This approach, endorsed by the UK Information Commissioner's Office (ICO), allows data to be rendered inaccessible and unusable without being fully erased.[125] The ICO explains that this option is relevant in scenarios where data still exists in residual forms, such as backup systems or shredded documents, and complete deletion would either harm other data or is not technically possible. For the "beyond use" test to be valid, certain conditions must be met: the data controller must ensure that the personal data are not used in decision-making or actions affecting the individual, not shared with any

[122] The European Data Protection Board, Opinion 28/2024 on certain data protection aspects related to the processing of personal data in the context of AI models Adopted on 17 December 2024, https://www.edpb.europa.eu/our-work-tools/our-documents/opinion-board-art-64/opinion-282024-certain-data-protection-aspects_en.

[123] Id. para. 114.

[124] Id. para. 115.

[125] Information Commissioner's Office, Right to erasure, https://ico.org.uk/for-organisations/uk-gdpr-guidance-and-resources/individual-rights/individual-rights/right-to-erasure/.

other entity, safeguarded with appropriate technical and organizational measures, and permanently deleted when feasible.[126]

The "beyond use" test is consistent with 2012 ENISA report, which suggests that strict interpretations of data deletion may be impractical, and that a more flexible approach to "forgetting" data could be necessary for the EU. As ENISA suggests, "a slightly weaker (and possibly more practical) interpretation" of the RTBF in the Digital Age "would allow encrypted copies of the data to survive, as long as they cannot be deciphered by unauthorized parties."[127] This perspective recognizes that complete data deletion may not always be feasible and permits residual information to remain, provided robust safeguards are in place.

The Article 29 Data Protection Working Party (now the EDPB) has further provided guidance on the practical implementation of the RTBF in the context of search engines.[128] According to this guidance, SAs should carefully assess data subjects' requests, without requiring the original publishers to delete the related content or engage directly with search engines or the individuals involved.[129] This approach implies context matters and that a complete, oblivion approach to forgetting may not be suitable.

Nonetheless, the EDPB emphasizes that "(...) search engine providers are not exempt in a general manner from the duty to fully erase."[130] In certain situations, they must perform actual erasure in their indexes or caches.[131] For instance, if search engine providers disregard robots.txt requests from original publishers, they would be required to fully erase the URL, not merely delist it based on the data subject's name.[132] A URL here is analogous to a ML model, acting as a downstream derivative

[126] Information Commissioner's Office, Deleting personal data, https://www.pdpjournals.com/docs/88043.pdf.

[127] Peter Druschel, Michael Backes, Rodica Tirtea (2011) The Right to be Forgotten–Between expectations and practice, ENISA-European Union Agency for Cybersecurity, 1-22,9 https://www.enisa.europa.eu/publications/the-right-to-be-forgotten

[128] Guidelines 5/2019 on the Criteria of the Right to be Forgotten in the Search Engines Cases Under the GDPR (Part 1), European Data Protection Board (7 July 2020).

[129] Id. para. 6–9.

[130] Id. para. 10.

[131] Id.

[132] Id.

of personal data, thus highlighting similar complexities in ensuring data erasure across derived forms.[133]

More recently, the CNIL has determined that under Article 17 of the GDPR, erasure of personal data should extend beyond simply deleting it from training datasets and backups, as ML models trained on such data may still retain its influence.[134] This requirement emphasizes the need for data controllers to integrate mechanisms from the system design stage to address erasure requests effectively.[135] However, the CNIL also recognizes that challenges arise when ML models contain residual personal data, either intentionally due to algorithm design or accidentally. It explains that in cases where the data subject cannot be re-identified without additional data collection—prohibited under Article 11—data controllers may be exempt from fulfilling erasure requests. Nevertheless, such exemptions must not harm the individual's rights. Importantly, the CNIL explicitly states, "Complying with a request to correct or delete learning data does not ... necessarily mean correcting or deleting the AI model(s) generated from this data."

This logic is further supported by recent advice from the Swedish Authority for Privacy Protection (IMY), which acknowledges that while some ML-generated outputs may not directly contain personal data, the underlying models may still be influenced by training data, necessitating mechanisms to address erasure requests at the system design stage.[136] It explains that in cases where fulfilling a deletion request is deemed infeasible, organizations should facilitate individuals' rights by directing them to the appropriate channels, such as the provider of the ML system, and providing clear justifications for any refusal.[137] It also clarifies that

[133] Bjørn Aslak Juliussen, Jon Petter Rui, Dag Johansen (2023) Algorithms that forget: Machine unlearning and the right to erasure. Computer Law & Security Review 51:105885, 1–12, 11.

[134] The Commission nationale de l'informatique et des libertés (CNIL)(2022) AI: ensuring GDPR compliance, https://www.cnil.fr/en/ai-ensuring-gdpr-compliance.

[135] Id.

[136] Swedish Authority for Privacy Protection | IMY (2025), GDPR vid användning av generativ AI: Integritetsskyddsmyndighetens del av regeringsuppdraget att ta fram vägledande riktlinjer för användningen av generativ AI inom offentlig förvaltning, Diarienummer IMY-2024-9162, 1–30, 20–21, https://www.imy.se/globalassets/dokument/rapporter/gdpr-vid-anvandning-av-generativ-ai_imy-2024-9162.pdf.

[137] Id.

organizations are not required to respond to requests that are manifestly unfounded or excessive.[138]

Collectively, these legal opinions tend to support a more flexible and pragmatic approach to implementing the RTBF in the digital age, particularly applicable to the legal regulation of approximate machine unlearning. They emphasize the importance of balancing the technical realities of modern systems, such as the challenges of full data erasure, with the need to uphold data protection principles. This flexibility recognizes that residual traces of personal data, if safeguarded, may satisfy compliance without requiring complete deletion.

6.7 Machine Unlearning as a Privacy Enhancing Technology

Even if machine unlearning cannot offer a silver bullet for meeting the requirements of Article 17 in the era of ML, its potential as a privacy-enhancing technology (PET) remains undeniable. This is especially true since "(t)here are many variables at play and each RTBF request will have to be evaluated individually."[139] Here, the European Data Protection Supervisor explains, "Machine unlearning should not be viewed as a 'band-aid solution', but as an integral part of the overall data management and privacy strategy to ensure long-term robustness and trustworthiness in AI systems."[140] For example, in cases where exemptions to the RTBF apply, and therefore complete erasure of the data is not required under the law, approximate unlearning provides a potential mechanism to at least reduce the influence of specific data on a ML model without requiring full erasure of the model.[141] This would allow a data controller to meet

[138] Id.

[139] Katie Hawkins, Nora Alhuwaish, Sana Belguith, Asma Vranaki and Andrew Charlesworth (2024) A decision-making process to implement the 'Right to Be Forgotten' in machine learning. In: K. Rannenberg, P. Drogkaris, C. Lauradoux (eds) Privacy Technologies and Policy. APF 2023. Lecture Notes in Computer Science, vol 13888. Springer, Cham, 20–38, 29.

[140] Saskia Keskpaik, Machine unlearning, European Data Protection Supervisor, https://www.edps.europa.eu/data-protection/technology-monitoring/techsonar/machine-unlearning_en.

[141] Katie Hawkins, Nora Alhuwaish, Sana Belguith, Asma Vranaki and Andrew Charlesworth (2024) A decision-making process to implement the 'Right to Be Forgotten' in machine learning. In: K. Rannenberg, P. Drogkaris, C. Lauradoux (eds) Privacy

its obligations under Article 25 of the GDPR (data protection by design) while also balancing the rights of data subjects with the controller's legitimate interests, ensuring a proportionate approach to data protection.

Furthermore, the RTBF might not apply if the data are deemed necessary for the purpose for which it was collected. With vague or broad purpose definitions, as are commonplace within the ML processing environment to allow for "unforeseen future uses," secondary uses of data can often be justified as relevant.[142] Additionally, if unlearning might result in reduced accuracy of the model, then this argument may be even more persuasive.[143] Here, data controllers may interpret "necessity" differently from data subjects, especially in an increasingly personalized digital landscape where nearly all personal data can be argued as relevant.[144] In light of the CJEU's decision in *Google Spain*, SA's should carefully balance the interests of all parties involved, with due consideration for their fundamental rights.[145] This balancing act highlights the potential role of PETs, such as approximate unlearning, in navigating these complexities. In other words, machine unlearning, even if not explicitly required under Article 17, may nevertheless still be required under Article 25.

Viewing machine unlearning techniques as PETs is consistent with the EDPB's opinion on the use of personal data in the development and deployment of AI models, where it acknowledges machine unlearning as a potential mitigating measure to limit the impact of the processing data subjects in the deployment phase.[146] More specifically, the EDPB

Technologies and Policy. APF 2023. Lecture Notes in Computer Science, vol 13888. Springer, Cham, 20–38, 31–33.

142 Helena U. Vrabec. The Right to Be Forgotten, data subject rights under the GDPR, In: Helena U. Vrabec (ed) Data subject rights under the GDPR, Oxford, 2021; online edn, Oxford Academic, 129–158, 142.

143 See further Sandra Wachter and Brent Mittelstadt (2019), A right to reasonable inferences: Re-thinking data protection law in the Age of Big Data and Ai, Columbia Business Law Review 2019: 494, 553–54.

144 Helena U. Vrabec. The Right to Be Forgotten, data subject rights under the GDPR, In: Helena U. Vrabec (ed) Data subject rights under the GDPR, Oxford, 2021; online edn, Oxford Academic, 129–158, 142.

145 Id.

146 The European Data Protection Board, Opinion 28/2024 on certain data protection aspects related to the processing of personal data in the context of AI models Adopted on 17 December 2024, para 107 https://www.edpb.europa.eu/our-work-tools/our-documents/opinion-board-art-64/opinion-282024-certain-data-protection-aspects_en.

opinion highlights measures that are designed to facilitate or expedite the exercise of individuals' rights during the deployment phase including techniques aimed at enabling the erasure of personal data from model outputs, supporting deduplication, and employing post-training methods to remove or suppress personal data.[147] These measures should be assessed on a case-by-case basis and importantly, "should not be confused with the measures that the controller is legally required to adopt anyway to ensure compliance with the GDPR."[148] That is, while machine unlearning can serve as a mitigating measure to limit the impact of data processing in ML, it does not replace the legal obligations of data controllers under the GDPR, which require lawful processing and full respect for data subjects' rights.

Ultimately, machine unlearning contributes to a deeper understanding of how models store and process information, making it a key component of privacy management.[149] It can support transparency, explainability, robustness, and accountability in ML, helping to mitigate risks associated with data retention and misuse.[150] It aligns with PETs by enabling targeted data removal, reducing the risk of unauthorized retention, and improving compliance with legal frameworks such as the GDPR.

6.8 Conclusion

Understanding the related concepts of deletion, erasure, and forgetting requires distinguishing between various interpretations of what it means to "remove" data.[151] Deletion generally implies the removal of data from storage systems, rendering it permanently unavailable. However, erasure goes a step further by ensuring that data cannot be recovered through any technical means, effectively making it inaccessible even to advanced recovery methods. Forgetting, particularly in the context of ML and the

[147] Id.

[148] Id. at executive summary.

[149] Emmie Hine, Claudio Novelli, Mariarosaria Taddeo, Luciano Floridi (2024) Supporting trustworthy AI through machine unlearning. Science and engineering ethics, 30(5): 43.

[150] Id.

[151] Elena Esposito (2017) Algorithmic memory and the Right to Be Forgotten on the web. Big Data and Society 4: 1–11; Luciano Floridi (2023) Machine unlearning: Its nature, scope, and importance for a "delete culture". Philosophy & Technology 36: 42.

RTBF, extends these concepts by aiming to eliminate the influence or residual effects of data on a model's behavior. This means not only making data unavailable or inaccessible but also addressing any remaining impact that the data may have had during model training. This layered understanding of deletion, erasure, and forgetting highlights the technical and legal challenges in fulfilling data privacy obligations, especially as they intersect with complex systems like ML models.

In today's intricate data ecosystems, personal data are rarely confined to neatly organized databases; instead, it is scattered across systems in diverse formats, creating challenges for ensuring adequate protection for data subjects. This data fuels ML models, drives statistical analyses, and informs decision-making across nearly all facets of society.[152] These varied applications make the implementation of the RTBF increasingly complex, as removing data often requires disentangling it from the systems and models in which it has been deeply embedded.[153]

Personal data may be simply stored and retrievable upon request but that they may also be used "as inputs to computations producing other correlated data that in turn can be stored and used in subsequent computations."[154] In other words, personal data may be transformed into new forms of data, creating a domino effect where each stage of processing generates additional derived data that can be further analyzed and utilized. For reasons such as efficiency, integrity, and accountability, the usefulness of such computed data may still rely on the presence (whether implicit or explicit) of the original data used in its creation.[155]

[152] Aloni Cohen, Adam Smith, Marika Swanberg, and Prashant Nalini Vasudevan (2023). Control, confidentiality, and the Right to be Forgotten. In Proceedings of the 2023 ACM SIGSAC Conference on Computer and Communications Security (CCS'23). Association for Computing Machinery, New York, NY, USA, 3358–3372. https://doi.org/10.1145/3576915.3616585.

[153] Aloni Cohen, Adam Smith, Marika Swanberg, and Prashant Nalini Vasudevan (2023). Control, confidentiality, and the Right to be Forgotten. In Proceedings of the 2023 ACM SIGSAC Conference on Computer and Communications Security (CCS'23). Association for Computing Machinery, New York, NY, USA, 3358–3372. https://doi.org/10.1145/3576915.3616585.

[154] Ivan Visconti (2024) The right to be zero-knowledge forgotten. In Proceedings of the 19th International Conference on Availability, Reliability and Security (ARES'24). Association for Computing Machinery, New York, NY, USA, Article 110, 1–9. https://doi.org/10.1145/3664476.3669973.

[155] Id.

As explained above, simply deleting the original personal data is generally insufficient for ensuring full erasure, as traces may remain embedded within the model's structure.

An "oblivion" approach to data deletion, however, should be rejected in the context of ML due to its impracticality and technical limitations.[156] Fully erasing all traces of data from ML systems is often unfeasible because models retain residual patterns and insights derived from the data, even after deletion attempts. These learned patterns are deeply embedded in the model's architecture and cannot be easily disentangled or removed without retraining from scratch. Enforcing complete data erasure in such cases would impose excessive burdens on organizations, requiring substantial computational resources and potentially undermining model performance. A more practical approach would focus on mitigating data retention risks through methods like certifiable machine unlearning, which aim to balance legal obligations with the technical realities of ML systems.[157]

References

Roger Brownsword (2008) Rights, regulation, and the technological revolution (Oxford University Press).

Gary E. Marchant, The growing gap between emerging technologies and the law (2011). In: Gary E. Marchant, Braden R. Allenby, Joseph R. Herkert (eds) The growing gap between emerging technologies and legal-ethical oversight. Springer Dordrecht, 19–33.

Tobias J. Oechtering, Sara Saeidian and Cecilia Magnusson Sjöberg (2023) Calculated privacy: tech meets law and law meets tech. Florida International University Law Review 17: 383–398.

Katie Hawkins, Nora Alhuwaish, Sana Belguith, Asma Vranaki and Andrew Charlesworth (2024) A decision-making process to implement the 'Right to Be Forgotten' in machine learning. In: K. Rannenberg, P. Drogkaris, C. Lauradoux (eds) Privacy Technologies and Policy. APF 2023. Lecture Notes in Computer Science, vol 13888. Springer, Cham, 20–38.

[156] Luciano Floridi (2023) Machine unlearning: Its nature, scope, and importance for a "delete culture". Philosophy & Technology 36: 42.

[157] Siva Sai, Uday Mittal, Vinay Chamola, Kaizhu Huang, Indro Spinelli, Simone Scardapane, Zhiyuan Tan and Amir Hussain (2024) Machine un-learning: An overview of techniques, applications, and future directions. Cognitive Computation 16: 482–506, 488.

Anvith Thudi, Hengrui Jia, Ilia Shumailov, Nicolas Papernot (2022) On the necessity of auditable algorithmic definitions for machine unlearning. 31st USENIX Security Symposium (USENIX Security 22), 4007–4022.

Haibo Zhang, Toru Nakamura, Takamasa Isohara and Kouichi Sakurai (2023) A review on machine unlearning. SN Computer Science 4: 337, 1–13.

Lucas Bourtoule, Varun Chandrasekaran, Cristopher A. Choquette-Choo, Hengrui Jia, Adelin Travers, Baiwu Zhang, David Lie and Nicolas Papernot (2021) Machine unlearning. In 2021 IEEE Symposium on Security and Privacy, 141–159.

Min Chen, Zhikun Zhang, Tianhao Wang, Michael Backes, Mathias Humbert, Yang Zhang (2021) When machine unlearning jeopardizes privacy. In Proceedings of the 2021 ACM SIGSAC Conference on Computer and Communications Security (CCS '21), November 15–19, 2021, Virtual Event, Republic of Korea. ACM, New York, NY, USA.

Herke Kranenborg (2020) Article 17 Right to erasure ('right to be forgotten'). In: Christopher Kuner, Lee A Bygrave, Christopher Docksey, Laura Drechsler (eds) The EU General Data Protection Regulation (GDPR): A commentary, Oxford, 475–484.

Eugenia Politou, Alexandra Michota, Efthimios Alepis, Matthias Pocs, Constantinos Patsakis (2018) Backups and the Right to Be Forgotten in the GDPR: An uneasy relationship. Computer Law & Security Review Volume 34: 1247–1257.

Aleksandra Kuczerawy and Jef Ausloos (2016) From notice-and-takedown to notice-and delist: Implementing Google Spain Colorado Technology Law Journal 14: 219–258.

Eugenia Politou, Efthimios Alepis and Constantinos Patsakis (2018) Forgetting personal data and revoking consent under the GDPR: Challenges and proposed solutions, Journal of Cybersecurity 4:1–20.

Jay Kaganoff (2021) Send the word over there: An offshore solution to the Right to Be Forgotten, Northwestern Journal of International Law and Business 41: 245–271.

Alan Westin, *Privacy and Freedom* (New York, Atheneum: 1967)

Helena U. Vrabec (2021) The Right to Be Forgotten, data subject rights under the GDPR. In: Helena U. Vrabec (ed) Data subject rights under the GDPR, Oxford, 2021; online edn, Oxford Academic, 129–158.

Sebastian Schelter, Stefan Grafberger, and Ted Dunning (2021) HedgeCut: Maintaining randomised Trees for Low-Latency Machine Unlearning. In Proceedings of the 2021 International Conference on management of data (SIGMOD'21). Association for Computing Machinery, New York, NY, USA, 1545–1557. https://doi.org/10.1145/3448016.3457239

Bert-Japp Koops (2011) Forgetting footprints, shunning shadows: A critical analysis of the "right to be forgotten" in Big Data Practice. SCRIPTed 8: 229–256.

Eduard Fosch Villaronga, Peter Kieseberg, Tiffany Li (2018), Machines remember: Artificial intelligence and the Right to Be Forgotten. Computer Law & Security Review 34: 304–313.

Jef Ausloos (2011) The 'Right to Be Forgotten'—Worth remembering? Computer Law & Security Review 28: 143–152.

Meem Arafat Manab (2024) Eternal sunshine of the mechanical mind: The irreconcilability of machine learning and the Right to be Forgotten. arXiv:2403.05592

Bjørn Aslak Juliussen, Jon Petter Rui, Dag Johansen (2023) Algorithms that forget: Machine unlearning and the right to erasure. Computer Law & Security Review 51:105885, 1–12.

Luciano Floridi (2023) Machine unlearning: Its nature, scope, and importance for a "delete culture". Philosophy & Technology 36: 42.

Jie Xu, Zihan Wu, Cong Wang, and Xiaohua Jia (2024) Machine unlearning: Solutions and challenges. IEEE Transactions on Emerging Topics in Computational Intelligence 8: 2150–2168.

Heng Xu, Tianqing Zhu, Lefeng Zhang, Wanlei Zhou, and Philip S. Yu. 2023. Machine unlearning: A survey. ACM Computing Surveys 56, 1, Article 9 (January 2024), 1–36.

Kairan Zhao, What makes unlearning hard and what to do about it, https://arxiv.org/html/2406.01257v1

Korbinian Koch; Marcus Soll, No matter how you slice it: Machine unlearning with SISA comes at the expense of minority classes," 2023 IEEE Conference on Secure and Trustworthy Machine Learning (SaTML), Raleigh, NC, USA, 2023, pp. 622–637.

Lilian Edwards and Michael Veale (2017) Slave to the algorithm? Why a "Right to an Explanation" is probably not the remedy you are looking for. Duke Law and Technology Review 16: 18–84.

Maria Rigaki and Sebastian Garcia (2023) A survey of privacy attacks in machine learning. ACM Computing Surveys 56, 4, Article 101, 1–34.

Nadezhda Purtova (2018) The law of everything. Broad concept of personal data and the future of EU data protection law. Law, Innovation and Technology 10: 40–81.

Data Protection Working Party Opinion 04/2007 on the Concept of Personal Data, at 10 (June 10, 2007), https://ec.europa.eu/justice/article-29/documentation/opinion-recommendation/files/2007/wp136_en.pdf [https://perma.cc/W6Y4-DM39

Helena U. Vrabec, The Right to Be Forgotten, data subject rights under the GDPR. In: Helena U. Vrabec (ed) Data subject rights under the GDPR, Oxford, 2021; online edn, Oxford Academic, 129–158.

Elena Esposito (2017) Algorithmic memory and the Right to Be Forgotten on the web. Big Data and Society 4: 1–11.

Bateson G (1972) Steps to an Ecology of Mind. New York: Ballantine Books.

Eduard Fosch Villaronga, Peter Kieseberg, Tiffany Li (2018) Humans forget, machines remember: Artificial intelligence and the Right to Be Forgotten. Computer Law & Security Review 34: 304–313.

Stephen Pastis, A.I. trained on private user data never really "forgets," Fortune Eur. (2023), https://fortune.com/europe/2023/08/30/researchers-impossible-remove-private-user-data-delete-trained-ai-models/

Stephen Pastis (2023) A.I. trained on private user data never really "forgets," Fortune Eur., https://fortune.com/europe/2023/08/30/researchers-impossible-remove-private-user-data-delete-trained-ai-models/

Claudio Novelli, Federico Casolari, Philipp Hacker, Giorgio Spedicato, Luciano Floridi (2024) Generative AI in EU law: Liability, privacy, intellectual property, and cybersecurity. Computer Law & Security Review 55: 106066.

Ronen Eldan and Mark Russinovich (2023) Who's Harry Potter? Making LLMs forget, Physics of AGI, https://www.microsoft.com/en-us/research/articles/whos-harry-potter-making-llms-forget-2/

Quang-Vinh Dang (2021) Right to Be Forgotten in the age of machine learning. In: T. Antipova (ed.) Advances in Digital Science. Springer International Publishing, Cham, pp. 403–411.

Nicholas Carlini, Evaluating and testing unintended memorization in neural networks, https://bair.berkeley.edu/blog/2019/08/13/memorization/ accessed: 15.07.2023.

Chang, Yi, Zhao Ren, Thanh Tam Nguyen, Wolfgang Nejdl, and Björn W Schuller (2022) Example-based explanations with adversarial attacks for respiratory sound analysis. In Interspeech 2022 September 2022, Incheon, Korea, 18–22.

Quoc Phong Nguyen, Bryan Kian, Hsiang Low, Patrick Jaillet (2020) Variational Bayesian unlearning. In Proceedings of the 34th International Conference on Neural Information Processing Systems (NIPS '20). Curran Associates Inc., Red Hook, NY, USA.

Chunxiao Li, Haipeng Jiang, Jiankang Chen, Yu Zhao, Shuxuan Fu, Fangming Jing, Yu Guo (2024) An overview of machine unlearning. High-Confidence Computing 100254, 1–11.

Weiqi Wang, Zhiyi Tian, Chenhan Zhang, Shui Yu (2024) Machine unlearning: A comprehensive survey arXiv:2405.07406.

Hongsheng Hu, Shuo Wang, Jiamin Chang, Haonan Zhong, Ruoxi Sun, Shuang Hao, Haojin Zhu, Minhui Xue (2023) A Duty to Forget, a Right to be

Assured? Exposing Vulnerabilities in Machine Unlearning Services, https://arxiv.org/abs/2309.08230.

Chuteng Zhou, Quntao Zhuang, Matthew Mattina and Paul N. Whatmoug, "Strong data processing inequality in neural networks with noisy neurons and its implications," 2021 IEEE International Symposium on Information Theory (ISIT), Melbourne, Australia, 2021, pp. 1170–1175.

Saskia Keskpaik, Machine unlearning, European Data Protection Supervisor, https://www.edps.europa.eu/data-protection/technology-monitoring/techsonar/machine-unlearning_en

Emmie Hine, Claudio Novelli, Mariarosaria Taddeo and Luciano Floridi (2024) Supporting trustworthy AI through machine unlearning. Science and Engineering Ethics 30: 43, 1–13.

Alex Oesterling, Jiaqi Ma, Flavio Calmon, Himabindu Lakkaraju (2024) Fair machine unlearning: Data removal while mitigating disparities. Proceedings of The 27th International Conference on Artificial Intelligence and Statistics, PMLR 238:3736–3744.

Ivan Visconti (2024) The right to be zero-knowledge forgotten. In Proceedings of the 19th International Conference on Availability, Reliability and Security (ARES'24). Association for Computing Machinery, New York, NY, USA, Article 110, 1–9.

Cassandra Lindstrom (2024) Evaluation metrics for machine unlearning. Preprints 2024, 2024091925, https://www.preprints.org/manuscript/202409.1925/v1

Peter Seipel (2006) "Nordic School of Proactive Law Conference, June 2005 Closing Comments," In: Peter Wahlgren (ed.), *A Proactive Approach, Scandinavian Studies in Law Volume 49* (Stockholm Institute for Scandinavian Law): 359–363.

Peter Druschel, Michael Backes, Rodica Tirtea (2011) The Right to be Forgotten--Between expectations and practice, ENISA-European Union Agency for Cybersecurity, 1–22. https://www.enisa.europa.eu/publications/the-right-to-be-forgotten

Sanjam Garg, Shafi Goldwasser and Prashant Nalini Vasudeva (2016) Formalizing data deletion in the context of the Right to Be Forgotten. In: Anne Canteaut, Yuval Ishai (eds) Advances in Cryptology—EUROCRYPT 2020. EUROCRYPT 2020. Lecture Notes in Computer Science, vol 12106. Springer, Cham.

In the Matter of Everalbum, Inc., United States of America Before the Federal Trade Commision (May 7, 2021), available at https://www.ftc.gov/system/files/documents/cases/1923172_-_everalbum_complaint_final.pdf

US Federal Trade Commission Press Release (2021) California Company Settles FTC Allegations It Deceived Consumers about use of Facial Recognition in Photo Storage App (January 11, 2021) available at https://www.ftc.gov/news-events/news/press-releases/2021/01/california-company-settles-ftc-allegations-it-deceived-consumers-about-use-facial-recognition-photo

Tiffany C. Li (2022) Algorithmic destruction, SMU Law Review 75: 479.
Joshua A. Goland (2023) Algorithmic disgorgement: destruction of artificial intelligence models as the FTC's newest enforcement tool for bad data, Richmond Journal of Law and Technology 29: 1–51.
European Data Protection Board, The French SA fines Clearview AI EUR 20 million (20 October 2022), https://www.edpb.europa.eu/news/national-news/2022/french-sa-fines-clearview-ai-eur-20-million_en
Restricted Committee Deliberation No. SAN-2022-019 of 17 October 2022 concerning CLEARVIEW AI, https://www.cnil.fr/sites/cnil/files/atoms/files/deliberation_of_the_restricted_committee_no_san-2022-019_of_17_october_2022_concerning_clearview_ai.pdf
The European Data Protection Board, Opinion 28/2024 on certain data protection aspects related to the processing of personal data in the context of AI models Adopted on 17 December 2024, https://www.edpb.europa.eu/our-work-tools/our-documents/opinion-board-art-64/opinion-282024-certain-data-protection-aspects_en
Information Commissioner's Office, Right to erasure, https://ico.org.uk/for-organisations/uk-gdpr-guidance-and-resources/individual-rights/individual-rights/right-to-erasure/
Information Commissioner's Office, Deleting personal data, https://www.pdpjournals.com/docs/88043.pdf
Guidelines 5/2019 on the Criteria of the Right to be Forgotten in the Search Engines Cases Under the GDPR (Part 1), European Data Protection Board (7 July 2020)
The Commission nationale de l'informatique et des libertés (CNIL)(2022) AI: ensuring GDPR compliance, https://www.cnil.fr/en/ai-ensuring-gdpr-compliance
Swedish Authority for Privacy Protection | IMY (2025), GDPR vid användning av generativ AI: Integritetsskyddsmyndighetens del av regeringsuppdraget att ta fram vägledande riktlinjer för användningen av generativ AI inom offentlig förvaltning, Diarienummer IMY-2024-9162, 1–30, 20–21, https://www.imy.se/globalassets/dokument/rapporter/gdpr-vid-anvandning-av-generativ-ai_imy-2024-9162.pdf
Helena U. Vrabec. The Right to Be Forgotten, data subject rights under the GDPR, In: Helena U. Vrabec (ed) Data subject rights under the GDPR, Oxford, 2021; online edn, Oxford Academic, 129–158.
Sandra Wachter and Brent Mittelstadt (2019), A right to reasonable inferences: Re-thinking data protection law in the Age of Big Data and Ai, Columbia Business Law Review 2019: 494–620.
Emmie Hine, Claudio Novelli, Mariarosaria Taddeo, Luciano Floridi (2024) Supporting trustworthy AI through machine unlearning. Science and engineering ethics, 30(5): 43.

Aloni Cohen, Adam Smith, Marika Swanberg, and Prashant Nalini Vasudevan (2023). Control, confidentiality, and the Right to be Forgotten. In Proceedings of the 2023 ACM SIGSAC Conference on Computer and Communications Security (CCS'23). Association for Computing Machinery, New York, NY, USA, 3358–3372. https://doi.org/10.1145/3576915.3616585

Siva Sai, Uday Mittal, Vinay Chamola, Kaizhu Huang, Indro Spinelli, Simone Scardapane, Zhiyuan Tan and Amir Hussain (2024) Machine un-learning: An overview of techniques, applications, and future directions. Cognitive Computation 16: 482–506, 488.

Case-Law, Directives, and Regulations:

Case C-131/12 Google Spain SL, Google Inc. v Agencia Española de Protección de Datos (AEPD), Mario Costeja González [2014] ECLI:EU:C:2014:317.

Criminal proceedings against Bodil Lindqvist Case C-101/01, 2003 ECR I-12971 (Nov. 6, 2003).

Patrick Breyer v Bundesrepublik Deutschland. Case C-582/14. ECLI:EU:C:2016:779.

Peter Nowak v Data Protection Commissioner. Case C-434/16. ECLI:EU:C:2017:994.

OT v. Vyriausioji tarnybinės etikos komisija. Case C-184/20. ECLI:EU:C:2022:601.

Council Directive No. 95/46/EC of 24 October 1995 on the Protection of Individuals with Regard to the Processing of Personal Data and on the Free Movement of Such Data, art. 2(c), OJ. L 281/31 (1995); Directive 2000/31/EC, of the European Parliament and of the Council of 8 June 2000 on Certain Legal Aspects of Information Society Services, in Particular Electronic Commerce, in the Internal Market, 2000 O.J. L 178 1, 1.

Regulation (EU) 2024/1689 of the European Parliament and of the Council of 13 June 2024 laying down harmonised rules on artificial intelligence and amending Regulations (EC) No 300/2008, (EU) No 167/2013, (EU) No 168/2013, (EU) 2018/858, (EU) 2018/1139 and (EU) 2019/2144 and Directives 2014/90/EU, (EU) 2016/797 and (EU) 2020/1828 ("AI Act")(2024) OJ L 1689.

CHAPTER 7

Towards a General Principle of Vulnerability: Is Private Law Ready for the Digital Age?

Begoña Gonzalez Otero

7.1 Introduction

The rise of artificial intelligence (AI) and other digital technologies has profoundly reshaped the dynamics of market interaction everywhere in the world. At the intersection of innovation, automation, and datafication lies a crucial but under-theorised legal challenge: how to conceptualise and regulate vulnerability in increasingly digitised environments. Once thought of as a marginal category applicable to specific at-risk groups, vulnerability is now emerging as a structural and universal condition of modern digital life. The implications for private law in general and for EU private law in particular are significant, prompting the question of whether there is a need for a general principle of law to help better address and mitigate digital vulnerability in private law contexts.

B. Gonzalez Otero (✉)
Max Planck Institute for Innovation and Competition, Munich, Germany
e-mail: begonia.otero@ip.mpg.de

The Governance Lab (GovLab), New York, USA

A. Aliu (ed.), *Artificial Intelligence and the Rule of Law*,
https://doi.org/10.1007/978-3-031-97389-5_7

The idea of vulnerability is as old as humanity itself, but its definition and conception have evolved significantly over time. A comparative review of the most representative vulnerability theories across different fields of science can yield a number of lessons and help us recognise the multidimensional ways in which AI technologies can affect human vulnerability.[1]

Vulnerability is an inherent aspect of humanity, specific to living beings and relational. Power imbalances are central to its theoretical conceptualization, and there are two approaches to addressing it: addressing harm collectively or empowering individuals. Ethics and law often take a labelling approach to vulnerability, providing lists of vulnerable populations or vulnerable groups.[2] Thus, it is layering that opens the door to a more intersectional approach and stresses its cumulative and transitory potential.[3]

From a private law perspective, the concept of vulnerability has long occupied a contested place in European consumer protection, traditionally understood through the lens of the 'average' versus the 'vulnerable' consumer.[4] However, digital technologies—especially those relying on pervasive surveillance, algorithmic personalization, and persuasive interface design—have collapsed this distinction. In digital markets, most if not all consumers are potentially vulnerable due to systemic power imbalances rooted in data asymmetries and the manipulative affordances of digital

[1] For a comparative overview see B G Otero, 'AI for Good: Questioning the idea of human vulnerability' (06 September 2024) *OdiseIA* https://www.odiseia.org/en/post/ai-for-good-la-idea-de-la-vulnerabilidad-humana-en-tela-de-juicio. Accessed 24 March 2025.

[2] For a review of the different classifications from institutional organizations and the ECHR see, L Cotino, 'Vulnerabilidad y colectivos vulnerables en el derecho: ¿quiénes son y cómo se definen?' (18 December 2024) *Revista Catalana de Dret Públic* Blog https://eapc-rcdp.blog.gencat.cat/2024/12/18/vulnerabilidad-y-colectivos-vulnerables-en-el-derecho-quienes-son-y-como-se-definen-lorenzo-cotino/ Accessed 24 March 2025.

[3] F Luna, 'Elucidating the Concept of Vulnerability: Layers Not Label' International Journal of Feminist Approaches to Bioethics 2(1) Transnationgal Dialogues (2009), pp. 121–139.

[4] Case C-210/96 *Gut Springenheide and Tusky* [1998] ECR I-4657, para 31.

infrastructures. Vulnerability is no longer an exception; it is embedded in the very architecture of digital marketplaces and commercial practices.[5]

Vulnerability is a concept that can be adjusted, dynamic, and especially adaptive and relational to the contexts in which it occurs and, obviously, to the specific person whose vulnerability is being claimed. This evolving notion of vulnerability calls for a reconceptualization of fairness (and agency) in EU private law. As Metzger, Schweitzer, and Wagner argue, the data economy presents profound structural market failures, including entrenched information asymmetries, the erosion of consent, and forms of behavioural manipulation that challenge traditional conceptions of autonomy and responsibility.[6] Their call for a rethinking of the legal framework towards a market order for the data economy includes protecting the decision-making process itself against manipulation—a form of structural vulnerability that current consumer law is ill-equipped to address.[7]

Luna's layered approach to vulnerability supports this need for conceptual innovation.[8] Helberger, Sax, Strycharz, and Micklitz have shown that digital architectures create systemic exposure, rendering vulnerability not accidental but engineered.[9] Acemoglu and Johnson further demonstrate that AI technologies amplify inequality and centralise power.[10] Floridi's ethics-by-design framework aligns with these insights, arguing that fairness, non-maleficence, and explicability must be embedded in AI systems

[5] N Helberger, M Sax, J Strycharz and H Micklitz, 'Choice Architectures in the Digital Economy: Towards a New Understanding of Digital Vulnerability' (2022) 45 *Journal of Consumer Policy* 175, 177–178.

[6] A Metzger, H Schweitzer and G Wagner, 'Datenschutz und Datenmarkt: Grundzüge einer Marktordnung für die europäische Datenwirtschaft' (2023) *Zeitschrift für die gesamte Privatrechtswissenschaft (ZfPW)* 227, 247–248.

[7] Ibid 255.

[8] See F Luna (n 3).

[9] See N Helberger, M Sax, J Strycharz and H Micklitz (n 5).

[10] Daron Acemoglu and Simon Johnson, *Power and Progress: Our Thousand-Year Struggle Over Technology and Prosperity* (PublicAffairs 2023) 344–349.

themselves.[11] Such embedding requires a corresponding legal transformation—from consent-based doctrines to principles that impose structural duties.

Yet, the EU legislature has not fully realised this shift. The tension between innovation and protection (of the vulnerable) in the EU Digital Single Market further highlights the limits of current legislative approaches. Despite the introduction of regulatory initiatives such as the Digital Services Act (DSA)[12] and the AI Act (AIA),[13] the response to structural vulnerability is still fragmented and insufficient. As noted in the Digital Fairness for Consumers report, EU law lacks a coherent framework to address what they term 'digital asymmetries'—deep-seated structural imbalances in knowledge and power between digital service providers and consumers.[14] Their analysis points to the need for a holistic and horizontal legal response rooted in value-based principles, rather than piecemeal legislative patchwork.[15] Vulnerability, in this account, is a systemic condition demanding legal recognition as a principle—not a category of exception.

From this perspective, the notion of a general principle of law gains renewed relevance. General principles have historically served as interpretive and gap-filling tools in EU law and have the capacity to respond flexibly to societal transformations.[16] However, this solution may also be kicking the can down the road.

[11] L Floridi and others, 'AI4People's Ethical Framework for a Good AI Society: Opportunities, Risks, Principles, and Recommendations' (2018) 28 Minds and Machines 689, 694–700.

[12] Regulation (EU) 2022/2065 of the European Parliament and of the Council of 19 October 2022 on a Single Market for Digital Services and amending Directive 2000/31/EC (Digital Services Act) [2022] OJ L277/1.

[13] Regulation (EU) 2024/1689 of the European Parliament and of the Council of 13 March 2024 laying down harmonised rules on artificial intelligence (Artificial Intelligence Act) and amending certain Union legislative acts [2024] OJ L134/1.

[14] N Helberger and others, *Digital Fairness for Consumers* (BEUC, March 2024) 10–13 https://www.beuc.eu/reports/digital-fairness-consumers Accessed 21 March 2025.

[15] Ibid 8–9, 22–24.

[16] A Metzger, 'General Principles of Law' in *Max Planck Encyclopedia of European Private Law* (Max-EuP 2012) https://max-eup2012.mpipriv.de/index.php/General_Principles_of_Law Accessed 21 March 2025.

While the Treaties of the European Union make only limited reference to general principles of EU law, these principles have been primarily developed through the jurisprudence of the CJEU. Core principles such as legal certainty, institutional balance, legitimate expectations, proportionality, and fairness have emerged not from codification but from judicial reasoning that compensates for legislative gaps. The recognition of fundamental rights as general principles likewise originates in the case law, and is now codified in Article 6(3) TEU, which refers not only to the European Convention on Human Rights but also to the constitutional traditions common to the Member States and the Charter of Fundamental Rights of the European Union.[17]

However, the structural evolution of European private law—characterised by its multi-level architecture and doctrinal pluralism—challenges traditional conceptions of how such principles function.[18] As scholarship has shown, general principles in EU law do not operate exclusively within statutory frameworks, but often derive their normative force from inductive legal reasoning, comparative analysis, and institutional recognition across national and supranational levels.[19] They play a critical role in unifying fragmented regimes and ensuring coherence across diverse legal traditions and regulatory domains.

In the context of a digital society, there is a growing recognition that the normative foundations of the legal order must adapt to new forms of power, opacity, and systemic asymmetry. A digital society may demand a recalibration of these principles—what some have termed 'General Principles 2.0'—which are not merely applied ex post but are embedded within the technical and organisational architecture of digital environments.[20] These principles must transcend doctrinal silos to address the structural

[17] Charter of Fundamental Rights of the European Union [2012] OJ C326/391 ('Charter').

[18] O Remien, 'Europäisches Privatrecht als Verfassungsfrage' (2005) EuR 699, 700–701.

[19] A Metzger, *Extra legem, intra ius: Allgemeine Rechtsgrundsätze im europäischen Privatrecht* (Mohr Siebeck 2009) 546–548.

[20] X Groussot, A Zemskova and E Gill-Pedro, 'Towards General Principles 2.0: The Application of General Principles of EU Law in the Digital Society' (2019) Lund University Legal Research Paper Series No 02/2019, 3–4 https://ssrn.com/abstract=3473681 Accessed 21 March 2025; N Helberger and M Sax, 'Regulating Personalisation: From the Normative to the Technical' (2021) 40(5) *Computer Law & Security Review* 105561.

challenges posed by automation, datafication, and behavioural manipulation, and to ensure that fairness, accountability, and fundamental rights remain enforceable within an increasingly algorithmic legal and economic order.

This chapter critically explores the need and feasibility of recognising vulnerability in the context of AI and other digital technologies as a normative concern of general private law. Drawing on legal scholarship and regulatory developments, it argues that vulnerability in a digital society is not merely a technical issue, but a structural and cross-cutting phenomenon that calls for the evolution—or indeed the development—of a general principle of law fit for the digital age.

While the term 'digital vulnerability' is increasingly employed in the literature to refer to forms of vulnerability emerging in the context of digital technologies and societies, this chapter opts for the more general term 'vulnerability'. The choice reflects the underlying hypothesis that, in a digital society, vulnerability is not an exceptional or situational condition, but rather a structural and systemic one. The chapter is structured as follows: Sect. 7.2 reconceptualises vulnerability in light of current scholarship; Sect. 7.3 evaluates gaps in the EU legislature response; Sect. 7.4 considers the role of private law in mediating digital asymmetries; Sect. 7.5 explores the normative potential of a general principle of law on vulnerability; and Sect. 7.6 offers concluding reflections.

7.2 Conceptualising Vulnerability

7.2.1 Rethinking Vulnerability in the Digital Society

'Despite its common use, the meaning of the concept of vulnerability is complex and vague'.[21] However, in the realm of law, one cannot evade the necessity of employing classifications and generalisations.

EU private law has traditionally associated vulnerability with specific categories of individuals—such as the elderly, minors, or persons with disabilities—often within the framework of consumer protection. This

[21] Council of Europe, *Access to Justice for Vulnerable Groups in Azerbaijan* (Council of Europe 2023) https://rm.coe.int/access-to-justice-for-vulnerable-groups-in-azerbaijan-eng/1680a31544. Accessed 24 March, 2025, p. 6.

approach, codified in instruments like Article 5(3) of the Unfair Commercial Practices Directive (UCPD),[22] reflects a view of vulnerability as an exception: a condition rooted in identifiable personal traits that require tailored legal safeguards. Yet, this targeted model does not account for how technological environments themselves can shape, intensify, or even produce vulnerability.

In a digital society, vulnerability is not an anomaly but a generalised structural condition. Increasingly, academic literature and policy reports point to how information asymmetries, predictive analytics, and persuasive interface design expose individuals to influence and manipulation irrespective of their demographic or psychological profile.[23] Vulnerability arises not merely from intrinsic characteristics, but from external conditions embedded in the architecture and logic of digital infrastructures.[24] It is these systems—platforms, algorithms, and data flows—that systemically reduce user agency and challenge the legal assumptions underpinning autonomy, consent, and responsibility.

The AI Act, adopted in 2024, reinforces this understanding. As Carmen Muñoz has pointed out, while the Regulation is a harmonised administrative framework—setting uniform obligations for AI operators across the EU—it does not directly regulate fundamental rights nor explicitly define protected groups.[25] Its normative ambition lies in preventing harm by obliging developers and deployers of AI to avoid infringing the rights guaranteed by the Charter and other areas of existing EU law, including consumer protection. In this structure, protection of vulnerable individuals is achieved indirectly: through stricter requirements, more rigorous ex ante risk assessments, and intensified post-market

[22] Directive 2005/29/EC of the European Parliament and of the Council of 11 May 2005 concerning unfair business-to-consumer commercial practices [2005] OJ L149/22, art 5(3).

[23] N Helberger and others (n 5) 177. OECD (2023), 'Consumer vulnerability in the digital age', OECD Digital Economy Papers, No. 355, OECD Publishing, Paris, https://doi.org/10.1787/4d013cc5-en. E. Terryn, S. M. Marquez, 'AI and Consumer Protection: An Introduction', in The Cambridge Handbook of the Law, Ethics and Policy of Artificial Intelligence, N. A. Smuha, Ed. (Cambridge: Cambridge University Press, 2025), pp. 192–210.

[24] N Helberger and others (n 14) 11–12.

[25] C Muñoz, '¿Protege el Reglamento de IA a los vulnerables?' (OdiseIA, 2024) https://www.odiseia.org/post/protege-el-reglamento-de-ia-a-los-vulnerables Accessed 24 March 2025.

surveillance where AI systems may impact those in particularly exposed positions. As noted by Malgieri and Rebrean, the Regulation contains at least 17 references to vulnerability, associating it with contexts of dependency, asymmetrical power, and threats to fundamental rights and dignity.[26] These references span key articles—such as Article 5(1)(a), which prohibits AI systems that exploit the vulnerabilities of specific groups, and Article 7(2)(h), which considers the position of vulnerable persons in assessing high-risk AI systems.

While the AI Act refrains from offering a single, uniform definition of vulnerability, it clearly conceptualises it as a legal criterion that interacts with social, contextual, and normative factors. In this way, the AI Act affirms that vulnerability is not confined to specific individuals or static traits but arises through structural relations and socio-technical environments. Furthermore, the absence of a clear definitional framework complicates the identification and visibility of such groups, but the regulation nonetheless mandates that governance, enforcement, and accountability mechanisms must be more rigorous in these contexts. For Muñoz, this underscores a central regulatory message: that the robustness of protections afforded to individuals and communities depends not only on the formal rights granted but also on how intensively the legal system monitors and constrains the operations of AI technologies across vulnerable contexts.[27]

As a consequence, one could argue that the AI Act provides a normative opportunity to recognise vulnerability not just as a condition to be remedied, but as a lens through which to assess the legitimacy of digital market practices more broadly. Accordingly, the call of this contribution for vulnerability to be treated as a transversal legal principle that supports the internal coherence of the EU's digital regulation landscape.

7.2.2 Systemic Harms in Digital Environments

As Helberger rightly proposed, the production of vulnerability in digital contexts can be analysed along three interrelated vectors: *architecture*,

[26] G Malgieri, M Rebrean, 'Vulnerability in the AI Act: Building an Interpretation' (2024) SSRN Working Paper 5,058,591, 4–6 https://papers.ssrn.com/sol3/papers.cfm?abstract_id=5058591 Accessed 24 March 2025.

[27] C Muñoz (n 25).

relational asymmetries, and *data-driven influence*.[28] First, the architectural design of user interfaces profoundly impacts user decision-making in the digital landscape, as it often uses features such as dark patterns and default settings that are intentionally crafted to nudge individuals towards choices that favour business interests rather than respecting personal autonomy. These are not neutral features but intentional strategies that exploit cognitive biases. Second, there exists a pronounced asymmetry between users and digital service providers, the latter of whom possess superior access to behavioural data, analytics, and optimisation tools. Third, continuous data surveillance and algorithmic profiling personalise the user experience in ways that reinforce predictability and suppress critical reflection, ultimately diminishing the agency of users in their interactions.

These dynamics do not simply affect marginal groups; they pervade everyday interactions online and constitute a new form of market power. A power rooted not only in the control over supply but also in the manipulation of demand.[29] In such a context, vulnerability is not limited to an individual's lack of information or capacity—it is embedded in a system of commercial persuasion and behavioural steering.

The CJEU has taken steps towards recognising this perspective. In *Commission v Belgium*, it found that pre-ticked boxes in online interfaces can mislead users, thereby acknowledging that design choices—not user traits—may generate conditions of reduced autonomy.[30] In *Orange România*, the Court similarly held that consent obtained through preformulated statements in contracts could not be considered freely given.[31] These rulings collectively reflect a move away from individualistic understandings of vulnerability, towards a more contextualised view that takes commercial architecture into account.

This trajectory continues in *Planet49*, where the Court confirmed that valid consent for cookie use cannot be obtained through pre-ticked boxes, reaffirming that meaningful control requires active and informed

[28] N Helberger and others (n 5) 179–181.

[29] A Metzger, H Schweitzer and G Wagner, 'Datenschutz und Datenmarkt: Grundzüge einer Marktordnung für die europäische Datenwirtschaft' (2023) ZfPW 227, 255.

[30] Case C-421/12 Commission v Belgium [2014] ECLI:EU:C:2014:2064, paras 17–21.

[31] Case C-628/17 Orange România [2019] ECLI:EU:C:2019:480, paras 44–46.

engagement.[32] The ruling reinforces that design choices that exploit inertia or cognitive bias are incompatible with data protection principles, further substantiating the claim that vulnerability may be systematically engineered. In *Schrems II*, the Court underscored the structural risks of data environments lacking adequate safeguards, invalidating the Privacy Shield framework on grounds that users could not meaningfully protect themselves against disproportionate surveillance.[33] Most recently, in *Bundeskartellamt v Meta* the Opinion of AG Rantos argued that Meta's extensive and undifferentiated processing of personal data for behavioural advertising—without clear user control—violated GDPR principles such as data minimisation and purpose limitation.[34] Rantos emphasised that such practices risk undermining user autonomy and distorting the notion of consent, particularly when carried out by dominant platforms. This reinforces the broader view that systemic vulnerability arises from the architecture and commercial logic of digital platforms, rather than from users' personal characteristics alone.

Together, these cases confirm that the legal system is increasingly alert to the ways in which digital infrastructures themselves shape user agency and generate systemic vulnerability, regardless of individual awareness or capacity.

7.2.3 Beyond the Binary: Reassessing the 'Average Consumer'

EU consumer law continues to rely heavily on the figure of the 'average consumer' as a benchmark for assessing unfairness and deception. This concept, defined in *Gut Springenheide* as someone 'reasonably well-informed, observant and circumspect', provides the normative baseline for evaluating commercial practices.[35] However, in algorithmically-driven

[32] Case C-673/17 *Bundesverband der Verbraucherzentralen v Planet49 GmbH* [2019] ECLI:EU:C:2019:801, paras 62–63.

[33] Case C-311/18 *Data Protection Commissioner v Facebook Ireland and Maximillian Schrems* [2020] ECLI:EU:C:2020:559, para 202.

[34] Case C-446/21 Bundeskartellamt v Meta Platforms Inc and Others, Opinion of AG Rantos, ECLI:EU:C:2022:658, 20 September 2022, para 22-28. In October 2024, the Bundeskartellamt closed the proceeding after accepting Meta's reforms as sufficient under competition law. Meta withdrew its appeal, making the 2019 decision final, Case C-252/21 *Meta Platforms Inc and Others v Bundeskartellamt* EU:C:2023:537.

[35] Case C-210/96 *Gut Springenheide and Tusky* [1998] ECR I-4657, para 31.

environments, even well-informed users are vulnerable to manipulation. Personalised persuasion, adaptive pricing, and A/B testing techniques affect all users, not merely the inattentive or uninformed.

As the authors of the *Digital Fairness for Consumers* report argue, the increasing complexity and personalisation of digital environments renders the average consumer construct functionally obsolete.[36] Hyper-targeted marketing exploits behavioural insights at a scale and depth that blur the boundaries between informed choice and automated response. These challenges the legitimacy of normative standards that assume a baseline of rational consumer behaviour. In short, vulnerability becomes universal—not because everyone is equally disadvantaged, but because digital infrastructures operate through mechanisms that structurally impair choice across the board.

Moreover, vulnerability should be understood as a normative and political category—one that emerges in relation to technological infrastructures and institutional conditions.[37] This view resonates with Muñoz's approach to the regulatory message of the AI Act, indicating a legal turn towards vulnerability as a systemic concern.

7.2.4 The Consumer-Citizen and the Multidimensional Nature of Vulnerability

In digital societies, users are not only consumers—but they are also citizens, workers, and members of social and political communities. The same algorithmic tools that recommend products also curate news, target political messages, and determine eligibility for welfare or employment.[38] This convergence of roles amplifies the stakes of commercial influence and extends the implications of vulnerability beyond market fairness into the domain of fundamental rights.

[36] M Sax and N Helberger, 'Digital Vulnerability and Manipulation in the Emerging Digital Framework' in N Helberger and others (n 14) 10–13.

[37] See Lorenzo Cotino citing B Otero in L Cotino, 'Vulnerabilidad y colectivos vulnerables en el Derecho: ¿quiénes son y cómo se definen?' (2024) EAPC-RCDP Blog https://eapc-rcdp.blog.gencat.cat/2024/12/18/vulnerabilidad-y-colectivos-vulnerables-en-el-derecho-quienes-son-y-como-se-definen-lorenzo-cotino/ Accessed 24 March 2025.

[38] R Schulze, 'Conclusions' in C Crea and F De Franceschi (eds.), *The New Shapes of Digital Vulnerability in European Private Law* (Nomos, 2024) 521–523.

Helberger has highlighted how digital environments fail to respect the contextual integrity of users' roles, leading to cross-contextual profiling and manipulation.[39] As individuals move between different digital contexts, the lack of boundaries facilitates a form of exploitation that affects both market participation and democratic agency. In this sense, vulnerability is not only legal—it is political, social, and ethical.

Accordingly, EU private law must respond not to isolated instances of market harm, but to systemic and cross-cutting forms of vulnerability that are deeply embedded in the digital infrastructure of everyday life. This requires moving beyond individualistic notions of harm and towards a legal framework attuned to collective, structural, and institutional dimensions of influence.

7.3 EU Legal Framework: Fragmentation and Gaps

7.3.1 *The Breakdown of Normative Coherence in EU 'Digital' Law*

The existing EU legal framework for a digital society is composed of several instruments that respond to discrete risks and in some instances, lack conceptual and normative coherence. For instance, the GDPR, the DSA, the DMA, the Data Act, or the AI Act regulate different aspects of digital life—personal data, content in digital platforms, markets contestability, access and use of sensors' data, algorithmic systems—yet none centrally address the systemic production of vulnerability across digital environments. This reflects a deeper conceptual fragmentation in EU private law, which continues to rely on outdated assumptions about consumer rationality and informed choice.[40]

Additionally, existing EU consumer protection law presumes a reasonably informed and circumspect consumer. But such a model is increasingly out of touch with the realities of digital commerce, which is structured

[39] M Sax and N Helberger, (n 36) in N Helberger and others (n 14) 22–24.

[40] H-W Micklitz, *The Politics of Justice in European Private Law: Social Justice, Access Justice, Societal Justice* (CUP 2018). M Grochowski, 'Digital Vulnerability in a Post-Consumer Society. Subverting Paradigms?' in C. Crea and A De Franceschi (eds.), *The New Shapes of Digital Vulnerability in European Private Law* (Nomos, 2024) 213.

around asymmetries of information, interface design, and personalisation.[41] In this regard, EU law remains largely tethered to transactional autonomy, neglecting how market infrastructures shape and exploit user behaviour. The result is a mismatch between the normative framework of private law and the architecture of digital markets.

This has profound implications for legal coherence. As Schulze observes, the concept of vulnerability currently operates in a fragmented and instrumental manner, invoked only to trigger specific duties in sectoral contexts.[42] There is no general legal concept of vulnerability capable of grounding systemic protection or guiding horizontal interpretation across EU law.

7.3.2 A concrete example: The AI Act—Risk Regulation Without Normative Anchoring?

The 2024 AI Act represents an important development in the governance of algorithmic systems. It adopts a risk-based approach that classifies AI systems by the likelihood of causing harm to safety or fundamental rights. Vulnerability plays a visible role: Art. 5 prohibits systems that exploit vulnerabilities based on age, disability, or social situation, while Art. 7 includes 'vulnerable persons' in its list of risk-enhancing factors.[43]

[41] See Recital 18 and Art. 5(2)(b) of Directive 2005/29/EC of the European Parliament and of the Council of 11 May 2005 concerning unfair business-to-consumer commercial practices in the internal market and amending Council Directive 84/450/EEC, Directives 97/7/EC, 98/27/EC and 2002/65/EC of the European Parliament and of the Council and Regulation (EC) No 2006/2004 of the European Parliament and of the Council (Unfair Commercial Practices Directive) [2005] OJ L149/22. Additionally, the CJEU has applied the 'average consumer' standard when interpreting adequacy of pre-contractual information in Directive 2011/83/EU of the European Parliament and of the Council of 25 October 2011 on consumer rights, amending Council Directive 93/13/EEC and Directive 1999/44/EC of the European Parliament and of the Council and repealing Council Directive 85/577/EEC and Directive 97/7/EC of the European Parliament and of the Council [2011] OJ L304/64, and fairness of contract terms in Council Directive 93/13/EEC of 5 April 1993 on unfair terms in consumer contracts [1993] OJ L95/29.

[42] R Schulze (n 38) 521–524.

[43] Regulation (EU) 2024/1689 of the European Parliament and of the Council of 13 March 2024 laying down harmonised rules on artificial intelligence (Artificial Intelligence Act) and amending certain Union legislative acts (AI Act) [2024] OJ L134/1, arts 5(1)(a), 7(2)(h).

Yet, the AI Act's logic is technical and administrative, not normative, even if one may concede it is meant to protect consumers. It imposes procedural duties—such as conformity assessments and documentation—but it does not establish vulnerability as a legal principle with doctrinal force. As Muñoz has remarked, the AI Act protects individuals indirectly, through obligations on developers and deployers, not by granting rights to the affected.[44] There is no attempt to define vulnerability, nor to anchor it in fundamental rights. Its function is limited to risk intensification, not legal transformation.

As Micklitz has argued elsewhere, this is symptomatic of the broader trend towards compliance-based governance, where the protection of autonomy and dignity is outsourced to algorithmic auditing and risk scoring.[45] Vulnerability becomes a tool for calibration—not a category of justice.

7.3.3 The Digital Fairness Act: A Missed Doctrinal Opportunity

The forthcoming Digital Fairness Act (DFA), expected post-2025, reflects the European Commission's recognition that existing consumer law no longer fits the realities of the digital market. It aims to tackle dark patterns, influencer marketing, and hyper-personalisation.[46] This signals a political willingness to address design-based harm, but not a conceptual re-foundation of private law.

The DFA is expected to complement—rather than replace or directly revise—existing directives such as the UCPD. Yet this incremental approach arguably perpetuates the transactional logic that underpins much of EU consumer law. By focusing primarily on individual symptoms—like manipulative design patterns or misleading digital practices—the regulation risks overlooking the deeper structural conditions that foster consumers (and users) vulnerability in digital environments. As such, the DFA remains tethered to an ex post enforcement paradigm

44 See C Muñoz (n 25).

45 H-W Micklitz, A Villanueva, 'Responsibilities of Companies in the Algorithmic Society' in H-W Micklitz and others (eds), Constitutional Challenges in the Algorithmic Society (Cambridge University Press 2021) 267–291.

46 European Commission, 'Digital Fairness Act: Call for Evidence' (2024) https://www.digital-fairness-act.com Accessed 21 March 2025.

that lacks the systemic foresight needed to address the dynamics of digital markets.[47]

The Commission's Staff Working Document for the Fitness Check acknowledges this limitation. It notes the legal uncertainty as regards the application of the three Directives in the digital area, in particular to new technologies and data-driven practices.[48] Similarly, the *Digital Fairness for Consumers Report* from 2024 report shows persistent fragmentation, weak enforcement, and poor cross-border coordination, even in areas of established consumer protection.[49]

Legal responses that merely address design practices or transparency miss the deeper structural transformation of market dynamics. Thus, the DFA, while politically valuable, cannot function as the foundation for systemic protection. It will remain as a legislative patch, lacking the conceptual ambition to address the transversal nature of vulnerability in digital societies.

7.3.4 The Role of Fundamental Rights and Their Limitations

EU digital regulations often invoke fundamental rights—such as dignity, autonomy, privacy, and non-discrimination—as core values underpinning legislative objectives. The Charter is frequently cited as a normative touchstone, with the AI Act, for example, referencing the protection of dignity and fundamental rights in Recital 16.[50] Yet, as scholars have shown, this invocation tends to remain rhetorical.[51] Rights language is often used to justify regulatory ambition but rarely functions as a structuring logic in the design, enforcement, or interpretation of digital norms.

[47] H-W Micklitz, 'Dissolution of EU Consumer Law Through Fragmentation and Privatisation.' in N Helberger and others (n 14) 69–144.

[48] European Commission Staff Working Document, Fitness Check of EU consumer law on digital fairness SWD(2024) 230 final, 44.

[49] M Sax and N Helberger, (n 36) in N Helberger and others (n 14)18–24.

[50] Regulation (EU) 2024/... on Artificial Intelligence (AI Act), Recital 16.

[51] M Sax and N Helberger (n 46) 11–13.

This disconnect reflects a deeper conceptual limitation. Due to the compliance-based governance trend,[52] even advanced legislative instruments like the AI Act protect individuals not by granting enforceable rights but by regulating the conduct of system operators. The result is an indirect protection model: the rights of individuals are safeguarded only insofar as AI providers fulfil compliance obligations. This disconnect creates a double asymmetry—between individuals and technologies, and between rights rhetoric and legal operationalisation.

Some scholars have articulated this limitation in more structural terms. Neither the general principles nor the fundamental rights enshrined in EU law are keeping pace with digital transformation, remaining aspirational and under-theorised in the face of algorithmic governance. The classical rights paradigm—focused on ex post remedies, individual standing, and identifiable harms—is poorly suited to the distributed, anticipatory nature of digital harms.[53] In algorithmic environments, influence is ambient, harms are probabilistic, and agency is diffused. The right to dignity, for instance, may be undermined not by a discrete act but by continuous micro-targeting, nudging, or exclusionary platform design. Yet EU law has still to integrate these realities into a rights-based framework.

Additionally, EU consumer law still privileges an economic logic, treating rights as secondary to market functionality.[54] The need for a reconceptualization of vulnerability is linked to non-economic consumer interests, such as psychological integrity and informational agency—interests which are largely underdeveloped in current rights protections (e.g. dignity in data protection, or non-discrimination in the 2024 Platform Work Directive).[55] Such criticism is echoed by others, who note that vulnerability in EU law remains instrumentalised, rather than recognised

[52] See J Black, 'Decentring Regulation: Understanding the Role of Regulation and Self-Regulation in a 'Post-Regulatory' World.' Current Legal Problems (2001) 54(1): 103–146. C Scott, 'Regulation in the Age of Governance: The Rise of the Post-Regulatory State' in David Levi-Faur and Jacint Jordana (eds), The Politics of Regulation: Institutions and Regulatory Reforms for the Age of Governance (Edward Elgar 2004) Chapter 7.

[53] X Groussot, A Zemskova, E Gill-Pedro (n 20) 11–12.

[54] M Grochowski (n 40) 201.

[55] Recital 2 of Directive (EU) 2024/2831 of the European Parliament and of the Council of 23 October 2024 on improving working conditions in platform work [2024] OJ L 2831/1, referring to Art. 21 of The Charter.

as a legal lens through which to reinterpret the scope and structure of fundamental rights.[56]

Ultimately, the lack of a substantive rights-based approach to digital vulnerability leaves individuals exposed to systemic manipulation without meaningful legal grounding for protection. While rights language persists, its application remains inconsistent, symbolic, and largely absent from enforcement practice. This underscores the need for vulnerability to be developed not merely as a trigger for risk regulation, but as a general legal principle capable of structuring legal obligations and systemic safeguards ex ante. Potentially, Art. 1 of The Charter (*human dignity*) could be the anchor for future doctrinal development, especially since both the AI Act and the GDPR invoke it without fully operationalising it.

7.3.5 *Enforcement Challenges and the Problem of Legal Design*

Even when protective rules exist, their practical effectiveness hinges on enforcement. Across the EU, enforcement of digital rights and consumer protections faces both structural and institutional weaknesses. The GDPR's decentralised enforcement architecture relies heavily on national Data Protection Authorities (DPAs), many of which are underfunded, overburdened, or constrained by political interference.[57] High-profile cases, such as those against Meta or TikTok, often stall due to jurisdictional disputes and inconsistent priorities across Member States.

Similar challenges affect the Consumer Protection Cooperation (CPC) Network. The *Digital Fairness for Consumers* 2024 report documents how the CPC has struggled to address cross-border digital harms, particularly those involving exploitative interfaces and manipulative design targeting children and vulnerable users.[58] The underlying problem is not

[56] R Schulze (n 38) 523–524.

[57] EC Communication, 'Evaluation of the General Data Protection Regulation (GDPR): Second Report on the application of the General Data Protection Regulation' COM(2024) 357 final, 7–8.

[58] N Helberger and others (n 14) 9, referring to M. Cantero Gamito, H.-W. Micklitz, 'Too much or too little? Assessing the Consumer Protection Cooperation (CPC) Network in the protection of consumers and children on TikTok' (BEUC, 17-02-23) Available at: https://www.beuc.eu/sites/default/files/publications/BEUC-X-2023-018_Assessing_CPC_Network_in_the_protection_of_consumers_and_children_on_TikTok-Report.pdf. Accessed 24 March 2025.

the absence of legal norms, but the limited capacity of enforcement bodies to act swiftly and at scale in fast-moving digital environments.

Legal design compounds this issue. Sound voices have argued that current EU frameworks remain anchored in abstract legal categories—such as consent, transparency, and fairness—that assume a degree of user autonomy and understanding that no longer exists in practice in data-driven markets.[59] These concepts are ill-equipped to deal with personalisation logics, behavioural adaptation, and real-time algorithmic decision-making. The result is a compliance regime that obscures systemic harm behind the appearance of formal legality.

This tension is also visible in the design of enforcement mechanisms. Increasingly, consumer protection is privatised—outsourced to platforms' terms of service, self-regulation, or informal dispute resolution systems. As it has been noted, this shift transforms public law values into private compliance obligations, often inaccessible to ordinary users.[60] The burden of proof frequently falls on consumers or under-resourced civil society actors, despite overwhelming asymmetries of information and power.

The Commission Staff Working Document accompanying the Fitness Check confirms these concerns. It highlights that legal uncertainty, enforcement fragmentation, and poor regulatory alignment all weaken the effectiveness of consumer law in the digital sphere.[61] Moreover, new risks like emotional manipulation or adaptive interfaces fall between the cracks of existing law, making enforcement either impossible or discretionary.

This landscape reveals the limits of ex post enforcement in a system that produces vulnerability by design. Without clear ex ante obligations and legal standards adapted to the architecture of influence, even the most well-crafted rules fail to protect. Therefore, a general principle of vulnerability could serve to anchor enforcement expectations, clarify interpretive standards, and re-centre EU law on the lived realities of structurally exposed individuals and groups.

[59] A Metzger and others (n 6) 255–259.

[60] H-W Micklitz, 'The Visible Hand of European Regulatory Private Law. The Transformation from Autonomy to Functionalism in Competition and Regulation' *Yearbook of European Law*, Vol. 28:1 (1 January 2009) 3–59.

[61] European Commission Staff Working Document, Fitness Check of EU consumer law on digital fairness SWD(2024) 231 final, 48–51.

7.4 The Role of EU Private Law: Autonomy, Consent, and Power

7.4.1 *Private Autonomy in Data Markets*

EU private law continues to rest on the normative premise of private autonomy—that legal subjects, as market actors, are capable of making free and informed choices. However, in digital markets, this assumption is increasingly contested. The asymmetries inherent in data-driven transactions often constrain meaningful choice, rendering the exercise of autonomy legally questionable.

As Micklitz argues, the tension between market liberalism and social justice is embedded within the architecture of EU private law itself.[62] Autonomy is upheld as an ideal, even as its practical conditions are systematically undermined. This contradiction suggests the need for a re-evaluation of how private law conceptualises autonomy in the context of digital transactions. As Schulze further contends, private law in the digital realm must transition from merely protecting transactional freedom to safeguarding the relational preconditions of agency.[63]

Furthermore, from the perspective of data protection law, the limits of an individualistic regulatory approach that relies on private autonomy and the initiative of the individual are also evident once again when it comes to law enforcement. The rational disinterest of the data subject, which torpedoes the consent solution, also calls private law enforcement into question.[64]

These shifts acknowledge that in digital environments, individuals often face structural conditions that impede genuine autonomy, necessitating a more protective legal framework.

7.4.2 *Consent, Manipulation, and Knowledge Asymmetries*

The legal centrality of consent can be seen as a symptom of private law's resistance to normative evolution. Consent-based frameworks rest

[62] See H-W Micklitz, *The Politics of Justice in European Private Law: Social Justice, Access Justice, Societal Justice* (CUP: 2018), in which this theme is central to Micklitz's analysis throughout the volume.

[63] R Schulze (n 38) 521.

[64] A Metzger and others (n 6) 265.

on the assumption that parties possess symmetrical knowledge and decision-making capacities.[65] But in digital infrastructures, asymmetries are not incidental—they are constitutive. As Helberger demonstrates, choice architectures are not neutral: they are structured to direct attention, suppress friction, and exploit known behavioural vulnerabilities.[66] Consent in such environments is not a manifestation of autonomy but a ritualistic exercise legitimising structural imbalance.

This criticism is confirmed by the AI Act, which ostensibly seeks to address high-risk systems but does so via provider compliance regimes, not enforceable user rights.[67] The Act's rights-protective ambitions are mediated entirely through ex ante obligations imposed on operators,[68] severing the link between rights discourse and individual empowerment.

Some have proposed a reconceptualization of consent as part of an ethically grounded system of digital governance, emphasising fairness, explicability, and non-manipulation.[69] Yet EU private law preserves the fiction of user agency in environments where users are designed to submit.

The CJEU has taken modest steps to challenge this. In *Planet49*, *Orange România*, and *Commission v Belgium*, the Court invalidated various forms of formalistic consent, recognising that legal validity must be context-sensitive.[70] However, as AG Rantos argued in *Meta Platforms*,

[65] Think for instance in 'consent-or-pay' or 'pay-or-okay' business models.

[66] N Helberger and others, 'EU Consumer Protection 2.0: Structural Asymmetries in Digital Consumer Markets' (BEUC 2021) 15–22; N Helberger, F C. J. Zuiderveen Borgesius and A Reyna, 'The Perfect Match? A Closer Look at the Relationship Between EU Consumer Law and Data Protection' (2017) 54 *Common Market Law Review* 1427, 1445–1450.

[67] See P Hense and T Mustać, *AI Act Compact: Compliance, Management & Use Cases in Corporate Practice* (DFV Mediengruppe 2025) 86–89.

[68] For the purposes of this analysis, 'operators' refers to providers, deployers, importers, and distributors as defined in Articles 3(2), 3(4), 3(6), and 3(7) of Regulation (EU) 2024/1689 (AI Act).

[69] L Floridi and others, 'AI4People—An Ethical Framework for a Good AI Society: Opportunities, Risks, Principles, and Recommendations' (2018) 28 *Minds and Machines* 689, 694–699.

[70] *Case C-673/17 Planet49* ECLI:EU:C:2019:801; *Case C-61/19 Orange România* ECLI:EU:C:2020:901; *Case C-421/12 Commission v Belgium* ECLI:EU:C:2014:2064.

systemic personalisation cannot be countered by disclosure alone.[71] What is needed is a shift in legal design, not just in enforcement.

7.4.3 *Lessons from Labour and Anti-discrimination Law*

EU private law has traditionally resisted acknowledging structural inequality, adhering instead to a model grounded in formal reciprocity and abstract autonomy. In contrast, labour law and anti-discrimination regimes are premised on the recognition of **relational asymmetry** as a source of legal vulnerability. These fields offer conceptual and doctrinal resources for reimagining the role of private law in digital societies.

This is the point of departure for Catanzariti to argue that labour and equality law are engaged in the **juridification of vulnerability, that is,** they treat relational exposure not as an exception but as a legal condition that necessitates structural correction.[72] In doing so, they introduce legal tools, such as contextual standards, group-based protections, and proactive duties, that could be transposed to the other legal spheres such as consumer protection law.

This logic aligns with Goanta's call to move beyond consumer law's economic reductivism. She highlights how digital platforms shape not only market functions but also **political and social roles**, giving rise to hybrid subjectivities that demand integrated legal responses.[73]

The role of private law, then, is not merely to restore choice, but to institutionalise safeguards against **structural dominance.**

The AI Act partially recognises these dynamics by classifying certain applications—such as biometric categorisation or real-time surveillance as **inherently high-risk,** based on power asymmetries. Yet, as others

[71] Case C-446/21 Bundeskartellamt v Meta Platforms Inc and Others, Opinion of AG Rantos, ECLI:EU:C:2022:658, 20 September 2022, paras 22–25.

[72] M Catanzariti, 'The juridification of vulnerability in the European legal culture', Oñati Socio-Legal Series, 12(6), pp. 1391–1416. https://doi.org/10.35295/osls.iisl/0000-0000-0000-1314, 1405.

[73] C Goanta, 'European Consumer Law: The Hero of Our Times' (2021) 9 *Journal of European Consumer and Market Law* 2, 5–7.

have observed, the absence of a binding concept of vulnerability highlights the limitations of a sectoral and instrumentalist approach.[74] Anti-discrimination law demonstrates that **normativity must precede compliance**: without a coherent legal principle of structural vulnerability, digital protections remain discretionary and fragmented.[75]

7.4.4 The Potential of Private Law in Embedding Vulnerability and Shaping Fair Digital Relations

EU private law operates within a fragmented, multi-level legal order shaped by national traditions, supranational instruments, and comparative methodologies.[76] This plurality presents both potential and limitations. On the one hand, private law retains flexibility to evolve through inductive reasoning and the development of general principles, enabling it to integrate normative shifts without formal codification.[77] On the other hand, this same fragmentation, combined with the absence of a unified constitutional framework, constrains its ability to provide consistent and enforceable safeguards across Member States.

As seen earlier, in the context of the digital economy, private law's traditional reliance on formal consent, autonomy, and post hoc remedies increasingly fails to address systemic vulnerabilities and structural power asymmetries.[78] Likewise, the average consumer standard, central to much of EU consumer law, presumes a level of agency and information that is often absent in digital markets characterised by behavioural profiling and manipulative design.[79] These conditions reveal the inadequacy of existing tools to protect autonomy and fairness under digital conditions.

[74] A Diurni and D Riccio, 'Persone vulnerabili e tecnologie predittive' (2023) *Rivista Critica di Diritto Privato* 1, 47–53.

[75] B de Witte, 'The Role of General Principles in European Union Law' in D. Hanf, E. Vos, and B. de Witte (eds), *The Many Faces of Differentiation in EU Law* (Intersentia 2001) 131, 136–138.

[76] O Remien, 'Europäisches Privatrecht als Verfassungsfrage' (2005) EuR 699, 700–701.

[77] A Metzger, *Extra legem, intra ius: Allgemeine Rechtsgrundsätze im Europäischen Privatrecht* (Mohr Siebeck 2009) 99–108.

[78] Natali Helberger and others (n 5) 176–179.

[79] European Commission, 'Fitness Check of EU Consumer Law on Digital Fairness' SWD(2024) 230 final, 17–18.

Nonetheless, private law remains central to shaping digital legal relations. It governs contracts, establishes duties of care, and provides mechanisms for enforcement and redress. Its transformative potential lies in its capacity to incorporate structural normativity through general principles. Recognising vulnerability as such a principle would enable a recalibration of fairness, good faith, and balance, shifting the focus from individualised harm to systemic justice. This would allow private law to play a constitutive role in embedding values such as dignity, relational autonomy, and solidarity into the governance of digital interactions. Vulnerability provides the normative lens to correct the distributive effects of asymmetrical market conditions.[80] It also offers a mechanism for aligning private law with the overarching aims of EU law, including the internal market, fundamental rights, and the rule of law.[81]

Yet limitations persist. The reliance on judicial interpretation and the lack of positive obligations in private relationships may hinder the full implementation of structural fairness. The varying degrees of institutional embodiment across Member States, and the tension between market integration and national autonomy, can slow convergence.[82] Moreover, the abstract nature of general principles necessitates careful operationalisation through legislative mandates, enforcement practices, and design standards.

Private law, therefore, should not be viewed merely as a corrective mechanism, but as an active normative field capable of structuring equitable digital relations. Its capacity to evolve through principle-oriented reasoning positions it as a key vector in addressing vulnerability in digital markets, provided that its pluralistic foundations are mobilised towards coherent and enforceable normative outcomes.

[80] M Catanzariti (n 72) 1394–1405.

[81] A Metzger (n 77) 546–548.

[82] R Schulze and H Schulte-Nölke (eds), Europäisches Vertragsrecht im Gemeinschaftsrecht (Nomos 2002) 14–16.

7.5 Towards a General Principle of Law on Vulnerability

7.5.1 General Principles in EU Law: Functions and Flexibility

General principles in EU law serve as foundational interpretive instruments, enabling coherence across fragmented legal regimes and facilitating the legal system's capacity to respond to emerging social and technological challenges. In areas where statutory rules remain underdeveloped or conceptually outdated, general principles operate as normative scaffolding, shaping both legislative evolution and judicial interpretation.[83]

This function becomes increasingly vital in digital markets, in which vulnerability emerges as a transversal concept capable of bridging disparate domains such as personal data protection, consumer law, market regulation, or digital platform governance. The concept aligns closely with core general principles like fairness and justice, particularly in their function of protecting weaker parties and counterbalancing structural asymmetries.

Metzger's theory of general principles in private law provides a methodological and doctrinal basis for this integration. He argues that general principles derive their normative authority from inductive legal reasoning[84] and institutional recognition, rather than codification alone, and thus difficult to integrate into the conventional doctrine of legal sources. However, this is not an impediment for their legal validity as an independent source of law.[85] Vulnerability, understood as a condition of relational dependency or systemic exposure, satisfies these criteria. It is increasingly recognised across legislative instruments and judicial discourse, and it reflects the internal teleology of private law to safeguard autonomy under conditions of inequality.

In this light, a general principle of vulnerability would not merely fill doctrinal gaps but recalibrate the interpretation of foundational concepts such as fairness, consent, and autonomy across legal regimes. It allows for the systematic integration of structural considerations into legal

[83] A. Metzger (n 77) 99–108.

[84] Unlike in the empirical sciences, induction in legal thinking is not about drawing conclusions from observations of nature to 'synthetic' judgements, but rather to the conclusion from man-made norms (rules) to man-made norms (principles). See A. Metzger (n 77) 49.

[85] Ibid. 107–108.

reasoning, facilitating responses to forms of digital exploitation that transcend individual fault and consent-based paradigms. Thus, general principles in EU law can evolve from interpretive devices into normative anchors, reorienting private law towards its constitutional and social justice functions.

7.5.2 General Principles 2.0

To fulfil a structural role in private law, general principles must be operationalised beyond textual interpretation. Legal norms must inform the design of digital architectures ex ante, establishing binding parameters for fairness and protection. This implies a shift from law as remedy to law as infrastructure.[86]

This approach requires embedding legal principles directly into technical systems, aligning with the approach of legal design. Legal design applies human-centred methods to legal systems to ensure that regulatory objectives are not only legible but also actionable within digital environments.[87] It offers a method to translate normative principles such as fairness and dignity into operative system constraints and affordances.[88]

Design obligations in the GDPR, the AI Act, and the Data Act remain limited in scope and fragmented (if not impossible) in application. While provisions on privacy-by-design, transparency-by-default, and access-by-design-and-default exist, they lack a coherent normative basis and often reduce to procedural formalities. A general principle of vulnerability may be able to unify and substantiate these obligations, shifting their function from compliance mechanisms to enforceable guarantees grounded in structural fairness. This reallocation of normative weight would not merely assist users in managing risk but would reassign responsibility to those designing and deploying digital systems. General principles would thereby serve a constitutive function, enabling legal consistency across regulatory silos and reinforcing the role of private law as a framework for equitable digital relations.

[86] N Helberger and M Sax, 'Regulating Personalisation: From the Normative to the Technical' (2021) 40(5) Computer Law & Security Review 105,561.

[87] UX Collective, 'Legal Design Explained' (16 December 2021), available at: https://uxdesign.cc/legal-design-explained-e43129710cd9. Accessed 24 March, 2025.

[88] See R Ducato, A Strowel and E Marique (eds), *Design(s) for Law* (Ledizioni 2024).

7.5.3 *Can Vulnerability Be Normatively Anchored as a General Principle of EU Private Law?*

The possibility of anchoring vulnerability as a general principle of EU private law requires consideration of both methodological challenges and evolving normative frameworks. The scholarship of Axel Metzger, Hans-W. Micklitz, and Natali Helberger has played a foundational role in theorising how vulnerability might be normatively integrated into EU legal reasoning. These authors propose distinct but complementary approaches that converge on the idea that digitalisation and structural asymmetries necessitate a shift in the understanding of vulnerability—from an exception to a systemic, pervasive feature of private law.

Metzger defines general principles of law not as part of classical statutory sources but as inductively derived legal norms that acquire validity through recognition by norm addressees and some degree of institutional embodiment.[89] He further develops a procedural theory of general principles of law based on pragmatic induction, stressing that principles are not derived from definitive propositions but from presumed validity shaped by legal experience and comparative analysis.[90] His research underscores that general legal principles emerge from multi-layered sources—national, supranational, and international—and fulfil critical functions such as systematisation, coherence-building, and legal development. Importantly, in the context of European private law, these principles are not limited to the *acquis communautaire* but extend to comparative legal traditions and transnational norms, including *lex mercatoria* and public international law.[91] Vulnerability, in this framework, may qualify as such a principle due to its growing institutional recognition and role in guiding legal interpretation and system coherence.

Micklitz and Helberger have shown how the evolving digital economy collapses the traditional distinction between consumer and citizen.[92] For them, vulnerability is no longer a marginal condition but a default feature of digital subjectivity, necessitating regulatory responses beyond traditional consumer protection. In his theory of European private law, Micklitz contends that law must confront the internal contradiction between

[89] A Metzger (n 77) 99–108.

[90] A Metzger (n 77) 547–548.

[91] Ibid.

[92] See (n 14), (n 36), (n40), (n 47).

its commitment to **individual autonomy** and the reality of **market-driven asymmetries**. Vulnerability, he argues, exposes this contradiction and demands a legal response capable of redistributing structural power.[93] He thus sees general principles as mechanisms for embedding **social justice** within integration, turning private law into an instrument of **access justice** and **societal fairness**. **Helberger**, in turn, demonstrates that in digital markets, vulnerability is not an exception to autonomy, but a **constitutive condition**. Through empirical and doctrinal analysis, she shows that choice architectures are designed to **channel behaviour**, exploit **predictable irrationalities**, and suppress meaningful resistance to data extraction.[94]

In this regard, both explicitly support the idea of developing overarching principles—akin to general principles of law—that capture the normative shifts underway in EU private law. This aligns with Metzger's account of general principles of law as legal norms that evolve pragmatically to address systemic regulatory deficits. Furthermore, they conceptualise vulnerability in digital markets as an inherent feature of datafied choice architectures. Vulnerability is not merely relational but architectonic: it is embedded in technological systems designed to extract, profile, and manipulate consumer behaviour.[95] This reconceptualization challenges the efficacy of existing legal tools like transparency and consent. Digital markets architectures exploit consumer susceptibilities dynamically and contextually, thus rendering all users potentially vulnerable depending on how digital environments are configured.

Furthermore, Metzger's theory that general principles can be extrapolated from diverse normative sources—such as the foundational values of the EU, The Charter, and comparative constitutional traditions—supports this anchoring. The ECJ's historic use of principles like proportionality and effectiveness as interpretative tools lays the groundwork for extending the logic to vulnerability, especially given its increasing appearance in digital markets.[96] In support, Catanzariti argues that the ECtHR has already introduced vulnerability as an interpretative tool in its case

[93] H-W Micklitz, *(n 62)* 113–120.

[94] N Helberger and others, 'EU Consumer Protection 2.0: Structural Asymmetries in Digital Consumer Markets' (BEUC 2021) 15–22.

[95] See (n14) 10–18.

[96] A Metzger (n 77) 358.

law, particularly in non-discrimination and socio-economic rights. This uncodified but normatively resonant use of vulnerability reflects what she calls the 'juridification' of vulnerability.[97]

Taken together, the three frameworks make a compelling case: vulnerability is not only **doctrinally recognisable**, but also **normatively urgent**.

7.6 Conclusions: Vulnerability and Fairness as Structural Principles for the Digital Legal Order

This contribution has shown that vulnerability is no longer an incidental element of digital market dynamics, but a structural condition deeply embedded in the design of digital services and infrastructures. In this context, fairness must be understood not only as a procedural safeguard or an ex post corrective mechanism, but also as a normative compass for shaping legal responses to digital asymmetries.

The systemic nature of vulnerability, evident in algorithmic opacity, data extraction, and interface design, calls for legal tools that operate proactively and preventively. Addressing these issues requires moving beyond the individualised lens of conventional consumer law towards an integrated model of regulation that builds safeguards into the architecture of digital systems.

This reorientation necessitates a recalibration of core legal concepts in EU private law. Existing constructs such as the average consumer, consent, and transparency are increasingly outpaced by the realities of profiling, manipulation, and ambient influence. Fairness, when grounded in vulnerability, offers a unifying principle capable of restoring balance and promoting relational autonomy in the face of structural digital power.

Recognising vulnerability as a general principle of EU private law provides the normative basis for this transformation. It enables consistency in legal reasoning, supports coherence across regulatory fields, and affirms the role of law in shaping equitable digital markets. By serving as a guiding norm, vulnerability informs interpretation, regulation, and enforcement across the digital legal landscape.

The to be proposed Digital Fairness Act can offer a key institutional opportunity to codify this development. But as both critical scholarship

[97] M Catanzariti (n 72) 1394–1405.

and regulatory experience suggest, codification alone is insufficient. For fairness to have transformative potential, it must be constructed collaboratively, through design mandates, empirical audits, and cross-sectoral engagement with technologists, legal scholars, and consumer advocates. Legal accountability must evolve accordingly: away from isolated breaches and towards system-level responsibility.

Further research is needed to assess how a general principle of vulnerability might operate across legal domains. Comparative studies could illuminate how other jurisdictions, especially in Latin America and Asia, are addressing similar challenges in their AI governance frameworks. Likewise, empirical legal research is essential to evaluate whether emerging interventions—such as fairness audits or algorithmic impact assessments—genuinely mitigate harm or merely simulate compliance.

In conclusion, vulnerability and fairness are not merely regulatory concerns, they are foundational legal questions for a democratic digital society. A principled approach to them will offer a path towards legal resilience, institutional coherence, and justice in the age of AI and other digital technologies.

References

Acemoglu D and Johnson S, *Power and Progress: Our Thousand-Year Struggle Over Technology and Prosperity* (PublicAffairs 2023).

Black, J 'Decentring Regulation: Understanding the Role of Regulation and Self-Regulation in a 'Post-Regulatory' World.' Current Legal Problems (2001) 54(1): 103–146.

Catanzariti M, 'The juridification of vulnerability in the European legal culture', Oñati Socio-Legal Series, 12(6), pp. 1391–1416. https://doi.org/10.35295/osls.iisl/0000-0000-0000-1314

Cotino L, 'Vulnerabilidad y colectivos vulnerables en el derecho: ¿quiénes son y cómo se definen?' (18 December 2024) *Revista Catalana de Dret Públic Blog* https://eapc-rcdp.blog.gencat.cat/2024/12/18/vulnerabilidad-y-colectivos-vulnerables-en-el-derecho-quienes-son-y-como-se-definen-lorenzo-cotino/.

Council of Europe, *Access to Justice for Vulnerable Groups in Azerbaijan* (Council of Europe 2023) https://rm.coe.int/access-to-justice-for-vulnerable-groups-in-azerbaijan-eng/1680a31544.

Crea C and De Franceschi A (eds), *The New Shapes of Digital Vulnerability in European Private Law* (Nomos 2024).

Diurni A and Riccio D, 'Persone vulnerabili e tecnologie predittive' (2023) *Rivista Critica di Diritto Privato* 1, 47–53.

European Commission Staff Working Document, *Fitness Check of EU Consumer Law on Digital Fairness* SWD(2024) 230 final.

European Commission, 'Digital Fairness Act: Call for Evidence' (2024) https://www.digital-fairness-act.com.

Floridi L and others, 'AI4People's Ethical Framework for a Good AI Society: Opportunities, Risks, Principles, and Recommendations' (2018) 28 *Minds and Machines* 689, 694–700.

Goanta C, 'European Consumer Law: The Hero of Our Times' (2021) 9 *Journal of European Consumer and Market Law* 2, 5.

Gonzalez Otero B, 'AI for Good: Questioning the Idea of Human Vulnerability' (6 September 2024) *OdiseIA* https://www.odiseia.org/en/post/ai-for-good-la-idea-de-la-vulnerabilidad-humana-en-tela-de-juicio.

Grochowski, M 'Digital Vulnerability in a Post-Consumer Society. Subverting Paradigms?' in C. Crea and A De Franceschi (eds.), *The New Shapes of Digital Vulnerability in European Private Law* (Nomos, 2024) 201–226.

Groussot X, Zemskova A and Gill-Pedro E, 'Towards General Principles 2.0: The Application of General Principles of EU Law in the Digital Society' (2019) *Lund University Legal Research Paper Series* No 02/2019, 3–4 https://ssrn.com/abstract=3473681.

Helberger N and others, 'EU Consumer Protection 2.0: Structural Asymmetries in Digital Consumer Markets' (BEUC 2021) 15–22.

Helberger N and others, *Digital Fairness for Consumers* (BEUC, March 2024) https://www.beuc.eu/reports/digital-fairness-consumers.

Helberger N, Sax M, Strycharz J and Micklitz H-W, 'Choice Architectures in the Digital Economy: Towards a New Understanding of Digital Vulnerability' (2022) 45 *Journal of Consumer Policy* 175, 177–178.

Hense P and Mustać T, *AI Act Compact: Compliance, Management & Use Cases in Corporate Practice* (DFV Mediengruppe 2025)

Luna F, 'Elucidating the Concept of Vulnerability: Layers Not Labels' (2009) 2(1) *International Journal of Feminist Approaches to Bioethics* 121–139.

Malgieri G and Rebrean M, 'Vulnerability in the AI Act: Building an Interpretation' (2024) *SSRN Working Paper* 5058591. https://papers.ssrn.com/sol3/papers.cfm?abstract_id=5058591.

Metzger A, 'General Principles of Law' in *Max Planck Encyclopedia of European Private Law* (Max-EuP 2012) https://max-eup2012.mpipriv.de/index.php/General_Principles_of_Law.

Metzger A, *Extra legem, intra ius: Allgemeine Rechtsgrundsätze im Europäischen Privatrecht* (Mohr Siebeck 2009).

Metzger A, Schweitzer H and Wagner G, 'Datenschutz und Datenmarkt: Grundzüge einer Marktordnung für die europäische Datenwirtschaft' (2023) *Zeitschrift für die gesamte Privatrechtswissenschaft (ZfPW)* 227.

Micklitz H-W and Villanueva A, 'Responsibilities of Companies in the Algorithmic Society' in H-W Micklitz and others (eds), *Constitutional Challenges in the Algorithmic Society* (Cambridge University Press 2021) 267–291.

Micklitz H-W, *The Politics of Justice in European Private Law: Social Justice, Access Justice, Societal Justice* (CUP 2018).

Muñoz C, '¿Protege el Reglamento de IA a los vulnerables?' (OdiseIA, 2024) https://www.odiseia.org/post/protege-el-reglamento-de-ia-a-los-vulnerables.

Remien O, 'Europäisches Privatrecht als Verfassungsfrage' (2005) *EuR* 699.

Sax M and Helberger N, 'Digital Vulnerability and Manipulation in the Emerging Digital Framework' in Helberger N and others, *Digital Fairness for Consumers* (BEUC, March 2024) https://www.beuc.eu/reports/digital-fairness-consumers.

Sax M and Helberger N, 'Regulating Personalisation: From the Normative to the Technical' (2021) 40(5) *Computer Law & Security Review* 105561.

Schulze R, 'Conclusions' in C Crea and F De Francheschi (eds), *The New Shapes of Digital Vulnerability in European Private Law* (Nomos 2024) 521–523.

Scott, C 'Regulation in the Age of Governance: The Rise of the Post-Regulatory State' in David Levi-Faur and Jacint Jordana (eds), The Politics of Regulation: Institutions and Regulatory Reforms for the Age of Governance (Edward Elgar 2004) Chapter 7.

UX Collective, 'Legal Design Explained' (16 December 2021) https://uxdesign.cc/legal-design-explained-e43129710cd9.

Case-Law.

Case C-210/96 *Gut Springenheide and Tusky* [1998] ECR I-4657, para 31.

Case C-421/12 *Commission v Belgium* [2014] ECLI:EU:C:2014:2064, paras 17–21.

Case C-446/21 *Bundeskartellamt v Meta Platforms Inc and Others*, Opinion of AG Rantos, ECLI:EU:C:2022:658, 20 September 2022, paras 22–25.

Case C-628/17 *Orange România* [2019] ECLI:EU:C:2019:480, paras 44–46.

Case C-673/17 *Bundesverband der Verbraucherzentralen v Planet49 GmbH* [2019] ECLI:EU:C:2019:801, paras 62–63.

Case C-673/17 *Planet49* ECLI:EU:C:2019:801; Case C-61/19 *Orange România* ECLI:EU:C:2020:901; Case C-421/12 *Commission v Belgium* ECLI:EU:C:2014:2064.

CHAPTER 8

International Law Between Enhanced Anthropocentrism and Post-anthropocentrism: The Need for an International Treaty on Bio-technological Ethics

Themistoklis Tzimas

Proposals such as those advocating the prevalence of human design over natural selection or different forms of digital immortality have moved from science-fiction to scientific discourse, raising serious ethical and legal questions. The present article attempts to distinguish between enhancement and techno-ontological post-anthropocentrism focusing on the role of biotechnologies, as well as to identify the legal principles that should guide us through a relevant international treaty, in order to preserve legal anthropocentrism.

T. Tzimas (✉)
Aristotle University of Thessaloniki, Thessaloniki, Greece
e-mail: thtzimas@polsci.auth.gr

A. Aliu (ed.), *Artificial Intelligence and the Rule of Law*,
https://doi.org/10.1007/978-3-031-97389-5_8

8.1 Introduction

What used to be the realm of science-fiction is quickly entering the area of scientific and public discourse[1] With artificial intelligence—AI—in combination with advanced biotechnologies, standing at the epicenter of techno-utopian promises and techno-dystopian threats simultaneously, a flux of promises and warnings is dominating the headlines: unprecedented wealth accumulation, longer, healthier or even eternal, digital and natural lives, human enhancement of various levels potentially reaching the era of transhumanism through the synergies of human and artificial intelligence; the fall of "Anthropocene" seems imminent in favor of an era of enhanced humans, machines or the hybrids of humans and machines.[2] An era in which humans will transform ontologically into something "other-than-human", "other-than-completely-human" or will be obsolete in favor of other, superior intelligent beings.

The concepts of "enhanced anthropocentrism" and "post-anthropocentrism" in such a framework are emerging as central in an interdisciplinary scientific and public debate, involving philosophy, law, engineering, biology, computer science, artificial intelligence, with the former referring mainly to enhanced humans—of whatever type—whereas the latter to "other-than-humans".[3] Enhanced anthropocentrism

[1] In the present article, the definition of AI that is adopted is the one of the EU AI act, which defines AI as "…a machine-based system that is designed to operate with varying levels of autonomy and that may exhibit adaptiveness after deployment, and that, for explicit or implicit objectives, infers, from the input it receives, how to generate outputs such as predictions, content, recommendations, or decisions that can influence physical or virtual environments".

Regulation (EU) 2024/1689 of the European Parliament and of the Council of 13 June 2024 laying down harmonised rules on artificial intelligence and amending Regulations (EC) No 300/2008, (EU) No 167/2013, (EU) No 168/2013, (EU) 2018/858, (EU) 2018/1139 and (EU) 2019/2144 and Directives 2014/90/EU, (EU) 2016/797 and (EU) 2020/1828 (Artificial Intelligence Act) (Text with EEA relevance), Article 3 (hereinafter, EU AI Act).

[2] Daniel Nemenyi,. 'Robot Makes Free: The Leibnizian Cryptowar of Norbert Wiener' [2023] 2.14 Radical Philosophy 3; Savin-Baden, M., D. Burden, 'Digital Immortality and Virtual Humans' [2019] 1, Postdigit Sci Educ, 87–103; Jenny Huberman, 'Immortality transformed: mind cloning, transhumanism and the quest for digital immortality' [2018], 23:1, Mortality, 50–64; Eric Charles Steinhart, Your digital afterlives (Palgrave MacMillan, 2014); David Burden & Maggie Savin-Baden, Virtual humans, (Taylor and Francis, 2019).

[3] Savin-Baden, M., D. Burden, 'Digital Immortality and Virtual Humans' [2019] 1, Postdigit Sci Educ, 87–103; Jenny Huberman, 'Immortality transformed: mind cloning,

can be identified with transhumanism at a significant extent, which is why in the section below transhumanism is analyzed.

In light of the two concepts and the uncertainty that they bring, law has to come forth with answers at the international level. Issues of biotechnological ethics and regulations guiding us regarding what can be in principle allowed and encouraged and what not, become a new necessity. In the part below, a more detailed examination of the afore-mentioned concepts is presented.

8.2 Characteristics of Transhumanism or Enhanced Anthropocentrism and Post-anthropocentrism

Human enhancement in principle refers to "...interventions [that] aim to improve the state of an organism beyond its normal healthy state".[4] The goal is to improve "human dispositions, capacities and well-being", through any kind of genetic, biomedical or pharmaceutical intervention.[5] While sounding quite exotic as a term, enhancement is in reality as old as humanity and omni-present. It is characteristic that one of the key-areas of enhancement, cognitive enhancement, involves technologies that transcend the boundaries of science-fiction such as synergies of human and artificial intelligence but also much more conventional tools such as caffeine, exercise, sleep and meditation.[6] The adoption of artificial intelligence and robotics interventions must also be mentioned.[7]

Human enhancement is not new. The efforts to enhance human nature are diachronically everywhere around us: from praying to education

transhumanism and the quest for digital immortality' [2018], 23:1, Mortality, 50–64; Eric Charles Steinhart, Your digital afterlives (Palgrave MacMillan, 2014); David Burden & Maggie Savin-Baden, Virtual humans, (Taylor and Francis, 2019).

[4] Nick Bostrom & Rebecca Roache, Ethical Issues in Human Enhancement, in J. Ryberg (Editor), T. Petersen (Editor), C. Wolf (Editor), New Waves in Applied Ethics (New Waves in Philosophy), 2007.

[5] Alberto Giubilini and Sagar Sanyal, Challenging Human Enhancement, in C. A. J. Coady, Alberto Giubilini, Sagar Sanyal eds., The Ethics of Human Enhancement: Understanding the Debate, (2016, Oxford University Press), at p. 1.

[6] Erden, Y. J., & Brey, P. A. (2022). Ethics guidelines for human enhancement R&D. Science, 378(6622), at pp. 835–838.

[7] Ibid.

systems, from personal exercise to modern day drugs, from eye-glasses to usual—or not so usual—prosthetics we humans have been trying to enhance our nature in every possible way.

A traditional dichotomy is the one between enhancement and therapy, according to which enhancement refers to improvement of the human organism beyond its normal status, whereas therapy to curing the human organism when it is in a state of disease or injury. Such distinction is problematic for various reasons. The definition of health by the World Health Organization is enlightening: "Health is a state of complete physical, mental and social well-being and not merely the absence of disease or infirmity".[8]

Such a holistic approach to health profoundly blurs the lines between the two concepts. For instance, what about cosmetic surgery that aims to improve the way that people feel about themselves? Geriatrics, vaccination, cognitive improvements and even glasses are all means to improve and enhance human organism but nobody will deny their therapeutic nature as well. In addition, aging is gradually approached as the ultimate disease and therefore its cure as the ultimate goal which transcends the boundaries between enhancement and therapy, making the aforementioned distinction almost obsolete.

As Eric Juengst and Daniel Moseley comment, the same technologies and practices can be used both for therapeutic and enhancement reasons, depending on the scope of their use.[9] Disease is a cultural project and even more so the physical, mental and social well-being. This does not mean however that the well-being and of course the absence of disease are arbitrary categorizations. It is on the grounds of medical experts, research, law but also "social contract" between the peoples and the governments to determine the outer boundaries of the interpretation of these terms.

Since the reference to therapy can be partially misleading, it is difficult to imagine how enhancement can be enhancement—and not merely an eccentricity—while not serving the well-being. Therefore, the most accurate definition in the framework of transhumanism could be rephrased as following: "enhancement are biomedical, AI and robotic interventions

[8] Constitution of the World Health Organization, Preamble.

[9] Eric Juengst and Daniel Moseley, 'Human Enhancement' in Edward N Zalta (ed), The Stanford Encyclopedia of Philosophy (Summer 2019 Edition) https://plato.stanford.edu/archives/sum2019/entries/enhancement/.

that are used to improve human form or functioning beyond what is necessary regarding the absence of disease or infirmity".

Once this distinction becomes obsolete or at least too vague to be sustained, the discussion about human enhancement deepens and is succeeded by a different distinction: the one between human enhancement or enhanced anthropocentrism and the technologies or procedures leading to beings "other-than-human", which fall in the wider framework of post-anthropocentrism.

The afore-mentioned "enhanced anthropocentrism" is widely described as transhumanism, given that it is founded on the concept of human enhancement. It is on the basis of this relationship that transhumanism is analyzed in the present chapter. Transhumanism in the well-known "Transhumanist Movement Manifesto" is defined as: "... a worldview that seeks a quality of life that brings about perpetual progress, self-transformation, practical optimism, visionary solutions, and critical thinking—the transhuman. The transhuman is a biological-technological organism, a transformation of the human species that continues to evolve with technology...".[10]

Transhumanism describes at its core the effort to transcend and enhance human biology through technology. As Dieter Birnbacher wrote: "Transhumanists want us to enter upon a process that will ultimately lead to "post-humanity" by attempting, now and in the near future, to transcend certain limits inherent in the human condition as we know it".[11] According to Nick Bostrom, transhumanism refers to human evolution in the sense of a "globally coordinated policy to control human evolution by modifying the fitness function of future intelligent life forms".[12] Transhumanism describes the modification of the human nature.

In Julian Huxley's, one of the founders of the transhumanist movement, own words: the truth of the transhumanist approach and its central conception is larger and more universal than any previous truth, and is

[10] The Transhumanist Manifesto, <https://www.humanityplus.org/the-transhumanist-manifesto>, access. 9/3/2024.

[11] Diter Birnbacher, 'Posthumanity, Transhumanism and Human Nature', in Bert Gordijn & Ruth Chadwick (eds.) Medical Enhancement and Posthumanity, (Springer, 2008), 95.

[12] Nick Bostrom, The Future of Human Evolution https://nickbostrom.com/fut/evo lution accessed 11 March 2024.

bound in the long run to supersede lesser, more partial or more distorted truths, such as Marxism, Christian Theology or liberal individualism.[13]

Transhumanism constitutes essentially a cultural movement. At its core, there is human enhancement through the use of various technologies and therefore the exercise of some type and extent of control of human evolution.[14] In all its different versions, transhumanism proposes the use of technology and some type of human design for the enhancement of the human nature instead—at least partially—of natural selection.

Extropians who constitute part of the wider transhumanist movement in their "manifesto" called "Extropian Principles", list 7 fundamental principles: perpetual progress, self-transformation, practical optimism, intelligent technology, open society, self-direction and rational thinking.[15] Perpetual progress is expected to lead us eventually to post-humanism.

For transhumanists, progress consists in the transcendence of human biological limits from an individualistic perspective, within which individual desire constitutes not only the driving force but also an individual right that must be respected and preserved in furtherance of human enhancement. The opponents of transhumanism have a lot to counter. Steven Hoffman argues that transhumanism is both materialistic and reductionist in terms of the interpretation of human nature.[16] This is what makes transhumanism philosophically untenable and scientifically unfounded according to Hoffman: the effort to reduce what it means to be human to biology and more specifically to the molecular level, therefore underestimating what can be categorized as the cultural aspects of humanity.[17] The afore-mentioned approach, identifying human nature with the mind and the mind with a neurobiological machine which can be emulated on another, non-organic, material basis explains the impact of

[13] Julian Huxley, New Bottles for New Wine (Chatto & Windus 1957) 260.

[14] Ibid. at p. 17; Francesca Ferrando, 'Posthumanism, Transhumanism, Antihumanism, Metahumanism, and New Materialisms: Differences and Relations' (2013) 8(2) Existenz 26, 27; Ronald Bailey, Liberation Biology: The Scientific and Moral Case for the Biotech Revolution (Prometheus 2005); James Hughes, Citizen Cyborg: Why Democratic Societies Must Respond to the Redesigned Human of the Future (Westview Press 2004).

[15] Max More, The Extropian Principles, Version 3.0, A Transhumanist Declaration (1998) https://www.mrob.com/pub/religion/extro_prin.html accessed 7 April 2024.

[16] Steven A Hoffman, 'Transhumanist Materialism: A Critique from Immunoneuropsychology' in Stefan Lorenz Sorgner (ed), Beyond Humanism: Trans- and Posthumanism (Peter Lang 2005) 274.

[17] Ibid., at p. 275.

AI on transhumanism but also—according to its opponents—shows the naivety and the risks of this movement.[18]

Post–anthropocentrism is—even—more complicated as it includes various versions. In philosophical terms, it has been described—in differentiation from transhumanism or enhanced anthropocentrism—as the approach suggesting that contrary to industrial revolution-oriented ideas, human is not dominant over nature and other beings but an integral part of the planet—or the cosmos. The philosophical argument for post-anthropocentrism fundamentally consists in that the idea of human dominance is outdated.[19] For a large part of "post-anthropocentrists", even transhumanism is the step toward at least some forms of post-anthropocentrism.

For post-anthropocentrists, the main goal is the substitution of human dominion. Such substitution can take various forms which may end up being contradictory: from the emergence of ultra-humans to the obsoleteness of humans due to the emergence of some hybrid form of human and artificial intelligence or the philosophical-legal adherence to a world view arguing that we, humans are only one of the various species instead of the dominant one. Post-anthropocentrism, essentially consists in that our world is not, should not or will not be human-centered. Pepperell argued that: "Humanists might regard humans as distinct beings, in an antagonistic relationship with their surroundings. Post-humanists, on the other hand, regard humans as embodied in an extended technological world».[20]

According to Max More—aka Max O' Conner-humanity is a "transitional stage standing between our animal heritage and our post-human future", which—the future—will be shaped by "genetic engineering, life-extending biosciences, intelligence intensifiers, smarter interfaces to swifter computers, neural-computer integration, world-wide data networks, virtual reality, intelligent agents, swift electronic communication, artificial intelligence, neuroscience, neural networks, artificial life,

[18] Nick Bostrom, 'Transhumanist Values' (2001) http://www.nickbostrom.com/tra/values.html accessed 14 September 2024.

[19] Francesca Ferrando, 'Existential Posthumanism: A Manifesto' in Rosi Braidotti, et al. (eds.) More Posthuman Glossary, (Bloomsbury, 2023), pp. 47–49.

[20] Robert Pepperell, 'Posthumans and Extended Experience' (2005) 14 Journal of Evolution and Technology 34.

off-planet migration, and molecular nanotechnology".[21] These supreme beings will be free of natural environment restrictions.

Post-anthropocentrism describes a procedure during which humans will have evolved to a different form of beings—a form of ultra-humanism-or will be obsolete—a form of antihumanism. Post-anthropocentric philosophers often expect "humans to think beyond their traditional humanist limitations and embrace the risks that becoming-other-than-human beings".[22] Or in other words: "In the post humanist thought, the human is no longer [...] the adoption or the expression of man but rather the result of a hybridization of man with non-human otherness".[23]

The relationship therefore between transhumanism or enhanced anthropocentrism and post-anthropocentrism is complicated. On the one hand, transhumanism can lead to some form of post-anthropocentrism—in fact it is expected to do so. As it is noted in the World Transhumanism Association: "post-human may be completely synthetic (based on artificial intelligence), or be the result of numerous, gradual, biological improvements, what will be ending with the creation of a new post-human race. Some post-humans may even acknowledge that it could be useful to get rid of their bodies and live as information patterns on huge, super-fast computer networks".[24] On the other hand, they are concepts of different philosophical foundation: the primary is founded on the goal of enhanced anthropocentrism. The latter on overcoming anthropocentrism in favor of "other-than-human" beings.

Transhumanism in addition, constitutes in principle an enlightenment-oriented approach in furtherance of an enhanced form of humanity, which however may eventually lead either to some form of ultra-humanism but

[21] Ibid.

[22] Roberto Braidotti The Posthuman. Cambridge: Polity Press. Review' (2013) Culture Machine 2.

[23] Roberto Marchesini, 'Ruolo delle alterità nella definizione dei predicati umani' in Pietro Barcellona, Fabio Ciaramelli e Roberto Fai (eds), Apocalisse e post-umano. Il crepuscolo della modernità (Dedalo 2007) 54.

[24] Ewa Walewska, 'Trans-, Post-/-Humanizm, -człowiek. Transformacje' (2011) 3(4) Cuadernos de Bioética 315, 316.

also of post-anthropocentrism.[25] Transhumanism is built on the assumption of human superiority and reason which is expected to be capable of mastering completely nature. As Julian Savulescu says: "Humanity until this point has been a story of evolution for the survival genes—survival and reproduction ... we are entering a new phase of human evolution—evolution under reason—where human beings are masters of their destiny. Power has been transferred from nature to science".[26]

Post-anthropocentrism constitutes a rupture with enlightenment theories, advocating the relativization or complete negation of human superiority.[27] Post-anthropocentrism de-constructs human primacy and supremacy.[28] Postmodernity and post-anthropocentrism involve voluntaristic individualism.[29]

Despite their differences in terms of philosophical orientation, post-anthropocentrism and transhumanism share the centrality of technology as means of altering human nature. Both concepts suggest that human nature can and must be transformed—improved, enhanced or substituted depending on the perspective. This goal, for certain "versions" both of trans and post-anthropocentrists passes through a fundamental transformation: the transformation consists in human interferences in natural selection which may escalate even up to complete substitution of natural selection by human design and selection.[30] This is the crux of confrontations around transhumanism and techno-ontological post-anthropocentrism.

[25] Bradley B. Onishi, 'Information, Bodies, and Heidegger: Tracing Visions of the Posthuman' (2011) 50(1) Sophia 101, 112.

[26] Julian Savulescu, 'Human-Animal Transgenesis and Chimeras Might Be an Expression of Our Humanity' (2003) 3(3) Journal of Bioethics 22, 24.

[27] Roland Barthes, The Death of the Author (Fontana 1977) 142–148.

[28] Gianni Vattimo, The End of Modernity: Nihilism and Hermeneutics in Postmodern Culture (trans Jon R Snyder, The John Hopkins University Press 1988).

[29] Amalia Quevedo, De Foucault a Derrida: pasando fugazmente por Deleuze y Guattari, Lyotard, Baudrillard (Eunsa 2001); Luis Miguel Pastor and José Ángel García Cuadrado, 'Modernity and Postmodernity in the Genesis of Transhumanism-Posthumanism' (2014) 25(3) Cuadernos de Bioética 335, 342–344.

[30] Stefan Lorenz Sorgner, 'Beyond Humanism: Reflections on Trans- and Posthumanism' (2010) 21(2) Journal of Evolution and Technology 1, 2.

These aspirations of transhumanism and post-anthropocentrism raise ethical and eventually legal issues in relation to their specific applications especially regarding interventions in human biology. The type of ethical approaches per se constitutes a matter of debate as well. Due to the need to foresee and regulate in advance technologies that bring with them the potential transformations of human biology, the concept of the so-called speculative ethics, which is based on "a set of unknowns, or unverified social, empirical, and scientific knowledge about the future" is emerging.[31]

While speculative ethics can help us raise issues regarding potential transformations of the human condition, it has also been criticized as overwhelming present problems and considerations.[32] It is in this framework that anticipatory ethics have been proposed, involving various methods: systematic, strategic and proactive approaches to emerging technologies in the framework of which, foresight is adopted as well.[33] They are mainly focused on foresight meaning on envisioning multiple futures in anticipation of which ethical guidelines are proposed.[34]

Ethics related to technology and in particular enhanced anthropocentrism and post-anthropocentrism in fact need to be focused on both the present and the future. While present problems are more obvious and, in this sense, they seem more important, the problems of the future can also be equally significant and fast approaching.[35] Therefore, the present problems are not necessarily the primary ones and the ethical debates can extend from the present to the future, not in a linear way. In addition, the formulation of ethical priorities constitutes also a matter of debate and concern, given the impact of market economy, as well as of various academic, political and philosophical "schools" of thought.

[31] Racine, Eric, Rubio, Tristana Martin, Chandler, Jennifer, Forlini, Cynthia, & Lucke, Jayne (2014). The value and pitfalls of speculation about science and technology in bioethics: The case of cognitive enhancement. Medicine, Health Care and Philosophy, 17(3), 325–337, at p. 327.

[32] Nordmann, Alfred (2007). If and then: A critique of speculative nanoethics. NanoEthics, 1(1), 31–46.

[33] Jon Rueda, The ethics of doing human enhancement ethics, (2023), 153, Futures.

[34] Gariboldi, Isabella, Maria, Lin, Vivian, Bland, Jessica, Auplish, Mallika, & Cawthorne, Amy (2021).Foresight in the time of COVID-19. The Lancet Regional Health—Western Pacific, 6, Article 100049.

[35] Zohny, Hazem (2021). Future versus present morality. In David Edmonds (Ed.), Future morality (pp. 3–12). Oxford: OUP.

Ethical debates are not only philosophical but normative as well. Law has to adapt in order to expand its regulatory capacity so that it can cover a period from the present until the various potential futures. In order to examine such potential transformations, we must first examine some basic elements of anthropocentrism of law in order to examine the limits and boundaries of law regarding the area under examination.

8.3 Legal Anthropocentrism

The theme under examination necessitates an understanding of anthropocentrism in law—i.e., legal anthropocentrism. Anthropocentrism in law does not necessarily imply a complete subjugation of all nature and non-human beings to humans or the exclusivity of humans as legal subjects. What is central under legal anthropocentrism is that humans are distinguished by "other-than-humans" in a binary relationship and that humans constitute the dominant species ontologically and in terms of legal personality.[36]

Under law, what it means to be "human" has been empirically and therefore legally, self-obvious, thanks to common sense.[37] Human is "human-in-nature" and has been recognized as self-obvious under law.[38] Historically there are legal differentiations and heated confrontations about the level of legal personality that each human must have, on grounds of biological conditions—age, disabilities, disease, gender—or legal conditions—national of a state or not, free or slave, free or imprisoned, male or female etc. For the most part, however, these are legal fictions not actual ontological debates. The ontology of humanness is not seriously doubted under legal systems—at least current ones and since decades ago—with the exemption of embryos where their non-presence

[36] Andy Miah, A Critical History of Posthumanism (Springer 2008) 86.

[37] Dieter Birnbacher, 'Posthumanity, Transhumanism and Human Nature' in Anthony Mark Cutter and others (eds), Medical Enhancement and Posthumanity (Springer 2008) 98.

[38] Historically and until the emergence of the cyberspace we could never see human out of nature.

independently in the natural environment has raised doubts about their ontological and legal identification as complete humans and since when.[39]

Therefore, legal anthropocentrism is primarily built on common sense and the prevalence of self-obviousness regarding who is human and who is not, which sustains the binary identification with all, "other-than-human" entities.[40] On the one hand, this binary distinction is also founded on common sense whereas on the other hand there is an additional reason: if we cannot be certain about what is human and what is not, how can we maintain an anthropocentric legal system?

In addition, legal anthropocentrism is also founded on our self-obviously superior intelligence and conscious existence, which in a deeper sense takes the form of a moral consciousness.[41] As Neil Levy explains "... consciousness of some of the facts that give our actions their moral significance is a necessary condition for moral responsibility".[42]

All major international, human rights treaties are characteristic in these regards. In the Universal Declaration of Human Rights, there is no definition of the term "human family". As the Universal Declaration of Human Rights-UDHR—and after UDHR a series of international treaties on human rights foresee all members of the "human family" possess "inherent dignity" "and ... equal and inalienable rights", merely from the fact that they are members of the "human family".[43] The term "human family" is not defined, exactly because we know who is human when we see one. The fact that merely from human nature a number of rights flows which are labeled as inherent and inalienable is indicative of a natural—law foundation of human rights. We have these rights simply because we

[39] The definition of ontology that is adopted in particular is the following: "[T]he science of categorization of objects and relations". It is founded on the empirical verifiability thanks to objective facts.

[40] Andrew Feenberg, Technosystem: The Social Life of Reason (Harvard University Press 2017) 20.

[41] Pauline Kleingeld, Moral consciousness and the 'fact of reason', in Jens Timmerman and Andrews Reath, Kant's 'Critique of Practical Reason': A Critical Guide. (Cambridge University Press, 2010), 55.

[42] Neil Levy, Consciousness and Moral Responsibility, (Oxford University Press, 2014), 1.

[43] Universal Declaration of Human Rights, Preamble https://www.un.org/en/about-us/universal-declaration-of-human-rights accessed 8 September 2024.

are born humans.[44] UDHR is built on the assumption of the existence of a common human nature. Such is the wording of the European Convention of Human Rights which refers to "fundamental freedoms" without any need of further ontological explanation, being also founded upon human rights and UDHR.[45] The African Charter of Human Rights—ACHR—holds in the preamble that "...fundamental human rights stem from the attributes of human beings..." and in article 4 that "Human beings are inviolable..."[46] There is no need to define who is human; we know one when we see her/him.

The afore-mentioned legal documents are characteristic in depicting legal anthropocentrism. The latter and human rights as part of it, are founded on natural law which, as already mentioned, implies a common human nature which defines us as humans, does not change over time and binds us all over some common experiences.[47] If it did change, then human rights would be conditional upon certain changing ontological preconditions which should be re-defined over time.

Legal anthropocentrism is not unbreachable obviously. Advocates of the recognition of environmental personhood have achieved significant breakthroughs in the expansion of legal personality to non-biological, environmental entities.[48] Legal anthropocentrism is accused of establishing intra-species and inter-species hierarchies.[49] While the critique to legal anthropocentrism can be helpful in relation to environmental issues and the attribution of legal personality to non-human entities, it

[44] "All human beings are born free and equal in dignity and rights. They are endowed with reason and conscience and should act towards one another in a spirit of brotherhood". Ibid, Article 1.

[45] Convention for the Protection of Human Rights and Fundamental Freedoms as amended by Protocol No 15 https://rm.coe.int/1680a2353d accessed 9 September 2024.

[46] African Charter on Human and Peoples' Rights https://www.oas.org/en/sla/dil/docs/African_Charter_Human_Peoples_Rights.pdf accessed 9 September 2024.

[47] William Starr, 'Law and Morality in HLA Hart's Legal Philosophy' (1984) 67(4) Marquette Law Review 673, 689.

[48] Jade-Ann Reeves & Timothy D. Peters Responding to anthropocentrism with anthropocentrism: the biopolitics of environmental personhood, (2021), 30:3, Griffith Law Review, 474 at 475.

[49] Anna Grear, Deconstructing Anthropos: A Critical Legal Reflection on 'Anthropocentric' Law and Anthropocene 'Humanity', (2015) 26, Law Critique, 225, at 230.

is not particularly helpful in relation to the area under examination. The afore-mentioned post-anthropocentrism primarily refers to a non-human-centered legal and philosophical approach, which can be insightful but still does not question the binary distinction between human and other-than-human, the self-obviousness of "Anthropos", the diachronic human nature, as well as the superiority of human in terms of intelligence and consciousness. In such a framework, legal post-anthropocentrism constitutes primarily a proposal about the formulation of law, not negation of the foundations of present legal anthropocentrism.

Summing up, present legal anthropocentrism is founded not primarily on hierarchies around "Anthropos" or the on preservation of the privilege of legal personality only for humans but the empirically verified, self-obvious ontological perception about who is human and who is not, subsequently about the existence of a unique, common among us all and diachronic human phenotype and nature which we understand as such when we see it, on the binary distinction between human and "other-than-human" as well as on the superiority of Anthropos as a moral, conscious person. There are two predominant manifestations of legal anthropocentrism: the superiority of humans in law as the sole complete legal personalities and the afore-mentioned binary relationship between humans and "other-than-human" beings. The framework of human rights law is not the only manifestation of legal anthropocentrism but also the most emblematic one. It is on such grounds that we must envisage legal principles ahead of the potential developments of enhanced anthropocentrism or transhumanism and techno-ontological post-anthropocentrism.[50]

[50] Arthur O Lovejoy, The Great Chain of Being: A Study of the History of an Idea (Harvard University Press 1936).

8.4 Legal Principles for an International Treaty, ahead of Enhanced Anthropocentrism/Transhumanism and Techno-ontological Post-anthropocentrism

In the previous parts the fundamental characteristics of enhanced anthropocentrism or transhumanism, and techno-ontological post-anthropocentrism are presented, as well as the fundamental elements of legal anthropocentrism.[51]

As mentioned above, transhumanism's main ambition is to enhance and transform human nature through technology. Gregory Stock characteristically wrote: "Humanity is leaving its childhood and moving into its adolescence as its powers infuse into realms hitherto beyond our reach".[52] Or as the similar term "participant evolution" which has been endorsed by transhumanists suggests, human enhancement can—and must—remove biological barriers.[53] The question therefore in relation to transhumanism is whether its methods and its goals align with present anthropocentric legal systems and if so under what conditions? Concerning techno-ontological post-anthropocentrism and its ambition to overturn the centrality of humanity, the question of alignment with legal anthropocentrism becomes even more pressing.

The legal challenges that are posed by the two concepts are not completely identical in their foundations but eventually coincide in the

[51] Andy Miah, 'A Critical History of Posthumanism' in Anthony Mark Cutter and others (eds), Medical Enhancement and Posthumanity (Springer 2008) 83; Richard Van Gulick, 'Consciousness' in Edward N Zalta (ed), The Stanford Encyclopedia of Philosophy (Winter 2021) https://plato.stanford.edu/archives/win2021/entries/consciousness/; While there is a growing tendency of recognition of rights to other beings or even entities, the legal personality of the latter remains at a lower level compared to humans and its recognition is dependent upon human decisions to do so. *See* Sirkku K Hellsten, 'The Meaning of Life during a Transition from Modernity to Transhumanism and Posthumanity' (2012) Journal of Anthropology 1, 1–7; Viola F, 'Umano e post-umano: la questione dell'identità' in F Russo (ed), Natura cultura libertà (Armando, Roma 2010) 90.

[52] Gregory Stock, 'Germinal Choice Technology and the Human Future' (2005) 10 Ethics, Law & Moral Philosophy of Reproductive Biomedicine 27, 34.

[53] Amar Sharon, Human Nature in an Age of Biotechnology: The Case for Mediated Posthumanism (Springer Science & Business Media 2013); Adele E Clarke, Laura Mamo, Jennifer Ruth Fosket, Jennifer R Fishman, and Janet K Shim, Biomedicalization: Technoscience, Health, and Illness in the U.S. (Duke University Press 2009).

culmination of their ambitions. With transhumanism, the main legal challenge is how far we can go with interferences in human nature. With techno-ontological post-anthropocentrism it is whether we can permit the emergence of "other-than-human" species or beings, with equal or superior intelligence compared to humans. Both though, attempt to transform human nature.

The afore-mentioned questions emerged in the last decades very persistently with biotechnologies and in particular gene editing. Gene editing has been a particularly challenging manifestation of biotechnologies. CRISPR technology for editing human genome was both a scientific breakthrough and a cause of concern. The gene editing interventions raised the prospect of various types of potential consequences: gene editing in existing humans—i.e., patients—and gene editing of embryos or gametes which affects not only the future person but also all the generations after her/him.[54]

Legal systems came forth with a delicate and not always coherent effort to balance between therapeutic and research goals that align with human dignity. The Declaration on the Human Genome and Human Rights in its articles provided that all interventions in the human genome must be for the benefit of the individual, under her/his consent, in line with human rights and that they cannot take place for purposes which are considered as contradictory to human dignity, with human cloning being one of them. The Declaration prohibited practices that completely contradict natural selection—such as cloning—but did not outlaw all interventions in human genome and its evolution, therefore to human nature and natural selection as well. The Convention on Human Rights and Biomedicine—Oviedo Convention—holds in article 13 that "An intervention seeking to modify the human genome may only be undertaken for preventive, diagnostic or therapeutic purposes and only if its aim is not to introduce any modification in the genome of any descendants".[55]

The 2015 Report of the International Bioethics Committee—IBC—on Updating Its Reflection on the Human Genome and Human Rights in paragraph 107 makes an important observation about the role of nature

[54] David Cyranoski, 'The CRISPR-Baby Scandal: What's Next for Human Gene-Editing' (2019) 566 Nature 440.

[55] Convention for the Protection of Human Rights and Dignity of the Human Being with regard to the Application of Biology and Medicine: Convention on Human Rights and Biomedicine (ETS No 164).

under legal anthropocentrism: "Nature is often understood as a limit to human freedom. At least in this case... it should be rather considered as its premise, so that interventions on the human genome should be admitted only for preventive, diagnostic or therapeutic reasons and without enacting modifications for descendants... The alternative would be to jeopardize the inherent and therefore equal dignity of all human beings and renew eugenics, disguised as the fulfillment of the wish for a better, improved life".[56]

The European Commission's European Group on Ethics in Science and New Technologies—EGE—which is an advisory body of the Commission, has argued against gene editing both for clinical and research activities "given the profound potential consequences of this research for humanity".[57]

Human gene editing has been generally dealt with extreme caution under most national legal systems.[58] The level of prohibitions varies from stricter ones—such as in EU countries—to relatively more flexible such as in the United States and China. Even in the latter cases, however, the regulations pose a quite strict framework.[59]

The Convention on Human Rights and Biomedicine also makes mention to "human being" that deserves respect "both as an individual and as a member of the human species".[60] Of course as it is analyzed below, the definition of health and disease is dynamic but still has certain limits. The prohibitions of the creation of human embryos for research reasons as well as of financial gain and disposal of a part of

[56] International Bioethics Committee, Report of the IBC on Updating Its Reflection on the Human Genome and Human Rights (UNESCO, SHS/YES/IBC-22/15/2 REV.2, Paris, 2 October 2015) para 107.

[57] European Group on Ethics in Science and New Technologies, Statement on Gene Editing https://ec.europa.eu/research/ege/pdf/gene_editing_ege_statement.pdf accessed 11 September 2024.

[58] Britta C van Beers, 'Rewriting the Human Genome, Rewriting Human Rights Law? Human Rights, Human Dignity, and Human Germline Modification in the CRISPR Era' (2020) Journal of Law and the Biosciences 1, 3.

[59] Di Zhang and Reidar K Lie, 'Ethical Issues in Human Germline Gene Editing: A Perspective from China' (2018) 36(1–4) Monash Bioethics Review 23.

[60] Council of Europe, Convention for the Protection of Human Rights and Dignity of the Human Being with regard to the Application of Biology and Medicine: Convention on Human Rights and Biomedicine https://rm.coe.int/168007cf98 accessed 9 September 2024.

the human body are also characteristic of the afore-mentioned position toward human nature as common, diachronic and unbreachable.

The Universal Declaration on the Human Genome and Human Rights is not coincidentally founded in its preamble on equality, human, economic, social, cultural, civil and political rights.[61] More explicitly in terms of its transcending spirit, the Declaration in article 1 states that "The human genome underlies the fundamental unity of all members of the human family".[62]

It must be mentioned however that the UK in a shift from stricter legislation has legalized "human nuclear genome transfer"—HGNT—for preventing mitochondrial disorders, thus proving that the "cracks" in the prohibition of gene editing and therefore, of the alteration of human nature have already appeared.[63] In addition, further calls for easing the restrictions on gene editing have surfaced from members of the scientific community.[64]

The balance that the various legal systems found is more or less that gene editing can be allowed for therapeutic reasons, provided that it does not affect the germline genetic identity, meaning humankind as such. Nature must not be transformed under human design but only "healed". Article 13 of the Oviedo Convention prohibits heritable genome editing, allowing only genes' modifications for preventive, diagnostic or therapeutic reasons. Article 14 foresees that "the use of techniques of medically assisted procreation [...] for the purpose of choosing a future child's sex,

[61] Universal Declaration on the Human Genome and Human Rights (11 November 1997) https://www.ohchr.org/en/instruments-mechanisms/instruments/universal-declaration-human-genome-and-human-rights accessed, [access. 10-9-2024].

[62] Ibid, Article 1.

[63] Samvel Varvastian, 'UK's Legalisation of Mitochondrial Donation in IVF Treatment: A Challenge to the International Community or a Promotion of Life-saving Medical Innovation to Be Followed by Others?' (2015) 22 European Journal of Health Law 405, 424.

[64] European Group on Ethics in Science and New Technologies, Statement on Gene Editing https://ec.europa.eu/research/ege/pdf/gene_editing_ege_statement.pdf accessed 11 September 2024; Eric Lander and others, 'Adopt a Moratorium on Heritable Genome Editing' (2019) 567 Nature 165; Federation of European Academies of Medicine, The Application of Genome Editing in Humans (October 2017) https://www.feam.eu/the application-of-genome-editing-in-humans/ accessed 19 July 2019; George Daley, Robin Lovell-Badge, and Julie Steffann, 'After the Storm: A Responsible Path for Genome Editing' (2019) 380 New England Journal of Medicine 897.

except where serious hereditary sex-related disease is to be avoided".[65] According to these provisions, the enhancement of offsprings is illegal but healing is not.[66]

The distinction however between permitted and prohibited acts on the basis of the distinction between therapeutic acts and germline modifications is far from simple. The controversy over the legality of the modification of mitochondrial DNA is indicative.[67] In addition, the reference to therapeutic reasons implies the distinction between therapy and enhancement, which as already mentioned is constantly blurring. The notorious and by now discredited experiment of Dr. He Jiankui who tried to design HIV-resistant babies constitutes a characteristic case of the thin line between the two.[68]

The Nuffield Council on Bioethics proposed a different guiding principle concerning genes' editing and subsequently interventions in human nature: the welfare of the future child.[69] The question of course then becomes, who determines the welfare of a child and how? Widening "cracks" in the regulatory frameworks are promoting more "realistic" approaches in favor of regulatory frameworks that rather control and guide than prohibit, while several scholars have talked in favor of a breach with our traditional and mainstream interpretation of human rights in relation to technology.[70] On the other hand they strengthen more polarized approaches, advocating a complete prohibition of such technologies.[71]

[65] Oviedo Convention, Art. 13 and 14.

[66] Frances M Kamm, 'Is There a Problem with Enhancement?' (2005) 5(3) The American Journal of Bioethics 5.

[67] Annelien Bredenoord and others, 'Ethics of Modifying the Mitochondrial Genome' (2011) 37 Journal of Medical Ethics 97.

[68] Eric T Juengst, 'Crowdsourcing the Moral Limits of Human Gene Editing?' (2017) 47(3) Hastings Center Report 15, 21; Antonio Regalado, 'China's CRISPR Twins Might Have Had Their Brains Inadvertently Enhanced' MIT Technology Review (21 February 2019).

[69] Nuffield Council on Bioethics, Genome Editing and Human Reproduction: Social and Ethical Issues (2018) 71, 91–92.

[70] Robin Alta Charo, 'Germline Engineering and Human Rights' (2018) 112 AJIL Unbound 344.

[71] Edward Lanphier and others, 'Do Not Edit the Human Germline' (2015) 519 Nature 411.

As technology advances, we tend to accept that we cannot harvest its benefits without exposing ourselves to the risks as well. Gene editing with the help of AI offers the potential of novel therapies but at the same time raises the risks of germline consequences, of the re-emergence of eugenics and of ontological established inequalities in the "human family".[72]

The Convention on Human Rights and Biomedicine makes mention to "human being" that deserves respect "both as an individual and as a member of the human species".[73] It is on these grounds that in article 13 prohibits the breach with natural selection by stating that "An intervention seeking to modify the human genome may only be undertaken for preventive, diagnostic or therapeutic purposes and only if its aim is not to introduce any modification in the genome of any descendants".[74] The convention preserves natural selection as a fundamental element of human nature. The prohibitions of the creation of human embryos for research reasons as well as of financial gain and disposal of a part of the human body are also characteristic of the afore-mentioned position toward human nature as common, diachronic and unbreachable.

While things are already complicated with gene editing, they become even more complicated, once the hybrid relationship of human and machine is involved as well, involving new forms of biotechnology. A large part of enhancement aspirations involves a gradual "cyborgization" of the human body and the digitalization of the human mind. Therefore, it also touches upon a species' perspective.

It is not coincidental that the UDHR, the ECHR and other similar texts are founded on a species' argument without further clarification and then move on to the establishment of individual and social rights. This is more or less what is suggested in the Explanatory Report of the Oviedo Convention and in UNESCO's IBC, which proposed that "ethics is not

[72] Report of the IBC on Updating Its Reflection on the Human Genome and Human Rights, UNESCO, SHS/YES/IBC-22/15/2 REV.2 (Paris, 2 October 2015) paras 103–108.

[73] Council of Europe, Convention for the Protection of Human Rights and Dignity of the Human Being with regard to the Application of Biology and Medicine: Convention on Human Rights and Biomedicine https://rm.coe.int/168007cf98 accessed 9 September 2024.

[74] Ibid, Article 13.

simply a matter of individual morality but it involves society as a whole' and 'must therefore also pursue the common good".[75]

Legal anthropocentrism necessitates a synthesis of the three aforementioned perspectives, meaning the individual, the social and the species. The synthesis of the three perspectives can offer insight on what enhanced anthropocentrism/transhumanism and techno-ontological anthropocentrism may or may not promote. Under transhumanism, human enhancement must be approached from the perspective of the impact of enhancement technologies on the individual, the society and the species. Once we reach the level of techno-ontological post-anthropocentrism, the question is not one of transformation but of substitution.

In the first case scenario, law must answer on the question of how far we can go with interfering in human nature. In the second scenario, the question is whether we can permit out substitution as the superior species or even our extinction.

When enhancement and therapy coincide in furtherance of the absence of disease or infirmity, the usual—but still often ambiguous—norms about medical deontology apply.[76] When however, enhancement lies outside this goal—or at least does not profoundly fall within such boundaries—then we then we have to re-interpret existing norms in order to answer the question of permissibility under law.

From the perspective of the adult individual, there is no reason to prohibit seeking enhancement techniques, provided that these interventions do no harm and that there is adequate information provided about their consequences. The provider of the interventions—doctor, private company, state, experts of any type—will have to assess also if it is ethical to answer positively to the request.

For example, let us assume that instead of prohibiting doping, "Super-Olympics" are organized even with equal access for all athletes to doping—drug, genetic or of whatever other type.[77] The athletes—let us

[75] International Bioethics Committee, Report of the IBC on Updating Its Reflection on the Human Genome and Human Rights, UNESCO, SHS/YES/IBC-22/15/2 REV.2 (Paris, 2 October 2015) para 30.

[76] This is also a theme that requires extensive analysis but evades the scope of this article.

[77] Christian Munthe, 'Selected Champions: Making Winners in the Age of Genetic Technology' in Torbjorn Tännsjö and Claudio Tamburrine (eds), Values in Sport: Elitism,

assume that all are adults—are informed about long-term repercussions in their health but still seek for such interventions. Their will seems to be free and mature. Still, the potential harm to their health should restrict experts from delivering them what they asked for. If no risk for health exists, then in principle there is no reason to prohibit such interventions from the perspective of the individual, other than possible internal norms and regulations in the "world of sports" in this case.

From the social perspective, the criterion is that of social cohesion, which means that if enhancement is accessible only for a few among us, then social inequalities can quickly transform in ontological inequalities, which will breach catalytically the legal "true-ism" of the relative equality among humans. Therefore, a social right guaranteeing equal and universal access to enhancement technologies is a sine qua non. In terms of these two perspectives there is no reason and no—anthropocentric—logic in principle, in denying futures with enhanced health, lifespan within which inequalities will be eased or even better potentially eclipse.[78] In addition, again from a social perspective whatever enhancement must not endanger the foundations of law, fundamental principles, norms and rights of other member of our societies.

The third perspective raises more complicated issues as it refers to the human species and therefore to human nature. The species' perspective is particularly complex because it involves a variety of factors both in terms of time as well as of determining factors. We must not forget that while law makes reference to human nature and human family thus implying the existence of the human species as its foundation, it does not define the human species as such. We must infer what law considers as critical for the nature of human species through other references.

Law as mentioned above adheres to the existence of a singular human nature which binds us all together. We must not forget that law works with abstractions and legal fictions. Nevertheless, human nature is not "sealed", not even under law, from any interventions. Human genome

Nationalism, Gender Equality and the Scientific Manufacture of Winners (Routledge 2000) 217–231.

[78] Peters, R. A. (2018, July). Re-creation, Consciousness Transfer and Digital Duplication: The Question of 'What Counts as Human?'in Charlie Brooker's Black Mirror. In Film-Philosophy Conference 2018.

is not sacred and frozen in time under all circumstances.[79] Even gene editing can be occasionally permitted. Therefore, is it possible to talk about the legitimacy of enhancement from a species' perspective?

A number of distinctions must be made. The one is between embryos and people who are born—predominantly adults. In the first case, there is no personality that can assess its own well-being, which is an element of health. For embryos, health is primarily limited to the absence of disease or infirmity. Therefore, enhancement is out of the question. Whatever interferences can be permitted only when attempting to avoid disease or infirmity on the basis of the research and the knowledge that we have acquired. Obviously, our current knowledge is incomplete. What offers health at the lifespan of one generation may have negative side effects for future generations. This is however a risk that we have to take, on the basis of our trust to the scientific knowledge that we have.

Things are different, when parents or other people make a decision to alter non-pathological characteristics of the embryo, effectively designing the future person partially or completely. In such cases the parents, a company, a state or whoever else other than the future person imposes his/her/its beliefs of well-being to the unborn human, completely objectifying the latter.

As mentioned before, the substitution of natural selection by human design constitutes a characteristic point of reference in the post-anthropocentric discussion. John Harris argues that: "If the goal of enhanced intelligence, increased powers and capacities, and better health is something that we might strive to produce through education, [...] why should we not produce these goals, if we can do it safely, through enhancement technologies or procedures?".[80]

For the advocates of human design, human dignity constitutes a metaphysical construction or at least a not well-defined one, regarding the specific obligations that flow from it.[81] Human dignity is considered not to be the end. As Bostrom said, there can be "post-human dignity"

[79] Jason Scott Robert, Françoise Baylis, 'Crossing Species Boundaries' (2003) 3(3) The American Journal of Bioethics 1–14.

[80] John Harris, Enhancing Evolution: The Ethical Case for Making Better People (Princeton University Press 2007) 2.

[81] Oktawian Nawrot, 'The Biogenetical Revolution of the Council of Europe—Twenty Years of the Convention on Human Rights and Biomedicine (Oviedo Convention)' (2018) 14:11 Life Sciences, Society and Policy 10; Timothy Caulfield, Roger Brownsword,

as well: "Transhumanists [...] see human and post-human dignity as compatible and complementary. What we are is not a function solely of our DNA but also of our technological and social context. Human nature in this broader sense is dynamic, partially human-made, and improvable".[82]

Bostrom is not wrong in principle. We are not solely our DNA. What is problematic is that such arguments are used in order to justify the restriction—even more at a prenatal age—of human freedom and autonomy. The substitution of natural selection by human design which in fact is exercised on the basis of the will and desire of someone else compared to the one who is designed constitutes a complete and ontological subjugation of the future person. Human freedom, human autonomy is what can be found at the core of human dignity as it applies at the individual, social and species level. Even if there is going to be post-human dignity, in order to actually be "dignity", it must be based on freedom. Human autonomy necessitates the non-instrumentalization of human at any stage of the existence. One could say even more when it is in a more dependent relationship as is the case at the prenatal level.

Obviously, every child suffers restrictions during the upbringing. In addition, the boundaries between biological characteristics and social influence such as through education are often blurred and shifted. But this is completely different from arguing that the "biological" and the "social" can be identical and that therefore as we regulate the social life of children, we can pre-determine them biologically too. What we would end up with would be a relationship of "masters and servants", by design and biology, with the latter instrumentalized by the former's wills.

The serious risks from the substitution of natural selection by human design are endorsed in the Council of Europe's Convention on Human Rights and Biomedicine (1997)[83] and UNESCO's Declaration on the

'Human Dignity: A Guide to Policy Making in the Biotechnology Era?' (2006) 7(1) Nature Reviews Genetics 72–6.

[82] Nick Bostrom, 'In Defense of Posthuman Dignity' (2005) 19(3) Bioethics 202, 213.

[83] "The treaty allows genetic engineering only for preventive, diagnostic or therapeutic reasons and only where it does not aim to change the genetic make-up of a person's descendants. It prohibits the use of techniques of medically assisted procreation to help choose the sex of a child, except where it would avoid a serious hereditary condition". Convention for the Protection of Human Rights and Dignity of the Human Being with regard to the Application of Biology and Medicine: Convention on Human Rights and Biomedicine (ETS No 164).

Human Genome and Human Rights (1997). They prohibit "the use of reproductive technologies, especially when used for human enhancement purposes, such as the genetic modification or sex-based selection of offspring, regardless of the reproductive preferences of the prospective parents".[84] The provisions of the two conventions are directly associated with human rights protection, with the preservation of human dignity and in this sense with the prevalence of the anthropocentric legal systems, in the wider framework of "homo sapiens species".[85]

For adults, the boundaries between what can be permitted and not in terms of enhancement are expectedly different. We know that our genes are affected by myriad factors. Even our civilization, our social and economic model—capitalism—affects our genes through its repercussions which are internalized for example through stress and our general way of life. Nevertheless, not all forms, neither all levels of interventions are the same. There is little ground to justify why it is problematic for our species to alter genes which are responsible for cancer or even for aging. While it will be a huge difference to live up to 125 years per average, humanity has experienced the prolongation of lifespan per average again, without anyone seriously doubting that we are still homo sapiens. We can use exoskeletons in order to increase our strength or implants to raise our IQ per average again, which will certainly give rise to new legal issues but it seems unlikely that because of such reasons alone, our human nature will be questioned.

In order to comprehend what type of enhancements and when may be questionable or even explicitly rejected under anthropocentric legal systems from the perspective of species, it is important to reflect on the fundamental components sustaining legal anthropocentrism.

As mentioned before, these are the prevalence of natural selection in the sense of preventing a situation of complete heterodetermination of future humans by their predecessors, the binary distinction between human and "other-than-human" and the dominion of the legal personality of humans, over all other beings because of humans' superior intelligence.

[84] Britta van Beers, 'A Better Way of Being? Human Rights, Transhumanism and 'The Utopian Standpoint of Man'' (p 254).

[85] Explanatory Report to the Convention for the Protection of Human Rights and Dignity of the Human Being with regard to the Application of Biology and Medicine: Convention on Human Rights and Biomedicine paras 14 and 15.

Therefore, from the species' perspective, enhancements should not create ambiguity about whether the enhanced person is human or "other-than-human". Such a transformation would create a situation that would be incomprehensible under law.[86] It is crucial to retain the binary distinction between human and "other-than-human".[87]

Further, enhancements that could create a different, other-than-human species such as for example a cyborg species, a being which is less human and more robot or the rise of AI to a level of intelligence equal or superior to human would overturn human dominion. Legal systems never had to deal explicitly with such issues until now. The dominion of Anthropos and of the human legal personality is characteristic of who should be sitting on the top of the pyramid of law according to anthropocentric legal systems. Superior and "other-than-human" cyborgs or AI would introduce us in an ontological "terra incognita" and in an era of great legal uncertainty. Under techno-ontological post-anthropocentrism, the ontological dominion of humans will have eclipsed and law—as we know it—does not have the time to adapt and adjust.

Such a transformation is not going to take place overnight. The boundaries between legal anthropocentrism and techno-ontological post-anthropocentrism will be blurring both in practice and in theory as technology advances for a relatively long time.[88] This is exactly why it is imperative to be able to distinguish under law, human enhancement acting as enhanced anthropocentrism from the negation of the dominion of human legal personality.[89]

Therefore, once the binary distinction between human and "other-than-human" or the legal dominion of humans are overturned, it is not only that some norms of current legal systems will be violated. The foundations of legal anthropocentrism of current legal systems will have eclipsed.

From the species' perspective while human enhancement or enhanced anthropocentrism, when exercised with free will and in the framework of law can be permitted, it is not lawful when it involves situations

[86] A post- mortem digitalization of human mind can be such a hypothetical situation.

[87] Peter Bloom, 'Legal Reboot: From Human Control to Transhuman Possibilities' in Identity, Institutions and Governance in an AI World (Palgrave Macmillan 2020) 225.

[88] Neil Kessler, Ontology and Closeness in Human-Nature Relationships: Beyond Dualisms, Materialism and Posthumanism (Springer 2018).

[89] Obviously there is a level of legal abstraction in all such distinctions.

that contradict natural selection, binary distinction between human and "other than human" and human superiority. If we project this conclusion in the concepts which we examine, while transhumanism can be in principle and at its initial stages lawful, transhumanism that leads to techno-ontological post-anthropocentrism, as well as the latter contradict the foundations of law.

There can be criticism of course to the "obsession" with our species. The insistence to "homo sapiens species" can be accused of biological reductionism. Why after all the superiority of "homo sapiens" must be maintained instead of making the leap to another species? Why cannot we share our dominion with other beings and regulate co-existence on the basis of Gray's "cyborg bill of rights",[90] Gunkel's "robot rights",[91] or in general the "digitalization" or "cyborgization" of human?[92]

Several transhumanists suggest a species' leap through which we have the potential of overcoming the most negative and destructive aspects of human civilization, such as Julian Savulescu's "moral enhancement" so that human civilization can be protected by its own's destructive inclinations.[93] Potentially, through a new form of democratic decision-making we can choose the ontological leap to our transformation to a new species or the emergence of a superior species that will absorb us.[94] Habermas has given a response through what he describes as a "supra-individual"

[90] Chris Hables Gray, 'The Ethics and Politics of Cyborg Embodiment: Citizenship as a Hypervalue' (1997) 1(2) Cultural Values 252–258.

[91] David Gunkel, Robot Rights (MIT Press 2018).

[92] Leopoldina Fortunati, 'The Human Body: Natural and Artificial Technology' in Machines That Become Us (Routledge 2017) 71–87; Christian Godin, 'What Would Human Rights with the Posthuman Become?' (2018) 29(3) Journal International de Bioéthique et d'Éthique des Sciences 154.

[93] Julian Savulescu, Unfit for the Future: The Need for Moral Enhancement (Oxford University Press 2012); Peter Sloterdijk, 'Rules for the Human Zoo: A Response to the Letter on Humanism' (2009) 27(1) Environment and Planning D: Society and Space 12, 20.

[94] Sheila Jasanoff, J Benjamin Hurlbut and Krishanu Saha, 'CRISPR Democracy: Gene Editing and the Need for Inclusive Deliberation' (2015) 32 Issues in Science and Technology 25; Donna Dickenson, Me Medicine vs We Medicine: Reclaiming Biotechnology for the Common Good (Columbia University Press 2013).

belief that we belong to a common species.[95] His argument explains at a significant extent why the protection of each species, including our own is deeply entrenched in present legal systems.[96]

The call for not being restrained by the foundations of legal anthropocentrism and what the latter dictates is a call for a leap to uncertainty and the incomprehensible. When projected in prenatal life through human design, it constitutes a profound violation of human dignity and freedom because of the objectification of a human by another.[97] In this sense, it constitutes in principle a case of clear boundary between permitted enhanced anthropocentrism and non-permitted post-anthropocentrism. While permitted human enhancement could refer and may include the prolepsis and cure of diseases at a prenatal level, the substitution of natural selection by human design objectifies future humans, imposes biological inequalities and, in this sense, diminishes human freedom and dignity, while at the same time it shifts humanity fundamentally outside nature, producing thus a phenomenologically similar but essentially other-than-human species.

When it is attempted after birth, enhancement must not endanger ontological inequalities or the transfer to an "other-than-human" species. Under such circumstances, enhancement would transfer us from enhanced anthropocentrism to techno-ontological post-anthropocentrism raising the prospect of the destruction of the human family or at least of a condition that neither ontologically, nor socially and legally is comprehensible in the present. None of these can be tolerated under law.

[95] Jürgen Habermas, Przyszłość natury ludzkiej. Czy zmierzamy do eugeniki liberalnej? [Die Zukunft der menschlichen Natur. Auf dem Weg zu einer Liberalen Eugenik?] (Warsaw 2003).

[96] It is in UNESCO 's documents that reference is made both to "common human destiny grounded on the essential values of mankind" as a benchmark for the assessment of such potential developments, as well as to the need for international coordination through the human rights' norms of international law. Federico Mayor, 'Preface' in Proceedings of the First Session of the IBC (UNESCO 1994); Roberto Andorno, 'Biomedicine and International Human Rights Law: In Search of a Global Consensus' (2002) 80(12) WHO Bulletin 959–963; Explanatory Report to the Convention for the Protection of Human Rights and Dignity of the Human Being with Regard to the Application of Biology and Medicine: Convention on Human Rights and Biomedicine, para 19; Case of Vo v. France para 84.

[97] Explanatory Report to the Convention for the Protection of Human Rights and Dignity of the Human Being with Regard to the Application of Biology and Medicine: Convention on Human Rights and Biomedicine, para 22.

On such grounds, the main argument of the present article is that enhancement that does not violate anthropocentrism must be permitted under an international law treaty, provided that the foundations of legal anthropocentrism are not put in question. On the contrary, techno-ontological post-anthropocentrism cannot be allowed under a relevant international law treaty, as well as transhumanism reaching the point of non-binary relationship between human and "other—than—human", as well as of human design.

Because of the gradual emergence of these technologies, the need for an international treaty applying human rights law on techno-biological issues becomes increasingly imperative, which should preserve as already mentioned the foundations of legal anthropocentrism and must also include a scale of risk factor for technological developments.[98] Most importantly it must be able to further establish its provisions on the three perspectives, meaning the individual's, the social and the species.

8.5 Conclusions

Public debate is full of concerns or expectations about the possibility of enhanced anthropocentrism and of a techno-ontological post-anthropocentric future. In particular these concerns about post-anthropocentrism emerge from non-organic, artificial intelligence but they are equally concerning when they are expected to emerge from digitalized human consciences or from other forms of post-anthropocentric beings.

Back in 1990, Marek Safjan in his thesis entitled "The Law in view of intervention in the nature of human procreation" stressed: "The question really comes down to whether the law, given the bitterness of the conflict and the dramatic contrast of the arguments being put forward, is really in a position to find its own solutions in this regard while not becoming

[98] Themistoklis Tzimas, 'Algorithmic Transparency and Explainability under EU Law' (2023) 29 European Public Law Issue 4, 385–411; Themistoklis Tzimas, 'Artificial Intelligence and Human Rights: Their Role in the Evolution of AI' (2020) 80 Heidelberg Journal of International Law 1–25; Paolo Giudici, Mattia Centurelli and Stefano Turchetta, 'Artificial Intelligence Risk Measurement' (2024) Expert Systems With Applications 235, 235–241; Chris Johnson, 'The Increasing Risks of Risk Assessment: On the Rise of Artificial Intelligence and Non-Determinism in Safety–Critical Systems'; Jay Wang et al., 'Probabilistic Risk Assessment: A Look at the Role of Artificial Intelligence' (1988) 106(3) Nuclear Engineering and Design 375, 375–387.

entangled in deep contradiction and not dismissing those fundamental, basic values which were at the root of the regulations in question and which are the result of centuries of tradition and of evolution".[99]

The main argument in the present chapter is precisely that while present legal systems can permit enhanced anthropocentrism, they must not leave space for a post-anthropocentric future.[100] Such must be the goal of a relevant international treaty, regulating the present and future technological advances.[101]

References

Andorno, R. (2002). Biomedicine and international human rights law: in search of a global consensus. *Bulletin of the World Health Organization*, *80*, 959–963.

African Charter on Human and Peoples' Rights, available at: https://www.oas.org/en/sla/dil/docs/African_Charter_Human_Peoples_Rights.pdf accessed 9 September 2024.

Bailey, R. (2005). *Liberation Biology: The Scientific and Moral Case for the Biotech Revolution*, Prometheus.

Barthes, R. (1977). *The Death of the Author*, Fontana.

Bioethics, N. (2018). Genome editing and human reproduction: social and ethical issues. *London: Nuffield Council on Bioethics*.

[99] Marek Safjan, Prawo wobec ingerencji w naturę ludzkiej prokreacji (Warsaw 1990).

[100] Catherine Waldby, The Visible Human Project: Informatic Bodies and Posthuman Medicine (Routledge 2003); Brendan Keogh, 'Cybernetic Memory and the Construction of the Posthuman Self in Videogame Play' in Design, Mediation, and the Posthuman (2014) 233–248; Stelarc, 'From Psycho-body to Cyber-systems: Images as Post-human Entities' in David Bell and Barbara Kennedy (eds), The Cybercultures Reader (Psychology Press 2000) 560–576, Andrew Pickering, 'Practice and Posthumanism: Social Theory and a History of Agency' in Karin Knorr Cetina, Theodore R. Schatzki, Eike von Savigny (eds), The Practice Turn in Contemporary Theory (Routledge 2001) 163–174.

[101] For such analyses, *See*: Nick Bostrom, 'In Defense of Posthuman Dignity' (2005) 19(3) Bioethics 202, 214; Francis Fukuyama, Our Posthuman Future: Consequences of the Biotechnology Revolution (Profile Books 2003); Robert Pepperell, The Posthuman Condition: Consciousness Beyond the Brain (3rd edn, Intellect Books 2003) (originally published 1995); Leon Kass, 'Ageless Bodies, Happy Souls. Biotechnology and the Pursuit of Perfection' (2003) 1 The New Atlantis 9, 12; Donna Haraway, Simians, Cyborgs, and Women: The Reinvention of Nature (Free Association Books 1991); Bruce Mazlish, The Fourth Discontinuity (Yale University Press 1993) 44.

Birnbacher, D. (2008). Posthumanity, transhumanism and human nature. In *Medical enhancement and posthumanity* (pp. 95–106). Dordrecht: Springer Netherlands.

Bostrom, N. (2001). 'Transhumanist Values' available at: http://www.nickbostrom.com/tra/values.html accessed 14 September 2024.

Bostrom, N. (2004). The Future of Human Evolution https://nickbostrom.com/fut/evolution accessed 11 March 2024.

Bostrom, N. (2005). In defense of posthuman dignity. *Bioethics*, *19*(3), 202–214.

Bostrom, N. & Roache, R. (2007). Ethical Issues in Human Enhancement, In Ryberg, J., Petersen, T. S., & Wolf, C. (Eds.) *New waves in applied ethics*. Houndsmills: Palgrave Macmillan.

Bloom, P. (2020). Legal reboot: From human control to transhuman possibilities. *Identity, Institutions and Governance in an AI World: Transhuman Relations*, 211–246.

Braidotti, R. (2013). *The Posthuman*. Review' Culture Machine 2. Cambridge: Polity Press.

Braidotti, R. (2006). Posthuman, all too human: Towards a new process ontology. *Theory, culture & society*, *23*(7–8), 197–208.

Bredenoord, A. L., Dondorp, W., Pennings, G., & De Wert, G. (2011). Ethics of modifying the mitochondrial genome. *Journal of medical ethics*, *37*(2), 97–100.

Burden, D., & Savin-Baden, M. (2019). Virtual humans: Today and tomorrow. Chapman and Hall/CRC.

Caulfield, T., & Brownsword, R. (2006). Human dignity: a guide to policy making in the biotechnology era?. *Nature Reviews Genetics*, *7*(1), 72–76.

Charo, R. A. (2019). Rogues and regulation of germline editing. *New England Journal of Medicine*, *380*(10), 976–980.

Charo, R.A. (2018). 'Germline Engineering and Human Rights', *AJIL Unbound*, 112.

Clarke, A. E., Mamo, L., Fosket, J. R., Fishman, J. R., & Shim, J. K. (Eds.). (2020). *Biomedicalization: Technoscience, health, and illness in the US*. Duke University Press.

Convention for the Protection of Human Rights and Fundamental Freedoms as amended by Protocol No 15 https://rm.coe.int/1680a2353d accessed 9 September 2024.

Council of Europe, Convention for the Protection of Human Rights and Dignity of the Human Being with regard to the Application of Biology and Medicine: Convention on Human Rights and Biomedicine, available at: https://rm.coe.int/168007cf98 accessed 9 September 2024.

Convention for the Protection of Human Rights and Dignity of the Human Being with regard to the Application of Biology and Medicine: Convention on Human Rights and Biomedicine (ETS No 164).

Cyranoski, D. (2019). The CRISPR-baby scandal: what's next for human gene-editing. *Nature*, *566*(7745), 440–443.

Daley, G. Q., Lovell-Badge, R., & Steffann, J. (2019). After the storm—a responsible path for genome editing. *New England Journal of Medicine*, *380*(10), 897–899.

Dickenson, D. (2013). *Me medicine vs. we medicine: Reclaiming biotechnology for the common good*. Columbia University Press.

Erden, Y. J., & Brey, P. A. (2022). Ethics guidelines for human enhancement R&D. *Science*, *378*(6622), at pp. 835–838.

European Group on Ethics in Science and New Technologies, Statement on Gene Editing, available at: https://ec.europa.eu/research/ege/pdf/gene_editing_ege_statement.pdf accessed 11 September 2024.

Feenberg, A. (2017). *Technosystem: The social life of reason*. Harvard University Press.

Federation of European Academies of Medicine, The Application of Genome Editing in Humans (October 2017) available at: https://www.feam.eu/the application-of-genome-editing-in-humans/ accessed 19 July 2019

Ferrando, F. (2023). 'Existential Posthumanism: A Manifesto' In Rosi Braidotti, et al. (eds.) *More Posthuman Glossary*, Bloomsbury.

Ferrando, F. (2013). 'Posthumanism, Transhumanism, Antihumanism, Metahumanism, and New Materialisms: Differences and Relations'. *Existenz*, 8(2), 26–27.

Fortunati, L. (2017). The human body: Natural and artificial technology. In *Machines that become us* (pp. 71–87). Routledge.

Fukuyama, F. (2003). *Our posthuman future: Consequences of the biotechnology revolution*. Macmillan.

Gariboldi, M. I., Lin, V., Bland, J., Auplish, M., & Cawthorne, A. (2021). Foresight in the time of COVID-19. *The Lancet Regional Health–Western Pacific*, *6*.

Grear, A. (2015). Deconstructing Anthropos: A Critical Legal Reflection on 'Anthropocentric' Law and Anthropocene 'Humanity'. Law Critique 26, 225–249.

Giubilini, A., & Sanyal, S. (2016). Challenging human enhancement. In C. A. J. Coady, Alberto Giubilini, Sagar Sanyal (eds.) *The ethics of human enhancement: Understanding the debate*, Oxford University Press.

Godin, C. (2018). What would human rights with the posthuman become?. *Journal International de Bioethique et D'ethique des Sciences*, *29*(3), 154–169.

Gray, C. H. (1997). The ethics and politics of cyborg embodiment: citizenship as a hypervalue. *Journal for Cultural Research*, *1*(2), 252–258.

Gunkel, D. J. (2018). *Robot rights*. MIT Press.

Haraway, D. (1991). *Simians, cyborgs, and women: The reinvention of nature*. Free Association Books.

Harris, J. (2010). Enhancing evolution: The ethical case for making better people. Princeton University Press

Hellsten, S. K. (2012). "The Meaning of Life" during a Transition from Modernity to Transhumanism and Posthumanity. *Journal of Anthropology*, *2012*(1), 210684.

Hoffman, S.A. (2005). 'Transhumanist Materialism: A Critique from Immunoneuropsychology' In Stefan Lorenz Sorgner (ed), *Beyond Humanism: Trans- and Posthumanism*, Peter Lang.

Huberman, J. (2018). Immortality transformed: mind cloning, transhumanism and the quest for digital immortality. *Mortality*, *23*(1), 50–64.

Hughes, J. (2004). *Citizen Cyborg: Why Democratic Societies Must Respond to the Redesigned Human of the Future*, Westview Press.

Huxley, J. (1957). *New Bottles for New Wine*, Chatto & Windus.

International Bioethics Committee, Report of the IBC on Updating Its Reflection on the Human Genome and Human Rights (UNESCO, SHS/YES/IBC-22/15/2 REV.2, Paris, 2 October 2015)

Ionescu, Ş., Dumitrescu, G., Ioanăş, C., & Delcea, C. (2024). Mapping the Landscape of Key Performance and Key Risk Indicators in Business: A Comprehensive Bibliometric Analysis. *Risks*, *12*(8), 125.

Jasanoff, S., Hurlbut, J. B., & Saha, K. (2015). CRISPR democracy: Gene editing and the need for inclusive deliberation. *Issues in Science and Technology*, *32*(1), 25–32.

Johnson, C. W. (2018, February). The increasing risks of risk assessment: On the rise of artificial intelligence and non-determinism in safety-critical systems. In *the 26th Safety-Critical Systems Symposium* (Vol. 15). Safety-Critical Systems Club York, UK.

Juengst, E. & Moseley, D. (2019). 'Human Enhancement' In Edward N Zalta (ed), The Stanford Encyclopedia of Philosophy, available at: https://plato.stanford.edu/archives/sum2019/entries/enhancement/.

Juengst, E. T. (2017). Crowdsourcing the moral limits of human gene editing?. *Hastings Center Report*, *47*(3), 15–23.

Kamm, F. M. (2005). Is there a problem with enhancement?. *The American Journal of Bioethics*, *5*(3), 5–14.

Kass, L. R. (2003). Ageless bodies, happy souls: biotechnology and the pursuit of perfection. *The New Atlantis*, (1), 9–28.

Keogh, B. (2014). Cybernetic memory and the construction of the posthuman self in videogame play. *Design, Mediation, and the Posthuman, Lexington Books, Lanham, United Kingdom*, 233–247.

Kessler, N. H. (2019). Ontology and closeness in human-nature relationships. *Beyond Dualisms, Materialism and Posthumanism*. Springer.

Kleingeld, P. (2010). Moral consciousness and the 'fact of reason', in Timmerman, J. and Reath, A. (eds.) *Kant's 'Critique of Practical Reason': A Critical Guide*. Cambridge: CUP.

Lander, E. S., Baylis, F., Zhang, F., Charpentier, E., Berg, P., Bourgain, C., ... & Winnacker, E. L. (2019). Adopt a moratorium on heritable genome editing. *Nature, 567*(7747), 165–168.

Lanphier, E., Urnov, F., Haecker, S. E., Werner, M., & Smolenski, J. (2015). Don't edit the human germ line. *Nature, 519*(7544), 410–411.

Levy, N. (2014). *Consciousness and Moral Responsibility*. Oxford: OUP.

Lovejoy, A. (2017). *The great chain of being: A study of the history of an idea*. Routledge.

Marchesini, R. (2007). 'Ruolo delle alterità nella definizione dei predicati umani' in Pietro Barcellona, Fabio Ciaramelli e Roberto Fai (eds), *Apocalisse e post-umano. Il crepuscolo della modernità*, Dedalo.

Mazlish, B. (1993). *The fourth discontinuity: The co-evolution of humans and machines*. Yale University Press.

Miah, A. (2008). A critical history of posthumanism. In *Medical enhancement and posthumanity* (pp. 71–94). Dordrecht: Springer Netherlands.

More, M. (1988). The Extropian Principles, Version 3.0, A Transhumanist Declaration available at: https://www.mrob.com/pub/religion/extro_prin.html accessed 7 April 2024.

Munthe, C. (2002). Selected champions: making winners in the age of genetic technology. In *Values in sport* (pp. 227–241). Taylor & Francis.

Nawrot, O. (2018). The biogenetical revolution of the Council of Europe-twenty years of the Convention on Human Rights and Biomedicine (Oviedo Convention). *Life sciences, society and policy, 14*, 1–24.

Nemenyi, D. (2023). The Leibnizian cryptowar of Norbert Wiener. Radical Philosophy, (214), 3–20.

Nordmann, A. (2007). If and then: A critique of speculative nanoethics. *Nanoethics, 1*, 31–46.

Onishi, B.B. (2011). 'Information, Bodies, and Heidegger: Tracing Visions of the Posthuman', Sophia 50(1), 101–112.

Quevedo, A. (2001). *De Foucault a Derrida: pasando fugazmente por Deleuze y Guattari, Lyotard, Baudrillard*. Eunsa.

Pastor, L. M., & Cuadrado, J. Á. G. (2014). Modernity and postmodernity in the genesis of transhumanism-posthumanism. *Cuadernos de bioética, 25*(3), 335–350.

Pepperell, R. (2005). 'Posthumans and Extended Experience'. *Journal of Evolution and Technology*, (14) 34.

Pepperell, R. (2003). The Posthuman Condition: Consciousness Beyond the Brain (3rd ed.) Intellect Books

Persson, I., & Savulescu, J. (2012). *Unfit for the future: The need for moral enhancement*. OUP Oxford.

Peters, R. A. (2018, July). Re-creation, Consciousness Transfer and Digital Duplication: The Question of 'What Counts as Human? In Charlie Brooker's Black Mirror. In Film-Philosophy Conference 2018.

Pickering, A. (2001). 'Practice and Posthumanism: Social Theory and a History of Agency'. In Karin Knorr Cetina, Theodore R. Schatzki, Eike von Savigny (eds), *The Practice Turn in Contemporary Theory*, Routledge.

Racine, E., Martin Rubio, T., Chandler, J., Forlini, C., & Lucke, J. (2014). The value and pitfalls of speculation about science and technology in bioethics: the case of cognitive enhancement. *Medicine, Health Care and Philosophy*, *17*, 325–337.

Reeves, J. A. & Peters, T. D. (2021). Responding to anthropocentrism with anthropocentrism: the biopolitics of environmental personhood. Griffith Law Review, 30(3), 474–504.

Regalado, A. (2019). China's CRISPR twins might have had their brains inadvertently enhanced. *MIT Technology Review, February*, *21*, 2019.

Robert, J. S., & Baylis, F. (2003). Crossing species boundaries. *American Journal of Bioethics*, *3*(3), 1–13.

Rueda, J. (2023). The ethics of doing human enhancement ethics. *Futures*, *153*, 103236.

Safjan, M. (1990). *Prawo wobec ingerencji w naturÄ™ ludzkiej prokreacji* (Doctoral dissertation, Uniwersytet Warszawski. WydziaĹ ,Prawa i Administracji).

Savin-Baden, M., & Burden, D. (2019). Digital immortality and virtual humans. Postdigital Science and Education, 1, 87–103.

Savulescu, J. (2003). 'Human-Animal Transgenesis and Chimeras Might Be an Expression of Our Humanity'. Journal of Bioethics, 3(3) 22–24.

Sellen, A., Rogers, Y., Harper, R., & Rodden, T. (2009). Reflecting human values in the digital age. *Communications of the ACM*, *52*(3), 58–66.

Sharon, T. (2014). *Human nature in an age of biotechnology*: *The Case for Mediated Posthumanism*, Springer Science & Business Media.

Sorgner, S. L. (2010). Beyond humanism: Reflections on trans-and posthumanism. *Journal of Evolution and Technology*, *21*(2), 1–19.

Starr, W. C. (1983). Law and morality in HLA Hart's legal philosophy. *Marq. L. Rev.*, *67*, 673.

Steinhart, E. (2014). *Your digital afterlives: Computational theories of life after death*. Springer.

Stelarc, D. (2000). From psycho-body to cyber-systems: Images as post-human entities. *The cybercultures reader*, 560–576.

Stock, G. (2005). Germinal choice technology and the human future. *Reproductive biomedicine online*, *10*, 27–35.

Sloterdijk, P. (2009). Rules for the Human Zoo: a response to the Letter on Humanism. *Environment and Planning D: Society and Space*, *27*(1), 12–28.

The Transhumanist Manifesto, (1988). available at: <https://www.humanityplus.org/the-transhumanist-manifesto>, access. 9/3/2024

Tzimas, T. (2023). Algorithmic transparency and explainability under eu law. *European Public Law*, *29*(4).

Tzimas, T. (2021). Artificial intelligence and human rights: their role in the evolution of AI. *Heidelberg Journal of International Law, ZaöRV*.

Universal Declaration on the Human Genome and Human Rights (11 November 1997) available at: https://www.ohchr.org/en/instruments-mechanisms/instruments/universal-declaration-human-genome-and-human-rights accessed, accessed 10 September 2024.

Universal Declaration of Human Rights, Preamble https://www.un.org/en/about-us/universal-declaration-of-human-rights accessed 8 September 2024.

Van Beers, B. (2022). A better way of being? Human rights, transhumanism and the utopian standpoint of man. In *Utopian Thinking in Law, Politics, Architecture and Technology* (pp. 246–266). Edward Elgar Publishing.

Van Beers, B. C. (2020). Rewriting the human genome, rewriting human rights law? Human rights, human dignity, and human germline modification in the CRISPR era. Journal of Law and the Biosciences, 7(1), lsaa006.

Van Beers, B. C. (2015). Is Europe 'giving in to baby markets?'Reproductive tourism in Europe and the gradual erosion of existing legal limits to reproductive markets. *Medical law review*, *23*(1), 103–134.

Van Gulick, R. (2021). 'Consciousness' In Edward N Zalta (ed), The Stanford Encyclopedia of Philosophy, available at: https://plato.stanford.edu/archives/win2021/entries/consciousness/

Varvaštian, S. (2015). UK's legalisation of mitochondrial donation in IVF treatment: A challenge to the international community or a promotion of life-saving medical innovation to be followed by others?. *European journal of health law*, *22*(5), 405–425.

Vattimo, G. (1988). The end of modernity: Nihilism and hermeneutics in post-modern culture. (trans Jon R Snyder), The John Hopkins University Press.

Viola F, (2010). 'Umano e post-umano: la questione dell'identità'. In F Russo (ed), *Natura cultura libertà*. Armando, Roma.

Walewska, E. (2011). 'Trans-, Post-/-Humanizm,-człowiek. Transformacje' *Cuadernos de Bioética*, 3(4), 315–316.

Waldby, C. (2003). *The visible human project: Informatic bodies and posthuman medicine*. Routledge.

Zhang, D., & Lie, R. K. (2018). Ethical issues in human germline gene editing: a perspective from China. *Monash Bioethics Review*, *36*, 23–35.

Zohny, H., & Edmonds, D. (2021). Future versus present morality. *Future morality*, 3–12.

CHAPTER 9

The EU AI Act and the Future of AI Governance: Implications for U.S. Firms and Policymakers

David Krause

U.S. policymakers must weigh the benefits of aligning with EU regulations against the risks of stifling domestic AI innovation. A strategic approach balancing regulatory compliance, innovation, and global competitiveness is essential to sustaining U.S. leadership in AI development. This chapter examines the implications of the EU AI Act, its compliance and audit requirements, and strategic considerations for U.S. policymakers in response to evolving international AI governance frameworks.

D. Krause (✉)
Marquette University, Milwaukee, WI, USA
e-mail: david.krause@marquette.edu

A. Aliu (ed.), *Artificial Intelligence and the Rule of Law*,
https://doi.org/10.1007/978-3-031-97389-5_9

9.1 Introduction

The European Union's Artificial Intelligence Act (EU AI Act) is the world's first comprehensive AI regulatory framework, designed to balance innovation, consumer protection, and ethical AI governance. By introducing a risk-based classification system, the Act imposes strict compliance requirements, particularly for high-risk AI applications in sectors such as finance, healthcare, and law enforcement. Given the EU's influence on global regulatory standards, this legislation will have far-reaching implications, affecting not only European companies but also U.S. firms operating in the EU.

A critical aspect of the EU AI Act is its robust compliance and audit framework, which mandates conformity assessments, risk management protocols, and continuous monitoring for high-risk AI systems. Organizations must implement quality management systems, maintain detailed technical documentation, and conduct internal and third-party audits to demonstrate compliance. These requirements impose significant operational challenges, particularly for U.S. businesses that must align with EU regulations while navigating potential discrepancies with U.S. policies.

For U.S. policymakers, understanding the EU AI Act is essential, as its provisions will shape global AI governance, international trade, and regulatory alignment between the U.S. and the EU. The Act classifies AI systems based on potential risks to fundamental rights and safety, imposing various levels of oversight. This regulatory structure seeks to promote trustworthy AI development, yet it also introduces compliance burdens that U.S. businesses must navigate, including stringent documentation, data governance, and transparency requirements, as well as regulatory misalignment risks.

This chapter examines the key provisions of the EU AI Act, its impact on U.S. businesses, and the regulatory conflicts it may create with U.S. AI policies, including the AI Executive Order and sector-specific guidelines.[1] It also explores strategies for U.S. policymakers, emphasizing the need for regulatory coordination, support for AI innovation, and international cooperation on AI standards. By proactively engaging with EU

[1] White House, 'Removing Barriers to American Leadership in Artificial Intelligence (2025, January 23). The White House, US GOV available at: https://www.whitehouse.gov/presidential-actions/2025/01/removing-barriers-to-american-leadership-in-artificial-intelligence/.

counterparts and developing a balanced national AI strategy, U.S. policymakers can ensure both competitiveness and responsible AI deployment in an evolving global landscape.

9.2 Key Provisions of the EU AI Act

The European Union's Artificial Intelligence Act represents the world's first comprehensive legal framework for regulating artificial intelligence systems. Entering into force on August 1, 2024, the AI Act establishes a complex regulatory landscape that differentiates obligations based on risk levels while creating new oversight mechanisms. This section explores the Act's core provisions, compliance requirements, and enforcement mechanisms that significantly impact both European and international businesses deploying AI technologies.

9.2.1 Risk-Based Classification System

The EU AI Act employs a sophisticated risk-based approach that categorizes AI systems into four distinct tiers with corresponding regulatory requirements. This tiered system ensures proportionality by applying the most stringent controls to higher-risk applications while allowing innovation in lower-risk domains.[2]

As shown in Exhibit 1, the EU AI Act employs a graduated regulatory approach, with the stringency of requirements increasing as the potential risk of an AI system escalates.[3]Minimal-risk systems are subject to no specific obligations, while unacceptable-risk systems are prohibited. The Act establishes defined legal parameters for these risk categories, effectively formalizing them beyond standard risk analysis. The Act also establishes a separate category for General-Purpose AI systems (GPAI), which exists alongside the unacceptable, high, limited, and minimal-risk classifications. A model is considered a GPAI if it is trained on a vast amount of data and can manage a wide variety of tasks, thus acting as a foundation for other AI applications (Fig. 9.1).

[2] Trail ML. (2025). 'EU AI Act: Risk-Classifications of the AI Regulation.' available at: https://www.trail-ml.com/blog/eu-ai-act-how-risk-is-classified.

[3] European Confederation of Institutes of Internal Auditing (ECIIA). (2025). 'The AI Act Road to Compliance.' available at: https://www.eciia.eu/wp-content/uploads/2025/01/The-AI-Act-Road-to-Compliance-Final-1.pdf.

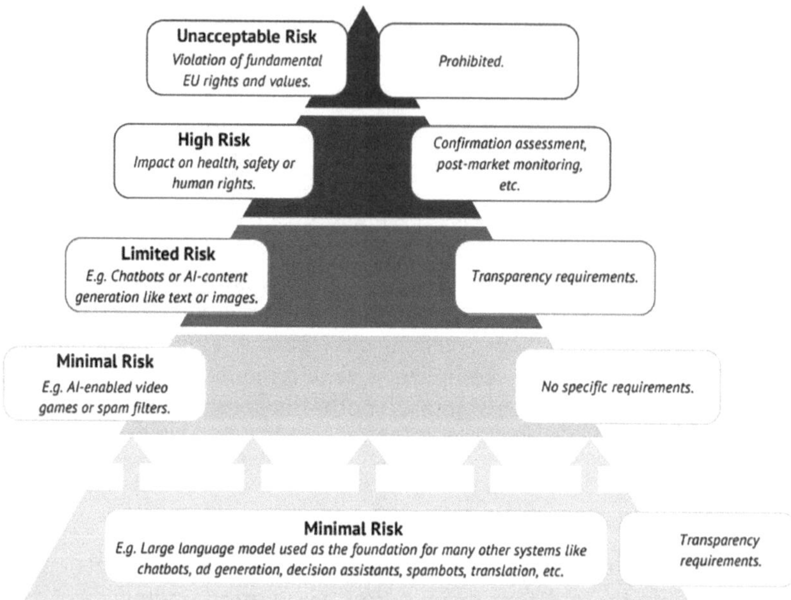

Fig. 9.1 The EU AI Act and the risk-based approach. *Source* European Confederation of Institutes of Internal Auditing

9.2.2 *Unacceptable-Risk AI Systems*

AI applications classified as presenting unacceptable risk are categorically prohibited under the EU AI Act, with this prohibition taking effect from February 2025. These explicitly banned systems include social scoring mechanisms that evaluate individuals based on social behavior or personal characteristics, predictive policing systems designed to forecast criminal acts by individuals, and technologies that create or augment facial recognition databases through scraped data.[4] Additionally, the ban extends to systems designed for cognitive behavioral manipulation of people (particularly vulnerable groups), emotion recognition deployments in workplace

[4] Autoriteit Persoonsgegevens. (2025). 'EU AI Act risk groups.' available at: https://www.autoriteitpersoonsgegevens.nl/en/themes/algorithms-ai/eu-ai-act/eu-ai-act-risk-groups.

and educational environments, and most forms of remote biometric identification in public spaces.[5]

The prohibition against biometric identification systems does include limited exceptions for law enforcement purposes. "Real-time" remote biometric identification systems may be permitted in specific serious cases, while "post" remote biometric identification systems can be deployed for prosecuting serious crimes following court approval.[6] These narrow exceptions reflect the EU's attempt to balance security concerns with fundamental rights protection.

9.2.3 *High-Risk AI Systems*

High-risk AI systems face extensive regulatory requirements while remaining permissible in the European Union market. This classification comprises two major subcategories: AI systems integrated into products already regulated under EU product safety legislation (such as medical devices, toys, and transportation), and standalone AI applications operating in specifically enumerated high-risk domains.

The high-risk categories explicitly identified in the legislation include systems used for managing critical infrastructure, educational and vocational training applications, employment and worker management systems, AI involved in access to essential private and public services, law enforcement technologies, and applications for migration, asylum, and border control management.[7] Systems facilitating legal interpretation and application also fall within this category, reflecting concerns about AI's potential impact on judicial processes and access to justice.

9.2.4 *Limited and Minimal-Risk Systems*

The AI Act establishes less onerous obligations for limited-risk systems, primarily focusing on transparency requirements. This category includes widely used consumer-facing AI applications like chatbots and systems

[5] European Parliament. (2025). 'EU AI Act: first regulation on artificial intelligence.' Available at: https://www.europarl.europa.eu/topics/en/article/20230601STO93804/eu-ai-act-first-regulation-on-artificial-intelligence.

[6] Id.

[7] Id para. 4.

generating synthetic content.[8] For minimal-risk applications, which comprise most AI systems currently in use, the Act imposes no additional regulatory requirements beyond voluntary adherence to codes of conduct, allowing continued innovation in these lower-risk domains.

9.2.5 *Compliance Requirements for High-Risk AI*

Organizations developing or deploying high-risk AI systems face particularly extensive compliance obligations under the Act, necessitating significant operational and technical adjustments across the AI development lifecycle.

9.2.5.1 *Technical Documentation and Conformity Assessment*

Providers of high-risk AI systems must ensure their technologies comply with specific requirements outlined in the legislation. Article 16 of the Act mandates that providers maintain comprehensive technical documentation, implement robust quality management systems, and undergo formal conformity assessment procedures before market placement.[9] These assessments evaluate whether systems meet EU safety, fairness, and transparency standards, with providers required to draw up an EU declaration of conformity and affix the CE marking to compliant systems.

Article 16 of the EU AI Act, in conjunction with related articles, mandates conformity assessments, quality management systems, and detailed documentation for high-risk AI systems, effectively requiring a form of audit through scrutiny and potential external review to ensure compliance. The documentation requirements extend beyond mere technical specifications to include detailed explanation of system design choices, development methodologies, and validation processes. This represents a significant administrative burden, particularly for organizations without established documentation protocols aligned with EU regulatory expectations.

[8] Frazier, T. (2024). 'EU AI Act and Its Relevance to US-Based Companies.' Class. Available at: https://www.class.com/blog/summary-of-the-eu-ai-act/.

[9] Artificial Intelligence Act. (2023). 'Article 16: Obligations of Providers of High-Risk AI Systems.' available at: https://artificialintelligenceact.eu/article/16/.

9.2.5.2 Data Governance and Risk Management

The Act establishes rigorous data governance requirements for high-risk AI systems, exceeding standards currently found in most U.S. regulatory frameworks. Providers must implement comprehensive risk management systems that operate throughout the entire lifecycle of high-risk AI applications.[10] These systems must identify, evaluate, and mitigate potential risks to health, safety, and fundamental rights.

Additionally, providers must establish data governance frameworks ensuring appropriate data quality metrics for training, validation, and testing datasets. This includes implementing procedures to examine datasets for biases and implementing mitigation measures where necessary. The emphasis on proactive bias detection and remediation reflects European concerns about AI systems perpetuating or amplifying social inequities.

9.2.5.3 Human Oversight and Transparency

A central requirement for high-risk AI systems under the Act is the implementation of appropriate human oversight mechanisms. These provisions are designed to minimize autonomous operation of high-risk systems without meaningful human intervention and understanding.[11] U.S. businesses operating in the EU market may need to develop costly compliance infrastructure to satisfy these requirements, potentially including new roles, training programs, and oversight processes.

Transparency requirements mandate that high-risk AI systems be designed to allow users to interpret system outputs and understand operational parameters. This includes providing clear information about system capabilities and limitations, enabling users to make informed decisions about appropriate use cases and potential risks.

9.2.6 Governance and Enforcement

The EU AI Act establishes a multi-layered governance structure combining centralized EU-level oversight with national enforcement mechanisms, creating a complex compliance landscape for businesses.

[10] Peaden, V. (2024). 'EU AI Act Tightens Grip on High-Risk AI Systems.' Baker Donelson. available at: https://www.bakerdonelson.com/eu-ai-act-tightens-grip-on-high-risk-ai-systems-five-critical-questions-for-us-companies.

[11] Frazier, T. (2024). 'EU AI Act and Its Relevance to US-Based Companies.' Class.

9.2.6.1 *The EU AI Office*

The European Commission has established a specialized AI Office to lead implementation and enforcement of the Act. This new regulatory body holds exclusive jurisdiction over certain provisions, particularly those relating to General-Purpose AI Models.[12] The AI Office will develop technical standards, provide implementation guidance, and coordinate enforcement actions across EU member states, serving as the central authority for AI governance within the European Union.

9.2.6.2 *National Regulators and Market Surveillance*

While the AI Office maintains central coordination, most compliance investigations and enforcement actions fall under the purview of national market surveillance authorities within individual EU member states. These authorities will exercise power in accordance with established EU market surveillance regulations, conducting inspections, requesting information, and initiating enforcement proceedings when necessary[13]. This distributed enforcement approach raises potential concerns about inconsistent application across different EU jurisdictions, creating compliance challenges for multinational organizations operating throughout the European market.

9.2.6.3 *Penalties and Sanctions*

The EU AI Act implements a three-tiered penalty structure with some of the most substantial financial sanctions found in any EU regulatory framework. Violations of provisions regarding prohibited AI systems can result in administrative fines of up to €35,000,000 or 7% of the organization's total worldwide annual turnover from the preceding financial year, whichever is higher[14]. This exceeds even the maximum penalties established under the GDPR, signaling the EU's commitment to rigorous enforcement.

[12] Apostle, J. (2024). 'The EU AI Act: Oversight and Enforcement.' Orrick. available at: https://www.orrick.com/en/Insights/2024/09/The-EU-AI-Act-Oversight-and-Enforcement.

[13] Apostle, J. (2024). 'The EU AI Act: Oversight and Enforcement.' Orrick.

[14] Güclütürk, O. and Hilliard, A. (2025). 'Penalties of the EU AI Act: The High Cost of Non-Compliance.' available at: https://www.holisticai.com/blog/penalties-of-the-eu-ai-act.

Violations of other obligations, including those related to high-risk AI systems, can trigger fines up to €15,000,000 or 3% of annual worldwide turnover. Meanwhile, providing incorrect, incomplete, or misleading information to authorities can result in penalties up to €7,500,000 or 1% of annual turnover[15]. The Act specifies that the lower amount applies to small and medium-sized enterprises (SMEs), while larger organizations face higher financial penalties. These substantial sanctions create significant financial risk for non-compliant organizations, particularly for larger technology companies with extensive AI deployments across the European market.

9.3 Compliance and Audit Requirements Under the EU AI Act

The EU AI Act establishes a risk-based regulatory framework for artificial intelligence, mandating comprehensive compliance and audit mechanisms to ensure accountability, transparency, and ethical AI deployment. The following is an analysis of key obligations and audit requirements under the legislation.

9.3.1 Compliance Requirements

The Act categorizes AI systems into four risk tiers: unacceptable, high, limited, and minimal. Systems deemed to pose an unacceptable risk—such as those enabling manipulative behavior or social scoring—are strictly prohibited. High-risk systems, including biometric identification and AI used in employment decision-making, require stringent oversight[16]. Organizations must maintain an inventory of AI applications and classify them accordingly to comply with these regulatory categories[17].

[15] Apostle, J. (2024). 'The EU AI Act: Oversight and Enforcement.' Orrick.

[16] Sullivan, P. (2025). 'Preparing for EU AI Act compliance with ISO 42001. A-LIGN.' available at: https://www.a-lign.com/articles/preparing-for-eu-ai-act-compliance; NAVEX. (2025). 'EU AI Act compliance requirements.' available at: https://www.navex.com/en-us/solutions/regulations/eu-ai-act/.

[17] European Confederation of Institutes of Internal Auditing (ECIIA). (2025). 'The AI Act Road to Compliance'.

9.3.1.1 Governance and Documentation

The legislation mandates a quality management system (QMS) for high-risk AI, requiring comprehensive documentation, risk management protocols, and post-market monitoring to ensure compliance[18]. Providers must retain records for at least 10 years as proof of compliance. Implementing frameworks like ISO 42001 can help organizations institutionalize governance through well-defined policies on accountability and risk mitigation[19].

9.3.1.2 Conformity Assessments

High-risk AI systems must undergo conformity assessments before deployment, ensuring adherence to key requirements such as data governance, transparency, and accuracy[20]. Depending on system complexity, these assessments can be conducted internally or by third-party auditors[21].

9.3.1.3 AI Literacy and Training

The Act emphasizes the importance of AI literacy, requiring organizations to ensure that employees involved in AI development, deployment, or oversight receive adequate training. Training programs must cover technical competencies, risk awareness, and ethical considerations[22].

[18] Id.

[19] Sullivan, P. (2025). 'Preparing for EU AI Act compliance with ISO 42001. A-LIGN'.

[20] Casovan, A., & Güclütürk, O. (2024). 'Top 10 operational impacts of the EU AI Act'.

IAPP. available at: https://iapp.org/resources/article/top-impacts-eu-ai-act-ai-assurance-risk-categories/.

[21] Jones Day. (2025). 'EU AI Act: First rules take effect on prohibited AI systems.' available at: https://www.jonesday.com/en/insights/2025/02/eu-ai-act-first-rules-take-effect-on-prohibited-ai-systems.

[22] NAVEX. (2025). 'EU AI Act compliance requirements.'; De Boel, L., Mithal, M., Nuding, M., & O'Neil, J. (2025). 'The EU's AI Act starts to apply as of February 2, 2025.' Wilson Sonsini. available at: https://www.wsgr.com/en/insights/the-eus-ai-act-starts-to-apply-as-of-february-2-2025.html.

9.3.1.4 Fundamental Rights Impact Assessments (FRIAs)

Organizations deploying high-risk AI systems must conduct FRIAs to evaluate potential risks to privacy, non-discrimination, and other fundamental rights. This requirement reinforces the Act's focus on ethical AI deployment and human rights protection[23].

9.3.2 Audit Requirements

9.3.2.1 Internal and Third-Party Audits

Regular audits are mandated for high-risk AI systems to ensure ongoing compliance. Internal audits assess adherence to technical documentation and risk management protocols, while external third-party audits are required for high-risk applications such as biometric identification[24].

9.3.2.2 Audit Challenges

The dynamic nature of AI, particularly adaptive algorithms, poses significant challenges for auditors in ensuring reproducibility and consistency in testing outcomes. Additionally, regulatory ambiguity complicates the translation of legal provisions into clear audit criteria[25].

9.3.2.3 Enforcement Preparedness

Organizations must maintain audit-ready documentation, including conformity assessments, risk mitigation measures, and employee training records[26]. Non-compliance with the Act's provisions can result in severe financial penalties, including fines of up to €35 million or 7% of global revenue[27].

[23] NAVEX. (2025). 'EU AI Act compliance requirements'.

[24] Casovan, A., & Güclütürk, O. (2024). 'Top 10 operational impacts of the EU AI Act'.

IAPP; European Confederation of Institutes of Internal Auditing (ECIIA). (2025). 'The AI Act Road to Compliance'.

[25] Gupta, P. (2024). 'European Union Artificial Intelligence Act: An auditor's perspective.' ISACA. available at: https://www.isaca.org/resources/news-and-trends/isaca-now-blog/2024/european-union-artificial-intelligence-act-an-auditors-perspective.

[26] Sullivan, P. (2025). 'Preparing for EU AI Act compliance with ISO 42001. A-LIGN.'; Sremack, J. (2024). 'Understanding the EU's Artificial Intelligence Act.' Marcum LLP. available at: https://www.marcumllp.com/insights/understanding-the-eus-artificial-intelligence-act-key-points-for-legal-and-compliance-professionals.

[27] NAVEX. (2025). 'EU AI Act compliance requirements'.

9.4 Implementation Timeline, Enforcement Mechanisms, and Global Policy

9.4.1 Implementation Timeline and Strategic Transitional Considerations

The EU AI Act introduces a phased implementation schedule with staggered compliance deadlines designed to provide businesses with sufficient time to adapt their AI development and deployment practices to the new regulatory framework. This gradual rollout reflects the European Commission's recognition of the operational and technical challenges associated with compliance[28]. The implementation timeline consists of the following key milestones:

- August 2024: The Act enters into force.
- February 2025: Bans on unacceptable-risk AI take effect.
- August 2025: Regulations for general-purpose AI (GPAI) models begin.
- August 2026: Full enforcement of high-risk AI requirements.
- August 2027: All compliance requirements fully applicable.

9.4.2 Entry into Force and Initial Prohibitions on Unacceptable-Risk AI

The EU AI Act formally came into force on August 1, 2024, marking the beginning of the compliance transition period. However, the first major regulatory deadline occurred on February 2, 2025, when prohibitions on unacceptable-risk AI systems became legally enforceable across the EU[29]. Organizations must ensure they are not developing or deploying AI systems that fall into prohibited categories, including:

- Social scoring systems that assess individuals based on personal characteristics or behaviors.

[28] Business Software Alliance. (2025). 'The EU AI Act: A Practical Guide for Businesses.' available at: https://www.bsa.org/policy-filings/eu-a-balanced-approach-to-general-purpose-ai-in-the-eu-ai-act.

[29] European Commission. (2024a). 'AI Act implementation timeline.' available at: https://digital-strategy.ec.europa.eu/en/policies/ai-act-implementation-timeline.

- Manipulative AI applications designed to exploit vulnerabilities of users.
- Remote biometric identification technologies used in public spaces, except in narrowly defined law enforcement scenarios[30].

Additionally, this phase introduces transparency requirements for AI-generated content, including deepfakes and other synthetic media. Providers must implement clear disclosure mechanisms to inform users when they are interacting with artificially generated content[31].

9.4.3 General-Purpose AI Model Regulations

The next enforcement deadline, August 1, 2025, focuses on GPAI models, particularly foundation models with systemic risks. Providers must comply with governance and transparency requirements, including:

- Documentation of training methodologies and datasets.
- Risk assessments to evaluate potential societal harm.
- Disclosure of copyright-protected materials used in model training[32].

For GPAI systems classified as posing systemic risks, additional obligations apply, such as adversarial testing, incident reporting, and safeguards against generating prohibited content[33]. This phase also marks the establishment of the AI Office, which will oversee compliance, issue guidance, and coordinate with national regulatory authorities[34].

[30] CNIL. (2024). 'AI Act: essential dates to remember.' available at: https://www.cnil.fr/en/ai-act-essential-dates-remember.

[31] Business Software Alliance. (2025). 'The EU AI Act: A Practical Guide for Businesses'.

[32] European Commission. (2024a). 'AI Act implementation timeline'.

[33] Hildebrand, M. and Rubin, J. (2024). 'EU AI Act: Implementation and enforcement explainer.' Lowenstein Sandler. available at: https://www.lowenstein.com/news-insights/publications/client-alerts/the-eu-artificial-intelligence-act-of-2024-what-you-need-to-know-privacy.

[34] Woodland, A. (2024). 'The EU AI Act: What does the EU AI Act mean for employers?' Clifford Chance. available at: https://publisher-prod65.cliffordchance.com/briefings/2024/08/what-does-the-eu-ai-act-mean-for-employers-.html.

9.4.4 *High-Risk AI System Requirements*

On August 2, 2026, full enforcement of high-risk AI requirements begins, concluding the primary 2-year transition period. Providers and deployers of high-risk AI applications must comply with:

- Conformity assessments to demonstrate compliance.
- Quality management systems ensuring AI system reliability.
- Human oversight mechanisms to prevent automation bias.
- Robust data governance frameworks to ensure ethical AI development[35].

Industries affected include healthcare, transportation, education, employment, financial services, and critical infrastructure. Organizations operating in these sectors must conduct risk assessments, system audits, and operational adjustments to ensure compliance readiness.

9.4.5 *Full Regulatory Application*

The final implementation phase, commencing August 2, 2027, extends the AI Act's requirements to all applicable AI systems, including those functioning as safety components in products covered under EU legislation[36]. From this date, the AI Act operates at full capacity, enforcing penalties for non-compliance and ensuring AI systems meet EU regulatory standards.

9.4.6 *Enforcement Mechanisms and Compliance Infrastructure*

The EU AI Act establishes a multi-layered enforcement structure that combines centralized oversight with national regulatory implementation.

- The European AI Office and AI Board. At the EU level, the European Artificial Intelligence Office plays a central role in overseeing GPAI compliance, issuing guidance, and coordinating national regulators. Working alongside it, the European Artificial Intelligence

[35] CNIL. (2024). 'AI Act: essential dates to remember.'

[36] European Commission. (2024a). 'AI Act implementation timeline.'

Board provides advisory functions and ensures harmonized enforcement across member states[37].

- National Market Surveillance Authorities. Member states designate national market surveillance authorities to conduct inspections, investigate violations, and initiate enforcement actions[38]. This decentralized approach, however, raises concerns about regulatory inconsistencies across different jurisdictions, which the AI Act seeks to mitigate through coordination mechanisms[39].
- Compliance Verification and Technical Standards. The AI Act employs a mix of self-assessment and third-party verification:
  - Providers of high-risk AI systems must conduct internal conformity assessments and document compliance[40].
  - Certain high-risk applications require third-party certification from notified bodies, independent organizations designated by member states to assess regulatory compliance[41].
  - The EU standardization bodies are developing harmonized technical standards to ensure consistent compliance evaluation across AI systems.
- Enforcement Actions and Penalties. The AI Act grants regulators extensive enforcement powers, including system withdrawals, suspension of operations, and financial penalties. The three-tiered sanction framework includes fines up to:
  - €7.5 million or 1% of global turnover for minor violations.
  - €35 million or 7% of global turnover for serious infringements[42].

[37] Id.

[38] Hildebrand, M. and Rubin, J. (2024). 'EU AI Act: Implementation and enforcement explainer'.

[39] Woodland, A. (2024). 'The EU AI Act: What does the EU AI Act mean for employers?' Clifford Chance.

[40] European Commission. (2024a). 'AI Act implementation timeline'.

[41] Business Software Alliance. (2025). 'The EU AI Act: A Practical Guide for Businesses'.

[42] Conventus Law. (2024). 'The EU AI Act: Implications for Non-EU Businesses.' available at: https://conventuslaw.com/featured-content/new-eu-ai-act-guidelines-what-are-the-implications-for-businesses/.

- These penalties exceed GDPR fines, reflecting the EU's strong commitment to regulatory enforcement and AI safety[43].

9.4.7 Global Policy Implications and U.S. Considerations

The EU AI Act has far-reaching implications beyond Europe, particularly for U.S. companies operating in global AI markets.

- The Brussels Effect and Regulatory Influence. The AI Act exemplifies the Brussels Effect, wherein EU regulations influence global standards through market access requirements[44]. Like GDPR, the AI Act extends compliance obligations to any company serving EU customers, effectively setting international AI norms[45].
- Strategic Considerations for U.S. Policymakers. The EU's first-mover advantage in AI regulation raises strategic challenges for the U.S.:
  - Competitive Disadvantages—American firms face EU regulatory burdens without a comparable U.S. framework[46].
  - Pressure for U.S. Regulation—The Biden Administration's AI Executive Order and AI Risk Management Framework[47], was revoked by President Trump on January 20, 2025. The Office of Management and Budget (OMB) has been directed to revise the guidance on AI to "sustain and enhance America's global AI dominance"[48].

[43] European Commission. (2024a). 'AI Act implementation timeline'.

[44] Bradford, A. (2020). *The Brussels Effect: How the European Union Rules the World*. Oxford University Press.

[45] Hildebrand, M. and Rubin, J. (2024). 'EU AI Act: Implementation and enforcement explainer'.

[46] KPMG. (2024). 'How the EU AI Act affects US-based companies.' available at: https://kpmg.com/us/en/articles/2024/how-eu-ai-actaffects-us-based-companies.html.

[47] Engler, A. (2023). 'The EU and U.S. diverge on AI regulation: A transatlantic comparison and steps to alignment.' Brookings available at: https://www.wilsoncenter.org/publication/transatlantic-perspectives-artificial- intelligence-regulation.

[48] Alder, M. (2025, January 23). 'Trump orders review of Biden admin's AI work, creation of new AI action plan.' FedScoop. Available at: https://fedscoop.com/trump-orders-review-of-biden-admins-ai-work-creation-of-new-ai-action-plan/.

- Transatlantic Coordination—Enhanced cooperation on AI governance could mitigate compliance burdens and foster regulatory alignment.

- Cross-Border Data Flows and Market Access. The AI Act's data governance and documentation requirements introduce challenges for U.S. firms managing cross-border data transfers. Companies must navigate overlapping compliance obligations between EU AI laws and U.S. privacy frameworks[49].

U.S. policymakers could:

- Develop parallel AI regulations aligned with EU standards while preserving U.S. innovation priorities[50].
- Establish bilateral agreements for mutual regulatory recognition[51].
- Influence global AI standards through ISO, IEEE, and other technical organizations[52].

The EU AI Act's implementation signals a defining moment in AI governance, with significant transatlantic implications. Ongoing dialogue between the EU and the U.S. will be critical in balancing regulatory effectiveness with innovation-friendly policies. However, the Trump administration revoked Biden's AI Executive Order because it "established unnecessarily burdensome requirements for companies developing and deploying AI that would stifle private sector innovation and threaten American technological leadership"[53].

[49] Bradford, A. (2020). *The Brussels Effect: How the European Union Rules the World*. Oxford University Press.

[50] KPMG. (2024). 'How the EU AI Act affects US-based companies.' available at: https://kpmg.com/us/en/articles/2024/how-eu-ai-actaffects-us-based-companies.html.

[51] Engler, A. (2023). 'The EU and U.S. diverge on AI regulation: A transatlantic comparison and steps to alignment.' Brookings.

[52] Bradford, A. (2020). *The Brussels Effect: How the European Union Rules the World*. Oxford University Press.

[53] Ochs, D., Betts, J. G., & Zagger, Z. V. (2025, February 7). 'Trump administration unveils new AI policy, reverses Biden's regulatory framework.' Ogletree Deakins. available at: https://ogletree.com/insights-resources/blog-posts/trump-administration-unveils-new-ai-policy-reverses-bidens-regulatory-framework/.

9.5 Challenges for U.S. Companies Operating in the EU

The Trump administration's recent AI policy shift introduces significant challenges for U.S. companies operating in the European market, where regulatory frameworks differ markedly[54]. The contrast between the EU's risk-based approach and the U.S.'s innovation-driven policies creates legal uncertainty, compliance burdens, and potential market barriers for American firms.

9.5.1 Risk Classification and Legal Uncertainty

U.S. firms must navigate the complexities of self-assessing their AI models under the EU AI Act, a process complicated by the divergence between U.S. and EU regulations. Trump's Executive Order 14,179, issued on January 23, 2025, prioritizes "sustaining and enhancing America's global AI dominance"[55]. This approach departs from the EU's emphasis on risk assessment and mitigation, increasing compliance uncertainty for U.S. firms operating in Europe.

The EU AI Act lacks clear definitions for many AI risks, forcing U.S. companies to interpret ambiguous guidelines while adhering to a U.S. regulatory framework that emphasizes market-driven governance. As a result, American firms face significant legal uncertainty when deploying AI solutions in the EU, potentially exposing them to regulatory penalties for non-compliance[56].

[54] Krause, D. (2024, November 12). 'Artificial Intelligence and the Changing Political Landscape: The Impact of Trump's Return on AI Governance and Policy.' Available at: SSRN. https://ssrn.com/abstract=5018240.

[55] Huffman, R., Lee, N., Burnette, R., Shapanka, M., & Gweon, A. (2025, February). 'January 2025 AI developments—Transitioning to the Trump administration. Inside Government Contracts.' available at: https://www.insidegovernmentcontracts.com/2025/02/january-2025-ai-developments-transitioning-to-the-trump-administration/.

[56] 2021.ai. (2025). 'Understanding the EU AI Act penalties and achieving regulatory compliance.' available at: https://2021.ai/news/understanding-the-eu-ai-act-penalties-and-achieving-regulatory-compliance.

9.5.2 *Compliance Burdens for High-Risk AI*

The EU AI Act imposes significant compliance costs, particularly for AI models classified as high-risk. Estimates suggest that compliance expenses range from €400,000 to €2 million per system, with annual governance costs of approximately €52,000, including certification and documentation expenses[57]. In contrast, the Trump administration's policies emphasize minimizing regulatory burdens, with Executive Order 14,179 advocating the removal of "unnecessarily burdensome requirements"[58].

For U.S. companies, these divergent approaches create operational challenges. While firms must meet stringent EU documentation and transparency mandates, their domestic counterparts operate under a less restrictive regime. This dual regulatory framework may reduce incentives for U.S. companies to expand into the European market, given the financial and administrative burden of compliance.

9.5.3 *Potential Market Barriers for U.S. AI Firms*

The disparity in AI regulation may disproportionately affect U.S. startups and SMEs, which often lack the financial resources to navigate complex compliance frameworks. Large firms such as Google, OpenAI, Meta, and Microsoft are better positioned to absorb regulatory costs, potentially leading to market consolidation in favor of major industry players. Additionally, the Trump administration's policy focus on "enhancing America's global AI dominance"[59] does not address the regulatory challenges smaller U.S. AI firms face in international markets. Without targeted support or policy alignment, these companies risk exclusion from the European market, limiting their global competitiveness.

[57] Id.

[58] Huffman, R., Lee, N., Burnette, R., Shapanka, M., & Gweon, A. (2025, February). 'January 2025 AI developments—Transitioning to the Trump administration. Inside Government Contracts'.

[59] Huffman, R., Lee, N., Burnette, R., Shapanka, M., & Gweon, A. (2025, February). 'January 2025 AI developments—Transitioning to the Trump administration. Inside Government Contracts'.

9.5.4 *Policy Considerations for U.S. Policymakers*

To address these challenges, U.S. policymakers must consider several key issues:

- Regulatory Alignment: The U.S. must assess whether closer alignment with EU AI regulations is necessary to facilitate market access for American firms. While the Trump administration has resisted EU-style oversight, failing to adapt could disadvantage U.S. companies operating internationally.
- Balancing Innovation and Regulation: While reducing regulatory barriers is central to current U.S. policy[60], excessive deregulation may hinder market access for AI firms needing to comply with foreign regulatory regimes.
- Support for SMEs: Policymakers should explore mechanisms to help smaller AI firms navigate international compliance requirements, such as financial incentives, regulatory guidance, or bilateral agreements with the EU.
- International Cooperation: Despite the administration's focus on U.S. AI leadership, fostering international regulatory cooperation could reduce compliance costs and mitigate barriers to entry for American firms in the European market.

The U.S.-EU regulatory divide presents substantial challenges for American AI companies. Without strategic adjustments to policy, U.S. firms may struggle to compete in the European market, underscoring the need for a balanced approach to AI governance that fosters innovation while ensuring international compliance.

[60] Milaninia, N., O'Brien, A. C., Radin, O., Vermynck, E., Apte, E. R., & Zaldivar, R. (2025). 'Trump administration early executive orders signal shift in AI policy.' King & Spalding. available at: https://www.kslaw.com/news-and-insights/trump-administration-early-executive-orders-signal-shift-in-ai-policy.

9.6 U.S.-EU Regulatory Conflicts and Policy Implications

The Trump administration's recent shift in AI policy has created significant regulatory divergence between the U.S. and the European Union, leading to potential conflicts and policy implications for both regions.

9.6.1 Differences Between the EU AI Act & U.S. AI Policy

The contrast between the EU's comprehensive AI regulation and the Trump administration's deregulatory approach is stark. Executive Order 14,179 seeks to remove regulatory barriers to AI innovation[61]. This order represents a significant departure from the previous administration's focus on AI safety and security.

Key differences include:

- Regulatory Approach: While the EU AI Act mandates compliance with strict guidelines and imposes legal penalties for violations, the Trump administration emphasizes reducing regulatory burdens on AI developers and deployers.
- Risk Classification: The EU AI Act categorizes AI systems based on risk levels, requiring specific compliance measures for each category. In contrast, the U.S. approach under the Trump administration does not include a formal risk classification system for AI[62].
- Enforcement Mechanisms: The EU AI Act includes clear investigatory powers and the ability to impose significant fines for noncompliance. The U.S. lacks explicit legal authority to regulate AI algorithms, relying instead on existing laws and potential litigation to address AI-related issues.

[61] Milaninia, N., O'Brien, A. C., Radin, O., Vermynck, E., Apte, E. R., & Zaldivar, R. (2025). 'Trump administration early executive orders signal shift in AI policy.' King & Spalding. available at: https://www.kslaw.com/news-and-insights/trump-administration-early-executive-orders-signal-shift-in-ai-policy.

[62] Ganesh, H. (2024). 'EU and US AI Regulation Differences: Compliance Guide for Tech.' The National Law Review. available at: https://natlawreview.com/article/difference-between-eu-and-us-ai-regulation-foreshadowing-future-litigation-ai

9.6.2 *Potential Conflicts with U.S. Tech Policy*

The divergent approaches to AI regulation between the U.S. and the EU are likely to create several areas of conflict:

- Global Standards: There is concern that the EU AI Act may become a de facto global standard, like the GDPR precedent. This could force U.S. companies to comply with EU regulations to maintain access to the European market, potentially increasing operating costs and compliance responsibilities[63].
- Data Sovereignty & Privacy Laws: The different rules for AI data collection and use between the U.S. and EU may create challenges for U.S. companies operating in both markets. The Trump administration's emphasis on reducing barriers to AI development may conflict with the EU's stricter data protection requirements[64].
- Trade Implications: U.S. AI firms may face barriers in the EU market due to the stringent requirements of the AI Act. This could potentially lead to trade tensions, as the Trump administration has expressed opposition to foreign AI regulations affecting U.S. businesses, framing them as barriers to innovation and economic growth.
- Content Moderation and Free Speech: The Trump administration's "free speech" agenda for AI platforms contrasts sharply with the EU's push to regulate AI-driven misinformation and disinformation. This divergence creates significant challenges for U.S. companies operating in both jurisdictions.

9.6.3 *What U.S. Policymakers Should Consider*

Given these conflicts and implications, U.S. policymakers face several critical considerations:

[63] Ganesh, H. (2024). 'EU and US AI Regulation Differences: Compliance Guide for Tech'.

[64] Milaninia, N., O'Brien, A. C., Radin, O., Vermynck, E., Apte, E. R., & Zaldivar, R. (2025). 'Trump administration early executive orders signal shift in AI policy'.

- Federal AI Law: While the Trump administration has moved away from comprehensive AI regulation, policymakers should consider whether developing a federal AI law to align with the EU could benefit U.S. companies operating globally. This could help prevent regulatory fragmentation and ease compliance burdens for U.S. firms[65].
- Supporting Innovation: U.S. regulators must balance the administration's goal of promoting AI innovation with the need for some level of oversight. This could involve developing flexible regulatory frameworks that adapt to rapidly evolving AI technologies without imposing excessive compliance burdens[66].
- International Cooperation: Despite the current administration's focus on U.S. AI dominance, exploring avenues for international cooperation on AI governance could help reduce regulatory divergence and ease the burden on U.S. companies operating globally.
- Sector-Specific Approaches: Given the diverse array of AI legislation being considered at the state level, federal policymakers might consider sector-specific AI regulations that address high-risk areas while maintaining a permissive approach to AI development[67].
- Small and Medium-Sized Enterprises: Policymakers should consider measures to support SMEs in navigating international regulatory landscapes, ensuring that the U.S. AI sector remains diverse and competitive globally[68].

The regulatory conflicts between the U.S. and the EU in AI policy present significant challenges and opportunities for U.S. policymakers. Balancing the promotion of innovation with the 'need for responsible AI development and international competitiveness will be crucial in shaping the future of AI governance in the U.S.

[65] Ganesh, H. (2024). 'EU and US AI Regulation Differences: Compliance Guide for Tech'.

[66] Johnson, J., Ponder, J., & Gweon, A. (2025). 'State legislatures consider new wave of 2025 AI legislation.' Inside Privacy. available at: https://www.insideprivacy.com/artificial-intelligence/blog-post-state-legislatures-consider-new-wave-of-2025-ai-legislation/.

[67] Johnson, J., Ponder, J., & Gweon, A. (2025). 'State legislatures consider new wave of 2025 AI legislation'.

[68] Ganesh, H. (2024). 'EU and US AI Regulation Differences: Compliance Guide for Tech'.

9.7 Strategic Recommendations for U.S. Policymakers

Considering the Trump administration's recent shift in AI policy and the growing regulatory divergence between the U.S. and the European Union, U.S. policymakers face several important challenges. The following recommendations seek to address these challenges while aligning with the current administration's focus on maintaining U.S. global AI dominance and reducing regulatory burdens.

9.7.1 Regulatory Coordination

While the Trump administration has emphasized deregulation and the removal of barriers to AI innovation, some level of coordination with the EU remains crucial. U.S. policymakers should engage in bilateral AI policy discussions with the EU to prevent conflicting standards that could hinder U.S. companies' global competitiveness. However, these discussions should focus on identifying areas of mutual interest rather than adopting EU-style regulations.

The administration's "AI Action Plan," currently in development, offers an opportunity to address international regulatory coordination[69]. Policymakers should ensure that this plan includes strategies for engaging with international partners while maintaining the U.S. commitment to AI leadership and innovation.

9.7.2 AI Safety and Innovation Balance

Instead of adopting strict regulations like the EU AI Act, the U.S. could develop a sector-based AI risk framework that aligns with the administration's goal of promoting innovation. This approach would focus on high-priority sectors such as finance, healthcare, and defense, where AI applications pose the greatest potential risks or benefits to national security and economic competitiveness.

The Trump administration's emphasis on "free speech" in AI development and opposition to content restrictions presents a unique challenge

[69] Huffman, R., Lee, N., Burnette, R., Shapanka, M., & Gweon, A. (2025, February). 'January 2025 AI developments—Transitioning to the Trump administration. Inside Government Contracts'.

in balancing innovation with responsible AI development[70]. Policymakers should consider developing guidelines that promote responsible AI use without imposing burdensome regulations that could stifle innovation.

9.7.3 Support for U.S. AI Competitiveness

To help U.S. firms adapt to the EU AI Act and maintain their global competitiveness, policymakers should consider providing tax incentives and funding for AI compliance research. This approach aligns with the administration's focus on sustaining U.S. AI dominance while addressing the challenges posed by divergent international regulations.

The recently announced "Stargate" partnership, which aims to invest $500 billion in AI infrastructure in the U.S., demonstrates the administration's commitment to maintaining U.S. leadership in AI technology[71]. Policymakers should leverage this initiative to support U.S. companies in developing AI solutions that can compete globally while meeting varying regulatory requirements.

9.7.4 Harmonization with International AI Governance

While the Trump administration has prioritized U.S. interests and sovereignty in AI development, some level of international cooperation remains necessary. The U.S. should lead efforts at organizations such as the OECD, G7, and UN to establish global AI standards that align with both U.S. and EU policies while preserving the flexibility and innovation-focused approach favored by the current administration.

These efforts should be carefully balanced against the administration's stance on protecting U.S. interests. As evidenced by recent actions, such as the memorandum threatening tariffs on countries deemed

[70] Milaninia, N., O'Brien, A. C., Radin, O., Vermynck, E., Apte, E. R., & Zaldivar, R. (2025). 'Trump administration early executive orders signal shift in AI policy.'

[71] Huffman, R., Lee, N., Burnette, R., Shapanka, M., & Gweon, A. (2025, February). 'January 2025 AI developments—Transitioning to the Trump administration. Inside Government Contracts.'

to be hindering American companies' global competitiveness, policymakers must navigate a complex landscape of international relations and economic priorities[72].

U.S. policymakers face the challenge of maintaining global AI leadership while addressing the regulatory divergence with the EU and other international partners. By focusing on sector-specific approaches, supporting U.S. AI competitiveness, and selectively engaging in international cooperation, policymakers can work toward achieving the Trump administration's goals of AI dominance and reduced regulatory burdens while still addressing critical issues of AI governance and safety.

9.8 Conclusion

The EU AI Act represents the most comprehensive artificial intelligence regulatory framework to date, setting a precedent for global AI governance. Its risk-based classification system imposes obligations that scale with the potential risks posed by AI applications. Minimal-risk AI systems face no compliance requirements, whereas unacceptable-risk AI systems, such as those involving manipulative behavior and social scoring, are outright banned. High-risk AI systems, including those used in biometric identification and employment decision-making, must adhere to stringent transparency, documentation, and oversight protocols. The Act's risk categories provide a legal framework for AI classification, transforming AI risk analysis from a subjective business decision into a structured regulatory requirement. For U.S. companies operating in Europe, compliance with the EU AI Act will require substantial adjustments in governance structures, data management practices, and audit mechanisms. Organizations must integrate AI risk assessments into their broader compliance frameworks and ensure that AI applications align with EU-defined transparency, accountability, and risk management standards.

Beyond corporate compliance, the Act poses critical strategic questions for U.S. policymakers. With AI governance frameworks diverging globally, the U.S. must determine whether to align its regulatory stance with the EU or adopt a distinct approach emphasizing innovation-driven

[72] European Union Institute for Security Studies (ISS). (2025, February 27). 'Trump takes aim at 'overseas extortion' of American tech companies.' https://www.iss.europa.eu/publications/commentary/trump-takes-aim-overseas-extortion-american-tech-companies-eu-us-rift.

policies. While regulatory alignment could facilitate market access and standardization, it may also introduce constraints that hinder technological progress and competitiveness. Conversely, pursuing an independent AI governance framework could bolster U.S. innovation but create challenges for multinational companies navigating conflicting regulatory landscapes.

A balanced strategy is essential—one that upholds AI safety and ethical considerations while fostering an innovation-friendly ecosystem. U.S. policymakers should explore sector-specific AI regulations tailored to industry risks rather than adopting a blanket regulatory framework. Additionally, proactive engagement with international AI governance bodies, such as the OECD and G7, can help shape global standards that support AI growth without imposing undue regulatory burdens.

The EU AI Act signals a pivotal shift in AI governance, prompting both companies and policymakers to reassess compliance strategies and regulatory approaches. For U.S. stakeholders, navigating these evolving requirements will be crucial in sustaining AI leadership while mitigating legal and operational risks associated with global AI regulation.

References

2021.ai. (2025). Understanding the EU AI Act penalties and achieving regulatory compliance. https://2021.ai/news/understanding-the-eu-ai-act-penalties-and-achieving-regulatory-compliance

Alder, M. (2025, January 23). Trump orders review of Biden admin's AI work, creation of new AI action plan. FedScoop. https://fedscoop.com/trump-orders-review-of-biden-admins-ai-work-creation-of-new-ai-action-plan/

Apostle, J. (2024). The EU AI Act: Oversight and Enforcement. Orrick. https://www.orrick.com/en/Insights/2024/09/The-EU-AI-Act-Oversight-and-Enforcement

Artificial Intelligence Act. (2023). Article 16: Obligations of Providers of High-Risk AI Systems. https://artificialintelligenceact.eu/article/16/

Autoriteit Persoonsgegevens. (2025). EU AI Act risk groups. https://www.autoriteitpersoonsgegevens.nl/en/themes/algorithms-ai/eu-ai-act/eu-ai-act-risk-groups

Bradford, A. (2020). The Brussels Effect: How the European Union Rules the World. Oxford University Press. https://global.oup.com/academic/product/the-brussels-effect-9780190088583

Business Software Alliance (BSA). (2025). The EU AI Act: A Practical Guide for Businesses. https://www.bsa.org/policy-filings/eu-a-balanced-approach-to-general-purpose-ai-in-the-eu-ai-act
Casovan, A., & Güclütürk, O. (2024). Top 10 operational impacts of the EU AI Act.
IAPP. https://iapp.org/resources/article/top-impacts-eu-ai-act-ai-assurance-risk-categories/
CNIL. (2024). AI Act: essential dates to remember. https://www.cnil.fr/en/ai-act-essential-dates-remember
Conventus Law. (2024). The EU AI Act: Implications for Non-EU Businesses. https://conventuslaw.com/featured-content/new-eu-ai-act-guidelines-what-are-the-implications-for-businesses/
De Boel, L., Mithal, M., Nuding, M., & O'Neil, J. (2025). The EU's AI Act starts to apply as of February 2, 2025. Wilson Sonsini. https://www.wsgr.com/en/insights/the-eus-ai-act-starts-to-apply-as-of-february-2-2025.html
Engler, A. (2023). The EU and U.S. diverge on AI regulation: A transatlantic comparison and steps to alignment. Brookings. https://www.wilsoncenter.org/publication/transatlantic-perspectives-artificial-intelligence-regulation
European Commission. (2024a). AI Act implementation timeline. https://digital-strategy.ec.europa.eu/en/policies/ai-act-implementation-timeline
European Parliament. (2025). EU AI Act: first regulation on artificial intelligence. https://www.europarl.europa.eu/topics/en/article/20230601STO93804/eu-ai-act-first-regulation-on-artificial-intelligence
European Confederation of Institutes of Internal Auditing (ECIIA). (2025). The AI Act Road to Compliance. Retrieved from https://www.eciia.eu/wp-content/uploads/2025/01/The-AI-Act-Road-to-Compliance-Final-1.pdf
Frazier, T. (2024). EU AI Act and Its Relevance to US-Based Companies. Class. https://www.class.com/blog/summary-of-the-eu-ai-act/
Ganesh, H. (2024). EU and US AI Regulation Differences: Compliance Guide for Tech. The National Law Review. https://natlawreview.com/article/difference-between-eu-and-us-ai-regulation-foreshadowing-future-litigation-ai
Güçlütürk, O. and Hilliard, A. (2025). Penalties of the EU AI Act: The High Cost of Non-Compliance. https://www.holisticai.com/blog/penalties-of-the-eu-ai-act
Gupta, P. (2024). European Union Artificial Intelligence Act: An auditor's perspective.
ISACA. https://www.isaca.org/resources/news-and-trends/isaca-now-blog/2024/european-union-artificial-intelligence-act-an-auditors-perspective
Hildebrand, M. and Rubin, J. (2024). EU AI Act: Implementation and enforcement explainer. Lowenstein Sandler. https://www.lowenstein.com/news-insights/publications/client-alerts/the-eu-artificial-intelligence-act-of-2024-what-you-need-to-know-privacy

Huffman, R., Lee, N., Burnette, R., Shapanka, M., & Gweon, A. (2025, February). January 2025 AI developments—Transitioning to the Trump administration. Inside Government Contracts. https://www.insidegovernmentcontracts.com/2025/02/january-2025-ai-developments-transitioning-to-the-trump-administration/

Huffman, R., Lee, N., Burnette, R., Shapanka, M., & Gweon, A. (2025, March 14). February 2025 AI Developments Under the Trump Administration. Inside Global Tech. https://www.insideglobaltech.com/2025/03/14/february-2025-ai-developments-under-the-trump-administration/

European Union Institute for Security Studies (ISS). (2025, February 27). Trump takes aim at 'overseas extortion' of American tech companies. https://www.iss.europa.eu/publications/commentary/trump-takes-aim-overseas-extortion-american-tech-companies-eu-us-rift

Johnson, J., Ponder, J., & Gweon, A. (2025). State legislatures consider new wave of 2025 AI legislation. Inside Privacy. https://www.insideprivacy.com/artificial-intelligence/blog-post-state-legislatures-consider-new-wave-of-2025-ai-legislation/

Jones Day. (2025). EU AI Act: First rules take effect on prohibited AI systems. https://www.jonesday.com/en/insights/2025/02/eu-ai-act-first-rules-take-effect-on-prohibited-ai-systems

KPMG. (2024). How the EU AI Act affects US-based companies. https://kpmg.com/us/en/articles/2024/how-eu-ai-act-affects-us-based-companies.html

Krause, D. (2024, November 12). Artificial Intelligence and the Changing Political Landscape: The Impact of Trump's Return on AI Governance and Policy. SSRN. https://ssrn.com/abstract=5018240.

Milaninia, N., O'Brien, A. C., Radin, O., Vermynck, E., Apte, E. R., & Zaldivar, R. (2025). Trump administration early executive orders signal shift in AI policy. King & Spalding. https://www.kslaw.com/news-and-insights/trump-administration-early-executive-orders-signal-shift-in-ai-policy

NAVEX. (2025). EU AI Act compliance requirements. https://www.navex.com/en-us/solutions/regulations/eu-ai-act/

Ochs, D., Betts, J. G., & Zagger, Z. V. (2025, February 7). Trump administration unveils new AI policy, reverses Biden's regulatory framework. Ogletree Deakins. https://ogletree.com/insights-resources/blog-posts/trump-administration-unveils-new-ai-policy-reverses-bidens-regulatory-framework/

Peaden, V. (2024). EU AI Act Tightens Grip on High-Risk AI Systems. Baker Donelson. https://www.bakerdonelson.com/eu-ai-act-tightens-grip-on-high-risk-ai-systems-five-critical-questions-for-us-companies

Sremack, J. (2024). Understanding the EU's Artificial Intelligence Act. Marcum LLP. https://www.marcumllp.com/insights/understanding-the-eus-artificial-intelligence-act-key-points-for-legal-and-compliance-professionals

Sullivan, P. (2025). Preparing for EU AI Act compliance with ISO 42001. A-LIGN. https://www.a-lign.com/articles/preparing-for-eu-ai-act-compliance
Trail ML. (2025). EU AI Act: Risk-Classifications of the AI Regulation. https://www.trail-ml.com/blog/eu-ai-act-how-risk-is-classified
White House. (2025, January 23). Removing Barriers to American Leadership in Artificial Intelligence. The White House, US GOV. https://www.whitehouse.gov/presidential-actions/2025/01/removing-barriers-to-american-leadership-in-artificial-intelligence/
Woodland, A. (2024). The EU AI Act: What does the EU AI Act mean for employers?
Clifford Chance. https://publisher-prod65.cliffordchance.com/briefings/2024/08/what-does-the-eu-ai-act-mean-for-employers-.html

CHAPTER 10

Conclusion: Future of AI and the Rule of Law—Ethics and Regulatory Framework in Legal Tech and Digital Governance

Armando Aliu, Rūta Liepiņa, Sofia Klymchuk, Ikran Abdirahman, Beatrice Panattoni, Josh Lee Kok Thong, and Hellen van der Kroef

10.1 Embrace the Future of Digital Ethics and AI Regulation with Enthusiasm

The debates on ethics of *AI* and the need for *AI* regulation are unfolding across the world. Algorithms are extensively employed to make decisions that have profound impacts on societies and individuals, and these

A. Aliu (✉)
Institute of European Studies, Faculty of Social Sciences, University of Wrocław, Wrocław, Poland
e-mail: armando.aliu@uwr.edu.pl

R. Liepiņa
ALMA-AI Bologna Interdisciplinary Research Center for AI and Law, University of Bologna, Bologna, Italy
e-mail: ruta.liepina@unibo.it

A. Aliu (ed.), *Artificial Intelligence and the Rule of Law*,
https://doi.org/10.1007/978-3-031-97389-5_10

lead to social discrimination, violation of privacy and property rights, algorithmic biases, censorship, manipulation, etc. These concerns and challenges sparked academic debates and triggered regulating *AI* and designing digital ethics.[1] There is a necessity to develop regulations on AI governance and prepare for a world with many more privacy[2] and moral issues, copyright violations, and externalities than exist today.[3]

Although the regulators are in a rush to catch up with disruptive technological innovations and to create a regulatory framework for advanced

S. Klymchuk
Ministry of Digital Transformation of Ukraine, Kyiv, Ukraine
e-mail: sofia.klymchuk@gmail.com

I. Abdirahman
High Court of Kenya & the DIFA Legal, Nairobi, Kenya
e-mail: ikran@difaconsultancy.com

B. Panattoni
Department of Law, University of Verona, Verona, Italy

Faculty of Law, Economics and Finance, University of Luxembourg, Luxembourg, Luxembourg

B. Panattoni
e-mail: beatrice.panattoni@uni.lu

J. L. K. Thong
Department School of Law, University of California, Berkeley, Berkeley, USA
e-mail: joshleekt@berkeley.edu

H. van der Kroef
Law & Tech Lab, Faculty of Law, Maastricht University, Maastricht, Netherlands
e-mail: h.vanderkroef@maastrichtuniversity.nl

[1] Ebers, M. (2020). Regulating AI and robotics: Ethical and legal challenges. In: Ebers, M. & Navas, S. (eds.) *Algorithms and Law* (pp. 37–99). Cambridge: CUP, pp. 37–38.

[2] Many people think that *AI* apps in smartphones already know too much about us. Yet these *AI* apps and synchronized advanced technologies offer '*digital immortality*' and '*digital reincarnation*', the issue of protecting digital data and dead people privacy (*post-mortem privacy*) is becoming problematic.

[3] Lee, K. F. & Qiufan, C. (2021). *AI 2041: Ten Visions for Our Future*. London: WH Allen, p. 209.

technologies, regulation on the ground is likely to be years away.[4] In this regard, the future of regulation for *AI* will likelihood remain fragmented due to the lack of collective vision, common objectives, and diverging interests in implementing policies, strategies, and practices in the field of *AI*. Ethics has become embedded in social and political responses to algorithms and *AI* and their deployments in more and more spheres of social life.[5] In this context, three ethical principles form the cornerstone of an effective *AI* model—i.e. transparency, explainability, and accountability.

Transparency means that "*AI* systems are developed and used in a way that allows appropriate traceability and explainability, while making humans aware that they communicate or interact with an *AI* system, as well as duly informing deployers of the capabilities and limitations of that *AI* system and affected persons about their rights"[6]. **Explainability** means being able to explain on the level of individual users, as well as on a collective level if the system affects groups[7]. **Accountability** is closely linked to the principle of **fairness**, and it necessitates that mechanisms be put in place to ensure responsibility and accountability for *AI* systems and their outcomes, both before and after their development, deployment, and use.[8] Beside these three ethical principles, the future regulation of *AI* must take into account the following ethical themes and related issues[9]:

1. **Justice** in terms of fairness, prevention/mitigation of algorithmic biases that can lead to discrimination, and fair access to the benefits of *AI*,

[4] Sinha, G. & Dunbar, R. (2022). Artificial intelligence and its regulation in the European Union. In: Bielicki, D. M. (ed.) *Regulating Artificial Intelligence in Industry* (pp. 3–20). Abingdon: Routledge, pp. 4–5.

[5] Aradau, C. & Blanke, T. (2022). *Algorithmic Reason: The New Government of Self and Other*. Oxford: OUP, pp. 139–140.

[6] The European Parliament and the Council of the European Union (2024). The European Union's Artificial Intelligence Act—Regulation (EU) 2024/1689. *Official Journal of the European Union*, p. 8.

[7] Dimatteo, L. A., Poncibò, C. & Cannarsa, M. (eds.) (2022). *The Cambridge Handbook of Artificial Intelligence: Global Perspectives on Law and Ethics*. Cambridge: CUP, pp. 12–13.

[8] High-Level Expert Group on Artificial Intelligence—AI HLEG (2019). Ethics guidelines for trustworthy AI. Brussels: European Commission, pp. 19–20.

[9] Dimatteo, L. A., Poncibò, C. & Cannarsa, M. (eds.) (2022). *The Cambridge Handbook of Artificial Intelligence: Global Perspectives on Law and Ethics*. p. 12.

2. **Nonmaleficence** and **privacy**, misuse via cyberwarfare, and malicious hacking,
3. **Responsible*AI*** including *AI* developers, designers, and the entire industry sector,
4. **Benefit-for-all principle** that means *AI* should benefit "everyone", "humanity", and "society",
5. **Freedom** from technological experimentation, manipulation, or surveillance (transparent and explainable *AI*, raising *AI* literacy, etc.),
6. **Trustworthy*AI*** that is the control should not be delegated to AI and the integrity of AI systems and processes should be monitored and evaluated,
7. **Dignity**, protection, and promotion of **human rights**, etc.

The Council of Europe (*CoE*) Ad hoc Committee on Artificial Intelligence (*CAHAI*) structured an "*AI lifecycle approach*" to consider the development stage, the deployment, and use stages of *AI*. In this framework, the future regulation of *AI* must consider the impacts of *AI* on human rights, democracy, and the rule of law, as set out by the European Convention on Human Rights ("**ECHR**"), its Protocols, and the European Social Charter ("**ESC**")[10]:

1. ***AI* and respect for human value**: Liberty and security, fair trial, no punishment without law (art. 5, 6, 7 ECHR); private and family life, physical, psychological, and moral integrity (art. 8 ECHR),
2. ***AI* and freedom of the individual**: Freedom of expression (art. 10 ECHR); freedom of assembly and association (art. 11 ECHR),
3. ***AI* and equality, non-discrimination,and solidarity**: Prohibition of discrimination (art. 14 ECHR, Protocol 12),
4. ***AI* and social and economic rights AI in and around the workplace**: Right to just conditions of work, safe and healthy working conditions, dignity at work as well as the right to organise (art. 2 and 3 ESC),
5. ***AI* and democracy**: Social and political discourse, access to information and voter influence, inequality and segregation, and systemic

[10] CoE CAHAI (2020a). Towards regulation of AI systems. Strasbourg: Council of Europe, pp. 23–32.

failure or disruption (e.g. systemic risks, digital power concentration, etc.),

6. ***AI* andthe rule of law**: *AI* can increase the efficiency of institutions, courts, and law enforcement. If developed and used responsibly, *AI* can empower agencies to identify corruption, detect, and defend against cyberattacks.

The future of digital ethics and *AI* regulation ought to consider practical mechanisms as a toolkit that presents ample opportunity for further regulatory innovation and refinement[11]:

1. **Human rights impact assessments**: Organisations should perform a fundamental rights impact assessment. These assessments validate conformity with principles outlined in the legal framework (e.g. human rights, data protection, transparency, accountability, competence, etc.). Conducting human rights due diligence is also recommended by the United Nations Guiding Principles on Business and Human Rights (*UNGPs*). According to the EU *AI* Act, deployers of high-risk *AI* system, in particular when AI systems are used in the public sector, could involve relevant stakeholders, including the representatives of groups of people likely to be affected by the *AI* system, independent experts, and civil society organisations in conducting such impact assessments and designing measures to be taken in the case of materialisation of the risks.[12].
2. **Certification and quality labelling**: Such schemes could be made voluntary or mandatory, depending on the maturity of the *AI* ecosystem. The certification process should be subject to regulation regarding auditors' qualifications, the standards adopted, and how conflicts of interests are managed.
3. **Audits**: Audits facilitate a move towards more transparent and accountable use of *AI*-enabled systems and verify the integrity, impact, and robustness of them.

[11] CoE CAHAI (2020b). Ad Hoc Committee on Artificial Intelligence (CAHAI) Policy Development Group (CAHAI-PDG) Draft Feasibility Study V.0.3. *CAHAI-PDG(2020)01*, Strasbourg: Council of Europe, p. 49.

[12] The European Parliament and the Council of the European Union (2024). The European Union's Artificial Intelligence Act—Regulation (EU) 2024/1689. *Official Journal of the European Union*, p. 26.

4. **Regulatory sandboxes**: Regulatory sandboxes enable closer regulatory support and present an agile and safe approach to testing new technologies. Regulatory sandboxes are used to strengthen innovative capacity in the field of *AI*.[13]

The emergence of regulation in tech industries and *AI* supremacy could be explained as the product of powerful sectional interests of tech-innovation superpowers, primarily powerful business interests of tech multinational enterprises (*MNCs*) and bureaucrats, rather than a need to protect the interests of the general public.[14] Thus, practical mechanisms (i.e. human rights impact assessments, certification and quality labelling, audits, and regulatory sandboxes) can help to measure both the interests of the general public and business interests of tech *MNCs* and offer a roadmap to advance the interests in favour of societies and individuals.

Considering the future of ethics in *AI* research, the great majority of university-based *AI* research is done without any ethical review process. Compared to the R&D activities of tech companies, universities (e.g. California Institute of Technology–Caltech, Massachusetts Institute of Technology–MIT, Stanford University, etc.) specialised in high-tech research areas are far beyond in *AI* research. Once *AI* moved out of the laboratory contexts into real-world situations, the potential harms expanded and affected communities and individuals. However, there is still a presumption that publicly available datasets pose minimal risks and therefore should be exempt from ethics review.[15] Universities should be more open to play a key role in mitigating the risk of data misuse and prioritising ethical consideration and moral conduct in research projects. In this context, ethics advisory group (EAG), ethics advisory board (EAB), and/or institutional review board (IRB) should be tightly engaged in the implementation phase of *AI* research projects.

The future of AI regulation and digital ethics will be much more complexified and new holistic frameworks will require reasoning and

[13] CoE CAHAI (2020b). Ad Hoc Committee on Artificial Intelligence (CAHAI) Policy Development Group (CAHAI-PDG) Draft Feasibility Study V.0.3. *CAHAI-PDG(2020)01*, Strasbourg: Council of Europe, p. 50.

[14] Young, K. (2010). The regulatory state. In: Baldwin, R., Cave, M. & Lodge, M. (eds.) *The Oxford Handbook of Regulation* (pp. 64–86). Oxford: OUP, p. 68.

[15] Crawford, K. (2021). *Atlas of AI: Power, Politics, and the Planetary Costs of Artificial Intelligence*. New Haven: Yale University Press, pp. 115–116.

factual thinking of breakthrough *AI* innovations and new emerging advanced technological developments. Tech futurists foresee that *GPT-23* (of the year 2041, anticipating the *NLP* model parameters growing by ten times per year) will read every word ever written, watch every video ever produced, and build its own model of world. This all-knowing sequence transducer would contain all the accumulated knowledge of human history. Eventually, deep learning (*DL*) will become artificial general intelligence (*AGI*), matching human intelligence in every way possible. Lee and Qiufan recommended to develop useful applications suitable for *AI* and seek to find "human–*AI* symbiosis", rather than "*DL* becoming *AGI*".[16] Otherwise, the "*DL–AGI* transformation" will complexify the ethical dilemma and pose a high level of risk in *AI* research field in 2040s.

10.2 Future of the Rule of Law and Ramifications of AI's Use

The legal profession is undergoing rapid transformation with the advent of advanced AI tools. This is prompting jurists worldwide to reconsider how technology and the rule of law will co-exist.

The permeation of "**AI**" into legal systems around the world is underway. This phenomenon is bringing unprecedented capabilities and complex challenges. In Singapore, for example, Chief Justice Sundaresh Menon cautioned in 2024 that the legal system's operating environment is "changing at a rate and scale that is simply astounding". He also warned that we "should not assume that the rule of law will continue to serve us as well as it has if we were simply to maintain the status quo".[17] This stark warning underscores the pressing need to examine how AI's growing influence can be managed to preserve and strengthen the rule of law. After all, the rule of law—the principle that laws are applied fairly, transparently, and equally to all—remains, in Menon CJ's words, not just an aspirational ideal, but an "existential necessity" for modern societies.

[16] Lee, K. F. & Qiufan, C. (2021). *AI 2041: Ten Visions for Our Future*. London: WH Allen, pp. 117–118.

[17] Singapore Judiciary (Chief Justice Sundaresh Menon), "Reimagining the Rule of Law: A Renewed Conception"—Speech at Conversations with the Community (20 September 2024).

Therefore, it is crucial to evaluate how AI's use in the legal domain might bolster or undermine these foundational principles.

In this section, we analyse the future of the rule of law in an era of proliferating legal AI tools. The chapter begins by weighing the benefits that AI brings to the legal profession against its corresponding risks and trade-offs. It then discusses how the rise of AI challenges established legal professional ethics and norms—from duties of competence and confidentiality to the integrity of courtroom advocacy. Next, it explores the implications of widespread AI adoption by users of the legal system, including litigants-in-person and self-help legal consumers, including what it entails for access to justice and equality before the law. Finally, the chapter examines how these developments collectively impact the rule of law itself and public trust in legal institutions. To conclude, we offer some preliminary suggestions on how to align AI deployment with the need to sustain the rule of law.

10.2.1 Balancing the Benefits and Risks of AI in the Legal Profession

AI has become a double-edged sword in the legal profession. On one hand, AI systems promise to greatly enhance efficiency and productivity in legal work. Machine-learning algorithms can sift through vast volumes of case law and evidence far faster than any human, pinpointing relevant authorities or patterns in data. Law firms and courts are already using AI-driven tools for e-discovery, document review, and contract analysis, dramatically reducing the time and cost required for these labour-intensive tasks. Notably, the latest generation of AI language models can even perform complex legal reasoning tasks. In 2023, OpenAI's GPT-4 system famously passed the US Multistate Bar Exam in the 90th percentile of test-takers, demonstrating that an AI can perform legal analyses on par with human lawyers in certain contexts.[18]

Such milestones suggest AI could become a powerful "force multiplier" that expands legal services and access to justice by augmenting human lawyers' capabilities. For instance, AI-assisted tools might help lawyers draft pleadings or research arguments more quickly, enabling them to serve more clients at lower cost. Courts, too, may deploy AI

[18] Daniel Martin Katz et al., "GPT-4 Passes the Bar Exam", Illinois Tech News (15 March 2023).

to automate routine administrative tasks and manage dockets more efficiently, potentially reducing case backlogs and speeding up the resolution of disputes.

On the other hand, these very advances give rise to an array of risks and concerns. If not used with care, AI could easily undermine the quality and fairness of legal outcomes. A primary worry is that AI systems might introduce errors or biases into legal decision-making. Unless rigorously verified, an AI's output can be unreliable—a lesson underscored by a high-profile incident in the United States where attorneys submitted a brief generated by ChatGPT that cited non-existent cases, resulting in court sanctions. Similar incidents have taken place in Singapore. Further, the opacity posed by AI systems may be at odds with the principle of transparency in justice systems.[19]

There is also the broader concern that over-reliance on AI could erode human judgement—a phenomenon known as "reliance bias". Judges and lawyers could lean too heavily on algorithmic suggestions, potentially diluting the human accountability and nuance (built on human experience) that underpins judicial decision-making.

In sum, AI in the legal profession presents a trade-off: it can augment accuracy, consistency, and access to justice, but, if deployed recklessly, can also erode those very same qualities. Hence, the task ahead is to harness AI's potential while instituting safeguards that mitigate its risks—in short, to ensure the technology is a boon rather than a detriment to the rule of law.

10.2.2 *Impact of AI on Legal Professional Ethics and Norms*

The incorporation of AI into legal practice will prompt a deep re-examination of core and long-held professional ethics and norms. Duties that legal professionals are bound by—to their clients, the courts, and the justice system—must now be interpreted in light of AI-based tools functioning as an undeniable part of legal work.[20]

[19] Reuters (Sara Merken), "New York lawyers sanctioned for using fake ChatGPT cases in legal brief" (26 June 2023).

[20] Council of Europe, European Ethical Charter on the Use of AI in Judicial Systems (2018); Singapore Academy of Law, Research on Legal Technology 2023; Florida Bar, Proposed Advisory Opinion on AI in Legal Practice (2023); Nairobi Statement on AI (2024).

The first, and perhaps most immediate ethical implication, is to the **duty of competence**. To use AI responsibly, lawyers should be required to have a basic understanding of the technology's capabilities and limitations. To this end, bar associations worldwide are increasingly affirming that technological competence is part of a lawyer's professional obligations. In 2024, the International Bar Association ("**IBA**") updated its principles of professional conduct to emphasise that lawyers should "keep abreast of changes in the law" and be **technologically competent**, explicitly including engagement with AI, while remaining conscious of the accompanying risks and ethical challenges.[21] Similarly, the American Bar Association ("**ABA**") has issued formal guidance instructing that lawyers employing generative AI must "fully consider their applicable ethical obligations", such as duties of competent representation, confidentiality, candour to the court, and fairness. In Singapore, Menon CJ has highlighted the "paradigm shift" that generative AI brings to legal practice, urging new lawyers to combine technological adeptness with sound ethical judgement. The evolving consensus is that ignoring AI is no longer an option: **competent** lawyers must learn to use these tools effectively, but in a manner that upholds long-held ethical norms.[22]

A second implication is on the **duty of supervision**. In most legal systems today, lawyers retain ultimate responsibility for legal advice and work, and cannot abrogate this responsibility—be it to non-lawyers or technology tools. The aforementioned case of the sanctioned lawyers in New York illustrates this point vividly: there is nothing "inherently improper" about using AI for assistance, the judge there noted, but professional rules impose a **gatekeeping role** on attorneys to ensure the accuracy of their filings. While an AI application may provide a draft contractual clause or suggest case citations, the lawyer must diligently review and validate them (just as she would review the work of a human junior colleague). Failing to do so not only risks embarrassment or malpractice, but also undermines the integrity of the judicial process.

In many jurisdictions, ethical bodies have rushed to issue guidelines on this front. For example, bar authorities in Australia and England have stressed that any use of generative AI must preserve lawyers' core duties

[21] International Bar Association (IBA), "The Future Is Now: Artificial Intelligence and the Legal Profession", IBA Reports AIRe 4|2024 (2024), pp. 451–457.

[22] American Bar Association, Formal Opinion 512: Generative Artificial Intelligence Tools (2023).

of honesty, integrity, confidentiality, and independence. The consensus is that AI output should never be treated as infallible—it must be regarded as a tool to be supervised by the human expert. Lawyers are expected to understand, to the extent possible, how their AI tools work (at least enough to explain their use and verify results) and to refrain from using AI in areas where it would be impossible to meet their professional obligations. For instance, if an AI tool cannot ensure client confidentiality (perhaps because it processes data on external servers), a lawyer must think twice before using it with sensitive case information, or take steps to anonymise the data.

A third implication is the duty to maintain **public trust** and the reputation of the profession. Lawyers and judges are not only service providers but also officers of the legal system whose conduct affects societal confidence in the administration of justice. The legal profession has long upheld that appearance of impropriety can be as damaging as actual impropriety. In this light, unrestrained use of AI tools that the public views as untrustworthy could weaken confidence in court outcomes. Imagine a scenario where a litigant learns that a judge's decision was heavily influenced by an algorithm: if the reasoning cannot be explained in human terms, the litigant may feel cheated by "robot justice". To avoid such perceptions, some courts have adopted policies to limit autonomous AI decision-making. In the United States, at least one state judiciary (Florida) has issued guidelines warning that lawyers must not delegate their professional judgement to AI, and requiring that clients be informed when AI is used in their case preparation. We also see emerging norms around transparency in the use of AI—for example, attorneys might cite an AI tool as part of their research process in a footnote or affidavit to pre-empt concerns about "secret" AI influence. The fundamental ethical tenets of the legal profession—competence, diligence, loyalty, confidentiality, candour, and fairness—remain unchanged in the age of AI, but the means of upholding them are evolving. Every lawyer must now consider how to integrate AI into practice in a way that **reinforces** rather than violates these duties. In practical terms, this means continuous training on new technologies, careful selection of trustworthy AI vendors, implementation of verification protocols, and candid communication with clients and courts about the use of AI in legal tasks. Through such measures, the profession can adapt its norms to harness AI's advantages while keeping faith with the ethical infrastructure that undergirds the rule of law.

10.2.3 AI for Litigants and Laypersons: Access to Justice and Challenges

The potential for AI transformation extends beyond the Bench and Bar. Increasingly, ordinary users of the legal system are turning to AI tools for help in understanding and asserting their rights, resulting in significant implications for **access to justice**. On the positive side, AI has the potential to democratise legal knowledge, empowering individuals who could not otherwise afford professional counsel. A person with a legal question can now consult an AI-driven chatbot online and receive instant information that might previously have required an expensive consultation. In fact, the sophistication of answers that large language model AIs can provide has grown to the point that they can draft contracts, fill out legal forms, or even generate a basic court submission for a litigant-in-person. In theory, this trend could help balance the scales in legal disputes: a resourceful litigant-in-person armed with a well-designed legal AI might fare closer to an represented party than one who is entirely unaided. These speak to the potential for AI legal tools to make justice systems more inclusive and efficient.

The rise of the use of AI for self-help in legal matters, however, also comes with serious challenges for the rule of law. One concern is **accuracy and reliability**. While AI systems can produce answers with an authoritative tone, they do not guarantee correctness. Without legal training, a layperson may have no way to discern whether legal information or advice is sound or reliable. Unlike a human lawyer, current AI has no professional liability or regulatory oversight—if a free online chatbot misleads a user into missing a filing deadline or makes a critical procedural error, the user is often left with little recourse but to bear the consequences. This problem was highlighted when an AI-driven app widely touted as a "robot lawyer" offered to help individuals contest traffic tickets, only to be pulled back due to concerns that its guidance might amount to the unauthorised practice of law or expose users to harm. The lack of clear regulation for direct-to-consumer legal AI service leaves laypersons in a grey zone: they are receiving legal assistance from software that operates outside the traditional professional regulatory frameworks. Going forward, finding the right regulatory balance will be crucial—we should encourage innovation that improves access to legal help, but we also need sufficient safeguards to prevent the exploitation or endangerment of unrepresented litigants.

Another challenge is **inequality in access to quality AI**. Ironically, while AI could level the playing field by giving poor and rich litigants alike some access to legal insights, there is a risk of a new type of digital divide. Well-resourced parties might obtain premium AI tools—for example, a sophisticated predictive analytics platform fine-tuned for litigation strategy—while less wealthy individuals rely on basic or outdated AI apps. If one side in a dispute has cutting-edge AI assistance and the other has a subpar tool (or none at all), the imbalance could skew outcomes, raising fairness concerns. Moreover, even assuming equal access to AI, not all users will have the digital literacy to utilise them effectively. The courts may find themselves grappling with an influx of AI-generated filings that are incoherent or legally deficient, requiring judges to sift through voluminous but poorly crafted materials. Some judges have reported seeing briefs from self-represented litigants clearly composed with the help of form-generating software—sometimes these are quite cogent, but other times they reflect a lack of understanding of substantive law, merely copying boilerplate text that does not fit the situation. Hence, while AI can assist litigants-in-person, it is not a panacea; often it can only take a case so far, after which human judgement and legal knowledge are needed.

To truly improve access to justice, jurisdictions might consider providing **official** AI-guided tools that walk users through common legal processes (filling out court forms, calculating child support, etc.), combined with clear disclaimers and referrals to human attorneys for complex matters. Singapore, for instance, could integrate AI helpers into its e-filing systems to guide users step-by-step, ensuring they understand the requirements—an approach that would leverage technology while still operating under the supervision of the judicial system. Ultimately, broad use of AI by the public will require new forms of legal education and outreach, so that people understand both the powers and limits of these tools. Otherwise, there is a danger that AI will create a false sense of security, with litigants trusting algorithms blindly and unwittingly sacrificing their rights.

10.2.4 Implications for the Rule of Law and Societal Trust

The expansion of AI throughout legal systems begs the question: How will these developments affect the rule of law and the public's trust in justice? The rule of law is fundamentally about certain enduring values.

These include fairness, equality, transparency, consistency, and accountability in the application of laws. Each of these could be strengthened or strained by the advent of AI.

From an optimistic perspective, the judicious and responsible use of AI can reinforce the rule of law. AI-driven analytics might identify sentencing disparities and help act as a guide for judges to enhance the consistency and equitability in their treatment of litigants. Automation of routine processes could reduce court delays. For instance, in Singapore, the Small Claims Tribunal has announced a tie-up with Harvey AI to use generative AI systems to provide timely and helpful legal information to litigants-in-person. Increased use of AI could also free up human judges and lawyers to focus on the truly complex cases and on personal engagement where it matters, potentially improving the quality of legal reasoning and the perceived care with which decisions are made.

Yet one cannot ignore the **darker scenario**. If mismanaged, AI could impair key facets of the rule of law and erode public trust. For instance, when more advanced AI systems play a role in shaping or forming legal decisions without human users being able to have a sense of how these decisions were arrived at, the opacity can significantly erode trust and accountability in the legal system.

Another principle that could be challenged is thatof equality before the law. If AI tools are available unevenly, with parties of means being able to afford the most powerful versions, the inequality in effective recourse to the law could widen. Further, there is the risk of systemic biases. In some jurisdictions, predictive policing systems have resulted in heavier scrutiny of certain neighbourhoods, feeding a cycle of perception and enforcement.

Finally, we must address **societaltrust**. Public trust in the legal system is earned when people perceive the system to be just, impartial, and effective. The introduction of AI could affect these perceptions in significant ways. Should an AI-driven system allow a citizen to resolve a minor legal dispute online in days rather than spending months in court, that positive experience may increase trust in the law's ability to deliver timely justice. Conversely, highly publicised failures of legal AI (such as a fall in standards of the legal profession in ensuring the accuracy and veracity of legal precedents cited in cases, or a wrongful conviction traced to a flawed algorithm) could deeply shake public confidence. Even if justice were ultimately done, this is not sufficient—as the adage goes, "justice must not just be done; it must also be seen to be done".

In this regard, Menon CJ's call to "reimagine the rule of law" is a timely reminder that maintaining legitimacy in a high-tech future may require **adapting our institutions and norms** without losing the human touch and moral authority that give law its credibility. In practical terms, building trust will require: (a) transparency about how AI is used in the system, (b) opportunities for the public to provide input on its usage, and (c) potentially new oversight bodies (for example, an algorithm oversight committee within the courts) to ensure that the deployment of AI aligns with community values and legal principles.[23] The strength of the rule of law in the age of AI will depend on our success in crafting governance structures that keep this powerful technology in check and directed towards the public good.

10.2.5 Recommendations and Implications for the Future

The foregoing analysis reveals a landscape of both great opportunity and great risk at the intersection of AI and the rule of law. AI's burgeoning role in legal systems could, if properly managed, enhance the delivery of and fortify the rule of law in our societies. Conversely, unchecked or irresponsible use of AI threatens to inject opacity, bias, and unpredictability into legal decision-making, undermining public trust and the very ideals of legality and fairness. How we act now will determine whether the coming age of "AI-powered legal tech" and digital governance is one of renewed confidence in the rule of law or one of increasing public scepticism. In this concluding section, we offer several forward-looking suggestions aimed at ensuring that the rise of AI bolsters (rather than erodes) the rule of law.

1. **Developing robust regulatory frameworks for the use of AI in the legal system**: It is essential to establish clear and proportionate rules and standards governing the use of AI in judicial and legal processes. Jurisdictions should seek to provide regulatory clarity—through non-binding guidelines or even binding regulations—to delineate permissible uses of AI and provide safeguards. Meanwhile, the courts and professional regulators could also issue practice

[23] Straits Times (Tham Yuen-C), "Reimagining the rule of law: How Singapore is adapting for the future" (6 October 2024).

guides or codes of conduct to provide more granular guidance on AI. For instance, in 2024, the Singapore Courts issued a Guidance Note on the use of generative AI in court proceedings. Notably, the Guidance Note applies to both lawyers and litigants-in-person.

2. **Deep investment in training and capacity-building**: As AI becomes a fixture in legal work, continuous education, training, and upskilling are vital for all stakeholders. Judges, lawyers, and court officers should be equipped with an in-depth working understanding how AI tools function, their appropriate use parameters, and their pitfalls. Worryingly, a survey by UNESCO in 2024 showed that 91% of judges lacked institutional training on AI, despite nearly half using it daily.[24] Additionally, law schools should integrate interdisciplinary courses that cover law and technology, preparing new law students for the reality of practicing alongside AI. In addition, there must be significant public education campaigns so that ordinary citizens develop a baseline understanding of what AI legal tools can and cannot do. These steps will help mitigate misuse and unrealistic expectations.
3. **Developing transparency and accountability in AI adoption**: To maintain public trust, the deployment of AI in any legal decision-making role must be accompanied by robust transparency and accountability measures. Minimally, there should be disclosure when AI has been used to assist a judicial decision or the provision of a legal service. Lawyers, for instance, should seek their clients' assent in using generative AI tools to aid their provision of legal services. Developers and deployers providing AI to the legal system should be encouraged, or required, to ensure explainability around their systems' recommendations. Regular testing of legal AI systems—such as through AI governance testing frameworks like AI Verify—should become standard.[25]

   To address accountability, clear lines of responsibility must be drawn: a judge or lawyer who uses an AI aid remains responsible for the outcome and must be prepared to justify it on traditional legal grounds. Vendors might be held liable for egregious flaws in

[24] UNESCO, "Building AI and the rule of law in Eastern Africa" (23 October 2024).

[25] V. Austinin et al., "Artificial Intelligence, the Rule of Law and Public Administration: The Case of Taxation", Cambridge Law Journal 83, no. 3 (Nov. 2024): 437–464.

their software (for example, if an AI tool marketed to lawyers is found to consistently fabricate citations or leak confidential data, consumer protection agencies should step in). In other words, the use of AI should never be permitted as an excuse for diminished accountability.

4. **Encouraging innovation that focuseson access to justice**: Finally, stakeholders should leverage AI as an opportunity to strengthen the rule of law by addressing long-standing gaps in access and efficiency. This could mean incentivising the development of AI tools specifically targeted at unmet legal needs—for example, multilingual legal information chatbots for marginalised communities, or AI that helps triage cases for overburdened courts. Governments and allied legal institutions—such as bar associations or professional training academies—could fund hackathons to encourage tech innovators to work on problems like simplifying legal language or automating the handling of small claims and minor disputes (with appropriate oversight). To that end, there have been efforts in Singapore to provide prompt engineering guides to the legal profession to enhance the quality of output produced by generative AI systems. By channelling innovation to where it is most needed—rather than merely to serve the largest law firms—we can make AI a tool for reducing the justice gap. Such efforts, if successful, will enhance the legitimacy of the legal system by showing that technology is being harnessed not just for efficiency's sake or profit, but to ensure that the legal system serves all.

The age of AI in the legal domain is upon us. While a powerful tool, the legal system's use of it comes with a responsibility to preserve the integrity of the rule of law. Achieving this balance will require vigilance, creativity, and collaboration across disciplines and borders. As Menon CJ aptly noted, there is no choice—we **must** reimagine and adapt our conception of the rule of law for the digital era. By doing so, we can strive to ensure that even in a fractured world, the rule of law remains a steady compass—guiding the deployment of AI in service of justice, and not vice versa.

10.3 Future of AI Systems, Robotics and Criminal Policies

The involvement of AI in criminal activities presents a complex and multifaceted challenge for contemporary legal systems. As AI technologies continue to evolve and integrate into societal functions, the legal and criminological implications of their use, misuse, or abuse require pressing and interdisciplinary attention.

One of the earliest concerns raised by criminal law scholars is the problem of emergence and unpredictability in AI behaviour.[26] If an AI system, for example, causes a death due to a malfunction or a "misbehaviour" (an unpredictable execution of its task), determining liability for an offence such as manslaughter becomes problematic. Traditional criminal law concepts such as *mens rea* and causality are difficult to apply when control is distributed across multiple actors or obscured by the opacity of algorithmic decision-making. As a result, assigning blame to a single operator becomes less feasible, and a model of shared responsibility among designers, deployers, and other stakeholders is likely to dominate future legal frameworks.

Yet perhaps a more immediate concern (one that has received relatively less scholarly attention) is the intentional abuse or misuse of AI technologies to commit crimes. As AI systems become more integrated into daily life, their potential to be used to commit criminal activities by malicious actors increases. Legal systems have not yet fully mapped the terrain of AI-enabled crime, and comprehensive taxonomies are not yet widely discussed. This legal uncertainty calls for collaboration between criminology and criminal law to develop an integrated methodology that can assess the roles AI plays in facilitating new forms of criminal activity and evaluate whether current legal provisions are adequate to address them, or whether there are gaps in the legislation that need addressing.

An important contribution to this emerging field is the work of the International Association of Criminal Law (*Association Internationale de Droit Pénal*, AIDP), which has begun to document and analyse the legal

[26] One of the first scholarly paper in European academia is on harm caused by incidents involving self-driving cars. See Sabine Gless, Elimity Silverman, Thomas Weigend, (2016). If robots cause harm, who is to blame? Self-driving cars and criminal liability. *New Criminal Law Review*, *19*(3): 412–436.

implications of AI-driven crime.[27] The reports of the Association aim to lay the groundwork for national and international criminal policy agendas that will need to adapt quickly to the challenges posed by AI.

To begin charting the intersection of AI and crime, a crucial distinction must be made between software-based AI systems and cyber-physical (or embedded) AI systems—namely, robots. These two forms of AI raise both overlapping and distinct regulatory issues.

Focusing on the differences, while software-based systems interact digitally, since they do not have a "body", embedded systems interact physically, through sensors, actuators, and robotic bodies. Therefore, the affordances of these two technologies might be different. How people interact with an artificial body or with a system of information cannot be framed in the same way on a normative level. Recognising these differences does not imply encouraging a rigid dualism, rather acknowledges that varying forms of AI generate different types of shared agency and social contexts, each with their own potential for enabling both traditional and novel criminal behaviours (they are different, not necessarily separated). Since the interactions with users and professionals might be distinctive based on the type of AI system involved, the specific shared agency social context created by those interactions might open to new and different ways to commit known crime or generate completely new criminal phenomena.

Software-based AI is already widely distributed online, with generative AI and algorithmic governance in contents generation raising particular concerns from a criminal law standpoint. Generative AI models (particularly large language models, image and video generators, and voice synthesis tools) can produce hyper-realistic content that is virtually indistinguishable from authentic human-generated material. This has profound implications for crimes involving deception, manipulation, and reputational harm. In other words, the ability to generate artificial content (which can be also, but not necessarily, false) creates new vectors for harm, ranging from fraud, identity theft to non-consensual pornography.[28] The scale and speed at which such content can now be produced and disseminated online exacerbate the challenge. Unlike earlier forms

[27] See the reports published in the Revue Internationale de Droit Pénal, 2023, issue 1, and 2024, issue 1.

[28] See OpenAI, GPT-4 System Card, 23 March 2023, available at <https://cdn.openai.com/papers/gpt-4-system-card.pdf>.

of online manipulation, which often required significant technical expertise or human labour, generative AI drastically lowers the threshold for content-based harm. In response, several jurisdictions are considering or have already introduced new criminal offenses targeting the creation and dissemination of artificial content which causes harm to a person.[29]

Nonetheless, expanding criminal law to confront these new technological realities must be approached with caution. The historical trajectory of cybercrime legislation offers a cautionary tale: the "digitalization" of crime, which widened the phenomenon from cybercrime in a *stricto sensu* to cyber-enabled crime,[30] cannot entail automatic new criminalization, where jurisdictions have already a high number of criminal offences that can be applied to these evolving criminal phenomena, or that might only need updating to the new challenges of the algorithmic society. Overcriminalization can result in legal inflation, where overlapping or redundant laws create confusion, inconsistent enforcement, and excessive burdens on judicial systems. It can also chill freedom of speech and press, particularly when content moderation is delegated to private platforms operating under vague or overly punitive legal frameworks.

A more prudent and sustainable approach may lie in developing integrated policy strategies that align criminal policies with complementary regulatory tools. These might include proactive compliance measures for developers and distributors of generative AI, mandatory transparency obligations for content platforms, and clear frameworks for corporate responsibility and algorithmic accountability, as the package of European regulations (among them, the AI Act and the Digital Service Act) began to do. Regulatory agencies could work in tandem with law enforcement to establish standards for risk assessment, harm mitigation, and ethical deployment of AI tools. Moreover, public–private partnerships can foster shared responsibility, ensuring that technological advancement is matched by safeguards that protect against its misuse. However, the due diligence obligations provided by the EU regulations should integrate with each other, especially the DSA and the AI Act. Without such integration, there is a risk of creating a fragmented

[29] Italian Bill A.S. 1146 suggests to introduce article 162 *quater* in the Italian Criminal Code, punishing the unlawful dissemination of content generated or altered with AI systems.

[30] See Anastasia Powell, Gregory Stratton, Robin Cameron, Digital Criminology. Crime and justice in digital society, Routledge, New York, 2018.

legal landscape, a dual-track system where content creation and content dissemination are governed by disconnected or inconsistent legal regimes. This not only undermines coherence and fairness in enforcement but also makes it more difficult to hold actors accountable across the entire lifecycle of harmful content. Effective governance, therefore, requires a harmonised framework that acknowledges the distinct stages of AI-driven content production and distribution while maintaining a unified vision of the phenomenon, fostering a coherent and proportionate responsibility attribution mechanism.

Criminal law scholarships could bring its contribution in mapping the areas of risk (including the perimeter of AI "reasonable misuses") which need assessment and mitigation within this integrated strategy. Notably, these areas of risk may overlap for different types of providers: those who manage "content artificial moderation" (moderation by AI) and those who manage "content artificial generation" (generation by AI). Despite their different roles, both are exposed to similar vulnerabilities related to content-related harms, underscoring the need for a coherent legal framework informed by criminal law principles.

This is not to suggest that jurisdictions should exclude criminalization entirely from consideration; rather, this specific criminal policy must be approached with a high degree of caution and precision. Recalling the earlier methodological distinction, the case of robotics appears to align with scenarios that warrant such careful deliberation. As physically embodied social agents operating within human environments, robots possess a unique set of "criminal affordances" tied to their material presence and interactive capabilities. Foremost among these is their potential to cause physical harm.

Robot-related crime might represent, in future criminal policies, a distinct category of criminal activity, fundamentally different from harm caused by "objects". As American scholar Ryan Calo outlined, "there is a significant difference between a bullet and a robot: the prospect of programming. Programming dictates behaviour in complex ways".[31] Hence, the physical harm caused by abuses or misuses of robots is different than the one caused by the simple use of a "tool".

The robots' capacity for complex, autonomous behaviour significantly alters the nature of criminal interactions. Such interactions can

[31] Ryan Calo, (2015). Robotics and the lessons of cyberlaw. California Law Review, 103(3), 513–564, at 534.

result in more severe harm on both quantitative and qualitative levels. Quantitatively, robots (particularly autonomous drones) can facilitate the execution of offenses, in terms of victims' scale or personalised attacks (the debate on lethal autonomous weapons should be taken as an important reference in this case). Qualitatively, the implications go beyond physical harm, encompassing the misuse of programming functions themselves. Programming is not merely a technical process but a socially embedded activity that shapes autonomous agents capable of interacting with and influencing society. As such, it warrants legal recognition and protection, especially given that its outcomes (social artificial agents) are increasingly integrated into human environments and decision-making processes.

Therefore, future policies might need to recognise a social and legal interest in the normative protection of virtuous human–machine interactions, in other words, a normative protection of the trustworthiness of robots. The foundation of this trust relies on the belief that robots, as physical agents, will not intentionally or negligently inflict harm upon human beings. However, this supposedly straightforward principle conceals a series of complexities. Not all robots are designed to avoid physical contact with human bodies: surgical robots, rehabilitation devices, and certain caregiving technologies must, by necessity, engage directly with the human body. As such, harmfulness cannot be attributed merely to the robot's capacity to compromise physical integrity, but rather to the wrongful alteration or subversion of its functional programming in a way that is intended to cause injury or death. In this light, the issue of trustworthiness becomes not only a matter of design but also of legal and ethical governance.

To prevent such scenarios, it may be necessary to anticipate the scope of criminal protection to include preparatory behaviours that could lead to the criminal use of robots, such as the "weaponization" of robots (either by repurposing civilian machines or designing robotic systems specifically for harmful purposes). To address this threat, criminal law may need to extend its reach beyond the moment of harm to the preparatory acts that enable such outcomes. This includes the development, distribution, or deployment of programming that facilitates the transformation of otherwise benign robots into instruments of violence. Anticipatory criminalization in this domain could serve a dual purpose: deterring malicious innovation and preserving public trust in robotic technologies as reliable and socially beneficial agents.

In conclusion, the future of criminal policy must be guided by a careful and principled approach that respects the foundational principles of criminal law. While the emergence of AI and other technologies may lead to the criminalization of new behaviours, such measures, though potentially necessary in narrowly defined cases, should remain a last resort due to their severity and long-term implications. Greater emphasis should instead be placed on developing a robust criminological understanding of emerging threats, taking into account existing preventive measures, particularly those established through due diligence obligations under EU law.

10.4 Future of (Legal) Natural Language Processing and the Application of Computational Linguistics

This section offers a brief overview of current and emerging directions in the application of NLP and computational linguistics to the legal domain. Given the inherently textual nature of law, much of the early research in this area has focused on the systematic analysis of legally significant texts, including statutes, contracts, and case law.[32] In recent years, however, the scope of relevant data has expanded to encompass a wider array of textual and multimedia sources, such as social media content, court hearing transcripts, legal chatbots, and video recordings. This expansion has significantly broadened the horizons of computational legal studies. Simultaneously, we are witnessing substantial advancements in legal technologies developed by major corporations and government agencies.[33]

10.4.1 Current Landscape

The evolving intersection of artificial intelligence and the rule of law reveals a landscape defined by both opportunity and uncertainty. As computational capabilities surge, legal systems around the world are

[32] Villata, S., Araszkiewicz, M., Ashley, K., Bench-Capon, T., Branting, L. K., Conrad, J. G., & Wyner, A. (2022). Thirty years of artificial intelligence and law: the third decade. Artificial Intelligence and Law, 30(4), 561–591.

[33] Katz, D. M., Hartung, D., Gerlach, L., Jana, A., & Bommarito II, M. J. (2023). Natural language processing in the legal domain. arXiv preprint arXiv:2302.12039.

scrambling to interpret, regulate, and integrate these technologies. From predictive tools once used to flag fraud, to generative models now capable of drafting legal arguments, the pace of innovation continues to outstrip institutional preparedness. This chapter offers a computational linguistics perspective, grounded in multilingual, interdisciplinary experience, to explore the gaps, tensions, and opportunities that lie ahead in shaping ethical and effective legal tech governance. Moreover, generative models blur traditional boundaries in copyright, authorship, and legal accountability. As generative systems become ubiquitous in public and private legal contexts, new regulatory paradigms will be required to ensure transparency, traceability, and sustainability.

Much of the AI infrastructure underpinning legal technology is inherently biased towards English-language texts and common law principles. NLP models trained on case law from English-speaking countries often struggle when applied to civil law jurisdictions, where legal reasoning is organised differently. This creates a structural imbalance in legal tech development and raises questions about linguistic justice. For multilingual users and systems, the divergence in NLP performance between languages is not just a technical concern. Rather, it's a barrier to equal access to legal information and services.

Predictive AI systems, while often designed with efficiency or fairness in mind, can have deeply harmful effects when deployed in high-stakes government contexts without adequate oversight. A telling example is the Dutch "Toeslagenaffaire", a welfare fraud detection system that wrongly accused thousands of families, often with a migrant background, leading to financial ruin and public scandal. Cases like this highlight the dangers of outsourcing discretion to algorithms trained on historical data, which often amplify existing human biases. As a result, policymakers have grown wary of predictive tools, potentially jeopardising the adoption of even well-designed, evidence-based models. Any future framework must address these harms transparently and build mechanisms for compliance.

In public discourse and even policy documents, the term "AI" has become an overhyped term, often used interchangeably for everything from advanced neural networks to simple rule-based systems. This terminological vagueness distorts legal debates and contributes to regulatory misunderstanding. A complex decision tree is not a machine-learning model. A chatbot trained on FAQs is not a legal reasoner. This inflation of the "AI" label can lead to both overregulation and underprotection, depending on how legislation is drafted and enforced. Clarifying these distinctions is essential if the AI Act and similar instruments are to have meaningful impact.

The persistent gap between technological development and regulatory response is hardly new, but it is especially consequential in the case of AI. While the EU's AI Act is an ambitious step forward, public forums reflect significant mistrust in both the process and the institutions behind it. In online communities like the Dutch Tweakers tech forum, scepticism is palpable. Users frequently conflate different EU bodies, speculate about bureaucratic overreach, and express concern that policymakers lack the technical literacy to regulate effectively. This erosion of public trust could undermine otherwise thoughtful legislation. Closing this gap will require more than just transparency. It demands genuine public engagement and digital literacy on both sides of the table.

The environmental cost of generative AI, both in training and application, is increasingly hard to ignore. These systems consume huge amounts of electricity, much of it spent through hyperscale data centres operated by a handful of large companies from the USA. Despite the EU's emphasis on data sovereignty and green computing, there are still no major European-owned alternatives at the same scale, although there are plans in that direction. This dependence poses strategic risks. Europe remains tethered to external infrastructure for systems that may soon undergird everything from legal research to public service delivery. A sustainable and autonomous AI ecosystem will require investment not just in code, but in compute.

10.4.2 The Rise of Generative AI in Legal NLP

The field of AI and law has undergone a profound shift, moving from a large focus on systems designed for prediction tasks to the emergence of generative AI, particularly Large Language Models (LLMs). Earlier approaches conceptualised AI as "prediction machines", trained to output specific classifications or decisions based on structured inputs, for example, predicting case outcomes or identifying relevant legal statutes.[34] These models relied on annotated training data and were task-specific,

[34] Medvedeva, M., Vols, M., & Wieling, M. (2020). Using machine learning to predict decisions of the European Court of Human Rights. Artificial Intelligence and Law, 28(2), 237–266; Chalkidis, I., Androutsopoulos, I., & Aletras, N. (2019). Neural legal judgment prediction in English. arXiv preprint arXiv:1906.02059.

excelling in scenarios where inputs and expected outputs were clearly defined.

Generative AI, by contrast, represents a broader paradigm shift. Powered by transformer architectures and trained on massive textual corpora, LLMs such as GPT-4 are capable of generating human-like language and engaging in a range of text-based tasks without requiring extensive task-specific fine-tuning. Rather than merely classifying legal clauses or retrieving matching cases, LLMs can summarise court decisions, answer open-ended legal questions, or even draft clauses and documents, guided by natural language prompts.[35] This transition has opened the door to more flexible, conversational, and context-aware AI systems that better mirror the complexity of legal practice.

Importantly, generative AI allows researchers and practitioners to reframe traditional legal NLP problems—such as summarization, information retrieval, or clause classification—as text generation tasks. This has resulted in a more unified methodological approach, with many subtasks now addressable through prompt-based generation. These advancements reduce the need for task-specific annotated datasets and make the tools more accessible to legal professionals outside of technical disciplines.

However, generative models also introduce new risks, including the generation of plausible but inaccurate content (hallucinations), sensitivity to prompt phrasing, and difficulties in evaluating outputs.[36] Despite these challenges, the shift to generative AI represents a new frontier in legal research and practice, offering tools that are more aligned with how legal professionals think, communicate, and interact with information.

10.4.3 Possible Future Paths

The future development of NLP for legal applications will likely proceed along several interconnected paths. First, we can expect significant

[35] Akter, M., Cano, E., Weber, E., Dobler, D., & Habernal, I. (2025). A Comprehensive Survey on Legal Summarization: Challenges and Future Directions. arXiv preprint arXiv:2501.17830; Xu, H., & Ashley, K. (2023). A Question-Answering Approach to Evaluating Legal Summaries. In Legal Knowledge and Information Systems (pp. 293–298). IOS Press.

[36] Dahl, M., Magesh, V., Suzgun, M., & Ho, D. E. (2024). Large legal fictions: Profiling legal hallucinations in large language models. Journal of Legal Analysis, 16(1), 64–93.

progress in hybrid approaches that combine the strengths of both classical symbolic methods and LLMs.[37] While generative models excel at capturing language patterns and context, symbolic systems, such as rule-based logics or legal ontologies, provide structure, traceability, and interpretability. Combining the two may address limitations such as factual hallucinations and enhance model reliability for critical legal tasks.

Second, fine-tuning and domain adaptation of LLMs for specific legal subfields (e.g. tax law, criminal procedure, data protection) will become increasingly important.[38] Legal language is highly specialised and context-sensitive; even the most powerful general-purpose models struggle with sector-specific terminology and reasoning. Ongoing research into few-shot and zero-shot learning suggests that LLMs can be adapted to low-resource legal domains, especially where annotated data are scarce.

Third, the field is likely to see a rise in user-centric design of legal NLP tools. As generative AI enables more intuitive interactions, legal professionals and citizens alike will interact with NLP systems through conversational agents, voice interfaces, and context-aware prompts. These interfaces could democratise access to legal information and advice, particularly when paired with multilingual and multimodal capabilities.

Finally, regulatory and ethical considerations will shape the path of legal NLP. Future systems will need to be auditable, privacy-preserving, and legally compliant. As regulatory frameworks such as the EU AI Act evolve, the legal tech community will be pressed to build systems that align with both functional needs and normative commitments.[39]

Together, these directions suggest a rich research and development agenda: one that balances innovation with legal and social responsibility.

[37] Calegari, R., Ciatto, G., & Omicini, A. (2020). On the integration of symbolic and sub-symbolic techniques for XAI: A survey. Intelligenza Artificiale, 14(1), 7–32.

[38] Yue, S., Chen, W., Wang, S., Li, B., Shen, C., Liu, S., ... & Wei, Z. (2023). Disc-lawllm: Fine-tuning large language models for intelligent legal services. arXiv preprint arXiv:2309.11325; Satterfield, N., Holbrooka, P., & Wilcoxa, T. (2024). Fine-tuning llama with case law data to improve legal domain performance. OSF Preprints; Liga, D., & Robaldo, L. (2023). Fine-tuning GPT-3 for legal rule classification. Computer Law & Security Review, 51, 105864.

[39] Kenthapadi, K., Lakkaraju, H., & Rajani, N. (2023, August). Generative ai meets responsible ai: Practical challenges and opportunities. In Proceedings of the 29th ACM SIGKDD conference on knowledge discovery and data mining (pp. 5805–5806).

10.5 Future of Regulatory Frameworks on AI and AI Governance: Case of Africa

This section provides an overview of key considerations on the development and adoption of AI systems across the African continent, as a region within the broader context of the Global South.

It explores current applications of AI, including within legal and judicial functions, and examines the emergence of ethical and regulatory frameworks guiding responsible AI use. Particular attention is given to the extent to which these efforts seek to safeguard human rights.

Additionally, the involvement of African countries in global AI governance fora is covered, and the importance of multi-stakeholder engagement and the need for inclusion of African voices in these processes. In this discussion, the necessity of aligned data governance frameworks and collaboration in the development of AI regulatory processes in Africa arises.

10.5.1 Development of Ethical and Regulatory Frameworks on AI in Africa

African involvement in international discourse on AI governance remains sparse, even though such processes are crucial in shaping the future of these regulatory frameworks globally. Indeed, there is a critical role for multi-stakeholder involvement from the African region in international AI governance discourse as it provides diverse representation and collaboration in developing frameworks that benefit all. Through the incorporation of diverse voices in these discussions, countries in Africa can advocate for the prioritisation of AI safety standards, accountability, transparency, and human rights safeguards by frontier countries developing AI systems. As ethical principles and standards are developed, it is important to ensure that they are fair, inclusive, human-centric, and trustworthy.

10.5.2 Decolonizing and Democratising AI Governance

In international agenda-setting and the creation of AI governance mechanisms within international fora, representational inclusion is a key step towards development of effective frameworks and institutional reform. However, due to power imbalances in these fora, there emerges a form of coloniality within AI governance.[40] It is therefore essential to ascertain that the universal AI governance frameworks include diverse global voices representing a multitude of interests and promoting fairness.[41]

This challenge can be addressed through inclusive AI governance that addresses power imbalances and facilitates substantive engagement with marginalised stakeholders leading to the design of protective guardrails that acknowledge efforts of self-determination.[42]

10.5.3 Why Stakeholder Engagement is Essential

Stakeholder engagement should be a priority in the development of AI governance frameworks, including the necessary public participation systems, and engagement of diverse stakeholders in the general public, academia, civil society, and industry.

Through the inclusion of diverse perspectives, voices, and values in agenda-setting and decision-making processes, it will be possible to advocate for AI systems that benefit all communities and their interests.[43] This inclusivity of AI framework development also serves the function of effectively shaping local AI ecosystems together with regulation that is beneficial to the community. Carrying out such engagement processes democratically amplifies voices that would otherwise not be audible, and does not only develop effective governance mechanisms, but also promotes public trust and awareness of AI systems development and adoption.

10.5.4 Concerns on Digitalization in Africa

Even as there is a race to support AI development, adoption, and regulation, it is still clear that basic digitalization goals have not yet been

[40] Png, M.-T. (2022). The critical roles of global south stakeholders in AI governance. In: Bullock, J., and others (eds.) *The Oxford Handbook of AI Governance* (pp. 981–1014). Oxford: OUP.

[41] Gwagwa, A. (2024). Resisting colonialism—why AI systems must embed the values of the historically oppressed. Chatham House.

[42] Constanza-Chock, S. (2020). Design Justice. MIT Press.

[43] Ayana, G., et al., 2024. "Decolonizing global AI governance: assessment of the state of decolonized AI governance in Sub-Saharan Africa". R. Soc. Open Sci., 11, p. 231994.

accomplished in African countries.[44] Indeed, AI innovation and development in the continent is not as advanced as in other parts of the world.[45] Africa is scoring lower than many countries in the world in AI readiness and still depends largely on partners such as technology firms and international donors.[46] Various factors contribute to this lack of readiness including digital infrastructure limitations, insufficient regulatory oversight, fragmented and insufficient data, shortage of talent, and limited funding and investment. As such, it is clear that even in promoting the development of AI and its responsible adoption, it is important to that an enabling regulatory environment for AI is in place, that the pre-existing less advanced digitalisation goals are met, current structural challenges are addressed, and clear implementation strategies are put in place.[47]

At the same time, discourse on innovation versus regulation is pronounced in Africa, as it is in other parts of the world. While innovation should be encouraged, it is also important to create an enabling ecosystem supporting responsible AI development. A balancing act must be prioritised in ensuring that innovation is not stifled while acknowledging that robust governance frameworks are essential for the development of fair and trustworthy AI systems that safeguard human rights against potential AI harms.

In the development of AI governance frameworks, there should be a balanced approach to regulation, that promotes innovation. The use of regulatory sandboxes is a way in which the co-creation of innovation processes and regulations can be promoted between AI developers and

[44] Abdella, S., & Alayande, A. (2025). 'African Countries Are Racing to Create AI Strategies-But Are They Putting the Cart Before the Horse?' Global Center on AI Governance available at: https://www.globalcenter.ai/analysis/articles/african-countries-are-racing-to-create-ai-strategies-but-are-they-putting-the-cart-before-the-horse.

[45] Global Centre on AI Governance (2024). AI in Africa: A Landscape Study. https://www.globalcenter.ai/analysis/articles/ai-in-africa-landscape-study.

[46] Gwagwa, A., Kachidza, P., Siminyu, K., & Smith, M. (2021). 'Responsible Artificial Intelligence in Sub-Saharan Africa: Landscape and general state of play.' Artificial Intelligence for Development Africa.

[47] Abdella, S., & Alayande, A. (2025). 'African Countries Are Racing to Create AI Strategies-But Are They Putting the Cart Before the Horse?'.

regulators who seek to understand these technologies and concurrently develop regulatory frameworks.[48]

The countries in the African region should also consider their value systems and needs in developing ethical AI standards and principles. This includes a focus on ensuring access to basic digital infrastructure, promoting digital literacy and upskilling, use of diverse knowledge and languages in development of AI systems as well as ensuring protection of marginalised communities (Adams, 2022).

10.5.5 A United Continental Front in AI Governance

Historically, solidarity as a continent has been lacking, with misaligned approaches to the development of AI governance frameworks and contribution to global AI governance discourse being palpable.[49] This is visible through the fragmented AI and data ecosystem as well as the lack of aligned approaches as a continent.

The African region should make effort to present a united front in international discourse on AI governance, and this can be done through ensuring alignment in AI policy on the continent. So far, there have been positive steps with the development of the African Union Continental AI Strategy (AU AI Strategy) which prioritises the adoption of AI in various sectors such as agriculture, education, health, and public sectors.[50]

However, critics of the AU AI Strategy have posited that it does not adequately cover the risks posed by AI systems including existential risks. While developing strategies and regulatory frameworks, African countries should consider all potential eventualities in AI risk and must be prepared to address them (Chege, 2024).

In addition to the AU AI Strategy, countries are taking steps to develop AI strategies or policy frameworks to guide national regulation of AI

[48] Datasphere Initiative (2025). Sandboxes for AI: Tools for a new frontier. https://www.thedatasphere.org/wp-content/uploads/2025/02/Report-Sandboxes-for-AI-2025.pdf.

[49] Gwagwa, A., Kazim, E., & Hilliard, A. (2022, April 8). 'The role of the African value of Ubuntu in global AI inclusion discourse: A normative ethics perspective.' Patterns, 3(4), 1–7.

[50] African Union (2024). Continental Artificial Intelligence Strategy: Harnessing AI for Africa's Development and Prosperity. https://au.int/sites/default/files/documents/44004-doc-EN-_Continental_AI_Strategy_July_2024.pdf.

systems. At least 8 countries in Africa have finalised and adopted AI strategies including Mauritius, Egypt, Benin, Rwanda, Senegal, Zambia, Lesotho, and Kenya, with several more in the process of developing their strategies/policy frameworks.

10.5.6 AI Infrastructure and Data Sovereignty

In recent years, AI infrastructure and data sovereignty have emerged as a pain point in discussions on AI development in Africa. Data are considered the backbone of effectively functioning AI systems as they require large datasets in training and learning. However, where data are extracted from the Global South but stored by technology companies in developed countries, concerns of data sovereignty arise. The communities from which the data are sourced often no longer have access to these data and do not benefit from data use, whereas the foreign entities control and own these data, amounting to what scholars refer to as digital colonialism.[51] This control not only applies to data but also to AI technologies and infrastructure on the continent such as connectivity infrastructure, and is evident in the over-reliance on import of foreign AI technologies that are not tailored to local communities and amount to biased outcomes.[52]

Part of the contributing factors to these challenges on data and AI technology sovereignty is the overrealiance on connectivity systems controlled by foreign entities, weak data protection laws, and limited enforcement. There should be a focus on developing robust data protection frameworks that secure data rights, and equitable data practices which are key for addressing existing inequalities while fostering a fair AI ecosystem.

10.5.7 Fragmented Data Governance Frameworks in Africa

As AI governance frameworks are developed, the underlying regulations on data governance, which are critical to AI, should be harmonised across the continent to ensure that there are principles in place to protect data rights, relating to ownership, privacy, autonomy, and human dignity. This

[51] Etori, N., Dawson, M., & Gini, M. (2024). 'Double-edged sword: Navigating AI Opportunities and the Risk of Digital Colonization in Africa.' MWAIS 2024 Proceedings. Association for Information Systems.

[52] Id.

will enable Africans to have autonomy in the control, use, and transfer of their data.[53]

Existing standards on human rights in Africa such as the African Charter on Human and Peoples Rights (African Union, 1981), the African Union Convention on Cybersecurity, and Personal Data Protection (African Union, 2014), should be enforced in relation to protecting data rights. Unified data governance frameworks in Africa are fundamental as data are the basis of development and application of AI tools.[54] As envisioned under the AU Data Policy Framework, individuals and institutions should be empowered in harnessing the potential of their data, to promote trust in the ecosystem and align African stances in international discourse on data and AI governance topics.[55]

Indeed, with the adoption of AI across the continent, and the development of data centres as a shared resource, data governance frameworks that are aligned within the continent are imperative to maintain a well functioning AI ecosystem that serves the continent effectively.

10.5.8 Addressing Digital Divides and Ensuring "Benefit for All"

The development of Africa-centric AI, or AI developed for use on the continent, is crucial to address concrete challenges and developmental use cases. It is critical that these AI tools benefit all and do not deepen existing inequalities.[56] AI adoption must be of actual benefit to the communities in which they are being adopted, such as in the public sector functions like education and health, or in critical infrastructure. Auditing and accountability frameworks are also integral, especially for AI tools that present higher levels of risk to various aspects of society. Inclusivity and

[53] Effoduh, J. O., Akpudo, U. E., & Kong, J. D. (2024). 'Toward a trustworthy and inclusive data governance policy for the use of artificial intelligence in Africa.' Data & Policy, 6.

[54] Effoduh, J. O. (2021). 'Towards a Rights-Respecting Artificial Intelligence Policy for Nigeria.' Paradigm Initiative and Global Partners Digital.

[55] African Union. (2022). Retrieved March, 2025 from AU Data Policy Framework: https://au.int/en/documents/20220728/au-data-policy-framework.

[56] Gor, G., Ryan, F., Zoumpalova, T., & Lliadis, N. (2025). 'International Coordination for Accountability in AI Governance. The Athens Roundtable.' The Future Society.

democratising AI must take into account the cultural and linguistic diversity, and the unique contextual landscape of Africa ensuring no one is left behind.

As a highly linguistically diverse region, majority of languages in Africa are low-resource languages, and remain marginalised and underrepresented in the digital space despite their wide use on the continent.[57] In the past few years, however, there have been increasing efforts to develop Natural Language Processing (NLP) tools and datasets from the African continent to power NLP technology which is a move towards democratising AI and reducing the challenge of digital colonisation.[58]

10.5.9 Focus on Legal Tech

AI technologies have been adopted across various legal functions, including in legal practice and the judiciary. It has helped in the automation of repetitive tasks, document and case management, improvement of legal research and virtual legal assistance mechanisms (Olatunji, 2024). There is a demand by legal practitioners for legal technologies as evidenced in the AI chatbots providing legal information and consults for legal practitioners, as well as in AI systems which review and increase efficiency of the work of legal specialists (Centre for Intellectual Property and Information Technology Law—CIPIT, 2023).

Within judicial systems, AI use is visible in certain countries in Africa, such as Tanzania where an AI system is used for transcription and translation services, and in Morocco where AI is utilised to transcribe rulings, conduct research, and in retrieval of archived texts (Lawyers Hub, 2024). The benefits of using AI systems developed for a particular purpose and adapted to the linguistic needs of the user have been witnessed in the use of the Almawave technology which was trained to recognise and process speech patterns in both English and Kiswahili, and enables human oversight by judicial staff. The same has been observed in Morocco, where there is care to ensure that the different dialects present in the country are taken into account in adopting AI systems within the judiciary (Lawyers Hub, 2024).

[57] Amol, C. J., Chimoto, E. A., Antony, G., Gesicho, R. D., Kinyanjui, C., Etori, N.,… Tombe, R. (2024). 'State of NLP in Kenya: A Survey.' arXiv preprint.

[58] Etori, N., Dawson, M., & Gini, M. (2024). 'Double-edged sword: Navigating AI Opportunities and the Risk of Digital Colonization in Africa'.

In South Africa, AI tools are supporting judicial processes with predictive analytics assisting in streamlining case management and reduction of backlogs in cases (Olatunji, 2024). In Kenya, studies have shown that NLP technologies are advanced enough to effectively contribute to certain judicial functions such as digitization of court documents.[59]

10.5.10 Arising Concerns on the Use of AI Tools in Legal Functions

With the gradual adoption of AI within the legal space in Africa, certain risks arise specifically affecting human rights, for example, algorithmic bias, lack of transparency in AI use, and lack of explainability in AI-generated outcomes or decisions.[60] Further, the stand alone use of legal AI technology to provide legal advice independent of lawyers has been sanctioned highlighting the need for ethical dimensions and quality assurance in provision of services.[61]

Algorithmic biases emerge frequently as the output of such legal AI tools is most often a reflection of their input or training data that reflect inaccurate or incomplete data, and data that are not aligned with the societal needs of the specific African countries utilising such tools.[62] The lack of transparency in decision-making in such technologies is concerning with regard to determinations made on legal responsibilities and human rights.[63]

Due to these risks, human oversight is fundamental in dealing with AI-generated legal decisions or insights, to facilitate accurate output, and to ascertain that human rights are not violated. Long-term harms such as potential catastrophic risks should also be taken into account while considering the future of AI and the rule of law. This is especially the case

[59] Ogonjo, F., Gitonga, J. T., & Wairegi, A. (2022). 'Leveraging AI in the Kenyan Judiciary: A Case for Utilizing Text Classification Models for Data Completeness in Case Law Meta Data in Kenya's Employment and Labor Relations Court.' Centre for Intellectual Property and Information Technology Law (CIPIT).

[60] Nhemi, S. (2023). 'Law Without Lawyers: Examining the Limitations of Consumer-Centric Legal Tech Services.' *J. Intell. Prop. & Info. Tech. L.*, *3*, 15.

[61] Id.

[62] Wakunuma, K., Ogoh, G., Eke, D. O., & Akintoye, S. (2022, May). 'Responsible AI, SDGs, and AI governance in Africa.' In 2022 IST-Africa Conference (IST-Africa) pp. 1–13. IEEE.

[63] Nhemi, S. (2023). 'Law Without Lawyers: Examining the Limitations of Consumer-Centric Legal Tech Services'.

in Africa and other countries in the Global South where there may not be adequate mitigation or protection systems for the citizenry against such potential AI harms (Chege, 2024).

In efforts to regulate such legal use cases, steps towards development of sector-specific guidelines on ethical AI use have been commenced. For instance, the Judicial Service Commission in Kenya is in the process of convening the development of guidelines on the use of AI systems within the judiciary, highlighting rules and procedures for the ethical and responsible adoption of AI technologies.

A regulatory method of ensuring AI is used responsibly could be the adoption of risk-based standards that fit within the African context.[64] For instance, other regions have adopted risk based systems, such as in Europe where the EU AI Act (2023) highlights that the use of AI in legal functions, including within the public sector such as the judiciary, is a high-risk use of AI and is subject to robust regulatory measures. Beyond the use of AI in high-risk functions, the issue of lack of robust data sets which are the backbone of development of AI systems, and insufficiency in data governance frameworks should be considered as a high-risk factors that should be addressed promptly.[65] Considerations of cultural values and beliefs should nevertheless be prioritised in the creation and enforcement of policies by AI policymakers and developers.[66]

To address these risks, relevant existing laws may be amended to include arising policy considerations on ethical adoption of AI. Furthermore, AI specific regulatory frameworks may be developed to govern key concerns that arise from these technologies while simultaneously ensuring that innovation is not stifled. The African countries should also aim to promote trust in AI adoption within their countries by ensuring that there is an enabling AI innovation ecosystem, digital literacy and upskilling programmes are in place, and that ethical and responsible AI use is championed.

[64] Effoduh, J. O., Akpudo, U. E., & Kong, J. D. (2024). 'Toward a trustworthy and inclusive data governance policy for the use of artificial intelligence in Africa'.

[65] Effoduh, J. O., Akpudo, U. E., & Kong, J. D. (2024). 'Toward a trustworthy and inclusive data governance policy for the use of artificial intelligence in Africa'.

[66] Eke, D. O., Wakunuma, K., & Akintoye, S. (2023). 'Introducing Responsible AI in Africa.' In Responsible AI in Africa: Challenges and Opportunities (pp. 1–12). Palgrave Macmillan.

There is a critical need for intra-continental collaboration in shaping the future of AI and the rule of law, particularly through aligning interests and promoting unity among African countries to present a unified voice. Addressing digital colonialism requires the inclusion of Global South voices and diversity, ensuring that African countries actively participate in the international discourse on AI governance framework development.

It is vital to ensure that data are accessible to the communities that own them, and to establish strong AI and data governance frameworks that are aligned across the continent. The development of inclusive AI safety standards must prioritise the protection of fundamental human rights and foster public trust. Furthermore, guardrails must be placed on AI systems to ascertain they are fair, transparent, and accountable. Specifically, in the context of high-risk AI use in law and legal technology, it is imperative that the relevant human rights are safeguarded.

10.6 Future of Legal Tech and Digital Governance: Safeguarding Human Rights in the Age of AI

As states navigate the AI-augmented transformation race in the public sector, AI can emerge as a tool of innovation and disruption. Its potential to bolster public administration, especially in fragile or reforming democracies, is immense. Yet, integrating AI into digital governance simultaneously raises pressing concerns about ethics, fairness, and transparency, causing slow or rapid erosion of human rights. High-profile failures involving AI-driven human rights abuses, paradoxically occurring in established liberal democracies such as the UK and the Netherlands,[67] underscore the inherent risks. It raises the following discussion: *how can states harness the transformative potential of AI while foreseeing and mitigating its inherent threats to fundamental rights*? This discussion may also nudge scholars to study the potential paradox in this complex terrain: AI as a saviour of weak institutions—and a risk to established democracies—through the lens of AI legal tech, AI-enabled public service, and

[67] The Guardian. (2023) 'UK officials use AI to decide on issues from benefits to marriage licences'. available at: https://www.theguardian.com/technology/2023/oct/23/uk-officials-use-ai-to-decide-on-issues-from-benefits-to-marriage-licences; Amnesty International. (2021) 'Netherlands: Children's rights sacrificed in the fight against fraud.' available at: https://www.amnesty.org/en/documents/eur35/4686/2021/en/.

human rights frameworks around it. Durkiewicz and Janowski[68] argued that "digitalisation brings substantial benefits to structural change and transparency, but not to accountability". Thus, the way to explore future implications and learn from past mistakes emphasises that mitigating AI's risks is not merely reactive but foundational to guide us through the future of AI-enabled and human-by-default policy-making justly and sustainably.

10.6.1 From Bureaucratic Weakness to AI-Enabled Opportunities

Max Weber's (1994) ideal bureaucracy is characterised by four principles: power is concentrated in the office; civil servants are meritocrats; they are loyal to the service and stable from political interference. Yet, it remains elusive in many transitioning democracies grappling with institutional fragility, corruption, reconstruction, or conflict. As Newman et al.[69] suggest, advanced computing technologies could not only strengthen the ability of public sector organisations to deliver services to the public, but they could also enhance the inherent democratic nature of bureaucracy and further concretise its role in democratic governance. Building on this potential, AI-driven solutions offer compelling tools to accelerate public administration reform—often a decades-long process—and can serve as crucial *digital stabilisers* in times of crisis. AI tools can also help bridge institutional gaps and enforce complex procedures by embedding rule-of-law values directly into algorithmic design for nations pursuing EU accession.

Ukraine's e-government environment during the war exemplifies this: while the country has faced the war, online services and digital platforms like Diia kept services operational, sustaining government legitimacy and public trust.[70] It vividly illustrates that GovTech can become a substitute for missing institutional capacity, offering digital-by-default services

[68] Durkiewicz, J. & Janowski, T. (2018). 'Is Digitalization Improving Governance Quality? Correlating Analog and Digital Benchmarks in European Conference on Digital Government.' 2018 Reading: Academic Conferences International Limited. pp. 48–VIII.

[69] Newman, J. et al. (2022) 'Digital technologies, artificial intelligence, and bureaucratic transformation.' Futures: the journal of policy, planning and futures studies.

[70] Brookings. (2023). "Ukraine: 'Digital resilience in a time of war.'" available at: https://www.brookings.edu/articles/ukraine-digital-resilience-in-a-time-of-war.

that bypass slow bureaucratic reform or even curb corruption.[71] Ukraine is leveraging AI within its Diia platform with over 20 million users[72] through tools like the "Natalka" chatbot for service integration and is developing an AI assistant for user navigation, legal analysis,[73] EU integration and translation procedures, alongside exploiting sovereign AI applications in critical sectors such as national security and defence (United24 Media, 2025). Additionally, Ukraine focuses on personalising education, recognising the importance of human-centred and EU-compliant AI systems.[74]

In contexts where institutions are in transition or overburdened, AI doesn't just support reforms—it *canbecome human-centred governance*. However, realising this potential while avoiding the pitfalls inherent in AI development demands an unwavering commitment to protecting fundamental rights frameworks. Thus, the path from bureaucratic weakness towards AI-enabled opportunities is viable only when safeguarding human rights is embedded as a central pillar within the government's digital and AI strategy.

10.6.2 AI and Risk for Human Rights in Liberal Democracies and Digital Governance

By contrast, liberal democracies possess a much longer history of utilising algorithmic systems. Estonia, for instance, has announced over 130 AI initiatives in digital governance (e-Estonia, n.d.), while others have deployed AI for decades. Consequently, significant failures undermining human rights have already surfaced in these contexts, generating major scandals at the intersection of AI and the public sector and demonstrating that no democracy is entirely immune to AI risks. The UK's

[71] Ugale, G., & Hall, C. (2024). 'Generative AI for anti-corruption and integrity in government: Taking stock of promise, perils and practice' (OECD Artificial Intelligence Papers, No. 12). OECD Publishing. https://doi.org/10.1787/657a185a-en.

[72] EU4Digital. (n.d.) 'Building a Digital State: Ukraine's Diia App Now Boasts Over 20 Million Users.' available at: https://eufordigital.eu/building-a-digital-state-ukraines-diia-app-now-boasts-over-20-million-users/

[73] 35% of legal acts are processed by the AI tool within 72 h.

[74] Ministry of Digital Transformation of Ukraine. (2024). 'White Paper on AI regulation in Ukraine.' available at: https://thedigital.gov.ua/storage/uploads/files/page/community/docs/Біла_книга_з_регулювання_ШІ_в_Україні_АНГЛ.pdf.

deployment of AI in public services, for example, revealed significant racial profiling issues in facial recognition and immigration screenings.[75] The Home Office, for instance, unfairly targeted individuals from specific European countries suspected of sham marriages. Experts voiced concerns regarding the absence of a robust legal framework for AI accountability and transparency and the lack of a dedicated regulatory body to mitigate risks associated with biased data sets.[76] Similarly, in the Netherlands, a flawed algorithmic profiling system erroneously flagged thousands of families for welfare fraud, precipitating widespread financial ruin and a political crisis.[77]

These stark cases reveal how poor data quality, inadequate accountability mechanisms, and opaque algorithms can systematically exacerbate discrimination. In both instances, the state's attempt to digitise governance critically undermined public trust—the very foundation GovTech ostensibly aims to build. This aligns with Fukuyama's[78] observation that citizens' trust in government, not regime type, is the crucial determinant of crisis response. Therefore, a key imperative for the future deployment of AI must be to ensure it functions to restore, rather than erode, that essential trust.

While critics may dismiss these instances as isolated failures or unavoidable "bugs", such incidents expose systemic vulnerabilities and highlight AI bureaucracy's "red lines". When automation displaces ethical deliberation and human judgement, the rule of law suffers. AI may offer a potential shortcut to institutional credibility in low-capacity states—*if* deployed responsibly. Conversely, in high-capacity democracies, it risks inducing institutional atrophy by eroding transparency or citizen agency.

[75] The Guardian. (2023) 'UK officials use AI to decide on issues from benefits to marriage licences'.

[76] Digital Watch. (2023) 'AI use in the UK government sparks concerns over bias and transparency'.https://dig.watch/updates/ai-use-in-uk-government-sparks-concerns-over-bias-and-transparency.

[77] Amnesty International. (2021) 'Netherlands: Children's rights sacrificed in the fight against fraud.' Available at: https://www.amnesty.org/en/documents/eur35/4686/2021/en/; Politico. (2022). 'Dutch scandal serves as a warning for Europe over risks of using algorithms.' POLITICO. https://www.politico.eu/article/dutch-scandal-serves-as-a-warning-for-europe-over-risks-of-using-algorithms/

[78] Fukuyama, F. (2020) 'The Thing that Determine's a Country's Resistance to the Coronavirus', The Atlantic. Available at: https://www.theatlantic.com/ideas/archive/2020/03/thing-determines-how-well-countries-respond-coronavirus/609025/.

Ultimately, regardless of context, robust, rights-based safeguards are not optional but essential. This contrast sets the stage for exploring the future trends and necessary safeguards discussed next.

10.6.3 Future Trends in AI Legal Tech and Digital Governance

The full extent of future opportunities and challenges for human rights in the AI era will unfold simultaneously with how AI is integrated into government and legal systems.

AI Agents in Public Administration: Numerous national AI strategies outline the future of AI digital governance as personalisation of AI for citizens and civil service, utilising digital twins, AI agents, bots, and co-pilots to assist public policy delivery, enhance institutional capacity, and manage the crisis. For example, the EU is building a GPT@EU,[79] and the UK Minister trialled automated decision advisors as policy-making tools.[80] Furthermore, AI agents trained on specific legal frameworks, like the *EU acquis*, can assist in complex tasks such as policy alignment and engagement bureaucracy for EU candidate countries (e.g. Ukraine, Moldova, Albania, Serbia) navigating accession requirements[81] (United-Media24, 2025; Euroactiv, 2023). These trends promise faster decisions, cost reduction, and automation—whether by relieving staff, splitting tasks, replacing functions, or augmenting human capabilities.[82] However, it also raises serious concerns about ethics on automated systems, maintaining meaningful human oversight, and addressing data and privacy issues that cannot be overlooked in the drive for efficiency. Besides, incorporating solid AI literacy, grounded in human rights principles, into the

[79] European Commission. (2024a). 'AI Act implementation timeline.' available at: https://digital-strategy.ec.europa.eu/en/policies/ai-act-implementation-timeline.

[80] The Guardian. (2025). 'Technology Secretary Peter Kyle asks ChatGPT for science and media advice.' available at: https://www.theguardian.com/politics/2025/mar/13/technlogy-secretary-peter-kyle-asks-chatgpt-for-science-and-media-advice.

[81] EU4Digital. (2025). 'New EU4Digital activity to improve translation tools through language resource mapping.' Available at: https://eufordigital.eu/new-eu4digital-activity-to-improve-translation-tools-through-language-resource-mapping/.

[82] Eggers, W. D., Schatsky, D., & Viechnicki, P. (2017). 'AI-augmented government: Using cognitive technologies to redesign public sector work.' Deloitte Insights. https://www2.deloitte.com/content/dam/insights/us/articles/3832_AI-augmented-government/DUP_AI-augmented-government.pdf.

training and qualifications of public servants is crucial for developing and implementing practical and responsible AI policies.

Localisation and AI Sovereignty: Another significant development is the push towards localisation and "AI sovereignty". To reduce dependency on foreign tech, nations like Saudi Arabia, UAE, Sweden, Taiwan, France, and many others[83] are building state-driven local LLMs tailored to domestic law, economy, society, culture, and language peculiarities. The main goals are to improve national security, gain greater control over digital infrastructure, and ensure citizen data are managed within their borders according to local laws. However, pursuing AI sovereignty and developing national LLMs pose risks, such as reinforcing authoritarian control and creating "sovereignty traps" that challenge multi-stakeholder governance and democratic norms.[84] While framed as a tool for security and efficiency, concerns also persist about its potential misuse for digital repression, shaping public perception, computational propaganda, surveillance, and weaponisation. Moreover, this trend poses a significant threat to sustainable development and the environment, given that sovereign AI infrastructure requires an immense amount of scarce natural resources and electricity, spurring planet-warming.[85]

AI for Courts andthe Rule of Law Acceleration: AI can also help the justice system by managing evidence in war crimes, summarising legal arguments, or providing algorithmic paperwork automation. Other tools have already transformed litigation strategies, contract review and redlining, legal research, document analysis, and automated workflow tasks[86]. Dispute resolution and legal aid bots are a new epoch in safeguarding citizen protection in public administration. These innovations

[83] Chavez, P. (2024). 'Sovereign AI in a hybrid world: National strategies and policy responses.' Lawfare. Available at: https://www.lawfaremedia.org/article/sovereign-ai-in-a-hybrid-world--national-strategies-and-policy-responses; Bondarenko, M., Lushnei, S., Paniv, Y., Molchanovsky, O., Romanyshyn, M., Filipchuk, Y., & Kiulian, A. (2025). 'Sovereign large language models: Advantages, strategy and regulations' (arXiv:2503.04745v1). arXiv. https://arxiv.org/abs/2503.04745v1.

[84] Komaitis, K., Ponce de León, E., Thibaut, K., Ray, T., & Klyman, K. (2024). 'The sovereignty trap.' DFRLab. https://dfrlab.org/2024/07/17/the-sovereignty-trap/.

[85] UNEP (United Nations Environment Programme). (2023). 'AI has an environmental problem. Here's what the world can do about it.' available at: https://www.unep.org/news-and-stories/story/ai-has-environmental-problem-heres-what-world-can-do-about.

[86] Thomson Reuters. (2025). 'How AI is transforming the legal profession.' Available at: https://legal.thomsonreuters.com/blog/how-ai-is-transforming-the-legal-profession/.

increase access to justice, especially in under-resourced legal systems. However, an AI-powered court system may pose a significant risk to the rule of law and states' constitutions. For instance, in China, AI judges must consult AI recommendations and provide written justifications if they deviate from them,[87] raising concerns about judicial autonomy and the potential erosion of judges' discretion. Issues may arise in predictive decision-making with AI. Governments look for AI-driven analysis of Big Data for policy forecasting, anticipating crises, or adapting legal services. This creates a feedback loop between citizen needs and state action, but requires proper AI and data governance to overcome AI prejudice and discrimination.

10.6.4 Future Policy Responses: Predictions for a Human Rights-Centred AI Governance

As states increasingly embed AI innovations into public functions, the parallel necessity of embedding robust, rights-based safeguards throughout the entire AI lifecycle—from initial design to final deployment—becomes paramount. This brings into sharp focus the most debatable question for the next decade: *Can we achieveAI democracy without dehumanising it?* Recognising this, several research centres actively monitor AI's human rights impact, developing global indices that benchmark national policy frameworks against criteria of human rights, democracy, and the rule of law.[88] These studies offer vital insights and track the evolving dynamics at the critical intersection of AI and human rights.

Speaking of international treaties on AI, achieving a globally enforceable AI governance agreement appears increasingly utopian amidst current geopolitical tensions. This reality points towards inevitable regulatory fragmentation, with nations primarily developing distinct local AI regulations. Furthermore, potential regulatory simplification or even

[87] Eurasian Times. (2025). 'China's AI-Enabled 'Smart Courts' To Recommend Laws & Draft Legal Docs; Judges To Take Consult AI Before Verdict.' available at: https://www.eurasiantimes.com/chinas-ai-enabled-smart-court-to-recommend-laws-judges/.

[88] CAIDP (Center for AI and Digital Policy). (2025). 'AI and democratic values index 2025.' Available at: https://www.caidp.org/app/download/8557711863/AIandDemocraticValuesIIndex(CAIDP2025).pdf?t=1743613077.

backsliding has been signalled even by traditionally proactive regulators, such as the EU with its "AI Continent" plan.[89] Consequently, policy innovation presents itself as a strategic option for nations seeking to compete effectively in the global AI race, allowing them to foster progress while potentially navigating away from burdensome regulations that risk hindering crucial innovation.

Our predictions are quite balanced regarding diminishing public service due to AI development. AI will rather empower—not replace—public servants. AI is increasingly viewed as a tool to handle routine or complex analytical tasks, freeing public servants for critical and creative thinking, complex decision-making, and essential human interaction. In this context, establishing *meaningful* human oversight—the **"public-servant-in-the-loop** (*PSITL*)"—is paramount, particularly for high-risk applications. However, tackling the human biases of employees working with algorithms will be the central issue in safeguarding human rights.[90] Thus, training civil servants in AI ethics and giving them veto power over algorithmic decisions may ensure a necessary human oversight. Another response may be so-called **public-in-the-loop** (*PITL*) initiatives for transparent, trustworthy, and accountable AI GovTech developments. Meaningful public participation, through diverse mechanisms ranging from consultations and online platforms to citizen assemblies, allows for the incorporation of varied societal perspectives and values directly into the governance process.

The Council of Europe has made a substantial step in developing the risk and impact assessment of AI systems from the point of view of human rights, democracy, and the rule of law ('the HUDERIA') under the Framework Convention on Artificial Intelligence and Human Rights, Democracy, and the Rule of Law.[91] **HUDERIA** can help hone a comprehensive checklist for the public sector in developing and deploying AI systems that respect fundamental principles such as dignity, freedom of

[89] European Commission. (2025). 'AI continent.' European Commission. https://commission.europa.eu/topics/eu-competitiveness/ai-continent_en.

[90] Helmholtz Centre for Information Security. (2024). 'AI under supervision: Human-in-the-loop.' Alexander von Humboldt Institute for Internet and Society (HIIG). https://www.hiig.de/en/ai-under-supervision-human-in-the-loop/.

[91] Council of Europe. (n.d.). 'HUDERIA: Risk and impact assessment of AI systems.' available at: https://www.coe.int/en/web/artificial-intelligence/huderia-risk-and-impact-assessment-of-ai-systems.

expression, privacy, and non-discrimination. Another example may be testing of AI GovTech in a controlled environment, such as **"sandboxes"** that allow a preliminary trial of systems with high risk without causing harm to citizens.[92] Some scholars suggest that human impact assessment also helps to reduce "slow violence" of human rights, when AI affects freedoms invisibly.[93]

As AI systems become increasingly embedded within the public sector, robust ongoing monitoring and enforcement mechanisms are equally indispensable. Therefore, **human rights watchdogs and ombudsmen** must be provided with the necessary powers[94] and mandate to monitor AI use and algorithmic labelling (like 'AI-generated decision') and subsequently enhance AI accountability and traceability for the public good.[95] The critical importance of such oversight and effective implementation is underscored by real-world risks. For instance, algorithms have reportedly been used to undermine democratic processes, such as liberal elections in Romania,[96] demonstrating that even comprehensive regulations like those within the EU are insufficient without robust enforcement. This highlights a crucial lesson: safeguarding democracy in the age of AI requires moving beyond solely refining regulations to proven **best practices** for their effective implementation on the ground.

Another policy workflow should be concentrated on **tackling geopolitical biases** in AI systems that undermine freedom of expression and exacerbate societal polarisation. For instance, scholars investigated that multilingual LLMs recall information differently to "Who owns Crimea

[92] OECD. (2025). 'Steering AI's future: Strategies for anticipatory governance' (OECD Artificial Intelligence Papers, No. 32). OECD Publishing. https://doi.org/10.1787/5480ff0a-en.

[93] Teo, S. (2024). 'Artificial intelligence and its 'slow violence' to human rights.' AI Ethics. https://doi.org/10.1007/s43681-024-00547-x.

[94] Council of Europe. (2023). 'Human rights by design: Report of the Commissioner for Human Rights.' available at: https://www.theioi.org/downloads/6mqop/CoE%20%20Commissioner%27s%20report%20%20Human%20rights%20by%20design%20-%20EN.pdf.

[95] Burrus, O., Curtis, A., & Herman, L. (2024). 'Unmasking AI: Informing authenticity decisions by labelling AI-generated content.' Interactions, 31(4), 26–30.

[96] Bjola, C. (2025). *Algorithmic invasions: How information warfare threatens NATO's eastern flank*. NATO Review. available at: https://www.nato.int/docu/review/articles/2025/02/07/algorithmic-invasions-how-information-warfare-threatens-nato-s-eastern-flank/index.html.

peninsula?" across languages when answering equivalent queries, quantifies geopolitical bias in popular models, and explores how conversational context—such as using personas with specific geopolitical leanings—can amplify or mitigate that bias.[97] Another study showed that African journalists accused ChatGPT of following Western narratives, describing African leaders as corrupt ones, while King Leopold II is fairly described.[98] Addressing these issues connects directly to broader challenges of **"decolonisation of AI"**, resisting **tech oligarchisation**, ultimately underscoring the need to subject powerful LLMs to public control.[99] Last but not least, AI harms are often caused by poor and improper data that lacks transparent and inclusive **data governance**.[100] Datasets must reflect diversity to avoid algorithmic bias, discrimination, and the undermining of human dignity. Consequently, developing robust, transparent, and inclusive data governance practices alongside AI ethics policies is not merely a technical requirement, but a foundational step towards the democratisation of AI within digital governance.

10.6.5 Charting a Human-Centric Future for AI in Governance and Law

Legal tech and digital governance powered by AI offer tremendous promise for advancing the protection of human rights, yet simultaneously pose significant risks to democratic principles. As seen in current tendencies, AI can be a powerful equaliser in fragile states. However, it

[97] Li, B., Haider, S., & Callison-Burch, C. (2024). 'This land is your, my land: Evaluating geopolitical bias in language models through territorial disputes.' In K. Duh, H. Gomez, & S. Bethard (Eds.), Proceedings of the 2024 Conference of the North American Chapter of the Association for Computational Linguistics: Human Language Technologies (Volume 1: Long Papers) (pp. 3855–3871).

[98] Gondwe, G. (2023). 'ChatGPT and the Global South: How are journalists in sub-Saharan Africa engaging with generative AI?' Online Media and Global Communication. Available at: https://scholar.harvard.edu/sites/scholar.harvard.edu/files/ggondwezunda/files/chatgpt_article.pdf.

[99] Bajohr, H. (2024). Whoever controls language models controls politics. ResearchGate. available at: https://www.researchgate.net/publication/377656052_Whoever_Controls_Language_Models_Controls_Politics.

[100] Pahune, S., Akhtar, Z., Mandapati, V., & Siddique, K. (2025). 'The importance of AI data governance in large language models' [Preprint]. Preprints.org. https://doi.org/10.20944/preprints202504.0219.v1.

can erode trust if misapplied, even in liberal democracies. Therefore, the future of a rights-oriented digital state should be seen not in replacing public servants with algorithms but in building capacity through careful, transparent, inclusive AI transformation and policy innovations that bring added value to citizens, safeguarding human rights.

Navigating the future—marked by trends like the proliferation of AI agents, the pursuit of AI sovereignty, and the increasing automation of legal and judicial tasks—**demands a correspondingly proactive and adaptive governance approach. This necessitates** incorporating multiple layers of safeguards: **meaningful human oversight** ('public-servant-in-the-loop'), robust mechanisms for **public participation** ('public-in-the-loop'), rigorous **impact assessment frameworks** like HUDERIA, controlled **testing environments** like sandboxes, and empowered **independent regulators**. Crucially, real-world cases reveal **an urgent need** to address the **implementation gap** between regulation and practice, **while alsotackling algorithmic bias** at its source through transparent and inclusive **data governance**.

Ultimately, the future of AI in the public sphere hinges on a fundamental choice: whether to pursue automation potentially at the cost of human agency and democratic values, or to deliberately harness AI's power in service of them. The path forward lies not in replacing human judgement with algorithms, but in augmenting human capabilities responsibly. It requires fostering policy innovation that prioritises transparency, accountability, and equity, ensuring that AI acts as a **booster forthe rule of law**, not a shortcut around it. Building a truly rights-respecting digital state demands an unwavering and ongoing commitment to **human-centricity** in every stage of AI development and deployment.

References

Abdella, S., & Alayande, A. (2025). African Countries Are Racing to Create AI Strategies—But Are They Putting the Cart Before the Horse? From Global Center on AI Governance: https://www.globalcenter.ai/analysis/articles/african-countries-are-racing-to-create-ai-strategies-but-are-they-putting-the-cart-before-the-horse

African Union. (2022). Retrieved March, 2025 from AU Data Policy Framework: https://au.int/en/documents/20220728/au-data-policy-framework

African Union (2024). Continental Artificial Intelligence Strategy: Harnessing AI for Africa's Development and Prosperity. https://au.int/sites/default/files/documents/44004-doc-EN-_Continental_AI_Strategy_July_2024.pdf

Akter, M., Cano, E., Weber, E., Dobler, D., & Habernal, I. (2025). A Comprehensive Survey on Legal Summarization: Challenges and Future Directions. arXiv preprint arXiv:2501.17830; Xu, H., & Ashley, K. (2023). A Question-Answering Approach to Evaluating Legal Summaries. In Legal Knowledge and Information Systems (pp. 293–298). IOS Press.

American Bar Association, Formal Opinion 512: Generative Artificial Intelligence Tools (2023).

Amnesty International. (2021) Netherlands: Children's rights sacrificed in the fight against fraud. Available at: https://www.amnesty.org/en/documents/eur35/4686/2021/en/

Amol, C. J., Chimoto, E. A., Antony, G., Gesicho, R. D., Kinyanjui, C., Etori, N., . . . Tombe, R. (2024). State of NLP in Kenya: A Survey. arXiv preprint.

Aradau, C. & Blanke, T. (2022). *Algorithmic Reason: The New Government of Self and Other*. Oxford: OUP.

Austinin, V. et al., "Artificial Intelligence, the Rule of Law and Public Administration: The Case of Taxation", Cambridge Law Journal 83, no. 3 (Nov. 2024): 437–464.

Ayana, G., et al., 2024. "Decolonizing global AI governance: assessment of the state of decolonized AI governance in Sub-Saharan Africa". R. Soc. Open Sci., 11, p. 231994. https://doi.org/10.1098/rsos.231994

Bajohr, H. (2024). Whoever controls language models controls politics. ResearchGate. https://www.researchgate.net/publication/377656052_Whoever_Controls_Language_Models_Controls_Politics

Bjola, C. (2025). *Algorithmic invasions: How information warfare threatens NATO's eastern flank*. NATO Review. https://www.nato.int/docu/review/articles/2025/02/07/algorithmic-invasions-how-information-warfare-threatens-nato-s-eastern-flank/index.html

Bondarenko, M., Lushnei, S., Paniv, Y., Molchanovsky, O., Romanyshyn, M., Filipchuk, Y., & Kiulian, A. (2025). Sovereign large language models: Advantages, strategy and regulations (arXiv:2503.04745v1). arXiv. https://arxiv.org/abs/2503.04745v1

Brookings. (2023). Ukraine: Digital resilience in a time of war. https://www.brookings.edu/articles/ukraine-digital-resilience-in-a-time-of-war

Burrus, O., Curtis, A., & Herman, L. (2024). Unmasking AI: Informing authenticity decisions by labelling AI-generated content. Interactions, 31(4), 26–30. https://interactions.acm.org/archive/view/july-august-2024/unmasking-ai-informing-authenticity-decisions-by-labeling-ai-generated-content

CAIDP (Center for AI and Digital Policy). (2025). AI and democratic values index 2025. https://www.caidp.org/app/download/8557711863/AIandDemocraticValuesIIndex(CAIDP2025).pdf?t=1743613077

Calegari, R., Ciatto, G., & Omicini, A. (2020). On the integration of symbolic and sub-symbolic techniques for XAI: A survey. Intelligenza Artificiale, 14(1), 7–32.

Chavez, P. (2024). Sovereign AI in a hybrid world: National strategies and policy responses. Lawfare. https://www.lawfaremedia.org/article/sovereign-ai-in-a-hybrid-world--national-strategies-and-policy-responses

Constanza-Chock, S. (2020). Design Justice. MIT Press.

Council of Europe. (n.d.). HUDERIA: Risk and impact assessment of AI systems. https://www.coe.int/en/web/artificial-intelligence/huderia-risk-and-impact-assessment-of-ai-systems

Council of Europe (2018). European Ethical Charter on the Use of AI in Judicial Systems. Strasbourg: Council of Europe.

Council of Europe. (2023). Human rights by design: Report of the Commissioner for Human Rights. https://www.theioi.org/downloads/6mqop/CoE%20-%20Commissioner%27s%20report%20-%20Human%20rights%20by%20design%20-%20EN.pdf

Council of Europe CAHAI (2020a). Towards regulation of AI systems. Strasbourg: Council of Europe. https://edoc.coe.int/en/artificial-intelligence/9656-towards-regulation-of-ai-systems.html March 1, 2025.

Council of Europe CAHAI (2020b). CoE CAHAI (2020b). Ad Hoc Committee on Artificial Intelligence (CAHAI) Policy Development Group (CAHAI-PDG) Draft Feasibility Study V.0.3. *CAHAI-PDG(2020)01*, Strasbourg: Council of Europe. https://rm.coe.int/fs-clean-version-13-10-20-rev1/16809ff30f March 1, 2025.

Crawford, K. (2021). *Atlas of AI: Power, Politics, and the Planetary Costs of Artificial Intelligence*. New Haven: Yale University Press.

Dahl, M., Magesh, V., Suzgun, M., & Ho, D. E. (2024). Large legal fictions: Profiling legal hallucinations in large language models. Journal of Legal Analysis, 16(1), 64–93.

Datasphere Initiative (2025). Sandboxes for AI: Tools for a new frontier. https://www.thedatasphere.org/wp-content/uploads/2025/02/Report-Sandboxes-for-AI-2025.pdf

Digital Watch. (2023) 'AI use in the UK government sparks concerns over bias and transparency'.https://dig.watch/updates/ai-use-in-uk-government-sparks-concerns-over-bias-and-transparency

Dimatteo, L. A., Poncibò, C. & Cannarsa, M. (eds.) (2022). *The Cambridge Handbook of Artificial Intelligence: Global Perspectives on Law and Ethics*. Cambridge: CUP.

Durkiewicz, J. & Janowski, T. (2018). Is Digitalization Improving Governance Quality? Correlating Analog and Digital Benchmarks in European Conference on Digital Government. 2018 Reading: Academic Conferences International Limited. pp. 48–VIII.

Ebers, M. (2020). Regulating AI and robotics: Ethical and legal challenges. In: Ebers, M. & Navas, S. (eds.) *Algorithms and Law* (pp. 37–99). Cambridge: CUP.

e-Estonia. (n.d.). Facts and figures. https://e-estonia.com/facts-and-figures/

Effoduh, J. O. (2021). Towards a Rights-Respecting Artificial Intelligence Policy for Nigeria. Paradigm Initiative and Global Partners Digital.

Effoduh, J. O., Akpudo, U. E., & Kong, J. D. (2024). Toward a trustworthy and inclusive data governance policy for the use of artificial intelligence in Africa. Data & Policy, 6.

Eggers, W. D., Schatsky, D., & Viechnicki, P. (2017). AI-augmented government: Using cognitive technologies to redesign public sector work. Deloitte Insights. https://www2.deloitte.com/content/dam/insights/us/articles/3832_AI-augmented-government/DUP_AI-augmented-government.pdf

Eke, D. O., Wakunuma, K., & Akintoye, S. (2023). Introducing Responsible AI in Africa. In Responsible AI in Africa: Challenges and Opportunities (pp. 1–12). Palgrave Macmillan.

Etori, N., Dawson, M., & Gini, M. (2024). Double-edged sword: Navigating AI Opportunities and the Risk of Digital Colonization in Africa. MWAIS 2024 Proceedings. Association for Information Systems.

Euractiv. (2023). Albania to speed up EU accession using ChatGPT. https://www.euractiv.com/section/politics/news/albania-to-speed-up-eu-accession-using-chatgpt/

Eurasian Times. (2025). China's AI-Enabled 'Smart Courts' To Recommend Laws & Draft Legal Docs; Judges To Take Consult AI Before Verdict. https://www.eurasiantimes.com/chinas-ai-enabled-smart-court-to-recommend-laws-judges/

European Commission. (2025). AI continent. European Commission. https://commission.europa.eu/topics/eu-competitiveness/ai-continent_en

European Commission. (2024). Commission launches a new general-purpose AI tool—GPT@EC. https://commission.europa.eu/news/commission-launches-new-general-purpose-ai-tool-gptec-2024-10-22_en

European Commission. (2023) Ukraine Report 2023. https://neighbourhood-enlargement.ec.europa.eu/ukraine-report-2023_en

EU4Digital. (n.d.) Building a Digital State: Ukraine's Diia App Now Boasts Over 20 Million Users. https://eufordigital.eu/building-a-digital-state-ukraines-diia-app-now-boasts-over-20-million-users/

EU4Digital. (2025). New EU4Digital activity to improve translation tools through language resource mapping. https://eufordigital.eu/new-eu4digital-activity-to-improve-translation-tools-through-language-resource-mapping/
Florida Bar (2023). Proposed Advisory Opinion on AI in Legal Practice.
Fukuyama, F. (2020) 'The Thing that Determine's a Country's Resistance to the Coronavirus', The Atlantic. https://www.theatlantic.com/ideas/archive/2020/03/thing-determines-how-well-countries-respond-coronavirus/609025/
Global Centre on AI Governance (2024). AI in Africa: A Landscape Study. https://www.globalcenter.ai/analysis/articles/ai-in-africa-landscape-study
Gondwe, G. (2023). ChatGPT and the Global South: How are journalists in sub-Saharan Africa engaging with generative AI? Online Media and Global Communication. https://scholar.harvard.edu/sites/scholar.harvard.edu/files/ggondwezunda/files/chatgpt_article.pdf
Gor, G., Ryan, F., Zoumpalova, T., & Lliadis, N. (2025). International Coordination for Accountability in AI Governance. The Athens Roundtable. The Future Society.
Gwagwa, A. (2024). Resisting colonialism—why AI systems must embed the values of the historically oppressed. Chatham House.
Gwagwa, A., Kachidza, P., Siminyu, K., & Smith, M. (2021). Responsible Artificial Intelligence in Sub-Saharan Africa: Landscape and general state of play. Artificial Intelligence for Development Africa.
Gwagwa, A., Kazim, E., & Hilliard, A. (2022, April 8). The role of the African value of Ubuntu in global AI inclusion discourse: A normative ethics perspective. Patterns, 3(4): 1–7.
Helmholtz Centre for Information Security. (2024). AI under supervision: Human-in-the-loop. Alexander von Humboldt Institute for Internet and Society (HIIG). https://www.hiig.de/en/ai-under-supervision-human-in-the-loop/
High-Level Expert Group on Artificial Intelligence—AI HLEG (2019). Ethics guidelines for trustworthy AI. Brussels: European Commission. https://ec.europa.eu/newsroom/dae/document.cfm?doc_id=60419 March 16, 2025.
International Bar Association (IBA), "The Future Is Now: Artificial Intelligence and the Legal Profession", IBA Reports AIRe 4|2024 (2024), pp. 451–457.
Katz, D. M. et al., "GPT-4 Passes the Bar Exam", Illinois Tech News (15 March 2023).
Katz, D. M., Hartung, D., Gerlach, L., Jana, A., & Bommarito II, M. J. (2023). Natural language processing in the legal domain. arXiv preprint arXiv:2302.12039.
Kenthapadi, K., Lakkaraju, H., & Rajani, N. (2023, August). Generative ai meets responsible ai: Practical challenges and opportunities. In Proceedings of the

29th ACM SIGKDD conference on knowledge discovery and data mining (pp. 5805–5806).

Komaitis, K., Ponce de León, E., Thibaut, K., Ray, T., & Klyman, K. (2024). The sovereignty trap. DFRLab. https://dfrlab.org/2024/07/17/the-sovereignty-trap/.

Lee, K. F. & Qiufan, C. (2021). *AI 2041: Ten Visions for Our Future*. London: WH Allen.

Li, B., Haider, S., & Callison-Burch, C. (2024). This land is your, my land: Evaluating geopolitical bias in language models through territorial disputes. In K. Duh, H. Gomez, & S. Bethard (Eds.), Proceedings of the 2024 Conference of the North American Chapter of the Association for Computational Linguistics: Human Language Technologies (Volume 1: Long Papers) (pp. 3855–3871). Association for Computational Linguistics. https://doi.org/10.18653/v1/2024.naacl-long.213.

Medvedeva, M., Vols, M., & Wieling, M. (2020). Using machine learning to predict decisions of the European Court of Human Rights. Artificial Intelligence and Law, 28(2), 237–266; Chalkidis, I., Androutsopoulos, I., & Aletras, N. (2019). Neural legal judgment prediction in English. arXiv preprint arXiv: 1906.02059.

Ministry of Digital Transformation of Ukraine. (2024). White Paper on AI regulation in Ukraine. https://thedigital.gov.ua/storage/uploads/files/page/community/docs/Біла_книга_з_регулювання_ШІ_в_Україні_АНГЛ.pdf

Nairobi Statement on AI (2024).

Newman, J. et al. (2022) Digital technologies, artificial intelligence, and bureaucratic transformation. Futures : the journal of policy, planning and futures studies.

OECD. (2025). Steering AI's future: Strategies for anticipatory governance (OECD Artificial Intelligence Papers, No. 32). OECD Publishing. https://doi.org/10.1787/5480ff0a-en

Ogonjo, F., Gitonga, J. T., & Wairegi, A. (2022). Leveraging AI in the Kenyan Judiciary: A Case for Utilizing Text Classification Models for Data Completeness in Case Law Meta Data in Kenya's Employment and Labor Relations Court. Centre for Intellectual Property and Information Technology Law (CIPIT).

OpenGlobalRights. (2025). AI to detect human rights abuse. https://www.openglobalrights.org

Pahune, S., Akhtar, Z., Mandapati, V., & Siddique, K. (2025). The importance of AI data governance in large language models [Preprint]. Preprints.org. https://doi.org/10.20944/preprints202504.0219.v1

Percipient. (2025). Everything you should know about AI legal tech. https://percipient.co/ai-legal-tech/

Png, M.-T. (2023). The Critical Roles of Global South Stakeholders in AI Governance. In J. Bullock, Y.-C. Chen, J. Himmelreich, V. Hudson, A. Korinek, M. Young, & B. Zhang, The Oxford Handbook of AI Governance. Oxford: OUP.

Politico. (2022). Dutch scandal serves as a warning for Europe over risks of using algorithms. POLITICO. https://www.politico.eu/article/dutch-scandal-serves-as-a-warning-for-europe-over-risks-of-using-algorithms/

Reuters (Sara Merken), "New York lawyers sanctioned for using fake ChatGPT cases in legal brief" (26 June 2023).

Singapore Academy of Law (2023). Research on Legal Technology.

Singapore Judiciary (Chief Justice Sundaresh Menon), "Reimagining the Rule of Law: A Renewed Conception"—Speech at Conversations with the Community (20 September 2024).

Sinha, G. & Dunbar, R. (2022). Artificial intelligence and its regulation in the European Union. In: Bielicki, D. M. (ed.) *Regulating Artificial Intelligence in Industry* (pp. 3–20). Abingdon: Routledge.

Straits Times (Tham Yuen-C), "Reimagining the rule of law: How Singapore is adapting for the future" (6 October 2024).

Teo, S. (2024). Artificial intelligence and its 'slow violence' to human rights. AI Ethics. https://doi.org/10.1007/s43681-024-00547-x

The European Parliament and the Council of the European Union (2024). The European Union's Artificial Intelligence Act—Regulation (EU) 2024/1689. *Official Journal of the European Union*, PE/24/2024/REV/1. http://data.europa.eu/eli/reg/2024/1689/oj Accessed January 25, 2025.

The Guardian. (2025). Technology Secretary Peter Kyle asks ChatGPT for science and media advice. https://www.theguardian.com/politics/2025/mar/13/technlogy-secretary-peter-kyle-asks-chatgpt-for-science-and-media-advice

The Guardian. (2023) 'UK officials use AI to decide on issues from benefits to marriage licences'. https://www.theguardian.com/technology/2023/oct/23/uk-officials-use-ai-to-decide-on-issues-from-benefits-to-marriage-licences

Thomson Reuters. (2025). How AI is transforming the legal profession. https://legal.thomsonreuters.com/blog/how-ai-is-transforming-the-legal-profession/

Ugale, G., & Hall, C. (2024). Generative AI for anti-corruption and integrity in government: Taking stock of promise, perils and practice (OECD Artificial Intelligence Papers, No. 12). OECD Publishing. https://doi.org/10.1787/657a185a-en

UNEP (United Nations Environment Programme). (2023). AI has an environmental problem. Here's what the world can do about it. https://www.unep.org/news-and-stories/story/ai-has-environmental-problem-heres-what-world-can-do-about

UNESCO, "Building AI and the rule of law in Eastern Africa" (23 October 2024).

UnitedMedia24 (2025). Ukraine integrates AI into government services with launch of five new tools. https://united24media.com/latest-news/ukraine-integrates-ai-into-government-services-with-launch-of-five-new-tools-7229)

Villata, S., Araszkiewicz, M., Ashley, K., Bench-Capon, T., Branting, L. K., Conrad, J. G., & Wyner, A. (2022). Thirty years of artificial intelligence and law: the third decade. Artificial Intelligence and Law, 30(4), 561–591.

Weber, M. (1994) Weber: Political Writings. Ronald Speirs. Edited by P. Lassman. Translated by R. Speirs. Cambridge: Cambridge University Press (Cambridge Texts in the History of Political Thought).

Yue, S., Chen, W., Wang, S., Li, B., Shen, C., Liu, S., ... & Wei, Z. (2023). Disc-lawllm: Fine-tuning large language models for intelligent legal services. arXiv preprint arXiv:2309.11325; Satterfield, N., Holbrooka, P., & Wilcoxa, T. (2024). Fine-tuning llama with case law data to improve legal domain performance. OSF Preprints; Liga, D., & Robaldo, L. (2023). Fine-tuning GPT-3 for legal rule classification. Computer Law & Security Review, 51, 105864.

Young, K. (2010). The regulatory state. In: Baldwin, R., Cave, M. & Lodge, M. (eds.) *The Oxford Handbook of Regulation* (pp. 64–86). Oxford: OUP.

Index

A. Aliu (ed.), *Artificial Intelligence and the Rule of Law*,
https://doi.org/10.1007/978-3-031-97389-5

D

E

F

G

FSC
www.fsc.org
MIX
Papier | Fördert gute Waldnutzung
FSC® C083411

Kolibri 360 GmbH
Ferdinand-Jühlke-Straße 7
99095 Erfurt, Deutschland
produktsicherheit@kolibri360.de